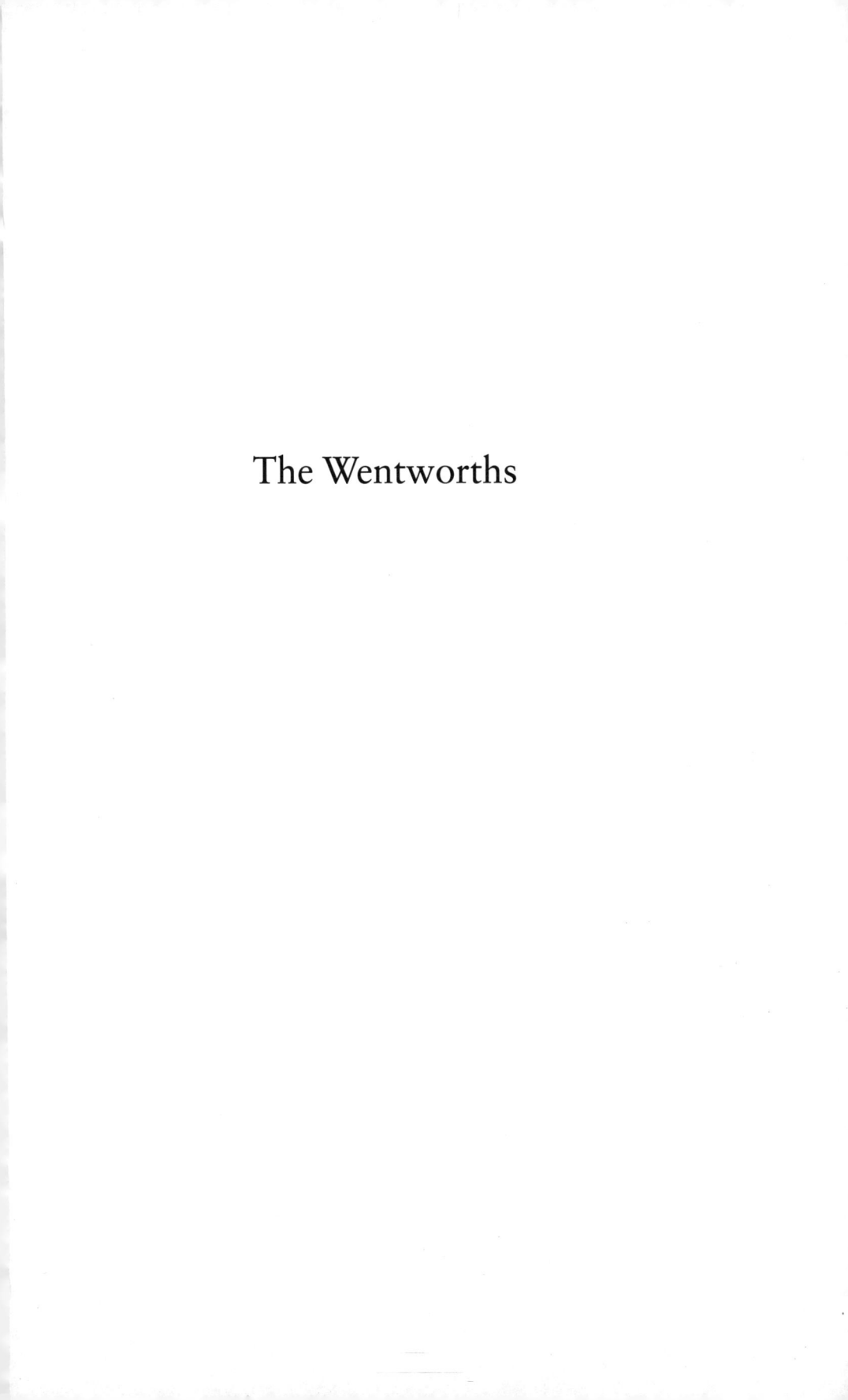

The Wentworths

JOHN RITCHIE

The Wentworths
Father and Son

MELBOURNE UNIVERSITY PRESS

Melbourne University Press
PO Box 278, Carlton South, Victoria 3053, Australia
info@mup.unimelb.edu.au
www.mup.com.au

First published 1997
Reprinted 1999

Text © John Douglas Ritchie 1997
Design and typography © Melbourne University Press 1997

This book is copyright. Apart from any use permitted under the Copyright Act 1968 and subsequent amendments, no part may be reproduced, stored in a retrieval system or transmitted by any means or process whatsoever without the prior written permission of the publisher.

National Library of Australia Cataloguing-in-Publication entry

Ritchie, John, 1941- .
 The Wentworths: father and son.
 Bibliography.
 Includes index.
 ISBN 0 522 84878 8.
 1. Wentworth, D'Arcy, 1764–1827. 2. Wentworth, W. C. (William Charles), 1790–1872. 3. Physicians—New South Wales—Biography. 4. Explorers—Australia—Biography. 5. New South Wales—History—1788–1900—Biography. 6. New South Wales—Politics and government—1788–1900. 7. New South Wales—Social life and customs—1788–1900. I. Title.
994.40099

for Christopher

Contents

Preface   xiii

1. Flame-coloured taffeta   1
2. The living and the dead   25
3. Remember not past years   48
4. Smile at the rising sun   72
5. Nets of wrong and right   101
6. To catch a thief   126
7. The greatest burden   151
8. What one is   177
9. Life's little day   204
10. Of graves and epitaphs   229

Abbreviations   240
Notes   241
Select bibliography   295
Index   297

Illustrations

between pages 168 *and* 169

D'Arcy Wentworth (1762–1827), silhouette by an unknown artist, *c.* 1815–20, from a copy held in the Mitchell Library, State Library of New South Wales.

William Charles Wentworth (1790–1872), lithograph by J. Allen, undated, from a copy held in the Mitchell Library, State Library of New South Wales.

Sarah Wentworth, née Cox (1805–80), watercolour and pencil by William Nicholas, *c.* 1852, in the possession of the Hon. W. C. Wentworth.

D'Arcy Wentworth's Family

Preface

Research for this book was facilitated by assistance from the Australian Research Grants Scheme in 1987 and 1988. The Faculty of Arts and the Research School of Social Sciences at the Australian National University provided me with opportunities to visit the Mitchell Library in Sydney on and off between 1987 and 1996, and the R.S.S.S. enabled me to travel to Britain and Ireland in 1993. In writing the manuscript I was aided by two periods of study-leave, six months in 1993 and five months in 1996. I thank the following people who helped me with their knowledge and kindnesses: John Barnes, Darryl Bennet, John Bennett, Paul Bourke, Janice and Michael Boyle, Geoffrey Brennan, Maureen and Rob Brooks, Martha Campbell, Paul Finn, Brian Fletcher, Iain Gosnay, John Griffiths, Kerrie and Peter Grundy, Ian Hancock, Alec Hill, John Knott, Roger Lovatt, Heather McCalman, Noel McLachlan, Brian Maher, Roderick Munday, Bede Nairn, George Parsons, Jill Roe, Peter Ryan, Alan Shaw, Margaret Steven, Gerry Walsh, Jim Walvin, Phillipa Weeks, the Hon. William Charles Wentworth, Brian Wilder, Sandy Yarwood and Peter Yeend. I am grateful to Anne-Marie Gaudry, Rachel Grahame, Jenny Newell, Alison Pilger, Gwyn Singleton, Sheila Tilse and Brian Wimborne who, at various stages, foraged and checked a range of material. Edna Kauffman and Karen Manning patiently taught me how to operate a computer. Ken Inglis, Iain McCalman, Oliver MacDonagh, Ken Miles (a great-great-grandson of D'Arcy Wentworth), John Molony and Barry Smith read the typescript and were, in their several ways, encouraging and constructive critics.

    I owe much to other people, too, my greatest debts being to scholars who preceded me. Of those who were primarily interested in D'Arcy

Preface

Wentworth, J. J. Auchmuty published a pioneering entry in the *Australian Dictionary of Biography* in 1967 and W. B. Lynch compiled a lengthy typescript in 1992. The best accounts of D'Arcy Wentworth have been written by two postgraduates, H. P. Barker who submitted an M.A. thesis at the University of New England in 1971 and Kathleen Dermody who completed her Ph.D. thesis at the Australian National University in 1990; I have drawn heavily on both these studies and thank the authors for permission to refer to their work. I also thank Michael Flynn whose outstanding book, *The Second Fleet*, Sydney, 1993, provided valuable material for Chapter 2 of *The Wentworths*. Of those who focused on William Wentworth, I am particularly grateful for the writings of G. W. Rusden (1883), G. B. Barton (1898–99), K. R. Cramp (1918), A. W. Jose (1928), A. C. V. Melbourne (1934), H. M. Green (1935), Vance Palmer (1940), Percival Serle (1949), G. V. Portus (1952), Michael Collins Persse (1966), John Senyard (1966), Manning Clark (1968), Carol Liston (1976 and 1988) and Don Fifer (1983 and 1991).

My deepest appreciation is to my wife, Joan, for sustaining me through hours, days and even weeks of doubt and uncertainty. To our son, Christopher, who rejuvenated us in his infancy and childhood, this book is fondly dedicated.

what's past is prologue

                Shakespeare, *The Tempest*, Act II, scene i

I

Flame-coloured taffeta

> ... hours were cups of sack, and minutes capons, and clocks the tongues of bawds, and dials the signs of leaping-houses, and the blessed sun himself a fair hot wench in flame-coloured taffeta.
>
> Shakespeare, *Henry IV*, Part 1, Act I, scene ii

All great families have their poor relations. In this regard the Fitzwilliams—singular in many ways—were no exception. William Wentworth Fitzwilliam, the 4th Earl Fitzwilliam, belonged to a family of means and consequence. Born in 1748, he traced his ancestry to Sir William Fitzwilliam and to the period of the Norman Conquest. Some time after 1117 one of Sir William's descendants had a cross erected in the main street of Sprotbrough, a village in Yorkshire close to the family seat, on which the following words were engraved:

> Whose is hungry, and lists to eate,
> Let him come to Sprotburgh to his meate;
> And for a night, and for a day,
> His horse shall have both corn and hay,
> And no man shall ask him where he goeth away.

About two hundred years later in their manorial grounds the Fitzwilliams founded a hospital and dedicated it to St Edmund. Another forebear, also named Sir William Fitzwilliam, served five terms under Elizabeth I as lord deputy of Ireland. His great-great-grandson became in 1716 Viscount Milton of County Westmeath and Earl Fitzwilliam of County Tyrone. From him the earldom passed, in turn, to his grandson William, the third earl, who, on 19 April 1742, was enrolled as an English peer in the dignity of Lord Fitzwilliam, Baron Milton of Northampton. In 1746 he was advanced as Viscount Milton and Earl Fitzwilliam of Norborough.[1]

William Wentworth Fitzwilliam succeeded to the earldom in 1756, at the age of eight. Educated at Eton, where he formed an enduring friendship with Charles James Fox, he proceeded to the University of Cambridge, then, in 1769, took his seat in the House of Lords. Next year he married Lady Charlotte Ponsonby, youngest daughter of the 2nd Earl of Bessborough and his wife the countess, formerly Lady Caroline Cavendish, a daughter of the 3rd Duke of Devonshire. On the death of his uncle, the 2nd Marquis of Rockingham, in 1782, William inherited estates valued at £40 000 a year. Adhering to the Whig politics of his family, he had steadily harassed the administration of Lord North. In 1783 Fox intended that Fitzwilliam should head the India board; and in their regency arrangements of 1788 the Whigs designed him for the lord-lieutenancy of Ireland. To this stage he had spent most of his parliamentary career in opposition and never held a ministry. He maintained Wentworth Woodhouse as his country seat. Set within ninety acres of parkland, some four miles to the north-west of Rotherham in Yorkshire, the Palladian mansion had a 606-foot frontage, 365 rooms and 1000 windows. At this princely establishment he was said to keep the finest stables and kennels in England. The motto on his coat of arms read: '*Appetitus rationi pareat*'—'Appetite should obey reason'.[2]

Thirteen years, eight months and fifteen days after Lord Fitzwilliam's birth, one of his poor relations greeted the universe with a bawl. As to time and place, this infant, who was to be named D'Arcy Wentworth, was born on 14 February 1762 in Portadown, County Armagh, Ireland.[3] A tiny twig on one of the farthermost branches of the Fitzwilliam family tree, D'Arcy came from modest circumstances but could boast of an ancestry that stretched, through twenty generations at least, to William of Wentworth Woodhouse in the thirteenth century. William's descendant, Thomas Wentworth, also of Wentworth Woodhouse, was appointed lord deputy of Ireland in 1632 and governed that country so sternly and effectively that he earned the appellation 'Black Tom Tyrant'. For his services he was created Earl of Strafford by Charles I in 1640. Strafford's efforts to retain for the

1 *Flame-coloured taffeta*

monarchy the authority which it had acquired under the Tudors, his imperious temper and his inability to quell a Scottish revolt so antagonized his enemies that they introduced a bill of attainder in parliament. All too late, he is said to have echoed the precept, 'Put not your trust in princes!' On 12 May 1641, watched by a jubilant crowd, he was beheaded on Tower Hill. His daughter, Anne, married Edward Watson, the 2nd Baron Rockingham. The eldest daughter of her grandson, Thomas Watson-Wentworth, 1st Marquis of Rockingham, married the 3rd Earl Fitzwilliam on 22 June 1744.[4]

During the reign of Charles II another descendant of William of Wentworth Woodhouse, D'Arcy Wentworth (b.1640), went to Ireland. He came from Mattersey Hall, South Elmsall, Yorkshire, and belonged to a collateral branch of Strafford's family. Steward in Athlone to the 4th Earl of Roscommon, D'Arcy was commissioned in the County Meath Militia and in 1692 established himself as a landholder at Fyanstown. A number of Irish Wentworths intermarried with leading Anglo-Irish families. Robert, the third Wentworth of Fyanstown, vaunted his relationship to the Marquis of Rockingham, remote though it was. Despite his boasting, he failed to realize his political ambitions, dissipated his family's resources and was reduced to being an impecunious barrister. The lands were mortgaged in 1730 and eventually sold in 1742. Robert had married Mary Walsh (d.1729). Their only son, D'Arcy (b.1722), was sent to Portadown where he began an apprenticeship in the linen trade. He married his master's daughter, Martha Dixon, on 8 January 1747, and set up as an innkeeper. However far these Wentworths had slid from high estate, they still claimed a connexion with the noble Straffords and the Fitzwilliams, with those who fell and those who rose on the shifting barometer of fame and fortune. They thought of themselves as 'cousins' of their social betters, a term which had the elasticity to encompass close and distant relationships, and which embraced sentiments that ranged from affection to contempt. Poor cousins in an alien land, they naturally placed greater store on their tenuous bonds of kinship than did the inheritors of Wentworth Woodhouse.[5]

The infant born to Martha and D'Arcy Wentworth on St Valentine's Day 1762 was the youngest of their four sons and the sixth of their eight children. His brothers were named William, Samuel and Gerrard, his sisters Mary, Dorothy, Martha and Mary Anne. Located in the staunch Province of Ulster, his birthplace lay on the banks of the River Bann, seven miles south of Lough Neagh, and some twenty-five miles south-west of Belfast, between the towns of Lurgan and Armagh. In the mid-eighteenth century fewer than two thousand souls lived in Portadown, a brisk, albeit small, market-town which was largely reliant on the linen industry. The spacious main street, town square, spruce and unpretentious shops, warehouses and the quay gave every indication of resolutely earned prosperity. Unlike their counterparts in the south, the women had their hair neatly braided up; the men dressed in jackets and trousers (rather than breeches), and wore caps, eschewing the hats (caibins) which were common in the southern part of the island. Sharp-featured and intent, the townspeople spoke bluntly, directly and to the point, their brogue carrying a Scottish inflection. English visitors saw in them the embodiment of thrift, prudence, perseverance and common sense, and ascribed these virtues to the influence of the Protestant religion.[6]

An ancient castle of the McCanns once stood beneath cloud-stacked skies on the strategic ground commanding the pass of the River Bann, but, like the nearby Elizabethan mansion formerly owned by John Obyns, it had crumbled into ruins. In emphatic contrast a stone bridge of seven arches was built over the river in 1764 (the only crossing for thirty miles) to link Portadown with the east. One mile off, on the road north-east to Lurgan, nestled the vicarage of Seagoe, the residence of the Reverend Blacker, a clergyman of the Church of Ireland. One of D'Arcy's brothers and a sister were baptized in the church adjacent to the vicarage, and his parents were to be buried in its graveyard. He was most likely christened by Mr Blacker and raised as an Anglican.[7]

The parish of Portadown comprised 3836 acres. While some inhabitants were engaged in the manufacture of linen, lawn, cambric and sheeting for the bleachers and factors of Banbridge, and others by slow degree turned their hands to weaving cotton goods for the merchants of Belfast, the land continued to employ the majority of the people. On undulating hills and dales the well-to-do ran horned cattle, sheep and horses, maintained small orchards and tilled the soil on farms of sixty acres; their inferiors, with five-acre holdings, grew corn, barley, oats, potatoes, flax or vegetables, owned a few goats, pigs and poultry, and even bred pigeons or kept an apiary. The lines of demarcation between grazier and cultivator were by no means as fixed as the careful fences that surrounded the farms, and many of the middling sort shrewdly combined husbandry with keeping a tiny herd or flock. Clean and trim, the farmhouses were almost all of one storey, with long thatched roofs and white exterior walls. Lower down the hierarchy—and only slightly above the vagrants, paupers and criminals—the tenant farmers and labourers made up the bulk of the population. Most of them lived in rude cottages and one-roomed cabins, without chimneys or glazed windows, and often in the company of animals. They clung to the Catholic faith and worshipped in the chapel at Drumcree. Barefoot and dirty, they appeared slovenly in gait and churlish in attitude, and were held to be lazy, superstitious and uncivilized. Their overlords treated them as lesser beings. In the main, they were malnourished, cold and frightened, and had been for generations. In Portadown and beyond, the bulk of Irish people rarely if ever moved beyond a radius of fifteen to twenty miles from their homes; most lived within a still more circumscribed area. Correspondingly, marriages within the native locality were the norm. Social life was thin and meagre, relieved only by feast-days and fairs, by gossip and storytelling, and by games, drinking, hilarity and fighting. Poverty, distress and starkness crushed the spirit, and, for the peasantry, the crowded countryside constituted so many square miles in which they swung between extroverted vivacity and introspective gloom.[8]

As a middling member of the middle orders, D'Arcy the innkeeper was 'above the common ground' and as far from impoverishment as he was from affluence. His children spent clamorous hours playing in and about the waters of the Bann where the river abounded in pike, trout and salmon. The family was closely knit. If there were fissures in its walls, they were small, scarcely more than hair-line breaks across the surface. Young, blue-eyed D'Arcy was the favourite child. His sisters dressed his hair, his father doted on him. With his friends James Hill and Leonard Dobbin, as well as other little Wentworths, he was sent to a local school to be taught by Mr McDowell. There he received an elementary grounding in the three Rs. Judging by D'Arcy's correspondence and strong handwriting, his education was effective and of a fairly high standard. In his boyhood he doubtless ran the gamut of family felicity and unhappiness, and began to appreciate the way in which they were interlaced. Little by little he came to know the crushing and sustaining forces, the narrowing and expansive tendencies, and the ups and downs implicit in family relations. From the trials of youth, and its myriad frictions, indignations and doubts, he emerged tall, stoutly built, charming in manner, and very handsome.[9]

About 1777, at the age of fifteen, D'Arcy was apprenticed to a surgeon, Dr Alexander Patton, in Tanderagee, six miles south of Portadown.[10] For a fourth son, with limited prospects and no wealth, the profession of medicine might give rise to opportunities in private practice, or to a post, perhaps, in the army, the navy or the colonies. He was commissioned in 1782 as an ensign in the 1st Provincial Battalion of the Ulster Volunteers, with which he served on a part-time basis for the next three years. The volunteers performed guard duties in garrison towns, dispersed unruly gatherings, apprehended suspected lawbreakers, escorted prisoners to and from gaol, supported magistrates and sheriffs in preserving the peace, and fought fires. In essence, they functioned as a police force.[11]

Wider, deeper and more restless forces lay behind the emergence and growth of the Volunteers. Stunned by the events in America of 1776 and their repercussions, and fearful that the floor of organized society might collapse, the established classes were suddenly reminded of the existence of dark passions, bestial ferocity and intense hatreds which they had hitherto relegated to a remote past in Britain's conquest of Ireland. The northern Protestants were self-consciously arriviste and a scattered ruling class, and felt beleaguered as an embattled yet enduring people in an island separate, mysterious and peculiar.[12] As recently as 1763 the peasantry had risen in protest against tithes and taxes. Calling themselves 'Oakboys', they had menaced gentlemen, insulted ladies, erected gallows and threatened widespread violence.[13]

Following the outbreak of war with the American colonies, troops stationed in Ireland had been called up for active service abroad. In 1778 the French signed a treaty with the Americans which effectively brought that nation into the war as their ally. Given France's hostility towards England and the weakened state of Ireland's defences, the twin phantoms of invasion and uprising haunted Protestants in the north. Like so many of his peers, among them merchants, shopkeepers, lawyers, physicians and noblemen, D'Arcy Wentworth had answered the call to the colours. James Caulfield, 4th Viscount and 1st Earl of

1 Flame-coloured taffeta

Charlemont, was commander-in-chief of the Ulster Volunteers which in 1782 numbered 100 000 men. Wentworth's battalion was led by Lieutenant-Colonel Thomas Dawson of the 36th Regiment, then stationed in Armagh. Each corps was made up of fifty to one hundred unpaid soldiers who were prepared to provide their own uniforms, arms and accoutrements. This expense, together with the time spent on military exercises, precluded the labouring orders and, inferentially, the majority of Catholics, from enlisting.[14]

Muted by the fear of dispossession should England's support ever weaken, a sense of grievance had slowly developed among the Irish Ascendancy in the eighteenth century and given rise to a native Whiggery. Through the volunteer associations Ulster Protestants succeeded in publicizing, dramatically, their discontent. As corps met with corps, citizen-soldiers aired their views, exchanged ideas and hammered out a political platform. They began to agitate for parliamentary reform, free trade and the right to constitutional independence. They targeted Poyning's law, a statute preventing any member of the Irish legislature from initiating a bill in either House at Westminster without prior approval from the Privy Council. On 15 February 1782 delegates from 143 corps met at Dungannon in County Tyrone and passed a series of resolutions which led the British parliament to repeal Poyning's law in June. The resentment of the bulk of Ulstermen expressed itself as mere demands for the same constitutional arrangements as the counterparts of the Ascendancy enjoyed in England. Their discontent was that of outer or transplanted Britons.[15]

On the shakiest of grounds—the anachronistic use of evidence drawn from Wentworth's subsequent career—historians have asserted or implied that he shared the egalitarian and democratic aspirations of extremists among the volunteers. Scarce though it is, contemporary evidence points quite the other way. The most that may be plausibly suggested is that D'Arcy may have been brushed by the eddies of temperate reform swirling among the citizen-soldiery, and that, even more likely, he shared in the camaraderie and joined in the drinking and roistering that characterized military life. Enlistment enabled him to parade in uniform and heightened his consciousness of belonging to a patrician caste. His period of service was brief. After the end of the American war in 1783, the volunteer battalions were gradually reduced. Lieutenant-Colonel Dawson signed a conventional statement attesting that

Wentworth had at all times conducted himself as befitted a good soldier. At the ensign's request, he also agreed to use his influence with Lord Charlemont to obtain a letter of recommendation for D'Arcy from the Marquis of Rockingham, but Rockingham's death had closed that avenue of patronage. Lacking gainful employment, and with no firm intention as to his future, Wentworth was rather at a loss as to what to do. His eldest brother, William, had entered the army and served as a sergeant in Holland. His sister, Dorothy, would later emigrate to America. D'Arcy turned his thoughts to India. He decided to write to the directors of the East India Company requesting an assistant-surgeonship in one of its settlements; their stock response indicated that his application would be considered—should a vacancy occur. Torn between accepting such a post, joining the army in some medical capacity, and remaining in Ireland where he was 'invariably popular with all classes and both sexes', D'Arcy temporized. Finally, in 1785, he left Portadown for London.[16]

One of the first people to whom he wrote was his mentor, Dr Patton. Believing that the wind sat in the shoulder of D'Arcy's sail and that his pupil would soon be bound for India, Patton replied on 30 November 1785. His letter gave fond counsel, much in the manner of Polonius's words to Laertes. Knowing full well the strengths and weaknesses of his protégé, Patton was confident that fortune would smile upon him, 'if you throw no impediment in its way'. He enjoined him to be industrious, diligent, prudent and cautious, to live within his income, and to respect his superiors, especially the 'Great People' who conferred favours. Further, he urged him to be regular in attending classes at the hospitals and to devote every spare hour to reading in his profession. In particular, he suggested that he seek advice from James Dawson at Lincoln's Inn, for few possessed a better head or heart than he. With acuity, he cautioned Wentworth to avoid 'idle, giddy and dissipated' friends, averring that 'there is something so fascinating in the Company of dangerous men that we cannot see it 'till it is too late; choose rather the orderly and sober than the pleasing and voluptuous for your companions'. Patton went on to remind D'Arcy that 'You have cost your father much', but added, 'I know your heart is good and I am sure you will endeavour to repay him with interest'. He concluded by wishing him every happiness. Aged in his early fifties, Patton hoped to live to see his erstwhile apprentice return home a nabob.[17]

1 Flame-coloured taffeta

The recipient of that letter was twenty-three years old. His preparation for London had been hasty and perfunctory, or so it proved. He began well enough, comporting himself sensibly and purposefully. The court of examiners of the Company of Surgeons recognized his qualifications as an assistant-surgeon on 1 December 1785. Having come to London to acquire further testamurs of medical proficiency, he 'walked the hospitals' to gain additional knowledge and skills by observing experienced physicians at work. His fellow students at St Bartholomew's Hospital were, for the most part, the clever sons of tradesmen. Medicine was not regarded as 'the profession of a gentleman'. Before issuing an aspiring doctor with a licence, the court of examiners required a certificate of hospital practice which was customarily granted after six to twelve months, or two to three years, depending on the applicant's term of apprenticeship. In Wentworth's case, the six months came and went, as did the twelve. He continued to equivocate. An opportunity arose to go to India, but he rejected it and sought a regimental post. He began to be late for engagements, then failed to keep them, much to Dawson's chagrin. D'Arcy shifted from shabby lodgings at No. 12 St Martin's-le-Grand (immediately north of St Paul's Cathedral) to 7 Great Russell Street in Bloomsbury, then to Islington, and from there to 68 Great Tichfield Street, Marylebone. As his addresses changed, his correspondence appears to have become desultory and erratic, and he wrote no more to Dr Patton.[18]

Threads survive of Wentworth's second year in London that enable one to weave the fabric of which they once formed part. With its forest of chimney-pots and slate roofs, its hurry and push, the metropolis seemed vast, unfamiliar, self-absorbed and unsympathetic. Paradoxically, the longer Wentworth remained there, the more he felt out of his element. Deprived of close friends in whom to confide, existing on the pin-money allowed by his father, and overwhelmed by the unfolding majesty and meanness of the great city, D'Arcy found that constraint brought no compensation. His education and upbringing had not equipped him to cope with his surroundings. He became inured to overcrowded wards where the stench was offensive, the diseases rife and the treatment of patients callous, but the daily round of calling at hospitals dulled by repetition. The noise and his needs ate continually into his concentration. Set apart by his accent and clothing, he appeared what he was—a country lad from Ireland, powerless, poor, devoid of luck, and a nobody. Want of money constituted a sort of underlying beat to the tempo of his existence. He did not have to look far to see the smart set who gratified their manifest superiority in station by spending lavishly on fads and fancies to pander to their hauteur. Contrariwise, he was compelled to be close-fisted. Whether he was envious or simply bored, he craved release and found it in dissipation.

Growing familiarity with the banter and argot of Oxford Market at the southern end of Great Tichfield Street may have drawn Wentworth south-east to the neighbourhoods of St Giles and nearby Seven Dials where the indigent, the alienated and the resentful made their rookeries. In the late eighteenth century London's underworld divided into two overlapping realms, the political and the criminal. The former sphere included a motley set of revolutionaries and insurrectionists, populists and radicals, infidels and Millenarians. In taverns, tap-rooms and candle-lit dens they gibbeted the rulers of state and church as grossly as they had been treated by them; with makeshift presses, they published books, pamphlets and broadsheets which varied from the rational to the bizarre, from polemic and cant to blasphemy and pornography. Sustaining one another through the uncertainties of betrayal and arrest, and through the misery integral to the lower social borderlands, they vented their visions and their caprice in a way that gave a chilling index of class distinctions. Yet it was not to their company that D'Arcy gravitated.[19]

London's population approached one million. Existence was precarious for one-tenth of that number. For some of them, crime was part and parcel of daily life. The Gordon Riots of 1780 provided an all too recent reminder of how close society was to civil unrest. Law and order depended on a network of marshals and constables who discharged their duties in twenty-six independent wards, but their movements were restricted to designated beats. This obsolete arrangement dated from the reign of Charles I and the officers were familiarly known as 'Charlies'. In the 1750s Henry and John Fielding had founded the 'Bow Street Runners', a small body of able and energetic 'thieftakers' who patrolled the city on foot and horseback to safeguard property and person. They often met their informants in 'flash houses' (which combined gaming and prostitution with the sale of liquor) and paid them a share of the rewards arising from the conviction of capital offenders. In spite of their efforts, crime appeared to be increasing and the prison hulks on

1 Flame-coloured taffeta

the River Thames were inadequate to confine the number under sentence. On 18 August 1786 Lord Sydney, secretary of state at the Home Office, wrote to the Treasury announcing his intention to establish a convict settlement at Botany Bay in antipodean New South Wales. This drift of events went unheeded by Wentworth.[20]

Impelled as much by instinct, gullibility and inexperience as by whim-driven design, he crossed the rim of the criminal underworld and moved towards its hub. His predilection for bravado and panache, together with an infatuation with role-playing, so drew him on that he was ready to live cheerfully beyond his means, to drink intemperately, to flirt with any pretty wench or agreeable trollop, and to succumb to the wiles of villains. He surrendered reason to appetite. Step by step, he trampled the accepted decencies, revelled in his amorality, and convinced himself that he had found a conduit to and from an irresistible nether region of colour and glow, of dash and daring. He had a mind for nothing else. Living as a man of two worlds, he sharpened his artifice and cunning, cloaked his better nature and masked the unworthiness of his actions. Cocksure and careless, he engaged in a charade which did not end even when his transgressions were made public.

The nadir was not slow in coming. By late 1786 Wentworth had formed a connexion with disreputable characters who frequented the Dog and Duck tavern in St George's Fields. An open common of great extent, lying south of the Thames between Southwark and Lambeth in Surrey, the fields had been used by the Romans as a camp-site, and by Shakespeare as the setting for Falstaff's night with Swallow. Lord George Gordon's rioters assembled in the area on 2 June 1780. During the Reformation martyrs had been burnt there; in the Age of Enlightenment it was a place where the hangman launched wretches into eternity. Built before 1642, and with a tabard depicting a dog, squatting on its haunches, with a duck in its mouth, the inn was located close to a spring whose waters were thought to cure gout, stone, the king's evil, sore eyes and cancer. In 1771 Dr Johnson recommended the medicinal wells of St George's Fields to Mrs Thrale. When a bowling-green, a bathing pool and a circus were opened in the vicinity, the tavern attracted more custom, but its reputation suddenly declined, and in 1787 its proprietor appealed—with temporary success—against the magistrates' decision to refuse him a licence. Twelve years later the

Dog and Duck was finally suppressed. In 1811–12 the premises were demolished and in 1815 a new Bedlam was built on the site.[21]

In early 1787 it was an easy ride east from the Dog and Duck to Blackheath, a windswept and lonely tableland south of Greenwich Park, through which passed the direct road from London to Canterbury and Dover. The Danes had camped at Blackheath in 1011–13, Wat Tyler assembled his peasants there in 1381, and there Henry V was welcomed after the Battle of Agincourt in 1415. There, too, John Wesley and George Whitefield held revivalist meetings earlier in the eighteenth century. By 1787, however, the heath had acquired a sinister name as a resort of highwaymen and footpads. A little to the east, at Shooters' Hill, there was a steep rise with gallows at its foot and a gibbet at its summit, but the sight of putrefying corpses failed to deter desperadoes.[22]

On Wednesday 10 January 1787, in the depth of winter, robbery with violence occurred on the king's highway at Blackheath. Dr James Irwin and Stephen Remnant were both waylaid under force of arms and the robbers made off with their watches, chains, seals and coins, later estimated to be worth £27. On the wet afternoon of the following Saturday, 13 January, at Shooters' Hill, three highwaymen bailed up Alderman William Curtis, Archibald Anderson and Claude Scott, ordered them to hand over their valuables, and escaped with jewellery and money worth £24. They subsequently robbed William Christopher of six half-pence. Once the alarm was raised, Mr Duncan rode after the culprits. The highwaymen separated, but Duncan managed to overtake and apprehend William Manning at the southern end of the road through Lewisham. Information in Manning's pocket-book led officers of the Bow Street patrol to Wentworth's London residence where they arrested him.[23]

Next Monday, the 15th, Manning and Wentworth appeared before the magistrates in the public office at Bow Street, charged with the commission of several robberies at Blackheath and Shooters' Hill during the previous week. Manning was committed for further examination. Found in possession of two watches which were sworn to be stolen property, Wentworth spoke of his family's good name, his training as a surgeon and his service as a commissioned officer in Ireland. He attributed his degraded situation to the evil influence of his companions at the Dog and Duck. Unimpressed, the magistrates bound him over to

1 Flame-coloured taffeta

stand trial at the Lent assizes. He remained in Newgate prison until 17 March when he was escorted to the common gaol in the County of Kent. On the 21st he came to trial at Maidstone on five charges of felonious assault on the king's highway, putting a person in fear and danger of his life, and violently taking from the person against his will such goods as a watch or a purse. Irwin, Remnant, Curtis, Anderson and Scott were his accusers. In a vain attempt to conceal his identity, Wentworth gave his occupation as labourer. He pleaded not guilty and was acquitted on all charges. Transcripts of the proceedings have not survived.[24]

In the month of Wentworth's trial eleven ships gathered at the Mother Bank prepatory to their voyage for Botany Bay. After collecting her cargo of convicts at Plymouth in January and February, the *Charlotte* anchored off Portsmouth on 17 March. John Harris, a naval surgeon, later stated that he met Wentworth on board this vessel, that D'Arcy was the ship's surgeon, and that he deserted before the flotilla sailed on the golden Sunday morning of 13 May. Wentworth never attempted to deny Harris's account. D'Arcy's friends had for some years endeavoured to find him a position overseas. The embarrassment of his appearance in court may have prompted them to try to secure his appointment to the First Fleet or to the medical establishment in New South Wales. Rather than abandoning his post, Wentworth did not sail in the *Charlotte* because the Home Office had not acceded to his patrons' requests.[25]

To salvage his reputation, he continued to solicit his friends to act on his behalf. Possibly through Robert Sinclair, a respected barrister with whom he had briefly resided in York, Wentworth contacted Lord Fitzwilliam. The two men met. If D'Arcy made any appeal for patronage, the responding silence was deafening. In July 1787 Wentworth received a letter from another contact, James Villiers, the representative for Old Sarum in the House of Commons and the second son of the Earl of Clarendon. Villiers advised him to seek out Henry Russell at Lincoln's Inn who might be able to convince Sir Charles Middleton, comptroller of the navy, of D'Arcy's suitability for a government post: 'a line from him . . . is the most satisfactory way . . . of obviating the objections to your appointment'. On 16 November Villiers wrote once more, regretting that he was unable to assist Wentworth in regard to a commission in a particular regiment of the army. Eleven days later D'Arcy was again apprehended by the law.[26]

The Wentworths

Hounslow Heath, a waste tract of 4000 acres strewn with gibbets, lay south-west of London and flanked the main road to the West Country. At dusk on Friday 23 November, while travelling with his clerk in a post-chaise *en route* to Hampshire, William Lewer was bailed up by a solitary highwayman near the powder mills on the heath. Without demur, Lewer handed over his silver watch, a seal and more than three guineas. His assailant appeared to be a large, lusty man who wore a black silk mask and a drab-coloured greatcoat. Next day a woman calling herself 'May Looking' sold a silver watch for one guinea to William Aldred, a pawnbroker of Berwick Street, Soho, whose shop was situated only three blocks from Wentworth's lodgings.[27]

Shortly before 5 o'clock on the evening of Tuesday 27 November John Hurst was returning from Slough to London, accompanied by his wife and their friend, Mrs Ann Grundy. A lone and solidly built highwayman, wearing a black silk mask which—save for the eye-sockets—completely covered his face, stood in wait at Hounslow Heath. Mounted on a chestnut horse with a white blaze on its head, he stopped their coach and robbed Hurst of his watch, chain, seal and key. Samuel Maynard and Edward Hughes, two officers of the Bow Street patrol, learned of the robbery and proceeded to the Notting Hill turnpike on the Uxbridge Road by the Kensington gravel pits. There, around 7.30 that evening, they intercepted Wentworth. Before dismounting from his chestnut horse, he stood in his stirrups and allegedly flung something 'a great way from him'. The patrolmen searched him. In the right pocket of his coat they found a loaded pistol, a wig, a black silk mask and a purse. From his waistcoat pocket they took a key which D'Arcy said belonged to a chest he kept in his rooms. He refused to disclose his address. A search by lantern-light revealed a metal watch some distance from the turnpike. It matched Hurst's description of the one stolen from him. Wentworth was taken into custody.[28]

He appeared before the magistrate, Sir Sampson Wright, at the Bow Street office on Wednesday the 28th and was committed to the bridewell at Tothill Fields. The *Daily Universal Register* (*The Times* from 1 January 1788) reported that he would soon be re-examined, and anticipated several additional charges being brought against 'this unhappy youth'. In the meantime Samuel Maynard, the arresting officer, went to 68 Great Tichfield Street where he recovered from a chest in the accused's rooms a seal similar to that taken from Lewer. At the

1 Flame-coloured taffeta

preliminary hearing before Wright and Nicholas Bond on Friday 30 November, D'Arcy initially seemed composed. It was quickly established that he and Mary Wilkinson lived together as man and wife. He had assumed the name 'Mr Fitzroy'. She was known as 'The Lady'. Mr Aldred alleged that it was she who had used the alias 'May Looking'. During the examination Wentworth declared that, if Miss Wilkinson were 'brought into trouble upon his account, he would destroy himself'. Described as a comely woman, she wore a white beaver hat adorned with a gold and silver band. The *Register's* reporter compared her with Sarah Millwood, a character in contemporary fiction who seduced a young apprentice, and enticed him to steal and murder. Once Lewer had identified the watch pawned by 'May Looking' as his own, Wentworth and Wilkinson were remanded for trial and sent to Newgate prison.[29]

On 1 December 1787 the *Register* used D'Arcy's plight as the basis for a homily. Exhorting magistrates to suppress 'flash houses', those moral cesspools which reduced young men like Wentworth to ruin, it asserted that he had already experienced 'several narrow escapes from an ignominious death', but, 'once initiated in the paths of vice he found it impossible to stop'. By the 6th the newspaper wrote pejoratively of the 'notorious D'Arcy Wentworth', a 'tall, personable man', 'well known on the road'. It referred to his previous trial at Maidstone where everyone had expected him to be convicted, but, 'through the ingenuity of his Counsel', he had been acquitted.[30]

In a dim, wood-panelled and musty courtroom of the Old Bailey on Wednesday 12 December 1787 Wentworth was indicted on three counts of highway robbery against William Lewer, John Hurst and Ann Grundy. Mary Wilkinson faced one charge of receiving stolen goods. Aldred swore that, when pawning the silver watch, Wilkinson had said that it belonged to her brother, and that she had used an alias and given a false address. Thomas Little, a carpenter and the landlord of 68 Great Tichfield Street, testified that D'Arcy and his lady kept regular hours and behaved like gentlefolk. Lewer, who had been nervous at the preliminary hearing on 30 November, steeled his resolve, and confidently identified as his own the watch pawned by 'May Looking' and the seal found by Maynard in Wentworth's trunk. Mr Knowlys, who appeared for Wilkinson, drew from Lewer the admission that such seals were common. Wentworth inveighed against the press for prejudicing the minds of the jury: 'I have been ranked among the most notorious of offenders; and I wish that any person that has published those paragraphs against me, would now come forth like a man'. Wilkinson denied that Wentworth had given her the silver watch. She swore that a 'much shorter' gentleman had handed it to another lady more than a fortnight earlier. Professing to be a needle-woman, Wilkinson said that she had previously lived with D'Arcy at Pleasant Row, Islington, where her sister, Elizabeth, had shared lodgings with them. Before that, Mary had worked as a servant on a farm near Faversham in Kent. Witnesses spoke of her good character. A point of law arose as to whether a 'wife' was a free agent or subject to her 'husband's' coercion. Although the judges, Sir Richard Perryn and Mr Justice Buller, found strong circumstantial evidence of guilt, the jury acquitted both Wilkinson and Wentworth.[31]

At the same Old Bailey session Wentworth immediately faced two further charges for crimes perpetrated against Hurst and Grundy. He retained Knowlys as his defence counsel. John Dunn, a stable-keeper of Three Horseshoe Yard, testified that he knew the accused and had, once or twice before, rented horses to him. Wentworth had used the name 'Fitzroy' when he hired the chestnut mare with the white face between noon and 1 p.m. on 27 November. Hurst showed a strong disinclination to establish Wentworth's complicity. According to Maynard, on the night of the offences Hurst had described the highwayman as a stout, lusty man who rode a chestnut horse. In court, Hurst swore that the person who robbed him rode a dark horse and was a tall, thin man, with little resemblance to D'Arcy. Ann Grundy supported Hurst's account. Knowlys seized on the discrepancies between Hurst's and Maynard's evidence. Wentworth, who cut a fine figure in court, was not examined, nor were witnesses called on his behalf. He was again found not guilty. The charge of feloniously assaulting Ann Grundy was dismissed.[32]

True to form, the *Daily Universal Register* ascribed Hurst's hesitancy in court to the darkness of the night on which he was robbed and to the difficulty of making accurate observations. It failed to discern that Wentworth was a beneficiary of Britain's bloody criminal code. By the late eighteenth century highway robbery was one of two hundred capital offences. The severity of sentences increasingly aroused sympathy for the criminal, and tempted prosecutors, witnesses, counsels,

1 Flame-coloured taffeta

juries, judges and advisers of the Crown to thwart the very laws they were meant to uphold. Moved by sentiments of mercy, on some occasions prosecutors mitigated offences, juries were reluctant to convict, and judges resorted to sentences of imprisonment or transportation as alternatives to the death penalty. In the cases of Wilkinson and Wentworth, compassion may have influenced the jury's verdict, as it may also have motivated Hurst and Grundy to give the evidence they did. It is even possible that Wentworth's friends could have attempted to influence the witnesses or members of the court. On 1 January 1788 the *Maidstone Journal* reported:

> When the notorious D'Arcy Wentworth escaped condemnation at Maidstone, it was said, some very powerful friends were to send him abroad in gratitude to the lenity which had been shown him; that gratitude, however, has evaporated, and to the shame of the police, he is let at large to prey still further upon the Public for otherwise how can he live?[33]

Rumours about D'Arcy crossed the Irish Sea to reach the ears of gossip-mongers at Portadown. He had, so the story ran, been drawn into fashionable society, and, in an attempt to meet his expenses, turned first to gaming before resorting to highway robbery. Such an account accorded with contemporary stereotypes. Novels, ballads, newspapers and folklore fanned popular imagination and pandered to a romantic fascination with 'gentlemen of the road'. Even hardened magistrates like Patrick Colquhoun classified highwaymen as a distinct group of criminals who were distinguished from 'the lower and more depraved part of the fraternity of thieves'. The *Criminal Recorder* was prescient in its observation:

> Many who have *taken the road*, as it is called, have been first induced either through necessity or extravagance; and being probably successful in their first attempts, they renew their depredations, notwithstanding they have procured a competency; but money thus obtained is soon spent; their success only tends to increase their audacity, and at length the constant repetition of their offence leads to a detection.[34]

The Wentworths

Polarity characterized D'Arcy Wentworth's being. Raised in the knowledge of the illustrious and ancient lineage of his family, he shared the opinion that its members were 'above the common ground'. In public he affected gentility and gained admittance to the homes of the respectable. His private life was raffish and clandestine, that of an outcast. It involved the temporary abandonment of his profession, the adoption of the alias 'Fitzroy' and a connexion with a mistress of dubious reputation in rooms near Oxford Market rented for half-a-crown each fortnight. It also entailed consorting with the rough coterie at the Dog and Duck and at the 'flash house' known as the Brown Bear, and gaining a reputation as a highwayman. Far from being bent on self-destruction, he was so possessed by arrogance and conceit that he had reached the point where he either would not, or could not, refrain from total recklessness. Vainglory and foolhardiness fed on each other.[35]

Within eighteen months of Governor Phillip's landing at Sydney Cove, George Washington was installed as president of the United States, the Paris mob stormed the Bastille and James Watt virtually completed his steam engine. Great shocks and small buffeted the fixed social order, even if it only existed as a reassuring frame of reference and as an abstract notion. About 11 o'clock on the damp summer morning of Sunday 5 July 1789 John Pemberton Heywood and Henry Russell, two circumspect barristers of Lincoln's Inn, were being driven across Finchley Common, north of Hampstead Heath, when their post-chaise was halted by a pair of masked highwaymen who demanded their money and watches. Heywood denied having a watch, but the taller highwayman brandished his pistol and said: 'Pho, Pho, I know who you are very well; I know you do travel with a watch, give it me'. Having collected their booty, they wished Heywood and Russell 'good morrow' and rode off. Heywood immediately remarked to his companion that, 'if I was not sure that D'Arcy Wentworth was out of the kingdom, I should be sure it was him'.[36]

Further and more desperate attempts by D'Arcy's friends to secure him a position overseas met with no success. On 16 October Villiers wrote to the Home Office. He stated that Wentworth was 'extremely desirous' to get to New South Wales where his training as a surgeon might prove useful; he asked that he be sent there, with a recommendation to the governor; and he further confided that, 'if he continues in

[18]

this country, it is scarcely possible for him to return to any honest course of life'. Villiers' letter was minuted: 'Nothing to be done'.[37]

By that month Wentworth was again under suspicion of involvement in a recent series of highway robberies. On Friday 6 November he approached a surgeon, Mr Howard, requesting his help to treat a man called 'Jack Day' who had been wounded by a pistol ball. Howard thought that Wentworth was a 'genteel young man', but became apprehensive when he was asked to keep the matter to himself because it concerned an affair 'which might occasion some uneasiness'. With much difficulty he persuaded Wentworth to allow the man, who appeared to be D'Arcy's servant, to be taken to Middlesex Hospital. At this time D'Arcy was living at 23 Clipstone Street, Marylebone, with another mistress who was to cling to him avidly over the weeks ahead. They were known as Mr and Mrs Wilson. Earlier on the 6th their landlord had overheard some of the conversation that passed between Wentworth and 'Jack'. On the 7th patrolmen visited the hospital and spoke with the patient. Thence they went to Clipstone Street where they arrested 'Mrs Wilson'. After dispersing the crowd which had gathered, they lay in wait for D'Arcy. On his return home they took him into custody. 'Jack Day' managed to slip away from the hospital when he heard of the arrest.[38]

Brought before the magistrate Nicholas Bond at Bow Street later that day, Wentworth disclaimed all knowledge of the wounded man, except that he had learned that his name was Jack and that he had been shot by someone who fired from a carriage. D'Arcy was again committed to the bridewell at Tothill Fields. He was re-examined four times, on 12, 14, 19 and 30 November, before being sent to Newgate to stand trial for the crimes committed against Heywood. On 13 November *The Times* posed the following enigma for its readers:

> Mr Wentworth's back papers shall be sent him with the future, but he must stop the paper sent from the former Hawker whose directions we have not. Nerva's favours are not forgot, but the lottery has engrossed much of our ransom.

Drawn by the coverage in *The Times*, a 'great concourse of people' attended the hearings, among them no lesser personages than the Duke and Duchess of Cumberland, brother and sister-in-law to the king, and

The Wentworths

His Grace the Duke of Hamilton, Scotland's premier peer. Two months earlier William Wentworth Fitzwilliam, the 4th Earl Fitzwilliam, had received the Prince of Wales at Wentworth Woodhouse and entertained 40 000 people in the park. Word of the earl's notorious relation may have spread during London's autumn season, whetting the appetite of those who found a divertissement in the discomfort of a fellow creature.[39]

Over the course of Wentworth's five examinations at Bow Street potential witnesses were rounded up or came voluntarily to the public office: they ranged from several gentlemen who had been robbed to post-chaise drivers and stable-keepers. Only Mr Howard positively identified him. Although Heywood was inclined to vacillate, he was subpoenaed for the prosecution. At the fifth hearing Wentworth proclaimed that he expected to be discharged, affirmed his innocence and expressed surprise at being remanded. Lamenting his situation, he said that he had resolved to amend his course of life, and he now feared that he would lose the berth which his friends had procured him to sail as a surgeon to Botany Bay. He added that 'his remaining in this country probably would be attended with the most fatal consequences to himself'.[40]

His trial at the Old Bailey took place on Wednesday 9 December 1789 before Sir Richard Perryn, one of the judges who had heard the case brought by Lewer against Wilkinson and Wentworth in 1787. By chance or by some arrangement, D'Arcy avoided appearing before Sir William Ashurst, who was also listed to sit that day and who had gained a reputation as a hanging judge. By circumstance or by some agreement, Russell did not prosecute, even though he—with Heywood—had been robbed on 5 July. Through Villiers, Russell had been acquainted with Wentworth since 1787. Lord Fitzwilliam had recently arrived in London where he assumed the expected role of a Georgian nobleman. As a representative of the ruling class he was accustomed to exercising paternal benevolence which created a 'mesh of vertical loyalties'. Such patronage, uneven, interrupted and frequently capricious in its operation, often found form in spontaneous and uncalculated acts to assist a relation in times of trouble. D'Arcy was enabled to retain the barrister William Garrow for his defence. A liberal Whig, and a friend of Thomas Erskine and Fox, Garrow was building a reputation as a consummate advocate in criminal cases.[41]

1 Flame-coloured taffeta

The indictment charged Wentworth with putting Heywood in fear and danger of his life, with feloniously taking from him a watch worth 40 shillings, four cornelian seals set in gold, a chain and a tweezer-case, valued in all at £8 2s 1d, and with robbing him of £7 in coins. Proceedings were managed with dispatch. Heywood swore to the events of 5 July and maintained that the wind had lifted the highwayman's crêpe mask, enabling him to see the lower part of his face. He verily believed that the prisoner in the dock was the man who had robbed him. Four years earlier, during the summer assizes, he had met and dined with D'Arcy at Robert Sinclair's home in York. Thinking him a most agreeable young gentleman from a good family in Ireland, he had helped to forward plans to enable Wentworth to leave England. Heywood concluded his evidence by stating that the highwayman had 'a pretty strong Irish brogue, as you will hear, if you hear him speak'.[42]

Under Garrow's cross-examination, Heywood admitted that Wentworth had grown much larger and stouter since those days in York, and agreed that he could not *positively* identify him as the tall highwayman. The court asked Wentworth if he wished to say anything. Garrow quickly rose to his feet and responded silkily: 'No, my lord, I would not advise him to say anything on this occasion'. No further witnesses testified for the prosecution. No witnesses were called by the defence. The case rested on the uncorroborated evidence of a single witness who was not prepared to make a definite identification. When the jury returned a verdict of not guilty, the prosecutor announced: 'My lord, Mr Wentworth the prisoner at the Bar says, he has taken a passage to go in a fleet to Botany Bay; and has obtained an appointment in it, as Assistant Surgeon, and desires to be discharged immediately'. The court granted his request. This arrangement may have stemmed from an out-of-court agreement between the prosecution and Wentworth's friends to have him acquitted on condition that he leave the country. Lord Fitzwilliam had agreed to fit his kinsman out and pay his fare to New South Wales. The press found the trial 'particularly uninteresting'.[43]

Eight cases were tried at the Old Bailey that day. Only two of the accused were acquitted. The remainder were sentenced to death. Of them, two were aged twenty, two eighteen, one was fourteen and one was twelve years old. Apart from Wentworth, the other person to be acquitted was George Barrington, a notorious pickpocket. *The Times* called them 'Lucky Dogs!'[44]

D'Arcy took only four days to finalize his affairs in London and to make his way to Portsmouth where the *Neptune* lay at anchor. Orders had been issued on 15 October 1789 that the *Neptune*, a transport ship in the Second Fleet, should move from the docks at Deptford to receive her complement of prisoners, together with a number of officers and men of the New South Wales Corps and their wives and children. By early November the soldiers and their families had been accommodated in the vessel. On the 11th the *Neptune* took on board four male and twenty-seven female convicts from Newgate prison. Sixty-one women from county gaols were also embarked, with nine of their children. Next day eighty-three males from the *Justitia* hulk and forty-one felons from the *Censor* at Woolwich were sent to the *Neptune*. On the 13th she sailed down the Thames from Long Reach to Gravesend, and thence for Plymouth. There, from 27 November, she embarked three hundred more male convicts from the hulk, *Dunkirk*. On 10 December she made for Portsmouth and three days later joined her sister ships, the *Scarborough* and the *Surprize*, at Stokes Bay.[45]

If Fitzwilliam were relieved at the prospect of having an irritating relation removed to an *ultima Thule*, he was not one to equate out of sight with out of mind. Referring to the events of 1789, he recalled that he had never approached the government or the civil service to obtain permission for D'Arcy to travel to New South Wales; nor had he sought any position for him, either in the *Neptune* or in the colony. For all that, Fitzwilliam was tolerant and humane, and willing to do more than provide money for D'Arcy's fare and outfitting. Black sheep have a place in a family, provided they roam faraway fields; stories about them can entertain guests at a dinner party or enliven clubland drollery. Given the mores of the eighteenth-century aristocracy, Fitzwilliam may have gained a certain éclat from D'Arcy's exploits, and it is likely that, from curiosity alone, he wished to know whether Wentworth would expiate his folly or die on a scaffold. Fitzwilliam instructed Charles Cookney, his London agent, to keep in touch with Wentworth and assist him as he could. Prudent and loyal, and unerring in his exactitude, Cookney was to act as Wentworth's counsel, accountant, intermediary and factotum for the rest of D'Arcy's life; furthermore, he would also

1 *Flame-coloured taffeta*

serve as agent to Lord Melbourne, and as guardian and adviser to Wentworth's children, and to his grandchildren.[46]

Replying to D'Arcy's missive of 13 December 1789, Cookney wrote to him on the 17th, sending his letter to the Crown Inn, Portsmouth, Wentworth's last land address in England. Cookney began by expressing his happiness at D'Arcy's account of being well received at the inn and in the *Neptune*. He indicated that he would gladly accept responsibility for managing his affairs; he assured him that, although he knew but little of him, he felt for him as if he were a relation; and he conveyed best wishes for his future welfare. Believing that ships might trade between India and Botany Bay, he asked Wentworth to attempt to gain information about John Parry, an East India Company marine officer who was Cookney's brother-in-law, and about George Wilson, a soldier whom Thomas Hill was endeavouring to contact in regard to a bequest. Both had last been seen in Bengal. Cookney went on to inform Wentworth that he had received no recent letter from Fitzwilliam in reference to him, nor had his lordship left any at Grosvenor Square. He then referred to Mrs Wilson, who was also known as 'Mrs Weaver' and 'Mrs Taylor'. He had given her only part of the money which Wentworth had left for her: 'indeed I was fearful lest I should pay her the whole that she would set out after you, which would have been a very silly pursuit, but there is no accounting for the action of a woman'. After receiving D'Arcy's letter of the 13th, Cookney had visited her lodgings, found that she was not at home and left a message for her to call on him. He ended his letter by telling Wentworth that he could rely on him to pay her the balance.[47]

It may have been as a result of Villiers' representations that Wentworth obtained permission to travel in the *Neptune*. When he boarded the ship in mid-December, he did so with official approval. D'Arcy had not, however, received any appointment as a surgeon, either to the *Neptune* or to the medical establishment in New South Wales. He attempted to gain a post, and the income and security it would bestow, by importuning his connexions to use their influence in his favour. In the light of his appearances in court, he showed little appreciation of the precariousness of his situation and the effrontery of his claims. D'Arcy was twenty-seven. Cookney had mentioned, in passing, the name of Thomas Hill, a lawyer of No. 8 Lincoln's Inn and an associate of Villiers. Without hesitation, Wentworth wrote to him from Portsmouth.[48]

Resentment and violence had erupted in the *Neptune* before D'Arcy joined the ship and ill feeling continued to simmer. It involved the captain, Thomas Gilbert, officers and men of the New South Wales Corps, and male and female convicts. As if in concert with the stormy passions on board, the weather off Portsmouth in December was tempestuous. Adverse winds kept the ship in Stokes Bay until 5 January 1790 when she sailed to Spithead and anchored at a point between the entrance to Portsmouth Harbour and Ryde. With the winds still against them, the flotilla sheltered off the coast of the Isle of Wight and tacked to the Mother Bank by 12 January.[49]

Thomas Hill wrote to Wentworth on the 16th. His letter was delivered to the *Neptune*. He informed D'Arcy that he had no doubts that Evan Nepean, under-secretary of state at the Home Office, had written to Governor Phillip about him, particularly as Nepean had been enjoined to do so by a duke of the realm. Hill had visited the Home Office, but was unable to see Nepean who was resting in Bath. None the less, Hill assured Wentworth that he would not be neglected. He could depend on him to make further application to Nepean, and he could also depend on Lord Fitzwilliam who 'is not a person that does things by halves'. As the wind in London was from the north, Hill wished D'Arcy a speedy and successful voyage, and signed himself his obedient and humble servant. Despite Hill's assurances, Wentworth's doubts were to be vindicated. Nepean did not instruct Phillip to forward Wentworth's prospects.[50]

Dawn on Sunday 17 January 1790 brought clear skies and a fine westerly breeze. The *Neptune* weighed anchor. Accompanied by the *Scarborough* and the *Surprize*, she sailed down the English Channel bound for the biggest penitentiary on earth. Years later Elizabeth Wentworth, D'Arcy's sister-in-law, reminded him of a Portadown legend which maintained that those who have drunk from the waters of the Bann, and are separated from their homeland, always return. He never did.[51]

2

The living and the dead

> both the living and the dead exhibiting more horrid spectacles than had ever been witnessed in this country
>
> David Collins, *An Account of the English Colony in New South Wales*

The six ships that composed the Second Fleet carried 1257 felons to the New World, but only three of the vessels sailed in convoy. In October 1788 Lord Sydney had expressed concern at the threat to public health posed by the state of his country's gaols. Newgate alone held more than 750 prisoners, and wards designed to house twenty-four were crammed with twice that number. On 2 February 1789 representatives of the Navy signed an agreement with the contractor, William Richards junior, commissioning the 401-ton *Lady Juliana* to be victualled, crewed and loaded with stores in readiness for a journey to Port Jackson. Captained by George Aiken, she left the Thames on 4 June and sailed from Plymouth on 29 July. On board were 226 female convicts under the care of the naval agent, Lieutenant Thomas Edgar, and the surgeon, Richard Alley, both of whom showed consideration for the women's physical welfare.[1]

Less attention was paid to their morals. According to John Nicol, the steward, when 'we were fairly out to sea, every man took a wife from among the convicts, they nothing loath'. Irons were removed, and the women were permitted access to the deck for fresh air and exercise. They were also allowed to move freely about the ship, to fraternize with the crew, to wear their own clothes and to buy wine at Port Praya Bay, Teneriffe, where the *Lady Juliana* anchored on 21 September. Lengthy

The Wentworths

calls at Rio de Janeiro (forty-one days) and at the Cape of Good Hope (nineteen days) enabled supplies of fresh meat and vegetables to be replenished. Seamen 'from every vessel in harbour were freely entertained' and there was 'no lack of either gaiety or liquor'. The officers made no attempt to suppress prostitution and the women created 'more noise than danger'. Pregnancies and births increased. Sarah Whitlam bore Nicol a son before the ship reached Sydney Cove on 6 June 1790, one year and two days after leaving the Thames. Only five of the convicts died during the passage. To Watkin Tench, a captain in the marines, the ship brought letters, the first direct word from England since he had sailed for Botany Bay over three years earlier: 'News burst upon us like meridian splendor on a blind man'. The arrival of the *Lady Juliana* raised the colonists' morale, not least because she carried limited supplies of food and clothing. Whether willing or unwilling partners in the debaucheries on board, her convicts doubled the number of women in the settlement. Nicol vowed to bring Sarah home once she had served her sentence. She promised to remain true when he sailed from Sydney on 25 July. Next day she married John Welch, a convict watchman.[2]

Back in England, additional stores were loaded into the Second Fleet's H.M.S. *Guardian* and the *Justinian*. Commanded by the 26-year-old Lieutenant Edward Riou, the *Guardian* was a frigate of 879 tons. Twenty-five male convicts were embarked at Spithead. They were all farmers and artificers from the hulks who were to help as seamen during the trip and to augment the few skilled workers in New South Wales. Seven free superintendents—two of whom came from the Royal Botanical Gardens at Kew—joined the ship, as did the daughter of one of them. The crew included the prime minister's cousin, 14-year-old Thomas Pitt, who had run away from Charterhouse and begged to be sent to sea. The *Guardian* sailed from English waters on 14 September 1789 with thirty-six passengers and a complement of eighty-eight. She called briefly at Teneriffe and anchored in Table Bay on 24 November. After leaving the Cape on 11 December, the vessel struck an iceberg, approximately at latitude 44° south and longitude 41° east, and was badly holed on Christmas Eve. A frantic effort ensued to keep the ship afloat and the deckhands operated the pumps to full capacity. Most of the animals, plants and stores were jettisoned. Sixty-three of the people on board were ordered to take to the boats; only fifteen of them were later rescued. With sixty companions, including twenty of the convicts, the badly injured Riou nursed the *Guardian* towards Table Bay and reached port by 21 February 1790. There the ship proved no longer seaworthy, and was beached and abandoned. Some of the meat and flour aboard was saved for transfer to other vessels in the Second Fleet. Riou's courage made him an instant celebrity, yet he remained unspoiled. He recognized his debt to the convicts who had assisted him and wrote to the British government requesting that they be pardoned.[3]

Having passed inspection at the Deptford naval dockyard on 19 November 1789, the *Justinian*, a three-decked, 398-ton storeship, was loaded in the Thames with 1400 casks of flour, 233 barrels of pork and smaller quantities of beef, peas, oatmeal, sugar, vinegar, oil and spirits, with 162 bales of clothing and a quantity of coverlets and blankets, and with a portable military hospital (valued at £690) which was dismantled into 602 pieces. Commanded by Benjamin Maitland and crewed by thirty-six men and boys, she sailed to Falmouth and left English waters on 17 January 1790. She called at St Iago in the Cape Verde Islands and completed her 154-day passage on 20 June. In all likelihood it was the *Justinian* that brought to the colony copies of *The Times* which contained accounts of Wentworth's committal hearings and trial in 1789.[4]

As early as July 1789 William Wyndham Grenville, the new secretary of state for the Home Office, had decided to dispatch one thousand convicts in the Second Fleet for New South Wales. Later that year an old lag on a hulk at Portsmouth blinded himself with a lancet so that he would never see Botany Bay. Preferring death to transportation, another hanged himself in Lancaster Gaol. Heedless of such reactions, the Navy Board complied with Grenville's wishes and invited merchants to submit tenders for supplying the requisite ships, provisions and stores. Economy ruled the transactions. Whereas William Richards junior had received £54 000 for transporting 770 First Fleet convicts, in August 1789 the board accepted the bid of a slave-trading firm, Camden, Calvert & King, to convey 1000 convicts for £22 370. Intent on profit, the contractors approached the East India Company for permission to carry home a cargo of tea from China. Evan Nepean and Charles Middleton harboured misgivings, particularly about the irons similar to those used in slave-ships: these shackles were fastened around the ankles by a 'short bolt' which prevented the wearer from extending his legs and restricted him to a shuffle. The contractors lodged bonds with the government which were liable to be forfeited if it were proved that their employees were culpable in allowing prisoners to escape. That month the board appointed Lieutenant John Shapcote as naval agent to sail with the flotilla. An ineffectual hack, he was aged fifty. It was his responsibility to see that the contractors and their agents transported the convicts in accordance with the contract. Camden, Calvert & King undertook through their broker to ensure that their three nominated transports were in good condition, fitted with secure accommodation for the convicts, and furnished with bedding, cooking equipment, cutlery and lamps. They also agreed to select and pay crews for the ships, and to enjoin their captains to obey the orders of the naval agent. A qualified surgeon was to be engaged for each vessel, medicines were to be provided for the sick, and, while visiting foreign ports, the soldiers and convicts were to receive fresh food—for two days per week to the value of one shilling—over and above their salt rations.[5]

By the terms of the contract, male and female convicts were to mess in groups of six, with weekly provisions of bread, flour, beef, pork, peas, butter and rice; in addition to these rations, the women were to be given tea and sugar. The allowance was reasonable in terms of quantity, though deficient in vitamin C and calcium. The soldiers received more—and doubtless better—meat and bread, as well as some cheese and oatmeal; their victuals also included one gallon of beer, or half a pint of rum, or a pint of wine a day. Each mess of convicts was to have 2 lb of soap per month; no provision of soap was made for the soldiers. Male and female felons were to be clothed according to specifications laid down by the Navy Office. The men were to receive a jacket, waistcoat, hat and worsted cap, two shirts, and two pairs of trousers, drawers, stockings and shoes, with a bag in which to carry their spare clothes. The women were to be given a jacket, two shifts, three petticoats, a pair of stays, a hat, two handkerchiefs, two pairs of stockings and shoes, and a bag. For all their range and detail, the clauses in the contract could be readily flouted.[6]

The soldiers belonged to a detachment of the New South Wales Corps which was to replace the marines who had accompanied Governor Phillip. On 20 May 1789 Sir George Yonge, secretary at war, promulgated the corps' formation; by September three hundred men had been recruited. Their commandant was Major Francis Grose. It was decided to dispatch about one hundred troops in the three ships,

2 The living and the dead

along with six officers and a surgeon's mate. Grose and the rest of the men would follow in due course. In the hurry and bustle no one delineated the respective authority of the ships' captains and the soldiers *vis-à-vis* the convicts. To carry the prisoners and troops, the contractors selected the *Neptune*, estimated at 809 tons, the *Scarborough*, 418 tons, and the *Surprize*, 400 tons, under the respective commands of Thomas Gilbert, John Marshall and Donald Trail. Gilbert and Marshall had sailed as skippers with the First Fleet; Trail had recently been employed by Camden, Calvert & King as master of a slaver on the Guinea run. By 13 November 1789 all the soldiers had been embarked. The *Neptune* then carried two officers, forty-three men, two wives and one child; the *Scarborough* two officers and thirty men; and the *Surprize* two officers, thirty men, seven wives and eight children. Accommodated where possible in the gun-room, the forecastle and the steerage areas of each ship, the soldiers were ordered to be brought on deck every morning so that their berths could be cleansed and their bedding aired. Smoking was not permitted between decks, and gaming and the sale of liquor were forbidden.[7]

Because a scattering of convicts received last-minute pardons or reprieves, there was room on board the ships for additional passengers. The male convicts were told that they could bring their wives and children on the voyage. Six chose so to do. In total, the three transports were to leave England with 1006 convicts, 78 females and 928 males. 504 male convicts were divided between the *Scarborough* and the *Surprize*, in roughly equal proportions. The *Neptune* alone carried female convicts, 78 out of her complement of 502. Shapcote received a warrant, dated 17 November 1789, specifically stating that the women were to be 'kept separate from the Men, and not abused or ill treated, but the contrary as far as is in your Power'. Quantities of linen, flannel and other supplies for pregnant women were ordered for the *Neptune*. Additional provisions were taken aboard, for consumption at sea and to feed the colonists in Sydney. Samuel Gates, the ship's steward, was to supervise the weighing and issuing of rations. Cooped and penned in the hold, poultry, pigs, sheep and cattle would consume fifty gallons of water per day in the tropics.[8]

Most of the 424 male convicts in the *Neptune* were housed in the orlop deck (third from the top) which was 75 feet long, 35 feet wide, and 6 ft 6 ins high between the beams and 5 ft 7 ins beneath them. They slept in bunks or hammocks in four rows of open-ended cabins, one row to the starboard, one to the port, and two in between. There were no portholes. Lights burned from dawn until 8 p.m. Each felon was chained by the wrists or ankles, and often to a companion. One man in a mess of six was released to collect a week's supply of rations and to cook meals daily. When a convict urinated, he used a bucket in his compartment; when he defecated, he used one of three large tubs on the orlop deck. Buckets and tubs were frequently overturned, by accident and by negligence. The stench of body odour, stale food, urine and faeces was noisome.[9]

Accommodated mainly in a section of the upper deck, the female convicts wore no chains. They were to be allowed range of the poop and quarterdeck while at sea. In contrast to the licence that prevailed in the *Lady Juliana*, a degree of order was enforced on board the *Neptune*. The crew requested access to the women, only to be denied. Undeterred, they frequently broke into the women's quarters at night, took them for their own use and procured them for the male convicts. Eventually, a section dividing the carpenter's berth from the women's compartment was surreptitiously removed. On numerous occasions when the sailors were found to have engaged in acts of illicit social or sexual intercourse with the female convicts they received a savage flogging. As the ship sailed from Plymouth to Portsmouth several prisoners died and were buried at sea. Carelessly weighted, four corpses floated with the tide to the shore at Gilkicker Point. During winter at Stokes Bay, Shapcote conducted a search of the convicts' quarters. Between seventy and one hundred knives were confiscated, most of them cutlery. Miscellaneous items, such as tin pots and chests with iron or brass fittings, were also appropriated. Assailed by fears that they might be fashioned into weapons for use in an uprising, Shapcote ordered these goods to be thrown overboard. As a pretext he proclaimed that he wanted to prevent the spread of gaol distemper. His action robbed many of the convicts of their personal clothing and private possessions, and diminished any respect they may have had for the naval agent who was charged with their welfare.[10]

Male convicts in the Second Fleet ranged in age from 10 to 68: one in twenty was under 16 years old, about a quarter between 16 and 20, around half were in the 21 to 30 bracket, and 2 to 3 per cent over 50; in this regard the females were almost identical, save that the youngest girl

2 The living and the dead

was an 11-year-old. More than half the men (53 per cent) had been tried in London, Middlesex or the Home Counties; of the remainder 16 per cent were tried in the South-West of England, 15 per cent in the Midlands, between 4 and 5 per cent in each of the groups of counties classified as belonging to the East, the North and the North-West, and 2.5 per cent in Wales. Almost three-quarters of the women in the *Lady Juliana* had been tried in London, Middlesex or the Home Counties, but only one-third of the women in the *Neptune* were tried in those districts and her complement included a higher proportion from the North. No male or female convict in the flotilla was tried in Scotland or Ireland. Eighty-six per cent of the males had been convicted of theft or burglary, usually involving domestic animals, clothing, shoes, linen, metal goods or food. No fewer than ninety-one men had been found guilty of highway robbery. There were two murderers, one rapist and one arsonist. Ninety per cent of the females had been convicted of theft or burglary. One in every four was a shoplifter. There were four pickpockets, two forgers, two perjurers and one who had absconded from a poorhouse. Nicol held that they were mostly 'disorderly girls' (by which he meant prostitutes) who had committed petty offences. At least one of the women was partially paralysed and two of the men were deemed to be 'idiots'. Probably half of the 1257 prisoners were illiterate. As a group, they were persistent criminals, guilty of more offences than that which resulted in their transportation. Youth was their major asset.[11]

Among the women in the *Neptune* was one named Catherine Crowley. Born in 1772, she was sentenced to seven years transportation on 30 July 1788 at the Staffordshire Assizes for stealing clothing from a house at Newcastle-under-Lyme. On 25 October 1789, with four other women, she was conducted from the gaol at Stafford to Woolwich on the Thames. When she boarded the *Neptune* for the long journey across the oceans she was seventeen years old. The destinies of her future lover and one of their progeny were to be inextricably linked with the vicissitudes of the early history of New South Wales, but the record of Catherine's appearance and character, her thoughts and her deeds, remains a blank.[12]

From the outset the issue of who held paramount authority over the convicts caused friction. The first dispute occurred in the *Surprize* and involved Captain William Hill of the New South Wales Corps and

[31]

the ship's master, Donald Trail. Well educated, upright in carriage and fastidious by disposition, Hill was aged thirty. Trail was fourteen years older. A Scot from the Isle of Orkney, he had served under Captain Horatio Nelson who thought well of him. Trail entered the African slave trade and became stubborn, foul-mouthed and brutal. On 18 November Hill boarded the *Surprize*. His sensibilities were affronted. From all he saw and heard, he was quickly convinced that his soldiers and the convicts had been badly accommodated, and had been fed salt rations even while the vessel lay in the Thames. Contemptuous of Trail for his incivility and lack of breeding, Hill was convinced that he, rather than the master, should decide when the prisoners would have their irons removed and when they would be allowed on deck. He threatened to use whatever force was necessary to take from Trail the keys to the hatches. While Hill complained to the Home Office, Trail informed Camden, Calvert & King of the incident. They in turn wrote to the Navy Board, condemning Hill's conduct and asking that he be removed from the ship. Shapcote sided with Trail. Several days later the board upheld Trail's authority.[13]

Hill's quarrel with Trail was to be mirrored in the rows on board the *Neptune*. Relations between Captain Gilbert and the military officers deteriorated from Friday 13 November, the day on which a 22-year-old army lieutenant joined the ship. That officer complained to Nicholas Anstis, the first mate, about the inadequacy of the cabin provided for himself, his wife and child, and their maid. Gilbert was furious at not being directly consulted which 'brought on some warm conversation' between him and the lieutenant. The two men refused to speak to each other while the ship plied to Plymouth. The lieutenant's anger grew as his family endured the shouting and swearing that emanated from the adjoining compartment housing the convict women, and the stench from their toilet buckets. The lieutenant complained to his superior, Captain Nicholas Nepean. Gilbert flew into a passion. On 27 November the lieutenant publicly rebuked Gilbert. They went on shore and fought a duel at 4 p.m. near the Fountain Tavern at Plymouth Dock. Two shots were exchanged. No injury was sustained, and the only damage was a hole in Gilbert's greatcoat. The seconds intervened and both men declared themselves satisfied. Next day Captain Nepean assumed charge of the convicts, averring that Gilbert had usurped too much power over him and his soldiers. Nepean

2 The living and the dead

took from Anstis the keys to the hatches and gave them to the lieutenant. He refused to surrender them to Gilbert. The master then assaulted and taunted a sentinel who vowed that he would use his bayonet to 'run him through'. Convinced that he had a mutiny on his hands, Gilbert left the ship to lobby for support. Captain Nepean appealed to his brother Evan, under-secretary of state at the Home Office. In this dispute Shapcote sided with Nicholas Nepean. The *Neptune* sailed from Plymouth Sound to Portsmouth. By 13 December officials in Whitehall had resolved, in principle, to uphold the authority of the ship's captain over the convicts, but, as a compromise, they decided to remove Gilbert from his command. Captain Trail took Gilbert's place in the *Neptune* and Anstis was made master of the *Surprize*. The lieutenant who had been at the forefront of the perturbation was John Macarthur.[14]

When the ships set sail at the Mother Bank on 17 January 1790 the potential of the army officers for disquiet was dispersed, but by no means dispelled. The *Surprize* carried William Hill, Ensign John Thomas Prentice, Hill's immediate subordinate, and John Harris, surgeon's mate to the corps, who had attended Wentworth's trial on 9 December 1789. On board the *Scarborough* were the lieutenants, John Townson and Edward Abbott. In the *Neptune* travelled Nicholas Nepean and John Macarthur, as well as John Shapcote, Trail's wife, Elizabeth, the ship's surgeon, William Gray, Macarthur's wife, Elizabeth, and their child, and the free passenger, D'Arcy Wentworth. Hill came from Gloucestershire, Townson from Yorkshire, Nepean from Cornwall and Elizabeth Macarthur from Devon; Abbott was Canadian born and Harris hailed from County Derry, Ireland; a minority of the convicts had Irish, Scottish or Welsh ancestry, or had been born in those countries; among the prisoners there was a Swede, a handful of Jews, and two or three Blacks from Africa or the West Indies; one of the superintendents was from Hamburg, one of the cooks was Portuguese and one seaman was Scandinavian. The flotilla was a floating commune, composed of heterogeneous elements as mixed as the waves and the weather it encountered throughout an odyssey of five months and sixteen days.[15]

John Macarthur was born near Plymouth on 13 August 1766, one of three known children of two expatriate Scots. As a youth he may have worked in his father's drapery business, for his opponents later ridiculed him as 'Jack Bodice', the staymaker's apprentice. He obtained an ensign's commission at sixteen, joined the 68th Regiment in 1788 and was promoted lieutenant when he transferred to the New South Wales Corps on 5 June 1789. Petulant, austere and resolved, with glowering eyes and a pouting lower lip, he had sharp features, a powerful voice and a face much marked by smallpox. By background and by temperament he had more in common with Wentworth than either would have conceded. A more tormented spirit, John was able to find serenity only in domestic life. In October 1788 he had married Elizabeth Veale, a timid, 22-year-old country lass, whose mother had regarded Elizabeth's ambitious but withdrawn suitor as 'too proud and haughty for our humble fortune'. A son Edward, born five months later, was a sickly and backward infant. On board the *Neptune*, Elizabeth was again pregnant. The family was increasingly isolated in the ship. Their closest ally, the squat and heavy-featured Surgeon Harris, John's second in the duel with Gilbert, had been ordered to sail in the *Surprize*. The Macarthurs ate together in their quarters, while Nepean dined and socialized in the captain's cabin with Trail and his wife, Shapcote and Gray. Starved of wider company, Elizabeth slowly developed inner resources. She kept a journal, but never mentioned Wentworth in its pages. Almost immediately on joining the *Neptune*, Wentworth had chosen Catherine Crowley, taken her to his cabin and made her his mistress, presumably with Trail's connivance. Shapcote had also selected a convict woman who 'constantly attended' him. Wentworth did not dine at the captain's table; nor did he mess with the surgeon, the soldiers, the superintendents or the sailors. Like the Macarthurs, he and Catherine kept to themselves. She, too, was pregnant.[16]

Saddened and depressed at parting with her only surviving parent, Elizabeth buoyed herself with the prospect of reaping material advantages from the land to which Mr Macarthur was taking her. No such hope consoled the prisoners, sixteen of whom had died before the *Neptune* left Portsmouth. Three days out to sea, on 20 January 1790 near the Bay of Biscay, a tempest battered the flotilla and the sea 'ran mountains high'. The bold were made craven. Next morning 'it was perfect calm', though the sea continued to be 'agitated by a swell'. Five days later a small vessel flying the French colours was seen in the distance. With the return of fair weather, opportunities arose to examine unfamiliar species of fish and seabirds, but, to the travellers' regret,

2 The living and the dead

Trail decided that the ships would not touch at Madeira or at Rio de Janeiro. Up to three months were to pass before they made port. Elizabeth soon learned a 'disagreeable truth'—that Trail was a 'monster', with a character of 'much blacker dye' than Gilbert's.[17]

Still resenting his allotted quarters, John Macarthur steeled his attitude towards Nepean for having moved from the great cabin, thereby allowing the contractors to subdivide it. One half housed the Macarthurs, the other some of the female convicts. Considering his superior to be guided by the maxim of 'every man for himself', John told Nepean that his action was 'highly indelicate'. It had exposed the Macarthurs to a 'set of abandoned creatures' from whom they were separated only by a thin partition. One concession was extracted: he and his family were permitted to use a passage through the gallery to the deck where they walked or sat together in the evenings. When a number of his men received short rations, Macarthur raised the matter with Nepean, whose reply was: 'Trail does everything to oblige me, and I must give up some points to him'. Subsequent requests were met with a terse: 'I will see into it'. By Elizabeth's account, unprovoked insults followed. On 31 January the door to the gallery was nailed shut, and the Macarthurs were compelled to share a common passage with the convict women 'and their constant attendants, filth and vermin'. John complained in writing to Nepean who told him that 'the master of the ship had a right to do as he pleased' and he would not quarrel with Captain Trail 'for any man'. Reason proved ineffectual in the altercation. Just as he had manipulated Shapcote, Trail had bent Nepean to his will or closed ranks with him. From this date the Macarthurs confined themselves to their quarters, except when John was on duty. Their servant caught a fever and they feared that the infection would spread. Edward became extremely ill and his mother expected the worst. Although his first birthday was imminent, he had not cut any teeth and was no bigger than a child of four months. On days when his health rallied, he appeared sensible and lively, and enchanted his parents. Elizabeth fretted over the delicate little creature and trusted that God would temper the wind to the shorn lamb.[18]

Another fracas over the soldiers' rations occurred on 10 February, four days before the twenty-eighth anniversary of Wentworth's birth. Furious at the steward, Samuel Gates, for cheating his mess of several pounds of meat, a sergeant requested Macarthur to intervene. William

[35]

Ellerington, the chief mate, overheard the discussion, called the sergeant a damned rascal and abused Macarthur. The matter was referred to Nepean. He dismissed it as a waste of time. Stung by this insult, Macarthur asked for a transfer to the *Scarborough*. Nepean agreed to expedite his request at the earliest opportunity, and was heartily glad to anticipate being rid of the lieutenant. Tempers frayed in the heat and humidity as the ships approached the Equator. Endeavouring to support her husband and to cope with their sick son, Elizabeth felt her strength and spirit desert her. In further acts of harassment the Macarthurs were deprived of their full victuals and their maid was closely watched to prevent the sailors from giving her more than the family's daily allowance of five quarts of water. To make matters worse, Elizabeth was taunted by the female convicts whose howls and insults showed the pleasure they took in aggravating her distress. On the 19th Lieutenant Townson exchanged places with John, and the Macarthurs were rowed with their baggage to the *Scarborough* in which they shared a small cabin with Lieutenant Abbott. Marshall, the ship's captain, 'a plain, honest man', made them as comfortable as possible, amused them with his accounts of New South Wales, and was well disposed to Elizabeth and Edward. With Macarthur's removal, no man on board the *Neptune* had the temerity to challenge Trail or to temper his cruelties.[19]

Meantime, there had also been trouble in the *Scarborough*. On 12 February she lost sight of the *Surprize* and lagged behind the *Neptune*. Some convicts began to whisper about a plot to seize the *Scarborough*. They were denounced by one of their number, Samuel Burt, a young forger from London, who suffered from a hereditary mental illness. Shapcote boarded the vessel. The ringleaders were ferreted out, severely flogged and chained to the deck. Regardless of whether or not they confessed, others were also punished. In all, Shapcote suspected that seventeen prisoners were involved. While it was never conclusively established whether the mutterings amounted to a conspiracy or were only wild fantasies fomented by rage and resentment, the alarm 'occasioned future circumspection' and led to a tightening of security. New procedures restricted the number of convicts who were allowed to exercise together on deck and the recalcitrant were kept in irons. None the less, due to Marshall's common sense, the convicts experienced better conditions than their fellows in the other two vessels. Four more convicts had died in the *Neptune*. On the 22nd that ship hove alongside a

2 The living and the dead

French Guineaman laden with slaves for Martinique. It was a symbol of Trail's past and an analogue to his present cargo.[20]

With her sister ships in her wake, the *Neptune* crossed the Line on 25 February. One morning in March a male convict was ordered on deck. Ellerington accused him of having slipped out of his wrist-irons at night. When the felon denied the charge, the chief mate asked the armourer to examine the irons to see if it were possible to shed them. The armourer thought that the shackles were riveted too closely for the prisoner to remove them. Ellerington was unsatisfied. 'Come over here and hold out your hands', he told the convict, ordering him to cover his thumbs with his fingers. The chief mate tried to pull the cuffs from his hands without success. He then placed his foot on the prisoner's stomach and wrenched the irons with greater force. 'Please don't use me ill Sir, please don't hurt me', pleaded the felon, but Ellerington tugged the irons so hard that one cuff was freed, tearing the flesh as it came. Convinced that he had proof of guilt, Ellerington sent for Trail and received his approval to inflict a flogging. The hapless man was tied to the bow of the longboat and a sailor was ordered to begin the punishment. The crewman hesitated, and Ellerington shouted that he would administer the cat himself if the flogging did not start at once. The punishment was brutal and the convict 'bled very much from the strokes'. When he was untied, his legs collapsed and he cried out that 'it was the last day he should live'. He begged the sailors to give him a draught of water. James Cowan did so. The felon drank deeply. Groaning in pain, he was left for three hours in the tropical heat and died where he lay. He had apparently been in good health before the whipping. With the exception of Cowan, no one brought him succour. Gray, the ship's surgeon, never examined the man. D'Arcy Wentworth did not go near him.[21]

Gates, Ellerington and Trail continued to maltreat the convicts as the *Neptune* rode the waters south-east to the Cape of Good Hope. In early April a violent storm tossed the flotilla for thirty-six hours and Hill was convinced that they were doomed to a watery grave. On the 13th, after a passage of eighty-six days, the ships entered False Bay and next morning dropped anchor by Simon's Town, in view of Table Mountain and twenty-five miles south of Cape Town. Landfall brought no peace. Hill had placed Prentice under arrest. At False Bay, Nepean arrested Hill. To prevent escapes, Shapcote directed all male convicts to be securely ironed. Trail allegedly allowed Dutch and British officers access to the female convicts for sexual purposes and even sent some of the women ashore for this end. Shapcote left the *Neptune* to visit the governor at Cape Town and to buy supplies of fresh food for the ships. He met Riou and arranged to take the twenty stranded convicts to New South Wales. Although the Dutch were charging exorbitant prices to store her cargo, Shapcote agreed to transfer only limited supplies of the *Guardian*'s salt meat and none of her flour. Riou thought him a fool. By the 24th, forty-five men and one woman had died in the *Neptune*, eight in the *Surprize* and fifteen in the *Scarborough*. The surgeons finally persuaded Shapcote to provide rations of fresh beef, vegetables and greens every day rather than twice a week as stipulated in the contract. Seasonal factors and demand may have raised the price of fruit that was high in vitamin C.[22]

For the fortunate, among them Wentworth, the fifteen-day call at the Cape afforded release: the relief of walking on land, a change of surroundings, the chance to make new acquaintances, and an opportunity to gain knowledge and broaden their experience. Mrs Macarthur was an inhibited tourist. She was received by the governor and introduced to his daughter, but, as the one lady spoke no Dutch and the other no English, all they could do was 'exchange dumb civilities'. In Simon's Town the houses were uniformly whitewashed and their doors and shutters painted green. Elizabeth paid ten and a half dollars per week to board with 'a genteel private family' whose spacious and airy home was kept spotless by a dozen slaves. John visited her daily, once he had finished his duty on board ship. With few exceptions, Elizabeth considered the Dutch no more friendly than the Cape's coastline. While she thought that those in positions of authority were rapacious in supplying any demand from ribbons to rum at a profit of 500 to 600 per cent, Mr Macarthur and Wentworth may have gleaned a lesson in colonial economics from their practices. For Elizabeth, the scenery was more romantic. She was impressed by the distant mountains and precipices, whither the Hottentots had been driven, and by the fertility of the lowland soil. Walking a mile and a half to the Dutch East India Company's garden to see the native shrubs and wildflowers, she had the practicality to observe the way in which vegetables flourished. It was autumn. Apples, pears and grapes abounded, wine cost one shilling a bottle, but

2 The living and the dead

the price of a cabbage was 1s 6d. Through her sojourn, Elizabeth's health and optimism were restored, though the respite was fleeting.[23]

Edward's condition deteriorated in their last days at the Cape and Elizabeth was terrified that each hour would be his last. John was attacked first by lumbago and secondly by a fever that raged until 'every sense was lost and every faculty but life destroyed'. Doubly afflicted as a mother and a wife, Elizabeth received assistance from Marshall and from Captain Reid, the commander of a visiting British East Indiaman. No officer in the New South Wales Corps helped her. A greater worry beset them. Scurvy was spreading through the ships. The symptoms were evident: swollen, bleeding and infected gums which loosened the teeth and made the breath offensive; soreness and stiffness in the joints and legs which blackened the limbs as the sinews contracted; spontaneous bruises under the skin and in deep tissues; anaemia; and, eventually, internal haemorrhages which could cause death. Those who suffered from scurvy experienced great difficulty in eating even soft foods such as rice. Thirty convicts in the *Surprize*, 10 soldiers and 57 convicts in the *Scarborough*, and 15 soldiers and 103 convicts in the *Neptune* had come down with the disease, which had broken out shortly before 24 April. No evidence exists that Wentworth tended any of the sufferers. Mrs Macarthur did not write one word of their plight.[24]

Despite the soldiers' and convicts' illness, a prolonged stay in port entailed the expense of fresh provisions. Trail was intent on sailing. The ships left False Bay on 29 April. Between decks, scurvy, dysentery and typhoid fever assumed epidemic proportions. Shapcote was an early casualty. At about 4 a.m. on 12 May a female convict informed Ellerington of the naval agent's sudden death. On board the *Scarborough* Edward Macarthur gained strength, but Elizabeth endured fresh misery in the Roaring Forties when she fought anew for her husband's life. She nursed John for five weeks, aided by one or two soldiers who sat with her and watched over him at night. Sleep came to her in snatches as she rested her head on a locker. Her husband hovered on the lip of eternity, yet clung precariously to life. The danger somehow passed and he became convalescent, though he could not walk without assistance. For all the resilience of her youth, the effort exhausted Elizabeth. Fatigue and anxiety brought on a premature labour and she gave birth to a daughter who lived 'but for an hour'. Meanwhile, in Wentworth's cabin in the *Neptune*, Catherine Crowley swelled with child.[25]

Midway between the Cape and Port Jackson autumn turned to winter. Heavy gales and high seas lashed the ships, interrupting the cooking of meals and preventing exercise on deck. The hatches were battened down, but not before water had cascaded through to the lower decks, drenching the guards, the prisoners and their pitiful possessions. The three vessels shipped so much that, for part of the final leg, some of the soldiers were hip-deep in water. In the orlop decks it rose to the convicts' waists. There they remained—wet, cold, sick, hungry and in chains. When the bad weather abated, no effort was made to dry or fumigate the compartments. Trail again withheld provisions for sale in Sydney. Starving felons ate the poultices from their own sores, stole tobacco plugs from the mouths of their sick companions, and tried to conceal the dead in order to obtain their rations. Moans of delirium mingled with screams and sobs, and with the incessant sounds of lapping water and whining cordage. In that pandemonium the healthy preyed on the sick. A black market emerged through which the crew sold food and drink to the prisoners. The price for a pint of fresh water was 2s 6d; a silk handkerchief bought two biscuits, a pair of shoes three, and a new shirt four. Sailors and convicts were routinely flogged for these and other offences.[26]

On 26 June the *Surprize* anchored in Sydney Cove. There, three days later, the *Neptune* and the *Scarborough* joined her. The passage from the Cape had taken sixty-one days. Of the 759 convicts in the First Fleet, 23 had died during the eight-month journey, a mortality rate of 3 per cent. Of the 1006 convicts who sailed in the *Neptune*, the *Scarborough* and the *Surprize*, 267 had died (256 men and 11 women), a staggering mortality rate of 26.5 per cent, with the male death rate (27.5 per cent) being almost double that of the female (14 per cent). *Neptune* lost 147 men and 11 women (31 per cent of her complement), 73 convicts perished in the *Scarborough* (28 per cent) and 36 in the *Surprize* (14 per cent). One soldier died *en route*. The voyage had ended but the nightmare had not. Only 248 prisoners—one in four—were landed in anything like fair health, and they were emaciated. A further 491 were either admitted to hospital or received medical treatment as out-patients: 269 from the *Neptune*, 96 from the *Scarborough* and

2 The living and the dead

126 from the *Surprize*. By the end of the year 117 of them (115 men and 2 women) had died, raising the number of dead males to 371 (40 per cent) and dead females to 13 (16.7 per cent), a total of 384, virtually two-fifths of those who had sailed. The mortality rate was the highest of any transports that came to the Australian colonies in the eighty-year history of convict transportation. It earned the ships the label of the 'Death Fleet'.[27]

Judge-Advocate David Collins looked aghast at the spectacle of the living and the dead in the little armada. One woman who had been transported in the *Lady Juliana* said that her heart bled at the 'melancholy sight'. The Reverend Richard Johnson was appalled to discover that the bodies of convicts who died as the vessels came up the harbour had been dumped overboard to be washed ashore. He boarded the *Surprize* and went down among the prisoners where he saw numbers lying naked or half-clad, 'without either bed or bedding, unable to turn or help themselves'. Johnson spoke to them as he passed by, but 'the smell was so offensive' that he 'could scarcely bear it'. The clergyman was persuaded not to venture into the *Scarborough*'s lower decks, and he did not attempt to visit the *Neptune* which 'was still more wretched and intolerable'. He did, however, watch the convicts being disembarked:

> The landing of these people was truly affecting and shocking; great numbers were not able to walk, nor to move hand or foot; such were slung over the ship side in the same manner as they would sling a cask, a box, or anything of that nature. Upon their being brought up to the open air some fainted, some died upon deck, and others in the boat before they reached the shore. When come on shore many were not able to walk, to stand, or to stir themselves in the least, hence some were led by others. Some creeped upon their hands and knees, and some were carried upon the backs of others.

Most of them were 'covered with their own nastiness, their heads, bodies, cloths, blanket, all full of filth and lice'. The local hospital, built of timber and shingles, was quickly overfilled with eighty patients. Thirty tents were pitched on the soaked earth near the gallows tree to accommodate the majority of the ill. On the first night they had only grass for

[41]

bedding. Blankets were soon unloaded, but it took two weeks to assemble the portable hospital. In the struggle for survival stronger convicts stole food from their weaker fellows, or, if compelled to share a bed, pulled the coverings from them. When a patient died, his body was stripped in minutes. At dusk the howls of dingoes could be heard as they fought for the corpses that had been thrown into a common pit.[28]

Inwardly seething over the calamity, Governor Phillip tersely informed Grenville that the contractors had packed too many convicts into the ships and that the masters had unduly confined them on the way. While Collins attributed the high mortality in part to the heavy irons and the manner in which prisoners were shackled together, he showed more perspicacity in seeing that the fault lay in the contract. The government had engaged to pay Camden, Calvert & King a set fee of £17 7s 6d for every felon embarked, irrespective of whether he or she lived or died; indeed, in terms of the ledger, the dead were more profitable than the living. The most trenchant criticism came from William Hill who was driven to rage and despair by the evil that had been done. In writing to his patron Samuel Wathen, an acquaintance of William Wilberforce, Hill singled out Trail and Anstis, and damned them for being barbarians, guilty of 'villainy, oppression, and shameful peculation'. The more provisions they withheld, the more they had available for sale at the journey's end; the sooner a convict died, the greater the profit. 'The slave trade' was 'merciful compared with what I have seen in this fleet', he concluded, for it was in the slave-traders' interests to preserve the health and lives of their captives. Harrowed by the misery, and by his impotence to mitigate the suffering, Hill doubted that he could ever regain his former vivacity. He eventually befriended an orphaned Aboriginal boy named Bondel.[29]

In July 1790 Donald Trail had opened a general store in Sydney. Although he was regarded as a pariah and charged extortionate prices, the food and clothing he sold drew eager customers. On 22 August he left Port Jackson in the *Neptune* to sail via Canton for England. Late in 1791 a London newspaper, the *World*, published an account of his nefariousness which created a public outcry. An attorney, Thomas Evans, went with several witnesses and depositions to the magistrate Nicholas Bailey at Bow Street, seeking a warrant for the arrest of Trail and Ellerington. He accused them of murdering the ship's Portuguese cook, John Joseph, and of causing excessive deaths among the convicts

2 The living and the dead

through neglect and mistreatment. Trail fled to Belgium. On 30 November Evans brought ten of the *Neptune*'s sailors to swear statements before Alderman Clark at the Guildhall. In February 1792 questions about the Second Fleet were raised in the House of Commons. One month earlier Henry Dundas, secretary of state at the Home Office, and his under-secretary, John King, had both written to Phillip to assure him that the strictest inquiry would be undertaken with a view to prosecuting those responsible for the 'inhuman treatment' of the convicts in the *Neptune*. The promiscuous Dundas (1st Viscount Melville from 1802), who owed his political career in part to William Pitt and stuck to him, as one contemporary put it, as fast as a barnacle to an oyster shell, usually seemed intent on employing his talents to the greatest personal advantage. On this occasion he was stung to take a selfless action. He asked the comptroller of the navy and the attorney-general to begin an investigation. Delay, denial and evasion followed, as civil servants tried to shield themselves from blame. Yet many were at fault: the Home Office for its wish to reduce the cost of transportation; the Navy Board for its want of supervision over the contractors; Camden, Calvert & King for its greed and negligence; and the firm's employees for their rapaciousness and cruelty. Finally, on 8 June, Trail and Ellerington appeared in the dock at the Old Bailey Admiralty Sessions, indicted for the murders of John Joseph and of Andrew Anderson, the sixth mate of the *Neptune*. No charge was laid against them for the death of a single convict. The prosecution was led by the attorney-general and the solicitor-general; William Garrow represented the defendants.[30]

Garrow discredited the witnesses, reprobated Evans's conduct as inflammatory, and convinced judge and jury that there was insufficient evidence to link Joseph's death with the flogging he had received. A verdict of not guilty was returned. The second indictment was dropped. On 6 July, within a month of Trail's acquittal, the attorney-general sent a report to the Home Office claiming that the contractors had described the *Neptune* as a ship of 800 tons when she was in fact only 400 tons in burthen, and that the provisions she had taken on board in 1789 were of poor quality. He recommended that the Navy Board should hold a full inquiry into the conduct of the contractors and into that of its own officers. Dundas referred the report to the Admiralty who in turn referred it to the Treasury. The issue was forgotten in the uproar that followed the execution of Louis XVI in January 1793 and France's declaration of war against Britain in the following month. Camden, Calvert & King escaped any prosecution for criminal liability. On 18 November 1790 the firm had signed a further contract to outfit the Third Fleet which sailed in February–March 1791 and reached New South Wales between July and October that year with a mortality rate of 10 per cent. The company was never again employed to transport convicts. Dundas introduced new arrangements whereby contractors were to be paid £17 per convict embarked, and an additional £5 for each one landed alive. Trail returned to naval service in 1792 and was appointed acting-master of H.M.S. *Temeraire* in 1799. Back at Simon's Town, from 1795 to 1798 he had held the post of master-attendant which authorized him to collect fees and taxes. He also entered into partnerships that dealt in slaves and in captured enemy vessels. With a fortune of £60 000, he returned to England in 1801, bought twenty-eight houses in London and an estate in Kent, and died in 1814. His wife and daughter survived him.[31]

Publishers alert to a market in the esoteric and the exotic had, in 1789–90, printed at least six books about New South Wales, among them the work of Phillip, Tench and Surgeon John White. For the most part these accounts presented glowing pictures of the infant colony by emphasizing the 'goodness' of the soil, the 'fineness' of the climate and the 'rapid progress' of the settlement. Before she sailed from England, Elizabeth Macarthur reassured her mother that she was going to a place of comfort, 'where nature had been so lavish' in her bounty. Her confidence was misplaced. The Second Fleet increased Sydney's population from a paltry 591 to 1715. When Mrs Macarthur and Mr Wentworth stepped separately ashore they gazed on a cheerless scene. Before them lay nothing more than a crude village, shaped like a crescent, clinging to the rim of a naturally contoured saucer. On one side the garrison was hemmed in by the waters of Port Jackson and the Pacific Ocean, and on the other by a grey-green, primeval wilderness which the Europeans had penetrated no farther than fifty miles. A primitive convict settlement nestled in the basin by the cove, but its denizens had known hunger, nakedness and despair before the arrival of the *Lady Juliana* and even the strongest were capable of no more than three hours toil a day. The remainder continued wayward, refractory and idle, dreading punishment less than they feared labour. If the human beings were

2 The living and the dead

unpromising, rain and drizzle did not help the aspect. To Surgeon Harris, Sydney was 'the most miserable place I ever beheld'.[32]

There were compensations. The light was vivid, the harbour and bays impressed onlookers with their beauty, the flora and fauna held the delight of novelty, and land offered freedom from the restrictions of shipboard life. But so much appeared mean and oppressive: the rude lines of barracks, the sagging tents along the waterfront, the sink of vice in the area of The Rocks to the west, the sad rows of thatched-roofed, wattle-and-daub cabins, the stone magazines—built without mortar—in which salt meat and grain were stored and rats ran riot, the governor's humble cottage on the slope of the eastern hill, the stump-strewn tracks, and the muddy banks of the Tank Stream which flowed into the head of the cove. There were no street lights, no shops, no theatre, no church and no sign of civilized amenities. Except for the clergyman's wife and Mrs Macarthur, no lady lived in New South Wales. Dirt tracks extended beyond the confines of the settlement, but it was unsafe to venture far and risk the Aborigines' spears. The camp was scarcely safer than the bush. Ninety per cent of its inhabitants carried the stigma of convictdom and a number of them were vicious and dangerous. Barefooted sentinels stood guard and patrolled the district, but even Phillip's home was not immune from burglary. Violence simmered on the surface of daily life. The sense of grievance and the despair of the gaoled was measured against the callousness and the sense of guilt of the gaolers. Some of the marines found mistresses among the female felons; others provided custom for the whores. Gaming and drunkenness in the mess gave rise to duels and the clamour for court martials. In that closed society men's minds fixed intensely on tiny matters and irritations expanded into obsessions. Civil, military and naval officers formed friendships and broke them, shared intimacies and betrayed them, as they swung between moods of headiness and despondency. Over their gatherings hung the consciousness that they were stranded at the end of the world and that their very existence depended on the arrival of the next food-ship. The alien soil had failed to support them. Wheat and barley often yielded less than thrice the quantity of seed sown. A few paddocks had been cleared and fenced in the off-chance that more cattle would arrive. Fresh meat cost 1s 6d a pound, a small pig 15 shillings, and even fish were expensive; the price of a dozen bottles of port wine was forty shillings and of sherry fifty; soap fetched four shillings a pound, Irish salt butter 1s 6d, sugar two shillings, flour—when it could be bought—one shilling, and tea was extraordinarily dear. The expense was more than Hill could afford, even on his captain's salary. Summer was to bring conditions to which the newcomers were unaccustomed: winds that seared, temperatures of 112°F, flies, mosquitoes, grubs, caterpillars and bull ants. The genialities of Hill's fellow exiles soon wore thin, and familiarity and routine made the longing for home more insistent. He was not alone in looking persistently to the sea whence rescue or escape might ultimately come.[33]

Wentworth's attitude to the colony was that of a transient, for he was determined to return, either to England or to Ireland. Memories of London and Portadown inhibited his immediate acceptance of the new land. According to the records that have survived, the only person who mentioned his name was Collins, and he did so in passing. In Sydney, as in the *Neptune*, D'Arcy was a man apart. On that ship he might have associated with Shapcote and William Gray, or mixed with the superintendents and crew, but he chose not to do so. Harris's gossip about the appearances at the Old Bailey prejudiced the Macarthurs against Wentworth, and their animosity became entrenched when he bedded the convict Catherine Crowley. He had the appearance and bearing of a gentleman, as well as influential connexions, but his behaviour did not accord with John Macarthur's ideal, or with that publicly upheld by the coterie of ramshackle military officers. To them, while he was not a convict, he was so near to that status as made no difference and they drew a line accordingly. He had reached some agreement with Trail, at least in regard to Catherine Crowley, but then steered clear of him. Like Nepean and Shapcote, he did nothing to oppose the ship's master. Wentworth neither attended the convict who was flogged to death in March, nor treated others who were sick and dying, though his profession laid claims on him. To continue as one of the living, he buried what humanity he possessed. Guided by the notion of 'every man for himself', he lay low, in eclipse, making himself a shadowy and unobtrusive figure.[34]

Anything more can only be conjecture. He may have read on the voyage; equally, he may not have. He probably thought that he had been shabbily treated by his companions in the *Neptune* and even by his friends in England; he possibly entertained no such ideas. He may or may not have harboured plans of vengeance or retribution. Perhaps he cast his mind over his early years, reflected on the crimes for which he was tried, contemplated his debt to Fitzwilliam and speculated that he had been given a chance to expiate his guilt. Perhaps he did not. He certainly conversed, long and often, with Catherine. What began as dalliance grew to affection, and, to some degree, he shared her hopes and fears as the child kicked within her. Both Wentworth and Crowley were strong and lucky. They retained their health. Unlike Hill, D'Arcy did not complain, officially or unofficially, to anyone about Trail's or Ellerington's conduct. Never once in the remaining thirty-seven years of his life would he refer in all his voluminous writings to his journey to Australia. Many years were to pass before his words disclosed some of the secrets of his past, even to his children. Over that shame he drew a veil, beneath which he concealed his hurt, his resentment and the days when he was green in judgement.

Having arrived in Sydney, Wentworth was an exile—at best, half-voluntary, at worst, against his will. Over the next thirty-two days he acquiesced in his obscurity and accepted what was decided for him. Bowed but unbroken, he retained a bitter pride, observed what he could, learned a lot, and bided his time. Only gradually would he find real purpose. Despite the advantages of employing Wentworth on the medical staff in Sydney, Phillip was cautious about offering him an appointment in the settlement. Instead, he directed him to proceed to Norfolk Island in the capacity of an acting assistant-surgeon. Wentworth was on probation. If he conducted himself well, he would be permitted to return to Sydney. Together with Catherine, 156 other female convicts, 37 male convicts, two superintendents and a deputy-commissary, D'Arcy boarded the *Surprize* and sailed on Sunday 1 August 1790 for the lonely outpost 920 miles east-nor-east in the Pacific Ocean.[35]

3

Remember not past years

> I loved the garish day, and spite of fears
> pride ruled my will; remember not past years
>
> John Henry Newman, *Lead Kindly Light*

On 11 October 1774, in the course of his second voyage around the world, Captain James Cook set foot on an uninhabited speck of land located in the midst of the vast Pacific Ocean at latitude 29° 02' south and longitude 167° 57' east. He named it Norfolk Isle. Cook was impressed by the fertility of the volcanic soil in which the cabbage tree, the flax plant and the giant spruce proliferated. After felling one of the smaller pines, the ship's carpenter told him that it resembled those that flourished in Quebec. Cook used the timber to replace a topmast in the *Resolution*. The island was five miles long and three wide; its average elevation was 350 feet, with two peaks rising to slightly over 1000 feet; the vegetation was that of a dense, subtropical rainforest, laced with vines and undergrowth. Breathtaking in its beauty, with green sloping hills and balmy weather that varied little from a minimum of 49°F in winter to a maximum of 85°F in summer, the island had a spectacular variety of birds, abundant fish, azure seas, white rolling surf and twenty miles of coastline mostly bounded by near-vertical cliffs about 300 feet high. In time this paradise would be rendered a hell-hole.[1]

Although there was no safe harbour, Cook's report of the island's flax and pines so dazzled government officials in London with the prospect of obtaining raw materials for rigging and masts that in 1787 they instructed Arthur Phillip to establish a settlement there. Shortly

3 Remember not past years

after moving his penal camp from Botany Bay to Sydney in the summer of 1788, the governor appointed Philip Gidley King as superintendent and commandant of Norfolk Island. Born on 23 April 1758 at Launceston in Cornwall, King—like John Macarthur—was a draper's son. At the age of twelve he joined the navy as a captain's servant and was commissioned eight years later. He had a sense of humour as a young man and played practical jokes. From the early 1780s he served with Phillip who formed a high opinion of his merits and chose him in October 1786 as second lieutenant to sail in the *Sirius* to Botany Bay. An able and energetic administrator, capable of advancing the public interest while feathering his own nest, King combined a benevolent concern for others with an irascible temper. On 15 February 1788 he sailed from Sydney Cove in the armed tender, *Supply*, under the command of Lieutenant Henry Ball. The superintendent's companions numbered twenty-two: a midshipman, James Cunningham, two surgeons, Thomas Jamison and John Altree, the seamen, Roger Morley and William Westbrook, two marines, Charles Heritage and John Batchelor, nine male convicts ranging in age from fourteen to seventy-two, and six female convicts, among them Ann Inett, a dressmaker and a thief who had been sentenced to seven years transportation. On board the *Supply* they took with them six months provisions, a four-oared boat, a few domestic animals and fowls, some tents and slops, and a small quantity of farm implements and flax-dressing tools. Thus equipped, they were charged with founding the second British settlement in the Pacific.[2]

The *Supply* reached her destination on 28 February and circled the coast for five days before finding an entrance to what would be known as Sydney Bay. People and provisions were landed by boat. Tents were pitched. On 6 March at Sydney (later called King's Town and subsequently Kingston) the colours were hoisted and King formally took possession of the island. Toasts were drunk to 'His Majesty', 'The Queen', 'The Prince of Wales', 'Governor Phillip' and to 'The Success of the Colony', after which those assembled gave three inebriated cheers. Two days later the ship departed for Port Jackson, leaving King and his party to fend for themselves. They began to clear the nearby ground, to sow grain and vegetable seeds, and to erect shelters. Despite numerous setbacks, King reported favourably on the settlement's progress, but death depleted the colonists' numbers. On 15 June Batchelor fell into the treacherous surf in Sydney Bay and drowned; the *Supply* returned with more provisions on 26 July and on 6 August heavy seas overturned a boat while it was attempting to reach the vessel, occasioning the deaths of Cunningham, Westbrook and Williams, a convict. The settlement was reduced to nineteen (an executive of five and fourteen prisoners) but the arrival of the *Golden Grove* on 13 October brought the population to sixty-four. The *Supply* came back with provisions in March, June and December 1789, and again in January 1790, by which time Norfolk Island's inhabitants had increased to 149. On 19 March the *Sirius* ventured too close to the reef at Sydney Bay and was wrecked, though no lives were lost. She brought Major Robert Ross, two companies of marines and more than two hundred convicts from Sydney; the eighty members of the crew of the *Sirius* were also landed and most of them endured eleven months of troubled sojourn. Their arrival raised the number of settlers to 498, more than trebling the demand for food. The thirty acres under cultivation could not fulfil the need, and survival largely hinged on the risky business of retrieving supplies from the wreck. Recalled by Phillip to carry dispatches to England, King sailed that month for Sydney in the *Supply*. Ross, his successor as commandant, remained at Kingston in charge of a group of people who had no means of escape or of communication with the world outside.[3]

Phillip had sent Ross to Norfolk Island to rid himself of a lieutenant-governor with whom he had been at odds since January 1788. A cantankerous, 50-year-old Scot, Ross had missed no opportunity to embarrass and hinder the governor, and Phillip was anxious to avoid an open quarrel with his deputy. Collins harboured 'inexpressible' hatred for the major; Lieutenant Ralph Clark thought that Ross was 'without exception the most disagreeable commanding officer' he ever knew. On Norfolk Island, Ross convinced himself that he faced a crisis which required desperate measures. His first official act was to proclaim martial law on 22 March 1790. Four days later he announced that plundering the public stores would be dealt with as a capital crime. Having reduced weekly rations to 3 lb of flour, 1.5 lb of salt beef and 1 pint of rice per person, next month he encouraged the settlers to satisfy their hunger by eating a species of petrel. This 'Bird of Providence' or Bill Hill Mutton Bird (*Pterodroma melanopus*) nested on Mount Pitt, 'a hill as full of holes as any rabbit warren'. Using torches made of pine knots to light their way, men, women and children joined in an eerie and primitive ritual as they made nightly excursions up the mountain to procure the birds and their eggs. The petrels 'had a strong fishy taste', commented Captain John Hunter, 'but our keen appetites relished them very well; the eggs were excellent'. Between April and August an estimated 170 000 birds were slaughtered, and, with the fish caught in calm water and the heads of palm trees eaten as cabbages, pressure on the public stores was relieved.[4]

Ross encouraged the convicts to maintain themselves by forming them into small parties, to each of which he allotted sections of cleared land and distributed one sow. He limited the hours of government labour for the convicts and envisaged the growth of self-supporting communes, but, since the majority of the prisoners had no experience of farming, the scheme created discontent and pilfering continued. Cohabitation between the felonry and the free was not uncommon, even if the dearth of eligible females meant that 'wives' were as young as fourteen. The marines lacked beds and blankets, and there was a shortage of cooking utensils, 'not a pot to every twelve men'. None the less, through Ross's efforts, good clay was found and twelve felons were employed in making bricks. The carpenters constructed two cobles (fishing boats) and a third was being built; they also made oars and one thousand axe-helves. A village was founded in the north at Phillipburgh, near Cascade Bay, where the dressers prepared two specimens of treated flax to be sent to Governor Phillip. Another outstation to the west at Charlotte Field had been established in an untimbered valley on the way to Anson Bay, and there the major planned to create a government farm. One ominous sign was the pests: caterpillars, flies and rats destroyed much of the crop before harvest, yet there were indications that wheat and barley could yield twenty-five times the seed sown, and that sugar-cane, oranges, potatoes and other vegetables would do well. The greatest rub was the absence of alcohol. By August 1790 Ross and Clark breakfasted on dry bread and on coffee made from burnt wheat. They had not tasted wine, beer or tea for months, and anticipated a 'dry' Christmas with nothing but cool water to greet the festive season.[5]

When hope was fast diminishing, and Ross proposed to reduce weekly rations to 2 lb of flour and 1 pint of peas per person, the *Justinian* came in sight of Norfolk Island on 7 August. She was laden with provisions and the residents rejoiced at their deliverance. After a speedy passage, the *Suprize* joined her late that afternoon. Both ships lay offshore. Next day the vessels moved closer to Sydney Bay. The weather was fine, the breeze a moderate north-westerly and the waters calm, but Hunter—the former commander of the *Sirius*—had learned from his ill fortune. He directed Lieutenant William Bradley and Mr Donovan to board the vessels and advise their masters on the peculiar dangers of the surf. Ross gave priority to the unloading of stores and ordered the convicts to remain on board. Hunter supervised the landing site, and the boats carrying provisions were manned by seamen from the *Sirius* as a precaution against accident. The weather was favourable for four days, during which all went without mishap. Then the wind freshened and the surf began to rise, forcing the ships to retreat to the northern side of the island where they sheltered in Cascade Bay. On Friday 13 August 1790 it blew a squall. That day, while the *Suprize* was anchored in the bay's protected waters, Catherine Crowley gave birth to a son who was to be named William.[6]

By the 16th the winds abated and the ships plied to Sydney Bay where the irksome job of unloading was resumed. On the 17th a sudden succession of large waves hit a boat which was ferrying female convicts and casks of salt meat from the *Suprize*. The sea lifted the boat, tossed it against the reef and split it in half. Thrown into the surf, the women and sailors fought against a strong tide running out from the shore. A crowd of nearly five hundred watched aghast at the water's edge. John Roberts, a convict, dived into the sea in an attempt to rescue some of the victims. He, too, was carried out by the current. Three women somehow managed to struggle ashore, but seven souls perished: three female convicts and a child, two seamen from the *Sirius*, and Roberts. The shocking sight afflicted all who witnessed it, heightening their recognition that life was precarious and fate random.[7]

Having taken almost three weeks to unload their provisions and convicts, the *Suprize* put to sea on the 29th and the *Justinian* on the 30th. Norfolk Island's contact with the wider world was again severed. Enlarged by new arrivals, the population totalled 718, comprising 197 free persons (including 78 men from the *Sirius*), 228 male convicts, 257 female convicts and 36 children. Ross discontinued martial law, restored full allowances, and turned the residents' attention to the immediate and pressing task of ensuring their survival. Labour recommenced on public works, and renewed effort went into clearing the land

3 Remember not past years

and sowing seed. Hunter observed how a spirit of defeat was temporarily transformed into a sense of purpose, how the pale and sickly regained their colour and health, and how common gloom gave way to cheerfulness.[8]

After nine months of disquiet, confusion and uncertainty, D'Arcy Wentworth had an opportunity to lay the foundations of a new life for himself, albeit on a remote and alien island. Driven by the experience of humiliation, he was to survive years of frustration and scorn through an elasticity of spirit which made him resilient, flexible, fertile in device and ready to be accommodated within the circle of the negotiable. He also possessed a steely resolve. His resentment was both intensified and balanced by a remarkable self-confidence. Yet, when it appeared that he could benefit by ingratiating himself with those for whom he had neither affection nor respect, he was prepared to comply. If need be, he would suppress his deepest yearnings, and accept relative poverty, neglect, insult, shame and degradation, while adjusting to his place of exile and currying favour with those who wielded power. He determined to be circumspect and discreet, to exercise tact and concession. He made up his mind to conform and to be obedient, not out of slavishness or subservience, but because he knew that a struggle lay ahead. He decided to be ruled, while still remaining sovereign of his own domain. As to his past, he wanted it forgotten and turned his back upon it. Nevertheless, it was precisely this past that pushed him on, prompted his endeavours, and induced him to look in the short term at the exigencies of the present and in the long term to a future that could be less fraught. He had seen a lot, yet observed little; the dimension of his experience was broad but shallow; he had gained in knowledge, though not in wisdom. Perhaps a turning point came with William's birth. At Cascade Bay he had helped him from his mother's womb, cut the cord, and washed, wrapped and warmed the babe. In that profound instant of becoming a father, D'Arcy saw Catherine at her most vulnerable. Their son was born at least five weeks premature. The infant's fight for life drew his father closer to him and placed D'Arcy's own struggles in perspective. The experience brought with it humility, as well as added resolution. He chose to bide his time.

Wentworth was part of a claustrophobic community fractured by division. Ross and his officials constituted the apex of the hierarchy; by degrees it descended through the naval and marine officers, then the civil and medical appointees, to the troops and seamen; the base was composed of the felonry, male and female. Dissatisfied with their living and working conditions, and restive under the constraints imposed by a penal establishment, a number of convicts resisted authority. Their offences included theft, neglect of duty, disobedience and insolence. On 4 September Thomas Street laid down his tools and escaped into the woods to live with two other runaways. Phoebe Flattery received twenty-six lashes at Charlotte Field on 6 October for repeatedly going to Kingston without permission. For encouraging their fellows to apply for additional free time, William Collingwood and James McKay were each sentenced to fifty strokes on 15 November. The tyranny of proximity meant that tensions were not confined to relations between the prisoners and their gaolers. Within the administration itself, rivalry, jealousy and discontent were barely held in check. Next to Ross in seniority came Captain John Hunter (who despised Ross for the treatment he had meted out to him in Sydney), Lieutenant William Bradley from the *Sirius*, and the marines George Johnston, John Creswell, Robert Kellow, John Johnstone, Ralph Clark and William Faddy. By the time Wentworth arrived, the officers of the marines had ostracized Lieutenant Kellow for his unbecoming conduct towards Lieutenant Faddy. Furthermore, Lieutenant Creswell was at odds with Lieutenant Clark, seeing him as the commandant's favourite. A more serious rift between the naval and marine officers resulted in firmer lines of demarcation being drawn, with the officers of the *Sirius* snubbing Major Ross and refusing to pay him the conventional compliments. The buoyant mood of August, which Hunter had sensed, soured and spent itself in factionalism. In this cauldron it behoved a shrewder Wentworth to accept much of Dr Patton's earlier counsel. He now proposed to be prudent, to live quietly, to remain unobtrusive and tight-lipped—regardless of provocation or injured feelings—and to be wary in forming friendships.[9]

Rather than finding that he had a joint practice, he quickly learned that there were four other surgeons on Norfolk Island: Thomas Jamison and John Altree, Dennis Considen, another First Fleeter who had accompanied Ross to the island in March 1790, and John Irving, a former convict who had been granted a pardon. Given the ratio of five doctors to a population of some seven hundred, it seemed that Wentworth's professional work would not be unduly onerous. It was

3 Remember not past years

the Irishman, Considen, who first befriended D'Arcy and tried to make his situation as comfortable as possible. As a keen natural historian and as a colleague, Considen taught him about the use of indigenous plants for treating illnesses. He had already demonstrated that the myrtle had properties which could help as a mild and safe astringent in cases of dysentery. Considen had sent specimens of native flora and fauna to Sir Joseph Banks in England. More importantly, Dennis offered D'Arcy guidance and support, advised him about their fellow colonists, and identified those who were turbulent and machinating. For his first eight months on the island Wentworth regularly walked two miles from Kingston to Charlotte Field where he had been assigned to attend the sick. Each day's journey allowed him to observe his surroundings. The land rose to hills and sloped to valleys which, in Hunter's eyes, resembled 'the waves of the sea in a gale of wind'. Wentworth used a track that cut through a wood which was choked with undergrowth and which echoed with the calls of colourful birds. Trees came into leaf and plants flowered, and from Mount Pitt flowed several streams that teemed with eels, no less than the Bann did.[10]

Irrespective of their station, the inhabitants praised Norfolk Island for its wholesome air and salubrious climate. Between March 1788 and August 1790 only two people died of natural causes. Most deaths were due to drowning, but some male convicts were killed while felling trees. One baby perished through neglect. The major illnesses that Wentworth treated were dysentery and diarrhoea. On 11 February 1791 the officers and crew of the *Sirius* boarded the *Supply* and sailed for Port Jackson, pleased to be leaving the scene of their vexation. To this stage Wentworth had managed to remain on amicable terms with members of both factions. Hunter, whom he had met at Charlotte Field, carried favourable reports about him to Governor Phillip; Clark, who stayed on the island, spoke of him with respect; and even Ross was being won round.[11]

Early in February 1791 convicts began to build a house for Wentworth at Charlotte Field, but he continued to feel insecure and uncertain about his prospects. On the 10th he wrote to Governor Phillip to seek clarification of his position in the colony. Through David Collins, the governor replied on 21 March, acquainting him that Hunter and Jamison had both expressed satisfaction with his conduct, and that Phillip would determine D'Arcy's future residence and employment as soon as he received directions from England. Wentworth remained sceptical. Fifteen months had passed since December 1789 when he had boarded the *Neptune* and nothing had been settled. He held his post of assistant-surgeon only in an acting capacity, and it carried no salary. Phillip's response was not reassuring. Even more galling was the implication that Fitzwilliam, Cookney, Villiers and Hill had either failed to advance his interests or that the Home Office had rebuffed their overtures. The awful truth that he was in the antipodes as a castaway dawned on him. If he were to advance at all, it would be solely by his own resourcefulness. He had, at least, made a start. The fact that he barely figured in official correspondence dealing with individuals and events on the island counted in his favour, for he was slowly being seen as one who was reliable and who kept out of trouble.[12]

Appointed in November 1790 to take charge of the building and development of Charlotte Field, Lieutenant Ralph Clark confirmed that the site was well chosen. Sawyers cut half-inch and two-inch planks, male labourers cleared the untimbered land of vines and the females hoed the soil. Clark was efficient, intelligent and capable, the pick of the officers on the island, and the type of man who began his work at daybreak and finished it at sunset. Relieved at being removed from the society of his querulous messmates, he was of D'Arcy's age and proved himself a good neighbour. He had been raised in Scotland and had married the object of his adoration, Betsy Alicia Trevan, in 1784; their only child, named after his father, was born next year. Clark continually regretted leaving them in England and carried a miniature of Elizabeth with him, which, in private moments, he kissed most fondly. He kept a journal, written up almost every day and sometimes at great length. Its idiomatic language, untidy hand, careless spelling and sparse punctuation were revealing in themselves; its informality and intimacy showed the spontaneity of a born diarist, and its concern for human beings sets it apart from most contemporary documents. Never at a loss for something to do, Clark collected butterflies and birds, and went fishing and shooting. He loved children and puppies. Superstitious, prone to nightmares and tormented by fears of a premature death, in temperament he was fastidious and quick to take offence. On 22 February 1791 he watched his charges raise the frame of Wentworth's cottage. In March the carpenters fitted logs to the structure. By April the home was completed and D'Arcy moved in with

Catherine and William. D'Arcy deliberately kept details of his domestic life private, not from the eyes of the Norfolk Islanders, but from his friends in Ireland. In his later letters home he often referred to William, but never mentioned Catherine. A subsequent list of local landholders recorded Wentworth's status as 'married', a term that encompassed de facto relationships. Cohabitation and illegitimacy were accepted features of colonial life. Lieutenants Johnston and Kellow were but two of the officers whose convict mistresses bore them children; Philip Gidley King had lived with Ann Inett by whom he fathered two sons before the family returned to Sydney in 1790; and even the lovelorn Ralph Clark had a daughter, Alicia, by Mary Branham.[13]

While it is possible that Wentworth may have married in Ireland or England, thus preventing the formalizing of his ties with Catherine, it is more likely that he callously chose to use her for the time being and to keep his options open. They had much in common as outcasts, and had shared the *Neptune*'s voyage from the moment he had selected her from the midst of her fellow female convicts and saved her from their lot. The birth of their son brought them closer. That Catherine was only eighteen years old and a prisoner did not diminish his regard for her. As she slowly gained in assurance and material comforts, her gait developed an air of flounce, though she inhabited a world she was powerless to alter. It was not for her to read the tides, let alone contest them. Catherine's essential simplicity complemented Wentworth's complexity. At night, when the infant lay at her breast, or in D'Arcy's arms, or in the rush crib at their feet, and on occasions when they joined in his babble or sang him to sleep, Wentworth dimly perceived that their needs were interdependent. The baby, no less than its mother, gave him his attention, then his trust, and ultimately his love. D'Arcy warmed himself by that fire. William gained in weight, but had heavy features and a badly inturned eye. It made no difference. Real love permits no rejection. D'Arcy loved the child so intensely that he was unable to articulate his feelings.

Beyond the intimacy of the Wentworth home a serious breakdown in military discipline occurred in April 1791. Disgruntled with their allowances and living conditions, and bored at having next to nothing to do, the rank and file of the marines shared common interests and an outlook which bordered on insurrection. In Clark's opinion: 'never was Club Law near taking place in any part of the World than it was in this

... for our men here are the Most Mutinious Set I ever was amongst and are ripe for rising against any Authority'. On the 9th Ross issued a direction that they should receive only three-quarters of the ration. Affirming their solidarity, the marines defied their officers and refused to take their provisions from the storekeeper, alleging that they were worse off than the convicts who could supplement their allowances with the produce of their gardens. Clark saw their stance as an attempt to challenge Ross's power. The commandant remained adamant. John Ascott was the first man to obey orders and accept the reduced rations. His comrades treated him with contempt, but they finally acquiesced and gave in. Their readiness to question the orders of their superiors set in place a pattern of behaviour which their successors, the soldiers of the New South Wales Corps, were soon to adopt.[14]

On the 15th the *Supply* brought a detachment of that corps to Norfolk Island. Captain William Hill, Lieutenant Abbott, Ensign Prentice (all of whom as fellow passengers in the Second Fleet knew something of Wentworth's past), a sergeant, a corporal, one drummer and ten privates replaced Johnston, Creswell and thirteen marines. The corps' numbers were to grow to three officers, a chaplain, and seventy-three non-commissioned officers and men by March 1793. Discord quickly arose between the officers of the marines and those of the corps. Hill quarrelled with Ross. Faddy refused to stable his horse with Hill's. On 13 August the commandant thought it advisable to separate the two factions and sent the detachment of the New South Wales Corps to a base at Phillipburgh. Over five months, rows among its officers and men led to nine courts martial. The motley settlement, which combined aspects of a garrison camp, a penal outpost and an incipient free colony, was riven with squabbles and feuds. Despite the military officers' disdain for him, Wentworth may well have considered them his inferiors. He had, after all, been an officer himself, and had served in a regiment in Ulster whose numbers, cohesiveness and importance made the members of the New South Wales Corps seem like a flock of cock sparrows.[15]

Obliged to rub shoulders with a wider community in which the military was merely one part, Wentworth saw similar bickering take on major proportions and consume his fellows. Frustration, rumour, suspicion and antagonism simultaneously stemmed from and fuelled envy and malice. Individuals and factions quarrelled over authority, status, privilege and possessions, over issues that counted and matters that appeared trivial. Holding a post on the civil staff, Wentworth belonged to a section of the establishment that had diverse occupations and interests. As a group the civil officials lacked a collective identity, as well as the *esprit de corps* of the soldiers—fractured though it was. D'Arcy already enjoyed the friendship of Considen and Jamison, and found a kindred spirit in William Balmain, another doctor who transferred from New South Wales to Norfolk Island in November. Bonded to some extent by their profession and by ties of mutual support, the surgeons were divided from one another by jealousy over seniority and by rivalry over reputation. They were, moreover, few in number and dispersed in three different centres, and spent their heat in quarrels with other civil and military officers rather than among themselves. Considen had a tiff with Ross, Jamison and Ross exchanged heated words, and Balmain fought a duel with James White. The ill feeling, however, remained on a personal level and never escalated into wider confrontation.[16]

D'Arcy was physically and emotionally distant from the dissonance at headquarters in Kingston. He performed his duties quietly and effectively at Charlotte Field (officially renamed Queenborough on 30 April 1791). The guard-house and the home of Denis Doidge, the superintendent of convicts, were situated on a gentle rise, overlooking the neat houses in the village spread below. In the government farm ten acres of wheat and thirty acres of Indian corn, sown during May and June, began to ripen in September and promised a bountiful harvest. The inhabitants watched apprehensively for any signs of the appearance of ground grubs, moths and caterpillars which had damaged previous harvests elsewhere on the island. By this time incidents of theft from the farm were few and the only danger to the crops came from a band of marauding convicts. The serenity of the setting contrasted with the brutality and suffering that were concomitant parts of life. Queenborough had its own gaol and stocks: the place of confinement, 'well spiked and framed', and the instruments of punishment were dual emblems of the penal system.[17]

Flogging was commonly used as a deterrent to further crime. Three women who had been apprehended for thieving were punished on 3 May. Clark ordered one of them, Mary Higgins, to receive fifty lashes. After twenty-six strokes had been administered, he remitted the remainder because of her advanced age. A man of almost seventy was given one hundred lashes for stealing wheat and neglecting his work; a young lad received thirteen strokes on the buttocks for robbing his master. As the resident surgeon at Queenborough, D'Arcy was obliged to attend the floggings: having ensured that life was not at risk, it was his duty to tend the victims' lacerations. Almost from the start there were times when he showed compassion for the female convicts. Clark sentenced Catherine White to fifty lashes on 3 May. She bore fifteen before fainting. Wentworth then asked Clark to have her taken from the triangles. D'Arcy's sympathy extended to felons who had committed offences against him. For abusing Wentworth, Sarah Lyons was ordered to receive fifty lashes on 6 June; when sixteen had been inflicted, D'Arcy begged Clark to dispense with the remainder; Clark complied with the request.[18]

Meantime, King made a brief and successful visit to London. Armed with Phillip's commendations, he had arrived in 1790, just before Christmas. He saw Lord Grenville, Sir Joseph Banks and Evan Nepean, discussed the problems of New South Wales with them and told them of his achievements on Norfolk Island. On 2 March 1791 he was promoted commodore. Nine days later he married Anna Josepha Coombe at the parish church of St Martin-in-the-Fields, Westminster. Commissioned as lieutenant-governor of Norfolk Island on a salary of £250 a year, and accompanied by his wife and his young protégé, Lieutenant William Neate Chapman, he returned to Sydney before reaching Norfolk Island in the *Atlantic* on 2 November. The ship also carried Captain William Paterson and his wife, the Reverend Richard Johnson, a detachment of the New South Wales Corps which was to replace Ross's marines, and thirty recently discharged marines and twelve ex-convicts intent on becoming free settlers. Anxious to inspect the improvements that had been set in train since his departure, King expressed guarded admiration for the settlements at Queenborough and Phillipburgh, and for the advanced state of the public farms and private gardens. Never one to understate his own accomplishments, he had the grace to concede that Ross had made fair progress—in some respects. The population was now 1008, of which the civil officials, military and free settlers numbered 131, ex-convicts 39 and male convicts 490; there were 263 women—bond and free—and 85 children. Yet Ross was not an easy commandant. Officials, soldiers, settlers and convicts had grown discontented under his rule. King found 'discord and strife on every person's countenance and in every corner and hole of the island', and informed Nepean that he was constantly 'pestered with complaints, bitter revilings, back-biting'. He took formal control of the administration on 12 November and learned that skilled labour and tools were in short supply, that theft was common and that there was no criminal court, despite the representations he had made in London on the need for better judicial arrangements.[19]

King's first deed on assuming office was to remit the sentences of those who had been imprisoned for offences committed on the island. He subsequently requested Richard Johnson to bestow the sacrament of marriage on couples who sought that blessing. More than one hundred people were wed in three days; Catherine and D'Arcy were not among them. Some convicts married in a vain effort to preserve their women from the soldiery. In November the *Queen* anchored in Sydney Bay with the balance of Paterson's contingent. She also brought a number of convicts who had come to Sydney in the Third Fleet. Many of them had been in poor health during their imprisonment in England. Like exhausted animals, they were hoisted on board the ships and deposited between decks. The voyage to New South Wales weakened them further. At Norfolk Island they were initially incapable of labour and their rehabilitation was protracted. On the 22nd Major Ross and his marines embarked for Port Jackson, Considen and Clark sailing with them. They left an island where an outbreak of dysentery had eroded the health of the community. Although the illness had rarely proved fatal, it occasioned widespread debilitation, reducing the number fit for work at precisely the time that the new arrivals increased the demand for food. Wentworth did his best to alleviate the suffering. Over the fifteen months in which he had practised at Queenborough he steadily forged a reputation for conscientiousness and reliability. In contrast, Denis Doidge had, through ignorance and ineptitude, become one of the banes of Clark's existence. When King reprimanded him for his improper behaviour, Doidge wrote two insulting letters in reply and submitted his resignation. On 10 December King appointed Wentworth to fill Doidge's post until Phillip's pleasure was known. In King's view, D'Arcy's actions and attitude did him credit. Wentworth had 'always behaved with the greatest propriety and attention to duty', and had 'fully answered the expectations' which he earlier formed of him. King believed that he would acquit himself with fidelity, both as acting-

The Wentworths

superintendent of convicts and as acting assistant-surgeon. It may have helped Wentworth's cause that he had been a consultant to Anna King in the last weeks of her pregnancy. He also assisted at the birth of her son on 13 December. The child was named Phillip Parker. He was the lieutenant-governor's first legitimate child and only legitimate son.[20]

With Catherine and William, who bore the surname Crowley, D'Arcy moved into the home on the rise that overlooked the village. A corporal and six privates of the New South Wales Corps lived in the nearby guard-house with an established garden adjoining it. As superintendent, Wentworth had responsibility for the management of one hundred convicts whose activities were largely geared to the tasks of clearing the land and cultivating crops in the public farm. He lacked knowledge of agriculture and had no experience in managing prisoners, but his previous daily visits to Charlotte Field and his residency at Queenborough enhanced his intimacy with the routine of the settlement and the character of the convicts, most of whom he knew by name. At a higher level, King's determination to overcome the difficulties he encountered was in tandem with Wentworth's. They were men of different stamp, though only four years separated them in age. The lieutenant-governor respected authority and was convinced that it behoved others to do likewise; he valued order, discipline and regularity; and he kept detailed records, journals and copies of his letters. More his own man, the acting-superintendent of convicts had a history of flouting the law, was more pliant in his outlook and easygoing in his conduct, and paid scant heed to paperwork. Each of them saw that his interests would be served by promoting the success of the Norfolk Island experiment. Wentworth sought to redeem his reputation, while King craved the approbation of his masters in Whitehall and the advancement that would flow from it. To realize his goal, the one needed acceptance and backing from the lieutenant-governor; the other relied on the support of people like Wentworth to secure the well-being and prosperity of the nascent colony.[21]

On 3 January 1792 Phillip wrote to King, informing him that he would allow Wentworth to return to Sydney, provided his conduct warranted the favour, but the governor suggested that it might be preferable if D'Arcy were to remain on Norfolk Island until his future prospects were decided for him. Wentworth accepted Phillip's advice, and stayed. In his dual roles of surgeon and superintendent, he faced a number of difficulties that affected productivity in his district. Dysentery continued to sap the health of the community. By February the majority of the inhabitants of Queenborough had fallen ill, with the recent arrivals suffering most of all. In the beginning, the control and management of convicts vexed him. One of his charges ate his weekly allowance in a single meal. Wentworth did what he could, but, after three days of excruciating pain, the man died. King regarded the felons as a set of miserable and lawless wretches. The female prisoners at Queenborough had so irritated and provoked Clark that he wrote in his journal, 'I never came a Cross Such a sett of D[amned] B[itches] in my life—they make me curs and swer my Soul out'. In addition to the usual instances of insolence, disobedience and neglect of work, a series of daring robberies had been committed in November and December 1791. King, Paterson and the Reverend James Bain, the new chaplain to the corps, were installed as magistrates and given the power to punish minor offenders. Those charged with serious crimes were shipped to Port Jackson for trial. Because witnesses had to be sent to testify, their absence for extended periods meant that farms were abandoned and the pool of labour reduced. It was seldom worth the trouble. In an effort to solve the problem King overreacted and increased the summary punishment for theft to a maximum of eight hundred lashes. In theory it amounted to a sentence of death, or of being crippled for life; in practice, once two hundred strokes had been inflicted, the remainder were suspended if the offender solemnly undertook to mend his ways.[22]

Perhaps remembering the savagery he had seen and heard in the *Neptune*, Wentworth sanctioned flogging only as a last resort. He preferred to stimulate his underlings by gentleness and encouragement. Rather than regarding the generous side of his nature as a weakness to be exploited, the convicts responded positively to his manner which differed so markedly from the way that Doidge had treated them. Joseph Smith, an overseer who worked under Wentworth, said that 'a better master never lived in the world'. Broadening his sphere as he built his reputation, D'Arcy came to know a range of people throughout the island: Captain Nicholas Nepean, another Second Fleeter, who acted as commandant for ten days in 1793, Lieutenant Chapman, the lieutenant-governor's secretary, Andrew Hume, who took charge of the growing and manufacture of flax at the Cascades, and James Sheers, the government butcher, whose daughter, Mary Anne, was to become the mistress of Captain John Piper. Wentworth also met the deputy-commissary, Zachariah Clark, later accused of incest with his daughter, the constable, James Belbin, the master carpenter, Nathaniel Lucas, whose wife Olive bore him thirteen children, eleven of them on Norfolk Island, and the soldier, Martin Timms, who transferred to the civil list as a superintendent. Wentworth's circle of acquaintances included the bushranger, Black Caesar, two Maoris, Hutu and Tuki, who had been kidnapped in the futile hope that they could help in treating flax, and three Lascars, Dinah, Francis and Maluai.[23]

D'Arcy continued to impress his commandant. On 9 March 1792 King wrote to Evan Nepean, extolling Wentworth's virtues and praising his propriety, punctuality and industry. The number of convicts at Queenborough increased to 150 and, on 8 May, the lieutenant-governor again wrote to the under-secretary reiterating his good opinion of Wentworth. He assured Nepean that the young surgeon's exemplary behaviour was obvious to all who lived on the island, and he suggested that Wentworth deserved a small remuneration for his efforts in performing the duties of two offices. In July King made an entry in his journal recording D'Arcy's attentiveness and activity in overseeing public work. Next month he appointed him a constable. His salary was £40 a year and he was charged with maintaining law and order in Queenborough and the surrounding district. On 21 September King brought Wentworth's services to Phillip's notice. And, at D'Arcy's request, he sent letters to Fitzwilliam and Villiers expressing satisfaction with his conduct. Through King, Wentworth had gained a channel to the Home Office and a fillip to his hopes for patronage. That year, in England, the *Advertiser* published the following paragraph: 'Wentworth, the highwayman, acts as assistant to the Surgeon General at Norfolk Island, and likewise behaves himself remarkably well'. While Wentworth was attempting by slow and dogged steps to establish his reputation in the colony, the press reminded the British public of his past.[24]

Hunter's book, *An Historical Journal of the Transactions at Port Jackson and Norfolk Island*, published in London in 1793, praised Wentworth's performances as doctor and superintendent, though the reference was tucked away near the end of the tome. The staff of the Home Office remained intractable. Without their approval Phillip was reluctant to acknowledge Wentworth as an official member of the medical staff. In his letter of 30 November 1792 the governor had chided King for including Wentworth's name as an assistant-surgeon in the return of the island's establishment and emphasized that it should only be listed under the minor heading of superintendents. The lieutenant-governor defended his action. Aware that D'Arcy had served without pay as an assistant-surgeon for some thirty-one months and as a superintendent of convicts for fifteen, King wrote once more to the Home Office on 4 March 1793. He reminded Nepean of Wentworth's consistent good conduct and deemed him 'a real treasure'; he reckoned that the inhabitants of Norfolk Island were indebted to him for 2000 bushels of maize and 500 bushels of wheat produced, under his supervision, for the government; and he asked that the Home Office pay him for his services, both as assistant-surgeon and superintendent. Furthermore, he revealed that Wentworth intended to leave the island and averred that he was at a loss as to how to replace him. Wentworth's intimation of departing for England was a ploy. He and King used it as a feint to prompt the Home Office to action and to rouse Fitzwilliam from his lethargy.[25]

Lord Fitzwilliam received King's letter, as well as one in which D'Arcy asked him to use his influence to obtain endorsement of the assistant-surgeonship. In response he wrote directly to Wentworth on 24 June 1793. Three and a half years had elapsed since D'Arcy's last trial, a decent interval by any standards. Still a member of the Opposition, Fitzwilliam had no political or personal connexions with Henry Dundas, the secretary of state for the Home Office, but he had spoken with one of his under-secretaries, John King, and was led to believe that Wentworth's appointment as assistant-surgeon would be confirmed. Addressing D'Arcy simply as 'Sir', his lordship related these details graciously, before revealing his affection. He informed Wentworth that he had sent him by the *William* a box containing 'an assortment of things that I fancy will be useful', and that he had asked Cookney to act as D'Arcy's attorney—'as you know him you will approve of the appointment'. Fitzwilliam concluded by wishing D'Arcy 'health, happiness and prosperity'. Wentworth's pleasure at reading this letter was diminished when Collins reported that the contents of the box had been stolen, either on the *William*'s voyage or in Sydney Town.[26]

Building on the achievements of the maligned Ross, King helped to improve conditions on Norfolk Island by his initiative, ability and perseverance. In October 1793 the Settlers and Landholders Society was formed, under the presidency of the provost marshal, Fane Edge. The lieutenant-governor was guided by its advice on regulating the prices of farm produce and the wages for labourers. 1794 and 1795 saw good harvests. By the end of the former year the island was self-sufficient in grain and had a surplus of 20 000 bushels of maize which it could send to Sydney; by the end of the latter, pigs had so multiplied that 4000 lb of fresh pork were cured, with some left over for export. In 1796 the population had fallen slightly to 889, of whom the civil officials and the soldiers, with their wives and children, numbered 120. Settlers, expirees and convicts made up the bulk of the remainder. They worked as farm servants, charcoal burners, carpenters, sawyers, butchers, bakers, blacksmiths, millers, barbers, brickmakers and school-teachers. A burgeoning colony had come into being. Two schools and an orphanage were functioning, 1528 acres were cleared of timber and vines, and the crops grown included wheat, maize, potatoes, sugar-cane, bananas, guavas, lemons, apples and coffee. There were 12 cattle, 6 horses, 12 asses, 374 sheep, 772 goats and 14 642 swine. Public buildings valued at £6000 had been erected, two windmills and a watermill constructed, and at Cascade Bay a wharf stretched 126 feet to a place of anchorage. The growth and treatment of flax, which had interested the British government from the outset, was a singular failure.[27]

King's health was also failing. He had been drinking heavily and was plagued by gout. In preference to other doctors, he chose to be treated by Wentworth who provided a panacea which temporarily relieved the agonies in his feet, legs, hands and elbow. D'Arcy's bedside manner engendered confidence, and he enjoyed the favour of the lieutenant-governor's wife. Whatever their rank, women were usually charmed by him. In December 1795 King's condition worsened. He suffered 'an almost fixed compression of the Lungs and Breast, with a difficulty of Breathing and a constant Pain in the Stomach'. Doubts were entertained of his survival, but, nourished by Wentworth's pigeon-broth, he rallied and recovered. Just as Lieutenant William Lawson felt beholden to Wentworth for showing him 'the greatest care and attention' throughout his illness, King, too, was grateful for D'Arcy's ministrations. The relationship between the two men was intriguing. By supporting King, Wentworth stood to gain in wealth and status. By favouring Wentworth, King cherished hopes—rather than expectations—of impressing a Whig nobleman who might assist in forwarding

3 Remember not past years

his claim to the governorship of New South Wales. In July 1794 the Duke of Portland and other Whigs joined Pitt in government. Fitzwilliam was appointed president of the council. In December he was sent as lord-lieutenant to Ireland. His mission, as he saw it, was to smooth the way for an almost complete Catholic Emancipation, but his plan was premature and impolitic as far as the British ministry was concerned. His actions ended in misunderstanding and bitterness, in débâcle and personal disgrace. He was replaced in March 1795. In his past there was neither striving nor disadvantage: nobility and privilege had been handed to him on a salver. The Irish imbroglio was bad enough; worse still, he had been humiliated by an English prime minister and a Tory. Fitzwilliam bided his time. Three years later he was sufficiently reinstated in Pitt's esteem to be given the lord-lieutenancy of the West Riding.[28]

Back on Norfolk Island matters were more mundane. Ground grubs had reappeared in July and August 1793, but King and Wentworth brought them under control by running fowls in the gardens and on the farms. At D'Arcy's behest, convicts cleared additional land at Queenborough and planted sugar-cane as protective borders around the plots. Following a break at Christmas, the labourers began gathering and husking maize for the government, and storing it in the outstation's 60-foot-long granary which was completed early in the New Year. King had allocated Wentworth a 60-acre block on which D'Arcy began, in his own right, to breed swine. On 7 May 1792 he received £11 2s for selling six sows to the government; on 3 May 1794 he sold 814 lb of pork for £20 7s and on the 18th an additional 900 lb which fetched £24 10s. By this time he had also become one of the largest private producers of maize on the island: between January and May in 1794 he lodged 436 bushels, worth £105 7s 4d in the public stores. The island's harvest glutted the market. Major Grose—who administered the government of New South Wales from December 1792 to December 1794 between the administrations of Phillip (1788–92) and Hunter (1795–1800)—refused to honour the bills which King had drawn on the Treasury until directions were received from England. His decision angered King and infuriated those farmers who were in financial straits. In March 1793 there were forty-five free settlers on Norfolk Island; by March 1795 only twenty-five remained. Wentworth took advantage of the situation by acquiring two additional farms, each of sixty acres. He ran goats on one, pigs on the other, and switched from maize to wheat-growing on his original grant. In November that year he received £39 for 78 bushels of wheat which he sold to the commissariat. Meanwhile, from his union with Catherine a second son, Dorset Crowley, was born on 23 June 1793 and a third, Matthew Crowley, on 13 June 1795; a daughter, Martha, died in infancy. At the age of five their brother, William, commenced his formal education by attending a nearby school where he was instructed by 'a woman of good character'.[29]

Because few ships called at the island, isolation exacted its toll. Tea and sugar became scarce, as did essential goods, especially clothing. In October 1793 the settlers formally complained to King. Next month, when the *Britannia* visited, he learned that its master, Captain William Raven, had allocated nearly all the space in his ship to carry cargo from India to the government in Sydney. Raven agreed to bring additional goods, to the value of £5 to £6, for each Norfolk Island family who could afford the outlay. Aware that Wentworth had pay due to him as a constable, the lieutenant-governor drew part of D'Arcy's salary as a bill on the Treasury, enabling Raven to buy articles at prime cost on his behalf. The venture underlined the lucrative profits to be made by importing articles for sale on the island, but even more so in the bigger market in New South Wales. To Chapman, the prices charged were 'amazing' and profits of at least 100 per cent were realized. The lesson reinforced what Wentworth had seen of trade at the Cape. On 3 October 1795 the *Asia*, an American ship from New York, berthed at the island to replenish supplies, the first vessel since the settlement's foundation to stop there without having previously touched at Port Jackson. D'Arcy was among the settlers who seized the opportunity to furnish her with meat and vegetables in exchange for tobacco and spirits. At the end of the month he received a shipment of goods conveyed in the *Supply*. By banking Wentworth's salary and using money advanced by Fitzwilliam, Cookney had been able to send D'Arcy such articles as cloth, linen, china, combs, paper, pens and groceries. Wentworth retained part of the consignment for his own and his family's use, but much of it was intended for sale—items like gowns and fancy ribbons of blue, lilac or pink, almost too beautiful to wear. The cargo cost £97 19s 9d; Cookney's annual fee for his services was two guineas. Wentworth charged moderate prices for what he sold. Profit was less important than maximizing good will at this point in his career.[30]

3 Remember not past years

A trading ring in Sydney, exclusively confined to the officers of the New South Wales Corps, exercised a virtual monopoly over articles brought by ships for private sale in the colony. King was less concerned by this operation than by being excluded from the transactions. Each officer at Port Jackson had the privilege of receiving goods based on a share of £60 per captain and £30 per subaltern. No one on Norfolk Island was party to the deal. In 1795, in an attempt to compensate his fellows who were unable to obtain liquor through trade, King began to distil rum from sugar-cane and produced a 'very good and wholesome spirit'. He had had a bellyful of the corps, irrespective of whether its members were based in Sydney or at Phillipburgh.[31]

The hotheads among the soldiers had been a constant nuisance to him from the time of their arrival. On 31 May 1792 the privates in William Paterson's company refused to draw their reduced rations. Eventually persuaded by their captain, they agreed to accept them, but with bitter complaints and sullen looks. When King found it necessary to issue maize in lieu of rice in July 1793, Edward Abbott's detachment protested belligerently until the lieutenant calmed his men. The corps' rank and file became familiar with the convicts, and ate, drank and gambled with them. By enticing convict women to leave their husbands or those with whom they lived, and by molesting and raping the wives of convicts and ex-convicts alike, the soldiers created widespread bitterness and unrest. Several disagreeable incidents culminated on the evening of 18 January 1794, the Queen's Birthday. A scuffle occurred during the public performance of a play at Kingston. The dispute continued in the streets, drawing more participants into a violent brawl. Intervening in the mêlée, King ordered them to return to their homes, and directed a soldier named Bannister and a convict named Cooper to be taken into custody for their part in the fracas.

Angered at the confinement of one of their number, the troops gathered on the parade-ground where they took an oath to be true to one another and declared that none of their comrades should be punished for an offence against a convict. King realized that the affair seemed likely to escalate and that public safety was in jeopardy. Supported by the officers of the corps, he disarmed the detachment, arrested the ringleaders and sent them to be court-martialled in Sydney. Some soldiers were dispatched to gather feathers on Phillip Island and others were ordered to perform menial duties at Queenborough. A citizens' militia was authorized to carry the soldiers' muskets. Nightwatchmen, armed with staves, ensured that the inhabitants remained indoors after 8 p.m. Offended by the treatment of his corps, Grose dismissed all charges against the mutineers, reprimanded King for his actions, and lugubriously advised Henry Dundas that Norfolk Island had dubious merit as a penal settlement and that there were dangers in sending ships there. The issue exposed the gulf between the felonry and the free, even though it was less conspicuous on Norfolk Island than in New South Wales. Wentworth had never been a convict and had received King's backing, but in the eyes of the exclusionists in the New South Wales Corps he was tainted by his past. For all his success in acquiring property, in breeding livestock and cultivating crops, in entering trade, in winning friends, in practising as a surgeon, and in holding office as a superintendent and a constable, he was regarded as having an affinity with the ex-convict segment of society. More often than not, he was to identify with people of that caste in a further struggle for emancipation.[32]

In July 1795 Wentworth wrote to David Collins, expressing his disappointment at the Home Office's failure to commission him as assistant-surgeon and asking to be allowed to return to England. King supported his request in a covering letter. He recorded his satisfaction with D'Arcy's conduct as a doctor and a superintendent. Attempting to elicit a final decision as to his friend's future, King wrote: 'How far Mr Wentworth can be spared, I must submit to the Governor; as well as the Propriety of his being detained to perform an Office, for which he does not receive any Emolument'. Hunter sympathized with Wentworth's predicament. But, in replying to King on 17 October, the governor admitted that, as the secretary of state had not responded to recommendations which had been forwarded home on Wentworth's behalf, he could see no point in pursuing the matter. He expressed regret at Wentworth's wish to quit a settlement where he had been of so much benefit to the public and gave him permission to repair to Sydney or to leave for England.[33]

On 23 January 1796 Wentworth again importuned Lord Fitzwilliam. He informed his patron that, because he had not been confirmed as an assistant-surgeon and could not expect to earn 'a single shilling', he had adopted the only alternative and decided to sail for Europe. Professing to have reached this determination reluctantly and

3 Remember not past years

with heartfelt sorrow, he trusted that he would not incur his lordship's censure. D'Arcy referred to his 'six years service' in the colony and described the circumstances under which subordinate officers worked. He assured Fitzwilliam that he had no desire to stay more than an hour in London, nor the smallest objection to re-embarking for New South Wales. Wentworth had sold one of his farms, but kept two others in the hope that he would obtain—through Fitzwilliam's kindness—a situation which would enable him to come back to the island. Sensible of his lordship's goodness to him, he prayed that Lord and Lady Fitzwilliam, and Lord Milton (their only child), might enjoy uninterrupted happiness and prosperity, and ascribed himself his lordship's most grateful and devoted servant, D. Wentworth. Just as he had done thirty-four months earlier, D'Arcy had resorted to a ruse. The immediate object of his leaving Norfolk Island was to live in Sydney. Only if he failed there would he consider departing for England. In the meantime he hoped that the renewed thought of having his maverick kinsman wandering the streets of London might impel Fitzwilliam to exert more pressure on civil servants in the Home Office.[34]

Complying with Wentworth's request, King once more acted in concert with him by writing to Fitzwilliam on 19 February, reinforcing all that D'Arcy had conveyed. He praised Wentworth's achievements in maintaining order in his district, and raising crops and stock. Oddly, he said nothing about his duties or performance as a surgeon. He did not allude to his wider entrepreneurial activities, nor to the network of contacts he had established: some were prisoners, others free; many were foolish, a few clever; almost all liked him and none was an inveterate enemy. He had walked with the Kings but retained the common touch. The lieutenant-governor concluded by confiding:

> Whatever may have been his former Errors I have no doubt but that his future Conduct in Life, will be mark'd by the same propriety of behaviour which has procured him the General Esteem of everyone here—And I sincerely hope the liberal & Good will consign his former Wanderings to Oblivion.

That day D'Arcy, Catherine and their three sons boarded the *Reliance*, captained by Henry Waterhouse, and sailed for Port Jackson. Henceforward the children bore the surname Wentworth.[35]

4

Smile at the rising sun

> I could not help foreboding that many of those who now smiled at the rising sun would change their ideas, when the proceedings, which the good nature of my predecessor had sanctioned should be any ways checked . . .
>
> P. G. King, September 1805, New South Wales, Colonial Secretary's Papers, MSS 681/2, f.245

The *Reliance* dropped anchor in Sydney Cove on 5 March 1796. D'Arcy and Catherine found that much had changed since their brief encounter with the mainland in 1790. The population of New South Wales now approached 4000, most of whom were concentrated in the capital, but others had fanned over the Cumberland Plain, settling at Parramatta and along the Hawkesbury River. Sydney had grown from a ramshackle garrison camp into a small town: barracks, store-houses, a church, a hospital, a magazine, a shipbuilder's yard, a market-place, shops, houses, taverns, huts, shanties and hovels had spread higgledy-piggledy along disorganized streets. Thriving crops, herds of cattle, flocks of sheep and visiting merchant ships attested to material progress.[1]

After Phillip's departure for England in December 1792, Lieutenant-Governor Grose had shifted the emphasis from public to private farming. He granted land to his civil and military officers, as well as to the rank and file in the corps, thereby giving them a share in the country's prosperity. This practice was continued by Captain William Paterson who, as administrator, directed the settlements from December 1794 until September 1795. While a number of officers and soldiers received grants of 130 acres, some obtained 1000 acres and more; they farmed mainly in the Parramatta district; and they gave predominant, though not exclusive, attention to producing beef and mutton. Alongside this trend, one of Phillip's policies survived: on the expiry or remission of their sentences, well-behaved convicts were rewarded with grants of 30 acres. Former felons gravitated to the Hawkesbury region where they mainly grew grain, fruit and vegetables; in their ignorance and poverty these small farmers of New Holland exhausted the soil and fell into debt. An economic or class division had arisen in the countryside, separating former rogues from the self-styled respectable, the ex-convict from the free, the 'emancipist' from the 'exclusive'. Whereas the New South Wales Corps ruled the colony *de jure* from December 1792 to September 1795, its members were effectively *de facto* controllers until August 1806, for neither of Phillip's two immediate successors as governor fully managed to curb their power. Throughout these years a breach opened between the governor and the military, between the legislative and executive authorities. When a naval governor attempted to implement any policy that ran counter to the vested interests of the army corps, he was checked and thwarted. The authoritarian rule of a virtual dictator was replaced, in practice if not in name, with government by an oligarchy.[2]

At its apex this clique came to include the military officers, a scattering of officials from the civil establishment, a few free immigrants and the wealthiest emancipists, but the junta broadened the base of its support and gained some popularity by widening the range of its transactions and by devolving day-to-day management of its proliferating ventures upon a set of agents. An entrepreneurial group, which incorporated numerous ex-convicts, emerged to manage farms and to muster cattle, to take produce to granaries and slaughter-yards, to vend spirits and to run shops, to buy and sell and keep accounts. The process trickled down to prisoners who were given opportunities, outside their hours of government labour, to work for wages in agriculture, retailing, services and incipient manufactories. The junta had succeeded in establishing stakes in property, labour, goods and markets; the oligarchs had deregularized the prison system, privatized the economy and unleashed commercial forces which benefited those who clung to their coat-tails. With no exports of which to boast, the penal colony enjoyed high living standards and an income per head comparable with the mother country. Prosperity was basically sustained by drawing on Paymasters' and Treasury bills to pay for imports and for local produce. The commissariat store represented the gaol's market, its bank and its mint.[3]

Wentworth's immediate concern was with rank rather than wealth, though he had brought £800 with him from Norfolk Island. Two additional assistant-surgeons had arrived in Sydney by September 1795. The Home Office appointed them long after D'Arcy had been encouraged in 1793 to believe that he would be commissioned as a member of the medical staff. Regarding this act as 'the greatest injustice', he fretted over his future. He was relieved when Governor Hunter found that Samuel Leeds, one of the new appointees, was an incorrigible inebriate and demanded that he return home. Leeds tendered his resignation on the grounds of ill health. On 1 April 1796, within a month of Wentworth's arrival in New South Wales, Hunter conferred the appointment on him. A down-to-earth Scot who took to sea as a 16-year-old, in his youth Hunter possessed a toughness which strengthened his power to endure hardship and pain. He loved music, drew with competence, looked to Providence as a prop and support, and was as unaware of women as they were of him. Having been associated with the penal colony from the beginning, he was pushed by ambition and circumstance into the office of its captain-general and governor-in-chief, and began duty on 11 September 1795 at the age of fifty-eight. Unlike Phillip, Hunter was prepared to assume responsibility for conferring the assistant-surgeonship on Wentworth. In explaining his motives, he simply informed the Home Office that Wentworth had assisted at the hospital on Norfolk Island since 1790, that he was a deserving man and that his case was a fair one. Hunter later said that the appointment would not have been made if Wentworth had been a convict. He did not mention how narrowly Wentworth had escaped that fate. D'Arcy's self-assurance grew as he proved his capability and as each year distanced him from his past. He never publicly attempted to explain, to justify, or to apologize for his mistakes; he pleaded neither 'victim' nor juvenile folly; he simply refused to acknowledge his troubled history. Although he dealt with the disgrace of his arrests and trials by blocking it from his mind, there were those about him—high and low—who would not hesitate to use his former notoriety to traduce him whenever they thought that he was overreaching his station.[4]

Deriving much satisfaction from the promulgation of his appointment on 4 April 1796, Wentworth thought that it heralded a new dawn in his fortunes. Since he had not solicited the post, its bestowal was doubly welcome and seemed further proof of the good will of his former neighbour at Charlotte Field. To D'Arcy the assistant-surgeonship meant a steady income, official status, an opportunity for respectability and scope for promotion. It also furnished him with a face-saving reason for postponing his return to England. Gratified with his success, he wrote at once to King. The news delighted his patron who suggested that he volunteer for a transfer to Norfolk Island, a proposal which Wentworth politely but promptly declined. He wrote, as well, to Cookney, with strict instructions to obtain his commission from the Home Office: if the under-secretary of that department were in any way to recoil or prove uncooperative, Cookney was to play Wentworth's familiar trump about leaving New South Wales. And he wrote, on 1 May, to Fitzwilliam. He relished the chance to besmirch Leeds's name by relating how he was 'in an almost constant State of Drunkenness'. Insensitive to Fitzwilliam's temporary political demise, D'Arcy urged him to use his influence with John King and the Duke of Portland to have his appointment as assistant-surgeon confirmed, and reminded him of his earlier failure in this regard.[5]

During the first months of his appointment Wentworth devoted long hours to his medical work in Sydney and travelled no farther than two miles beyond the perimeter of the town. His involvement with his new position, however, did not curb his ambition. He informed Fitzwilliam of Hunter's recommendation that Portland should appoint three or four officers to take charge of the outlying settlements, and solicited the earl's influence in obtaining one of these commands for him. His words showed his vanity and his deference:

> from the long Experience & the many Proofs which I have given of my Abilities in managing a distant Settlement, I presume I may say ... that I am in every way qualified for such a Situation & could I be so fortunate through your Lordship's goodness to obtain one of these Situations; it would be [the] constant study of my Life to prove myself not unworthy of so great a Favour, from that Moment I would relinquish every idea of returning to

England, & would endeavour to make myself as comfortable as possible here for the remainder of my Days.

He concluded with the invocation that 'Almighty God may take your Lordship ... under His Holy protection and grant you every wish of your heart shall always be the sincere prayer of ... [your] Ever grateful and devoted servant, D. Wentworth'.[6]

By September the Wentworths had settled into a regular pattern of existence in Sydney Town. In that month D'Arcy sent Cookney an inventory of items for his family, among them clothes, material for children's jackets, combs, silver spoons and a silver ladle, sealing wax and medical texts. One book he sought dealt with recent treatments for venereal diseases. He also requested the purchase of a cornelian stone, set in gold, with the arms of the Elmsall branch of the Wentworth family engraved upon it. On the 10th he wrote again to Fitzwilliam, entrusting this letter to his friend, Philip Gidley King, who was returning to England due to recurrent gout. He referred King to Fitzwilliam, emphasized the warmth of their friendship on Norfolk Island and extolled King's qualifications to govern New South Wales. In the six months of his residence Wentworth had witnessed the inhabitants' avidity for spirits which had, he primly confided, led to drunkenness, profligacy and a breakdown in public order. Owing to alcohol-induced idleness and indebtedness, many settlers had forfeited their farms.[7]

Believing that the colony would achieve independence only through exertion, David Collins had in May 1794 applauded the efforts of the civil and military officers in developing their land grants. Hunter commenced his term as governor by praising the enthusiasm of these individuals in raising crops and breeding livestock, but gradually began to question their activities. By March 1797 he concluded that they were motivated by self-interest and had scant regard for the common weal. The officers' greed to make money as fast as possible flowed into trade, engendering what Hunter saw as a 'rage' to buy goods cheaply from convict transports and merchant vessels and to sell them at the highest prices obtainable. Richard Johnson held such practices to be beneath the dignity of a gentleman; to Daniel Paine, a ship-builder in Sydney, the officers in the trading cartel were downright monopolists; and Robert Murray, one of the crew of the *Britannia*, lambasted their conduct:

The picture I form of an Officer, if married, with a Wife—a farm to exercise his leisure hours upon, and supply his family with grain and stock; is an amiable one. but, An Officer with a prostitute, and illegitimate offspring, Land added to their own possessions, purchased with enormous priced articles of the Soldiers, under their command—Publick duty neglected, The Officer standing forth in different characters—A Publican—Money Lender—Farmer—Chandler—and an Officer of the New South Wales Corps, forms one, which must strike a man of common feelings, with horror and detestation.[8]

Strong incentives propelled and enticed Wentworth into trading. According to the doctor, William Balmain, the clergyman, Samuel Marsden, and the soldier, William Paterson, most of the officers received salaries inadequate to provide for their comfort. Exorbitant prices for commodities such as tea, sugar, soap and clothing forced the cost of living upward. More than a sprinkling of those people who were beyond the pale of refined society in Britain cherished aspirations to respectability in New South Wales. Distinctions in status partly depended on birth, family and profession, but wealth made rank even more fluid than at home. In their quest for social standing, civil and military officers strove to acquire the trappings of respectability—broad acres, a stately house, servants, a carriage and pair. To achieve and maintain these symbols of gentility, they were prepared to undertake activities which genteel society deemed unbecoming. Wentworth always considered himself a gentleman. In his eyes he had education, bearing and an illustrious family heritage. Yet he still needed the means to support the way of life to which he aspired, and that involved substantially augmenting a salary which brought him less than £100 per annum.[9]

On 10 May 1796, barely two months after Wentworth had disembarked and while he was still familiarizing himself with his new surroundings, Captain William Raven returned to Port Jackson from a speculative voyage to India in the storeship, *Britannia*. On landing in Sydney, Raven was fêted. Leading officials met and attended him, the military band played stirring airs and he was conveyed in Captain Paterson's chaise to the market-place. Reflecting on the scene, Paine remarked:

Such were the *Honours* paid to this Great man ... much greater than those paid to Governor Hunter on his Arrival although his Character and Virtues were well known in the Colony. But he brought no supply of Rum with him.

Despite criticism from some quarters, and despite their own ambivalent feelings about being directly involved in trade, the officers felt that such public celebrations bolstered their standing in the community and legitimized their conduct. D'Arcy's activities on Norfolk Island further disposed him to enter the ranks of the entrepreneurs. Other than the officers, there were few settlers who had sufficient capital to undertake mercantile ventures. A small, exclusive and economically powerful clique had emerged to control the market. Its members permitted none but themselves to buy the cargoes of visiting vessels. In attempting to gain access to this trading ring, Wentworth was trebly advantaged. He held up to £800 in Treasury bills; he had an agent in England willing to send him articles for sale; and, from his dealings on Norfolk Island, he was acquainted with a few of Sydney's leading traders. But he had to tread warily.[10]

As the military officers' political and financial power grew, so did their arrogance and sense of superiority. Regarding themselves as leaders in the community, they thought themselves entitled to the cooperation of the governor, the respect of the free colonists, the deference of the emancipists and the obedience of the convicts. Maurice Margarot, one of the 'Scottish Martyrs' transported for sedition, saw that an *esprit de corps* united them: though they squabbled among themselves, any outsider who happened to offend one of their number incurred the wrath of the whole. In February 1796 Surgeon Balmain, in his capacity as magistrate, proffered legal advice to John Baughan, an ex-convict whose house had been wrecked by soldiers in Captain John Macarthur's company. Resenting Balmain's action, the officers of the corps—as one—expressed their indignation at his 'shameful and malignant interference'. Heated exchanges culminated in a threatened duel when Balmain told Macarthur that he thought him 'a base rascal and an atrocious liar and villain'. Both parties agreed to 'conditions of mutual forgiveness', but Macarthur continued to harass his gadfly.[11]

This incident was only one in a series of conflicts which sprang from deep-seated rivalry between the military authorities and those officials on the civil staff who remained loyal to the governor. In September that year the Reverend Johnson complained of an increase in 'party spirit'. Visiting the colony in 1800, John Turnbull was startled by the degree to which sour division paralysed the colony's administration. For five years Hunter struggled to wrest from the military officers the control they had acquired under Grose and Paterson. Trying in vain to curtail the traffic in spirits, he conceded that he could not prevent smuggling, even if he possessed the eyes of Argus. Whole cargoes of rum were landed in Sydney in open defiance of the governor's orders. Marsden railed against the profiteers: 'The greatest part of these officers sold spirituous liquor and enriched themselves at the expense of the morals of the people—the more drunkenness the more money returned to their pockets'. Characteristically, Wentworth avoided becoming too closely identified with either faction. He re-established amicable relations with Hunter and Balmain, while remaining on cordial terms with the corps. By 1797 he had eased his way into Sydney's business world without arousing party ire or losing the governor's friendship. At this time D'Arcy's letters home gave no hint of how deeply he was involved in the liquor trade.[12]

He began to prosper in 1797, when he was the plaintiff in no less than eight cases before the Court of Civil Jurisdiction. In February he sought the recovery of four debts that amounted to £91 2s 9d and in July another four that totalled £193 1s 8d. In the latter month he received from Hunter a Treasury bill for £502 10s and remitted it to Lord Fitzwilliam. Part of that sum was to repay D'Arcy's debts to his noble kinsman; the remainder was to cover Cookney's anticipated expenses in obtaining and shipping goods to him. Referring to the large amount of this bill, Cookney concluded that the items he had previously sent to Wentworth had found a ready market. So rapid was D'Arcy's rise to prominence in New South Wales that people in Britain importuned him to help their poor relations. One asked him to assist a young man transported for theft; another solicited his services in aiding a convict named Kennedy to return to the bosom of his family. Beyond the realm of commerce, in certain circles Wentworth was seen as one who might render assistance to those less fortunate than himself.[13]

Every omen seemed to augur well in the year of Wentworth's thirty-fifth birthday. On 19 August he wrote again to Fitzwilliam, craving a further boon. D'Arcy dwelt on a single issue: because Hunter had appointed him in 1796, he was the junior of other assistant-surgeons who had come to the colony while he was on Norfolk Island; this situation lessened his chances of succeeding by rotation to the office of principal surgeon. Wentworth asked that Fitzwilliam endeavour to persuade the Duke of Portland to grant him a commission from 10 December 1791, the date on which King had appointed him superintendent of convicts at Queenborough. If he were to be given a post in another department, he assured his lordship that he would continue the same honourable conduct which he had always pursued in the antipodes. It was his ambition to accumulate a handsome fortune, and to live in peace and quietness for the remainder of his years. He had every reliance that King would, upon his arrival in England, render him assistance from his 'most disinterested friendship'. Wentworth's patron and agent were not wanting in their constancy and support. In August 1797 Cookney conveyed the news that he had finally obtained D'Arcy's commission (bearing the date 1 April 1796) and enclosed a copy. Because of Fitzwilliam's intervention, the Home Office had agreed to recompense him £40 per annum for the four years he had acted as assistant-surgeon on Norfolk Island. Cookney had also received the £75 outstanding from Wentworth's salary as superintendent of convicts. He bought the goods that D'Arcy had requested (providing through his own thoughtfulness some fashionable caps for the boys) and shipped them on the *Barwell*. The cost of these items, and the merchandise he had earlier sent, amounted to about £300 a year and did not include spirits, for Cookney was a man who was convinced that 'drinking is the root of all evil'. At this stage the bulk of Wentworth's trading involved the purchase of shares in cargoes brought to the colony by the likes of William Raven. D'Arcy had taken his place among the gentlemen monopolists.[14]

Hunter realised that he alone could not suppress the officers' trading activities. On 25 May 1798 he advised Portland that the British government should lay an axe to the root of the colony's commercial dealings and order its servants in New South Wales to give less attention to their private concerns. Ultimately, Hunter's efforts had proved unavailing, and brought him nothing but odium and embarrassment. While the governor was hamstrung, the pace of Wentworth's successes accelerated. That month he received two Treasury bills, for £1000 and £500, and planned to invest them in the colony rather than remitting them to England. Dress and behaviour reflected his opulence: he took to wearing a watch, a ring and knee-buckles, and made a wager of fifty guineas with Captain Michael Hogan, master of the *Marquis Cornwallis*, that the French would not take the Electorate of Hanover by 15 November. D'Arcy won the bet. Impressed by his manner as much as by his industry and reliability, Hunter commented favourably on his conduct and invited him to dine at Government House at 3 o'clock on Christmas Day.[15]

A Government and General Order, promulgated on 11 May 1799, directed Wentworth to replace James Mileham, the assistant-surgeon at Parramatta. In that district he was to minister to the sick and run the local hospital. Located fifteen miles to the west of Sydney, the township stood on a large plain by the banks of a river. There were over one hundred and fifty houses in the main street. A wide road linked the outlying settlement to the capital, and boats regularly plied the river between the two towns. On 18 October, five months after his arrival in Parramatta, Wentworth took a fourteen-year lease on six acres in the township. The Macarthurs lived a mile away at Elizabeth Farm. Next month Hunter granted D'Arcy 140 acres. Bordered by creeks on either side, and by the road to Sydney on the south, the land lay four miles east of Parramatta. On this grant he was to establish a country seat, Home Bush. As Wentworth consolidated his position in colonial society, Hunter's hold on the command of New South Wales grew increasingly tenuous. His nominal supporters—who included the judge-advocate, Richard Atkins, the aide-de-camp, George Johnston, the clergyman, Marsden, the surgeon, Balmain, and the deputy-commissary, James Williamson—had failed either to steel his resolve or to give him the backing he needed to crush the leaders of the corps and constrain his principal adversary, John Macarthur. The realization of the need to replace Hunter with a more determined governor prompted speculation that King would succeed him. Hunter wanted to remain for two more years, but was recalled on 5 November 1799. Portland's dispatch, however, did not reach Sydney until the following April and King did not assume office until September 1800.[16]

In the meantime Hunter faced another problem. From 1794, when Irish convicts known as 'Defenders' had been transported to New South Wales, the free settlers had harboured apprehensions as to the security of the settlement. With the arrival of about 250 'United

Irishmen' late in 1799, fears of an uprising intensified. By September 1800 open rebellion seemed imminent. Those convicts suspected of disaffection were interrogated and sentenced to a public flogging. On the 6th the governor called on the settlers to form two volunteer associations—one in Sydney and the other in Parramatta—each comprising fifty armed men. Wentworth enlisted in the local body with the rank of lieutenant; his commandant was an emancipist, Andrew Thompson. In spite of Hunter's measures, rumours of an uprising persisted and, on the 27th, the volunteers assembled at Parramatta ready to resist any revolt. No such disturbance occurred. Those felons who appeared to have been the most forward in the supposed conspiracy were questioned and punished, and an uneasy calm settled on the countryside.[17]

If Wentworth remained little affected by these events, his composure was shaken by what he regarded as a personal affront. In February 1800 he confided some unpleasant intelligence to Fitzwilliam and Cookney. A number of individuals, through whim and caprice, had sought to render his residence in the colony disagreeable. D'Arcy weighed up the alternatives open to him: one was to return to England; the other was to ask his patron and agent to purchase him an ensigncy in one of the Duke of York's regiments so that he might obtain a lieutenancy in the New South Wales Corps. He disclosed nothing further about his ill-treatment or of those responsible for his unhappiness. In all likelihood his rise to affluence had occasioned envy and resulted in spite. Rather than maligning his performance as a doctor or reproaching him for his bastard sons, his critics probably seized on his past as his point of vulnerability. Margarot recorded the following passage in his journal:

> A noted highwayman after repeated escapes owing to great protection and interference is at last transported; he ranks as a gentleman, sits at the Governor's table, plunders the Colony and amasses a fortune after having twenty times deserved to be hanged.

His words showed the nature of the rumours about Dr Wentworth which circulated in New South Wales. Character assassination had greater potential to create mischief and to pierce a target if it followed the local pattern and found expression in scurrilous verse, known as 'pipes', that were left in the streets for all to read.[18]

Brigadier-General Grose wrote to Major Foveaux on 25 June 1799 noting that some officers of the New South Wales Corps had been so indiscreet as to admit Wentworth to their company. If the Duke of York should learn of any officer disgracing himself by such an association, Grose warned that he would turn them out of the service. Although no ban ever came into force in the colony, a number of officers used D'Arcy's reputation as a highwayman to scorn and shun him, particularly when competition for trade intensified and 'less elevated inhabitants' began to infiltrate the market. Years later Wentworth denounced a copy of Grose's letter as 'a vile and infamous forgery', but, by raising the possible purchase of a commission with Fitzwilliam and Cookney, he had clearly considered it as one means of rebuffing those among the military who had rejected or traduced him. The extent of his social ostracism was even wider. King maintained that, on returning to New South Wales in April 1800, he was advised by Balmain to exclude Wentworth from his table. Bond and free met and conversed in the daily round of work and business, and, as a professional and commercial colleague, Balmain found no difficulty in associating with D'Arcy. Yet, privately, Balmain had misgivings and thought that a governor should be discriminating in choosing who was invited to dine at Government House. Unaware of Balmain's ambivalence and reservations, Wentworth continued to count him among his closest friends.[19]

Catherine had died on 6 January 1800 at the age of twenty-seven; following a service conducted by the Reverend Samuel Marsden, she was buried in St John's churchyard, Parramatta. D'Arcy preserved the intimacies and the privacy of their domestic situation by remaining silent about her death. With her passing, he changed the names she had chosen for their sons: 6-year-old Dorset became D'Arcy and 4-year-old Matthew became John. William, who was nine, remained William. This little, clumsy, squinting, cloth-capped boy sometimes accompanied his father while D'Arcy transacted business in Sydney and Parramatta. More often D'Arcy walked alone. His mourning was brief and he provided relish for the town's talk. It is probable that he reverted to the ways of his youth and found fleeting solace in the arms of raw country girls or in the beds of strumpets; perhaps he sought oblivion at nights by draining cups in the company of the disreputable at a wayside tavern. If so, signs that he was, at best, unsteady, at worst, giddy, only convinced his opponents that he was a type of pariah, best excluded from polite society. Regular letters from his father and brother, William, reminded him of a larger family in which he was the prodigal son. The time was far from ripe to indulge in self-pity, whether over the past or the present. He could not silence his detractors in New South Wales, but he could defeat them at their own game. To this end he increased the level of his involvement in trade and set out to acquire one of the best houses in Sydney, in High (from 1810 George) Street, and a chaise and horses to go with it. In 1800 he employed two servants in Sydney, the convicts Laurence Carthy and John Kennedy, who were victualled by the government. Next year he also employed the assignee, Catherine Melling; she was listed as living at his Sydney home. For all that Wentworth had done to circumvent Hunter's policies, the governor stood by him and expressed pleasure in being able to testify that he had conducted himself 'not only in his Official Situation but upon all other occasions with the most exact propriety'.[20]

Long before he left England, King had considered measures to reduce colonial expenditure, lower the price of commodities, break the trading monopolies and curtail the traffic in spirits. He reached Sydney Cove on 15 April 1800, anxious to commence his administration. For over five months he waited impatiently while Hunter tarried. The 42-year-old governor-designate appreciated the impact that his reforms would have, not least of all on former associates, among them Wentworth whom he had known for almost nine years. While King's old acquaintances looked on him as a rising sun, he told George Suttor that 'friends had never been planted in the colony and if they had they would not grow'. King made his intentions obvious. Before taking command he put on notice his proposals to shatter the trading monopoly and control the import of spirits, and publicly voiced his determination to send home the first officer who disobeyed his orders. On 8 September he directed Lieutenant-Colonel Paterson, the lieutenant-governor and commander of the corps, to convene a meeting of the civil and military officers, and to read them a letter outlining the new regulations affecting trade. No spirits were to be landed from any vessel arriving at Port Jackson without prior consent and a written permit. Paterson was enjoined to prohibit any officer from disgracing the service by engaging in traffic which would tarnish the respect due to His Majesty's commission.[21]

King's pronouncements alarmed D'Arcy and his fellow merchants. In attempting to salvage the profits which they anticipated making on goods they had previously purchased but had yet to sell, Wentworth and Balmain unveiled the extent of their trading operations. On 14 September they wrote independently to King, divulging that they possessed large quantities of merchandise. Balmain had 1359 gallons of spirits and seven chests of tea in store; Wentworth had 3000 gallons of spirits and ten chests of tea. Pleading that these goods had been purchased before King's arrival, they promised not to dispose of them without permission. They said that they had bought the spirits at ten shillings a gallon and the tea at the same cost per pound. In a bid to be compensated for the money outlaid, the risks undertaken and the damages incurred, they offered their goods to the government at £1 a gallon for the liquor and the same price per pound for the tea. Wentworth pointed out that he would gain considerably more if he were allowed to sell on the open market. King felt that he was not at liberty, on the government's behalf, to give them the price they asked, but permitted them to retail their goods privately, subject to severe stipulations. They could only sell the spirits and tea at the same price they had offered them to the government; King had to approve the purchasers; and Wentworth and Balmain were required to give a written undertaking that they would not enter into any future speculations contrary to the tenor of His Majesty's orders. Given no real option, they agreed to King's conditions and pledged, as gentlemen, that they would not engage in trading practices incompatible with his recent orders. On the 28th King took command of the colony.[22]

With a sense of pity for Hunter's predicament, King saw his predecessor as an honest and upright man who was sadly duped by his designing friends. Hunter had attempted to appease the officers rather than alienate them. Contrariwise, from the beginning of his administration King was prepared to tear the mighty down. Save for Hunter and Paterson, he knew that every civil and military official had been more or less guilty of trafficking in spirits. In December 1800 he refused to allow the captains of two ships to land their cargoes of liquor. Throughout 1801 he continued to monitor and regulate the import of spirits and the sale of articles brought to the colony. He collected outstanding debts owed to government and restricted the settlers to receiving no more than two convict servants 'on the store'. Convinced that he was rescuing the inhabitants and the public purse from a gang of extortionists, he identified Macarthur as its leader and predicted that his intrigues would one day cause a conflagration. For their part, the officers had become accustomed to exercising control over land, labour and markets, and they resented any meddling by the government in their affairs. Their outlook blended Whiggery and *laissez-faire*, and their rhetoric drew on notions of liberty and natural rights to mask flagrant greed. In the face of King's resolve to pursue a course of action detrimental to the traders' interests, Wentworth was in no way disposed to defy the governor openly. He dutifully carried out his medical responsibilities while endeavouring to protect his mercantile concerns. In public he complied with King's orders; in private he did what he could to agitate for change.[23]

King's restrictive trade policies made it difficult for Wentworth to dispose of his merchandise. In letters to Fitzwilliam and Cookney, written in October 1800, he told them that the governor had behaved towards him in a manner he had little expected 'from his former professions of friendship'. Before King's intervention, D'Arcy had expected to realize some £7000 by selling his spirits and tea, but he now anticipated receiving only £5000, and, to secure even that amount, he feared he would have to resign his commission. Balmain left the colony in August 1801 and reached England in March 1802. In the following month he paid his respects to Fitzwilliam who received him 'like a Prince'. From Balmain, Fitzwilliam gained further details about colonial affairs in general and about Wentworth in particular. With Fitzwilliam's support, in December Cookney appealed to John Sullivan, the new under-secretary at the Home Office. Cookney outlined Wentworth's predicament and assured Sullivan that D'Arcy faced financial ruin. Sullivan defended the governor's actions, but agreed to advise him to buy Wentworth's goods at a moderate mark-up on the purchase price. Balmain thought that Sullivan's attitude would induce King, 'in spite of his cankered heart', to show D'Arcy a little more civility. Fitzwilliam's and Cookney's intervention had the opposite effect. Hostile to any move to frustrate his orders in the colony, King was infuriated by any wavering on the part of his political masters in Whitehall. Wentworth's supporters only succeeded in widening the breach between him and the governor.[24]

Both his agent and his patron gave Wentworth counsel. Cookney urged him to remain in New South Wales, to recover what he had outlaid on his goods and to refrain from injuring his own interests. In short, it was necessary to ride out the storm. As palliatives, he reported that he had shipped him goods to the value of £264 and advised D'Arcy that he would, according to his request, invest his salary in consolidated annuities, known as the 3rd Consols, which paid an annual dividend of 3 per cent. Fitzwilliam began his letter by reporting that Balmain had given her ladyship three beautiful parrots, and had brought him a fine pheasant of which he thought so highly that he sent it to be stuffed and mounted. They still awaited the delivery of some swans. His lordship then advised D'Arcy against returning to England. Expressing satisfaction with the numerous reports he had received of Wentworth's public service and of the success which had rewarded his private concerns, he assured him that:

> The circumstances of the Colony must afford to the contemplative mind, constant subjects of admiration and speculation. A New World rising into consideration, for you are young enough to live to see it reach a point of considerable importance . . . I hope . . . you will leave the name of Wentworth, one of the most considerable and most respectable in this New World.

It therefore behoved him to look to the future, and to behave responsibly and with circumspection.[25]

Independent of such exhortations, Wentworth had already demonstrated restraint. The Sydney market was glutted for much of 1801-02 and he waited for a more favourable time to unload his wares. Rather than panicking, he adopted a level-headed approach, as did the surgeon and sailor, George Bass, who remarked that, although the merchants had had their wings clipped, they would try to fall on their feet. Fitzwilliam's encouragement boosted D'Arcy's morale. He acknowledged his patron's praise, stating that it gave him pleasure and that he hoped his future conduct would elicit the same approbation. But he was either unable or unwilling to appreciate why King had turned his back on him. Balmain, who had served with both of them in happier days on Norfolk Island, offered an explanation:

perhaps you have not thought of a well known maxim, namely that Tyrants while they are dependent will apparently overflow with the full tide of thankfulness, but when placed in Power they throw of[f] the Mask and cannot brook the restraint which a retrospect of former obligations necessarily imposes on them, and thus it often turns out that he who served them in adversity is now an object hateful to their sight and the earliest victim of their rankling hearts, and such is that *man*.

Those injured by King's reforms refused to acknowledge his intention to enforce Home Office policy, uphold the law, stamp out abuses and govern in the interests of the majority of the colony's inhabitants. Instead of recognizing the governor's obligations and responsibilities, they attributed his conduct to personal malice and equated his rule with despotism. As early as August 1801, in his correspondence with Fitzwilliam, Wentworth depicted King as a tyrant who was universally execrated.[26]

John Macarthur articulated the grievances and demands of King's adversaries, mobilized support, and co-ordinated an extensive and subtle campaign to dismay and discredit the governor. When Paterson disagreed with Macarthur's suggestion that the officers should break off social relations with King, a quarrel developed. In the ensuing duel with Macarthur on 14 September 1801 Paterson was wounded in the shoulder. For openly flouting his orders, King placed Macarthur under immediate arrest and took the unusual step of dispatching him to England for court martial. The 'master worker of the puppets' sailed from Sydney in November. Accompanied by his sons, Edward and John, who were to be educated in England, Macarthur took with him a number of deputations from his friends, and proposed to use the arrest of Captain Piper, his second in the duel, as a *cause célèbre* to expose King's oppression and assist in his recall. By fortuitously acquiring the support of Sir Walter Farquhar, physician in ordinary to the Prince of Wales, and by soliciting the aid of Sir Joseph Banks, the pundit on all things antipodean, Macarthur set out to 'dish' King and his associates. He achieved less immediate notice than he had expected. Balmain had come to appreciate that big men in New South Wales were 'all very small folk' in Britain. Although the army's advocate-general eventually decided that Macarthur could not be court-martialled in England, official censure was liberally scattered—over Macarthur as well as the administration in Sydney. From his base in England the perturbator continued to rally his collaborators in the colony. Wentworth became increasingly drawn to the cause.[27]

While the market for his goods continued unfavourable, D'Arcy learned that James Thomson, the staff surgeon on Norfolk Island, intended to take leave and return to England. On 4 July 1802 Wentworth contacted the principal surgeon, Thomas Jamison, claiming a right to the appointment and indicating his readiness to embark at the governor's pleasure. Welcoming the prospect of being rid of another antagonist, King announced Wentworth's appointment two days later and gave him three weeks in which to prepare for the voyage. D'Arcy then wrote to the governor, informing him that he possessed a considerable amount of merchandise, asking if there were any objections to his taking it to Norfolk Island and volunteering to ship it at his own expense. King refused outright, whereupon Wentworth sought permission to leave it with a dealer in Sydney who would sell it in his absence. Again, King denied his request. Faced with the choice, Wentworth valued his commercial affairs more than his promotion to acting staff surgeon, and elected to remain on the mainland. He regarded King's actions as cruel and unjust, and as further evidence of his intention to injure him. Locked into a mutually antagonistic relationship with the governor, D'Arcy adopted a rhetoric that resembled Macarthur's.[28]

Private murmurings of discontent and secret denunciations of the governor's oppression found a public outlet and added to the rancour. Caricatures and anonymous writings reflecting on King were distributed in several parts of Sydney and the hinterland. On 13 January 1803 Lieutenant Thomas Hobby's servant found a paper in his master's chaise. It was addressed to Major Johnston. Hobby made a copy before travelling to Parramatta where he read it to Captain William Kent, Mr Jamison and Deputy-Commissary Williamson. Wentworth also read the pipe which contained the following lines:

> And to Ministers fates—Pitt and Portland are out,
> Then says K—g, 'I soon shall be put to the rout;
> But damn me, while powerful, I'll do what I can,
> According to what I proposed as a plan,
> To make all subservient, humble, and poor,

Take women and children all off from the store,
Crush all independence and poverty plant,
Ruin, tense, and distress, and make every one want
If my power was not stinted, I'd make the world shake,
Give serjeants commissions and officers break,
Which already I've tried, but in vain showed my spite,
And bit my own tongue when nought else I could bite;
I'd civilians give trust, confide in new faces,
Make magistrates of them and give them new places . . .

On the 17th King asked Wentworth, as an officer in His Majesty's service, to inform him—unequivocally—of the circumstances surrounding the reading and distribution of the anonymous pipe, and to reveal the time, place and those party to its circulation at Parramatta. Although he was not a principal figure in the affair, D'Arcy sided with the participants and maintained his silence. Despite the governor's strenuous efforts, the identity of the author of the libel remained a secret.[29]

    Continual confrontation with his enemies began to affect King and weaken his administration. Sickness and strain exacted their toll and he became overweight and heavy-eyed. The more the gap between his hopes and his achievements widened, the more he veered from outbursts of blustering pomposity to moments of near breakdown. He was confounded, too, by being unable to rely on his closest associates. Even Lieutenant-Governor Paterson lacked vigour in opposing the officers of the corps. As a result his relations with King deteriorated, and, though the two preserved an outward appearance of friendship for the sake of the government, they found renewed cause for friction. James Tuckey, an observer of colonial society, noted how King's suspicions fuelled distrust, setting in train a cycle of bitter, retaliatory measures. Clearly identified as belonging to the cabal which sought to undermine the government, Wentworth experienced King's petulance over a trivial matter. On 16 August 1802 Balmain informed D'Arcy that he had sent him, in the care of Assistant-Surgeon John Savage, a gift of a quarter-cask of madeira. It arrived on 11 March 1803 in the *Glatton*. Savage obtained the governor's permit to take possession of the wine. On being landed, the madeira and the longboat in which it was ferried were immediately seized on the ground that the permit had not been countersigned by the naval officer. The matter was reported to the governor who passed it to a civil court which found the seizure to be illegal. Displeased, King referred the finding to a bench of magistrates specially convened to hear the case. When this court upheld the original finding, the governor overruled both decisions and distributed the wine among those who had confiscated the cask. Wentworth then petitioned Lord Hobart (the secretary of war who had been given responsibility for the colonies) to afford him the redress to which he was entitled as a British subject. In his letters to Fitzwilliam he showed less restraint in airing his grievances against King's 'detestable tyranny'. D'Arcy's identification with the Macarthur faction was virtually complete.[30]

Balmain had appointed Wentworth his attorney in New South Wales, empowering him to recover money owed to him and to those clients on whose behalf he had acted. To this end D'Arcy set about recovering £1886 which George Crossley had drawn on a man named Schell, a pauper in an English workhouse. Crossley was a solicitor who had been transported for perjury in 1799. He opened a shop, acquired land, acted as an assistant to the judge-advocate and received a conditional pardon from Governor King in June 1801. At Wentworth's instigation, Crossley was arrested on 16 December for the bills he had dishonoured. The court found in D'Arcy's favour, but Crossley appealed to the governor. Instead of having his goods at once seized and sold, in an award on 9 January 1802 King permitted him to continue trading, subject to his accounting for his sales, in order that the loss to his creditors might be reduced. Crossley failed to observe this condition, and, on 14 September, the governor ordered his goods to be seized. With the assistance of the provost marshal, Thomas Smythe, Wentworth entered Crossley's home and removed his chattels. In retaliation Crossley prosecuted them for trespass. After much delay, Wentworth was acquitted on 10 July 1803 and Smythe on 17 February 1804. Crossley's projected appeal to the privy council lapsed because he lacked security for costs. Pitted against an opponent better versed in the law and as determined as himself, D'Arcy was tenacious in Balmain's cause. Yet he also revealed something else. The ex-convict Ann Inett (King's former mistress) had married Richard John Robinson. They held a licensed victualling house, known as the Yorkshire Grey, at

Parramatta, and two farms near by. According to Mrs Robinson, whose husband's property was tied to Crossley's debts, on one occasion Wentworth behaved like a wild animal, intimidating those who stood in his way and threatening to have them flogged or transported. The outburst may have been the result of frustration, but it provided a glimpse into the predatory side of D'Arcy's nature which was also evident in the way he treated his own debtors.[31]

Having sold his goods at a profit in 1803, in the following year Wentworth entered into a partnership in Sydney with the emancipist merchant, Simeon Lord. Spirits fetched between ten shillings and £1 a gallon, but, as a medium of exchange, their value was much higher. Sheep worth £3 were sold for a gallon and a half of rum. Enterprising and ambitious, D'Arcy continued to deal in spirits, though he carefully maintained the role of a sleeping partner in these transactions. Alongside his trading activities, his management of Balmain's business and his involvement in the Crossley affair, Wentworth practised as a surgeon. In November 1801 the government printer, a convict named George Howe, attributed his recovery from a serious illness to D'Arcy's skill and attentiveness, and thanked him for saving his life. Throughout November and December 1802 an unusually high number of deaths occurred in the Parramatta district. Many of the sick, suffering mainly from dysentery, were admitted to the local hospital under Wentworth's supervision. On 1 January 1803 he complained to Jamison of the chronic shortage of medicines, bedding and utensils, of the lack of barley, oatmeal and sago, and of the building's dilapidated state. That Wentworth adopted a peremptory tone showed the gravity of the existing situation, but it also indicated the low place he had assigned to his professional responsibilities over the preceding three and a half years. To some extent, overwork may have mitigated his neglect. Apart from the daily routine of ministering to the sick, colonial surgeons performed additional duties which entailed their attending corporal punishments, coronial inquiries and criminal trials. In January 1804 Wentworth appeared as a witness in the case of Richard Grimshaw who was accused of beating his infant daughter to death. By May 1803, however, D'Arcy had grown tired of his vocation. In that month he requested Fitzwilliam to use his influence with Lord Hobart to permit him to retire on half-pay. Wentworth still proffered alternatives. Were he to be appointed to the civil command at Parramatta, or to the post of naval officer in Sydney, it would render him infinitely more comfortable than his present lot, and he assured his lordship that he would not trouble him again for as long as he lived in New South Wales.[32]

Besides his official concerns, Wentworth was engaged in the management of his farms. In June 1800 he owned 160 acres on Norfolk Island, leased six acres in the township of Parramatta, held another property of 50 acres in the vicinity, and owned 140 acres at Home Bush on which he ran eight pigs, eight goats and one horse. By 1802 his holdings in New South Wales had increased to 245 acres, of which 24 were cleared and 16 under cultivation. Builders completed his new two-storeyed home at Parramatta in 1803. It was one of the finest country houses in the colony and he named it Wentworth Woodhouse. He continued to acquire property and in April 1804 spent 381 guineas on the purchase of five small farms at Parramatta, bringing his holdings to 340 acres. His livestock included 6 horses, 10 cattle, 72 sheep and 12 hogs. At the 1804 muster the largest landholdings were Macarthur's 3500 acres and the Balmain estate's 1480; Marsden had 1720 and Quartermaster Thomas Laycock 1365. In comparison, Wentworth was a modest landholder, but he was disposed to obtain more.[33]

By 1802 he had decided that his first and second-born sons should receive the benefits of an English education. He wrote to Balmain, requesting him to assist Cookney in finding an appropriate school for the children, with the proviso that its fees should not exceed his salary. He begged Balmain to see the lads as soon as possible after their arrival. Entrusted to the care of Captain Richard Brooks for their journey to England in the *Atlas*, 12-year-old William and 9-year-old D'Arcy sailed on 8 October. The ship traded goods in China and at Calcutta before they reached their destination safely. Although Brooks initially acted as their guardian and invited them to his home in Devon, Cookney soon took over the role of foster-father. William and D'Arcy waited on Fitzwilliam who seemed glad to see them and presented each of the boys with a guinea. They also met Balmain. Mr Taylor inoculated them with the cowpox and, though suffering fevers, the youngsters regained strength. Their surgeon was paid five guineas for his services. Cookney decided to send them to the Reverend Midgley's school in Bletchley, near Fenny Stratford, Buckinghamshire. Three of his own sons attended the same institution. While French was not on the curriculum, Latin was taught there, and the clergyman had a reputation for providing a sound grounding in grammar and arithmetic. The fees were twenty-three guineas per annum, excluding extras. William and D'Arcy started school in October 1803, conducted themselves to their master's satisfaction and received a good character from him. During their holidays Mrs Cookney was obliging and took them to a number of amusements. Their letters to their father kept him in countenance. The lads assured him that they appreciated the importance of a good education and that they were both well and happy at school; they gladdened his heart by relating how they bore in mind and looked with great pleasure to that day when they would have the irrepressible happiness of seeing again one of the best and kindest of parents. The correspondence was in William's hand, but jointly signed, 'Your dutiful and affectionate sons', W. C. and D'Arcy Wentworth.[34]

Neither duty nor affection filled the breasts of the predominantly Irish felons in government service at Castle Hill, eight miles to the north of Parramatta. At 11.30 p.m. on Sunday 4 March 1804 an express messenger leapt from his horse at Government House, Sydney, with the news that over three hundred convicts from Castle Hill and the surrounding region had armed themselves with muskets, pikes and cutlasses, and joined in open rebellion. Mrs Macarthur, Mrs Abbott and Mrs Marsden, together with their children and the Reverend Samuel Marsden, fled Parramatta by boat for Sydney. The free settlers who remained in that inland town either locked themselves in their homes or gathered at the barracks to resist the insurgents. Next day Major Johnston rode at the head of a detachment of twenty-five soldiers, a trooper and a dozen inhabitants of Parramatta in pursuit of the 'Croppies'. They came upon them seven miles from Toongabbie. Johnston apprehended two of the ringleaders, and, in the ensuing skirmish, twelve convicts were killed and six were wounded. By nightfall more than two hundred had been taken prisoner. Then the retribution began. In the following week eight prisoners were hanged for their part in the insurrection. Five others were flogged and thirty-odd sent to the Coal River. Wentworth, who was probably in Sydney at the time, did not mention the incident in his letters. He never wasted words in his correspondence on contemporary events, unless they directly impinged on him. Elements of self-centredness were intrinsic in his nature.[35]

4 *Smile at the rising sun*

On 3 January 1804 a Government and General Order had been issued announcing Wentworth's appointment as acting-surgeon at Norfolk Island. This transfer did not appear to threaten his entrepreneurial dealings and he had ample time to prepare for his removal. Simeon Lord acted as his agent. D'Arcy let his home in Sydney to Captain Kent, with strict instructions for its rent and repair, and for the safety of its contents. He sailed in the *Betsy* and, on 10 May, reached Norfolk Island which was then under the command of Lieutenant-Governor Joseph Foveaux, one of the junta which had farmed and traded in New South Wales before Hunter's arrival. Some things had changed, but much remained to trigger Wentworth's memories of the island he had first seen almost fourteen years previously. With Foveaux's approval he resumed his public and private activities. He acted as Jamison's attorney, as Lord's agent and as Piper's banker; he continued dealing in spirits, tea, sugar and clothing; and he turned his attention to farming. By December that year he received £1277 for the meat and grain which he sold to the commissariat store, and in the following year was paid £1493. After Balmain's death on 17 November 1803, Wentworth also accepted responsibility for administering his estate. He had requested Cookney to buy and send to the colony a still and a worm (a spiral pipe) for distilling. The importation of such apparatus was forbidden, unless it could be established that it was to be used in the production of essential oils from native plants. On one of his Parramatta farms D'Arcy had an orchard of peach trees. Anticipating the arrival of the still, he sent instructions from Norfolk Island to his agent on the mainland to have the juice on hand. Ten gallons of peach juice made one gallon of prized brandy. Despite Wentworth's assertion that the equipment was meant for experiments, the Home Office refused permission for the still to be shipped, and Cookney had never been warm in supporting the scheme. Rather lower on his scale of priorities, D'Arcy's official duties required him to give medical assistance to the detachment of the New South Wales Corps stationed on the island.[36]

In the month that Wentworth reached his destination, King received instructions from Britain to begin the evacuation of Norfolk Island and to move the inhabitants to Van Diemen's Land. During July or August D'Arcy learned that the governor intended sending him to Port Dalrymple. In an attempt to curry favour, he had sent a bonnet to the governor's lady. Anna King responded almost coquettishly. She thanked him for the pretty gift, so exactly to her taste, and for having had the kindness to send another bonnet for her 7-year-old daughter, Elizabeth. She expressed gratitude for the attentions that Wentworth had always shown her, and blamed Balmain's duplicity for the rift that had developed between Wentworth and her husband. And she assured him that he had no better well-wishers for his prosperity than King and herself. Wentworth was allowed to remain on Norfolk Island. None the less, news of the proposed resettlement prompted speculation about a reshuffle of the civil staff. One colleague, James Mileham, wanted to know Wentworth's intentions. On 18 August 1804 he wrote to D'Arcy to inform him that, according to what Judge-Advocate Richard Atkins had heard, Wentworth's friends in England were exerting themselves to obtain the principal surgeonship of New South Wales for him. The truth was more banal. Fitzwilliam, Cookney, Hunter, Waterhouse and Considen had lobbied the Home Office on his behalf, but only for salary increments and additional remuneration to which he was legitimately entitled. Before long, however, Wentworth had fixed his mind on the post of provost marshal. He told Fitzwilliam that the pay was only five shillings a day, but the additional emoluments could total £700 a year.[37]

Lieutenant-Colonel Foveaux had, from 1800, steadily acquired a reputation as an able and efficient administrator. His superiors in Sydney and Whitehall respected the strength and purpose he had exhibited in governing Norfolk Island. Among the convicts his name was loathed. In 1801 he had crushed an insurrection, summarily executed two prisoners and ordered floggings which continued for twenty days. Those who worked under him remarked on his cruelty and his passion for witnessing punishments. He was also condemned for his dubious morality in fathering a daughter (b. 1801) by Ann Sherwin, the wife of a sergeant in the New South Wales Corps, and for allegedly allowing female convicts to be sold to the settlers for a gallon of rum. By comparison, to convicts and overseers alike, Wentworth seemed kind-hearted. Although he had been a volunteer in Ireland and at Parramatta, and had taken a stand against Irish rebels *en masse*, D'Arcy showed consideration for a number of his fellow countrymen. Transported to Norfolk Island as a suspected leader of the 1804 uprising, Joseph Holt was assigned to heavy labour and placed on reduced rations. He soon fell ill. Wentworth raised his plight with Foveaux and persuaded him to be lenient. A mutual respect quickly developed between the lieutenant-governor and the doctor which blossomed into friendship. On 9 September 1804 Foveaux sailed for England where he did what he could to advance D'Arcy's interests and 'behaved very handsome' to his sons.[38]

Piper took command of Norfolk Island on Foveaux's departure. He was to enjoy the good will of those he governed. Wentworth liked the more relaxed style of his administration and the casual attitude he took towards King's regulations. In the governor's estimation Piper was unconscionably lax. Without authorization, he had allowed spirits to be landed and permitted a number of the inhabitants to depart on visiting ships. On 5 January 1805 King admonished him. Piper wantonly consorted with the local females, as did Wentworth who had an eye for Mary Ginders. She was a favourite of the soldiers and led the entertainment held on Thursday nights in the barracks. At these bacchanals women with numbers painted on their bare backs performed the salacious 'dance of the mermaids' to the applause of their admirers. The revelry ended in drunken debaucheries. D'Arcy's letter to Piper, advising him to make good use of his time among the young girls and 'Don't forget my old friend, Mary G.', showed how he savoured raffish company, whether at the Dog and Duck in St George's Fields or on an island in the Pacific. In writing to Cookney he admitted being happy.[39]

That year Wentworth sent his youngest son, 9-year-old John, to join William and D'Arcy at school in England. His passage took fifteen months, during which it was feared that the *Alexander*, the vessel in which he travelled, had either sunk or been captured by the French. Because of irregularities throughout the voyage, Captain Robert Rhodes, the ship's master, was arrested and confined in the King's Bench prison. On his arrival in June 1806, John was ill from scurvy. He recuperated under the watchful care of Mrs Cookney before joining young D'Arcy at Bletchley. It was more than three years since he had seen his brothers. For most of that time they had lived in a country which faced a threatened invasion by Napoleon. The Addington government had reintroduced income tax to finance the war with France, reducing their father's net salary—along with everyone else's—by 5 per cent, one shilling in the pound. *In loco parentis*, the ever reliable Charles Cookney had looked after the boys' material needs, settling accounts for their school fees, buying them greatcoats, suits, hats, gloves, shoes, stockings, trunks and bookcases, and meeting sundry costs which they incurred for transport, laundry and porterage. He also paid their doctors' bills. What was more, he showed genuine affection for Wentworth's sons. In midsummer holidays, and occasionally at Easter, they stayed at his home at 9 Castle Street, Holborn. He charged their father fifteen shillings a week for each boy's board and lodging, a minor recompense given that he once had two of the Wentworths, two children of a relation and nine of his own under the same roof. By July 1804 he thought that William should attend a superior school where French was offered. Five months later he wrote to Fitzwilliam, enclosing a page of the lad's handwriting and giving his opinion that it was high time that he should be placed out. Reminded that William had learned the elements of navigation, Cookney spoke with one or two naval commanders, but there appeared little chance that they would find a situation for him. He told Fitzwilliam that his kinsman's son was now 14, and—at 5 ft 8 ins—very tall for his age, in size more fit for a soldier than a sailor.

Cookney wrote to Wentworth on 13 April 1805, forwarding the boys' correspondence to their father. William had composed his own letter, but Midgley had given D'Arcy a little assistance with his. Cookney wanted to ascertain Wentworth's views on two matters. One was the question of pocket-money. As a parent who did not believe in giving boys very much, particularly at school where they mostly spent it on trash, Cookney allowed his three sons sixpence a week between them. Yielding more to the children of others than to his own, he suggested that William should now receive one shilling per week and D'Arcy sixpence, and added that the amounts were quite sufficient as they had necessaries in plenty. The other question related to William's future. Cookney asked Wentworth what he proposed for him, 'as he grows a great boy'. True to his word, Cookney again invited the lads to spend four weeks of their summer holidays at Castle Street. On 4 July young D'Arcy wrote to his father. He had seen St Paul's Cathedral, a painting of the Bay of Gibraltar, a panorama of the Battle of Agincourt and a play at Sadler's Wells. Better still, he had attended an 'Exhibition of Wild Beasts' at Exeter where he was much amused by a variety of birds and a kangaroo from Botany Bay. Best of all, in his judgement, was that most wonderful of beasts, the elephant, which stood more than 9 feet high and weighed 3 tons, and was so sagacious as to remove and replace a gentleman's hat. He had seen many other surprising things, but, because he was only 12 and quickly tired of writing, they were too numerous for him to mention. Kept to his desk, he did go on to say that on two or three occasions Foveaux had received his brother and himself most kindly, that he was to return with two of Cookney's sons to Bletchley and that William would be sent to another school. In conclusion, he trusted that his father and brother John were in good health.

Five weeks later William put pen to paper. He told his father that he had accompanied Mr Cookney to make inquiries at Dr Alexander Crombie's school in Greenwich. He would begin his studies there on 13 August. The institution was highly recommended and he was confident that his father would approve of it. Mrs Cookney added a postscript to William's letter in which she related that he had stayed with them for seven weeks and that he was a fine boy, but she doubted that he would ever make a surgeon because of 'the Cast in the Eye it leads Him differently to the object he intends'. On 8 October and 31 December 1805 Cookney provided Wentworth with more details of the school. The fees were forty guineas a year, plus four for dancing lessons, three for board during holidays and £2 15s 6d for extras. A liberal scholar whose writings ranged over philology, politics, economics, agriculture, science and theology, Crombie was a clergyman, a sharp disciplinarian and an excellent master. Although William did not like his situation as much as at Bletchley and wanted to join the navy, Cookney thought that no time should be lost in qualifying him for a vocation. Again and again he asked Wentworth to name the professions he intended for his sons. Too busy with his auditing to allow the Wentworth boys or even his own sons to come home that Christmas, Cookney undertook to have them in midsummer 1806 when the weather was conducive to outdoor activities. Wentworth found separation from his children painful and fretted when letters from or about them failed to reach him. With the intention of seeing the boys, he had requested Fitzwilliam to approach Lord Camden, the secretary for war and the colonies, to obtain leave of absence for him. According to Cookney, the matter languished, apparently due to wartime difficulties.[40]

Jamison had written to Wentworth on 8 February 1806, notifying him of his recall to New South Wales. The prospect of once more being in Sydney under King's sway dampened D'Arcy's spirits and prompted him to ask Cookney if Fitzwilliam had obtained permission for him to return to England. Concern for the welfare of his children added to his melancholy. He had not heard of them for over a year and waited anxiously for the arrival of every ship to learn if they were still 'in the land of the living'. On 12 March he begged Cookney to remember him to his dear sons in the most kind and affectionate terms. The same letter reiterated his request for a worm and still, but he stressed that the equipment would be used for experiments in distilling oils from native plants for medicinal use. Alert to the shortage of meat on the mainland, he made arrangements to ship a cargo of his pork from Norfolk Island to Port Jackson. He ceased duties on 30 March. In one of the rare written references which he ever made to a book, other than medical texts, he ordered the most recent edition of the *Encyclopaedia Britannica*. Restless and forlorn, he boarded the *Argo* to sail for Sydney.[41]

5

Nets of wrong and right

> Out-worn heart, in a time out-worn,
> Come clear of the nets of wrong and right;
> Laugh, heart, again in the grey twilight,
> Sigh, heart, again in the dew of the morn.
>
> W. B. Yeats, 'Into the Twilight'

After a swift but stormy passage the *Argo* reached Sydney Cove on 7 April 1806. About one week later Wentworth heard that King's successor, Captain William Bligh, was expected to arrive in New South Wales within six months. Cookney trusted that the new governor would make amends for the way in which King had treated D'Arcy. While his fellow colonists wondered what impact Bligh would have on their lives, Wentworth brooded over his personal disappointments. In April he lost his cargo of pork from Norfolk Island when the *Governor King* was wrecked in the Hunter River. He was seriously injured in an accident in June and confined to his house for nineteen weeks. His hope of becoming principal surgeon was dashed by rumours that James Thomson would return to the settlement in that office. There was talk, too, that William Gore had obtained the post of provost marshal. D'Arcy's application for leave had not been approved in Whitehall, nor would it be until December 1807, by which stage events overtook its granting. Bad tidings fell on bad. From Marsden he learned that Pitt was dead, and that the French had routed the allied armies and were carving Germany apart.[1]

In Lord Grenville's administration of 1806–07 Fitzwilliam achieved another milestone in his political career by entering the

The Wentworths

cabinet, first as president of the council and later as minister without portfolio. Wentworth, who was dispirited by a succession of setbacks and by a prolonged recuperation, wrote to his patron on 4 November 1806. He sent four black swans and several parrots, and told him that he was collecting the dried skins of different animals and birds which he would bring as gifts, if he were ever permitted to return to England. Characteristically, he blamed others for his unhappiness. He remarked on the high price of wheat, fresh meat, tea and coffee, and attributed it to a government run by a tyrant. Bligh had landed in the colony on 8 August and assumed command five days later. Before relinquishing office, King had improperly granted 1345 acres to Bligh and 600 to his daughter, Mrs Putland; with equal impropriety, Bligh had granted 790 acres to Mrs King. Although Wentworth detested King, he regarded his wife as 'a worthy woman' and gave her two guineas to pass on to William and D'Arcy whom she promised to visit in England. When he boarded the *Buffalo* on 15 August for the voyage home, King collapsed and could not sail until 10 February 1807. During the transfer of government and subsequently, he apprised Bligh of the state of New South Wales and of those who threatened its stability. He identified John Macarthur and D'Arcy Wentworth as troublesome characters.[2]

Macarthur had used his time in England profitably. Although Sir Joseph Banks showed increasing scepticism towards his schemes and doubts as to his motives, Macarthur secured permission through Lord Camden to resign from the army, to return to the colony and to receive a grant of 5000 acres in the Cowpastures on which to develop merino sheep. Accompanied by Walter Davidson, a nephew of Sir Walter Farquhar, who took up a grant of 2000 acres alongside the Macarthur lands, he arrived in Sydney on 8 June 1805. Between August and September Bligh received three addresses from the people he was sent to govern. Each of them congratulated him on his appointment and anticipated blessings from his rule. The first, dated 14 August, was signed by Johnston, Atkins and Macarthur, respectively, on behalf of the military, the civil officers and the free inhabitants. Within sixteen days the settlers of the Hawkesbury district presented theirs; it bore two hundred and forty-four signatures, nearly half of them made with a cross; Crossley was one of the small party who presented it to Bligh. On 22 September one hundred and thirty-five colonists designating themselves 'the free inhabitants of Sydney' presented the third; Simeon Lord figured prominently as a member of this group. The signatories to the second and third petitions expressed indignation that Macarthur had arrogated to himself the authority to represent their views. Wentworth signed none of them, but was acutely conscious that they reflected divisions in the penal outpost.[3]

A protégé of Banks, Bligh was a seasoned and resourceful naval officer who did not flinch when severity of discipline proved necessary. Chance and his own nature had made him the subject of abuse for his behaviour to the mutineers at the Nore and on the *Bounty*. Calumnies about him had circulated in the colony before he came to Sydney. It was said that, when anyone remonstrated against his conduct, rage distorted his features: he foamed at the mouth, shook his chubby fists, stamped on the ground and issued torrents of abuse. The traffickers in savagery might have cushioned their words had Bligh made his personal anguish known. His twin sons had died a day after their birth in 1795; one of his six daughters, an epileptic, had been declared insane; and his wife, Betsy, was so terrified by the sea that, after twenty-five years of marriage, he decided against bringing her to New South Wales even though he dreaded being separated from her. A little, corpulent man, with brilliant blue eyes and an alabaster complexion, Bligh was almost fifty-two when he took office, and had been well briefed on the task that confronted him. He resolved to crush the power of the corps, to exercise fiscal restraint, to govern for the common weal and to 'procure a little affluence' for himself. The man of the moment, he rose early, worked a fourteen-hour day and set about restoring government control.

The population of New South Wales was 7162 in 1806. There were 694 on Norfolk Island and 751 in Van Diemen's Land, 475 in the settlement of Hobart Town and 276 at Port Dalrymple. In the parent colony the civil establishment ran to 32, with 20 wives and 34 children; the soldiers numbered 474, with 61 wives and 196 children. There were 588 landed proprietors, comprising 74 who had emigrated from Britain, 80 discharged soldiers and sailors, and 434 ex-convicts; 412 women were attached to them. No fewer than 3620 people were off the stores; 2542 were victualled by the Crown. The government employed 1195 male convicts and 238 females, and these people had 200 children; the remainder of the convicts were assigned to the settlers. Bligh found great distress among the inhabitants, caused partly by the disastrous Hawkesbury floods in March that year, partly by the arrival of fewer ships with supplies and convict labourers after the renewal of the Napoleonic wars, and partly by the local trading sharks who had gained power as King's health worsened. With an eye on everything, Bligh curtailed land grants, alienating only 2180 acres whereas his predecessor had given 73 377; he clamped down on the import of spirits and restricted convict pardons; he also reduced the commissariat provisions bill on the Treasury from £32 351 in 1805 to £3264 in 1807, thereby staunching the major source of revenue to the junta and its supporters; and he surrounded himself with his own confidants—his secretary, Edmund Griffin, his aide-de-camp (and son-in-law), the consumptive Lieutenant John Putland, the provost marshal, William Gore, the commissary, John Palmer, the naval officer, Robert Campbell, and the clergyman, Henry Fulton—whose rivals branded them a cabal. Bligh's situation was arduous, but he thought the signs propitious.[4]

By October 1807 Wentworth owned 1219 acres, 290 sheep, 27 horned cattle, 14 horses and 30 swine. Most of his land was used for grazing, but he grew wheat on 20 acres and maize on 50, and had an orchard of 9 acres. He employed one overseer and five other servants, three of whom were convicts. In moments of relaxation he may have dipped into the twenty volumes of the *Encyclopaedia Britannica* which his agent dutifully sent him. Indicative of a change in Wentworth's domestic situation, Cookney also sent him silk hose, fine cotton gloves, a necklace that cost £2 12s 6d and a pair of earrings worth £1 11s 6d. Maria Ainslie, an illiterate, quiet and unassuming woman, generally acknowledged as D'Arcy's housekeeper, lived with him as his mistress. She was thirty-two years old and the mother of an illegitimate son, probably by a previous partner. Tried at Nottingham and sentenced to seven years transportation, she had sailed from England in October 1795 in the *Indispensable* and reached Sydney on 30 April 1796. After her sentence had expired she accompanied D'Arcy to Norfolk Island in 1804. There, she and Wentworth became familiar with another assistant-surgeon, the emancipist William Redfern, and his lady who later wrote to them from the island. Wentworth's union was far from unique. In New South Wales no more than 360 couples of every description were married. Among the civil and military officers and the landholders alone, 203 kept concubines: there were 900 legitimate and 908 illegitimate children in the colony.

5 Nets of wrong and right

Wentworth's bastard sons remained in England. William occasionally journeyed from Greenwich to see his younger brothers at Bletchley and spent further holidays with them at Castle Street. Apart from one incident when he broke a fellow pupil's flute and had to pay for a new one, he did well at school. Deemed 'a very clever fellow', he took tuition in French under Abbé de Roufigny and was made a monitor. In early manhood William stood taller than Cookney; he was given his first pocket-watch; he bought a one-sixteenth share in a lottery ticket for £1 7s. The lads wrote to their father, not as often as they could or should have, and less than Cookney, who was at his wit's end concerning their vocations. As one who advocated that young men should enter the world early, while their minds were supple, Cookney despaired of ever discovering Wentworth's aspirations for his sons. In 1807 young D'Arcy contracted scarlet fever. During his delirium it took two people to manage him, one of whom, a servant girl at Bletchley, caught the disease and died. Somehow the boy recovered. That year Wentworth's brother, William, wrote to tell him that their father had died on 14 November 1806 at the age of eighty-four, without fulfilling his hope to see again his prodigal son. Their mother had died on 17 July 1803, in her seventy-sixth year. Three of Wentworth's sisters—Dorothy, Martha and Mary Anne—were married and had large families. According to William, who was by then a lieutenant on half-pay in the 21st Dragoons and living in Dublin, D'Arcy had never written to his family since leaving England, in spite of their repeated letters to him.[5]

On 15 April 1807 Wentworth had once more taken charge of the hospital at Parramatta. In July he locked horns with Captain Abbott, the local commanding officer and chief magistrate for the district. The dispute originated early that month when an overseer, George Beldon, notified his superintendent, Richard Rouse, that Wentworth was employing convalescent prisoners from the hospital for his own advantage. Rouse informed the governor who directed Francis Oakes, the chief constable at Parramatta, to investigate the allegation, and, were it true, to remove such convicts from Wentworth's service. On the 3rd Oakes went to Wentworth's home and farms where he found five convalescing prisoners. James Griffin was working as a gardener, Lawrence Killaney as a house servant, Michael Downey and James McDonald as stockmen, and Thomas Steakham had charge of one of D'Arcy's farmhouses. Oakes took them from Wentworth's superintendence and

The Wentworths

placed them in government labour. Seething with indignation, Wentworth asked Jamison to seek an explanation from Bligh, but the principal surgeon was unable to obtain an audience with the governor. Four days afterwards Abbott directed a convict constable to escort two of the five prisoners back to the hospital. Killaney had an open wound on his arm and Griffin an ulcerated leg. Although he acknowledged that their condition warranted treatment, Wentworth refused to readmit them without an order from the governor or the principal surgeon. Abbott regarded Wentworth's action as defiance and took the matter further. On the 10th Wentworth was arrested. Because his commission was deemed to be essentially a military one, he was brought before a court martial on the 18th to face charges of contempt in disobeying Abbott's orders. The court was composed of Judge-Advocate Richard Atkins and eight officers of the New South Wales Corps who were disposed to support Abbott, their brother officer. Wentworth's case rested on four lines of defence. He argued that Abbott had no right to interfere in the running of the hospital. He submitted that the governor's written instructions to remove patients from a doctor's jurisdiction took precedence over a captain's oral request that they be returned to the hospital: if he had complied with Abbott's wish, he would have infringed Bligh's order. He asserted that it was a common practice of long standing for the colony's surgeons to allow convalescents to recuperate in domestic service. And he drew attention to his professional reputation as a conscientious and diligent surgeon. In the course of his evidence Wentworth censured Bligh for interfering in the management of the hospital and blamed him for the shortage of medical supplies at Parramatta. The court regarded his words as being highly disrespectful to the commander-in-chief. On the 21st he was found guilty as charged and sentenced to be publicly reprimanded in such manner as the governor thought fit. Two days later Johnston assembled the troops on the parade-ground in Sydney. At the head of this body, he called D'Arcy forward and expressed Bligh's displeasure at his behaviour. Wentworth submitted quietly to the humiliation.[6]

Having been directed on the 23rd to resume his duties at Parramatta, within forty-eight hours he was shocked to learn that Bligh had suspended him from his post as assistant-surgeon and withdrawn his salary until His Majesty's pleasure was known. D'Arcy asked Jamison to intercede on his behalf and to ascertain whether the suspension was a consequence of the court martial or whether it arose from fresh charges. The principal surgeon eventually saw the governor who, beyond stating that he disapproved of Wentworth's conduct, remained tight-lipped. Wentworth immediately applied for leave to return to England. Bligh refused permission. On 31 August Wentworth wrote to the governor, requesting him to disclose the nature of the charges to be preferred against him. Justice and humanity, he argued, entitled him to the right to defend his conduct. He received no reply. On 11 October he wrote again to Bligh to inform him that he had, one day earlier, drawn up a memorial to Viscount Castlereagh. He asked the governor to include this petition, together with the documents that accompanied it, among his official dispatches to the secretary of state. Bligh refused his request. Undeterred, Wentworth sent duplicates to England with a friend, Francis Williams—an associate of Simeon Lord and *persona non grata* with the governor—to be delivered through Fitzwilliam and Cookney to Castlereagh. By this means he ensured that the secretary of war and the colonies would receive the memorial, and that his position would be presented in the most favourable light. In a covering letter to his agent Wentworth explained that, in case illness prevented his patron from acting in his interests, he had taken the precaution of writing to James Villiers to plead his cause before Castlereagh.[7]

Using his memorial as a means of adumbrating the events that led to his suspension and of glossing over his behaviour, Wentworth stressed that the rights or wrongs of the court martial were not at issue. It was vital to him that Castlereagh should learn that a British subject had been suspended from public office without any charge being brought against him. He implored the secretary of war and the colonies to permit him to meet his accuser before an unbiased tribunal. In writing to Fitzwilliam, D'Arcy placed his suspension in a wider context by stating that, from the start, Bligh had displayed animosity towards him and made it clear that he would not rest until he had done him every injury in his power. Wentworth sought his patron's intervention not only to save him from disgrace and ruin but also to discredit the governor. Bligh, too, was busy with his correspondence. On 31 October he wrote both to William Windham, Castlereagh's predecessor as secretary of state, and to Fitzwilliam, curtly informing each of the action he had taken against Wentworth and of his grounds for so doing. He enclosed copies of the depositions which Oakes and Beldon had sworn on 23 July. In Bligh's judgement, the assistant-surgeon had employed convalescent convicts for his own advantage. His guilt was patent. When Atkins had voiced his misgivings and told Bligh that, because Wentworth had already undergone the sentence of the court martial, an additional penalty was improper and contrary to law, Bligh retorted: 'The law, sir! damn the law: my will is the law, and woe unto the man that dares to disobey it!' The governor somewhat disingenuously ignored the substance of Wentworth's complaint—that he was not allowed to defend himself. Cookney held no doubts that Fitzwilliam would see Wentworth righted, 'if you think with me he is an injured man'. Saddled with this further burden, Fitzwilliam saw Castlereagh. In April 1808 the secretary of state expressed measured disapproval of Bligh's action. The gulf between Regency civilization and Botany Bay society was immense. In Downing Street the affairs of a remote penal dumping ground made scarcely an impression. Parliament was weary, the ministry exhausted. Poor harvests had brought a rise in the price of corn, and the depressed state of trade and manufacturing had led to lower wages and reduced hours on wharves and in factories; the government's revenues fell short of expenditure; poverty stretched relief facilities beyond their limits; strikes and civil disorder occasioned fears of revolution in England and Ireland. Ministers had committed about one-third of Britain's gross national product to defeating Napoleonic France. Portugal and Spain obsessed them, at times to the exclusion of all else.[8]

In another hemisphere Bligh had continued to implement to the letter whatever directives British politicians saw fit to give him. He paid attention to the needs of the Hawkesbury settlers and they reciprocated with admiration and allegiance. To his enclave of advisers he admitted the surgeon, Edward Luttrell, the superintendent of convicts, Nicholas Divine, and the attorney, Crossley. The governor followed his instructions by taking another decisive step to regulate the rum traffic. On 14 February 1807 his Government and General Order prohibited all persons from exchanging spirits for grain, meat, labour, clothes, or any commodity whatsoever. Bligh largely succeeded in his intent. Given the shortage of specie in the colony, the inhabitants—for the most part—adopted different forms of barter, but the clergymen Rowland Hassall and Marsden were apprehensive that the regulation would goad the monopolists to undermine the government. Although several military and civil officers, and a number of free settlers, were annoyed by the governor's efforts to stem the liquor trade, they could not lodge any public or official complaint about his endeavours to control their lucrative business. They therefore scrutinized other aspects of his administration in the hope of finding a basis for legitimate criticism. Bligh believed that he had the measure of his enemies and confidently informed Sir Joseph Banks in October that he had checked the discontented in their machinations. That month Bligh's daughter, Mary, singled out John Macarthur as the government's foremost opponent, but she felt that her father treated him, as he did one and all, with his usual politeness.[9]

Elizabeth Macarthur found Bligh far from cordial. In complaining to her friend, Elizabeth Kingdom, that the governor was rash, tyrannical and violent, she evinced a loyalty to her husband which made her partisan. Her attitude to Bligh typified the brooding resentment which spread throughout a small and powerful section of the community. Free settlers such as John Townson, and his brother, Robert, who reached Sydney in July 1807, had brought letters from England indicating that the secretary of state intended to direct Bligh to grant them 2000 acres and certain indulgences; Bligh declined to locate their grants until he received specific instructions from London. Gregory Blaxland and his elder brother, John, who had arrived in April, thought themselves entitled to more land and assigned servants than they received; the governor seemed indifferent to their grumbling. John Harris was so irked by Bligh's incivility that in May he resigned as naval officer. In August three merchants, Simeon Lord, Henry Kable and Joseph Underwood, were sentenced to one month imprisonment and each fined £100 for writing a letter derogatory to the governor's rank and authority. In September Major Johnston called on Bligh, remonstrated against his interference in the internal management of the New South Wales Corps and threatened to bring the matter to the attention of the commander-in-chief. At this interview Jamison accompanied Johnston and stood by him as a friend; he was dismissed from the magistracy. More generally, Bligh aroused the hostility of the common soldiers in the corps by openly denigrating them; they despised him for his contempt. On 23 July the governor directed six men who had erected homes on land near the Domain to quit their premises. John Shea the fisherman, John Austin the watchmaker, Thomas Whittle a sergeant-major, John Davis a private, the constable John Redman and the millwright Nathaniel Lucas saw their thatched cottages demolished or the tattered huts of others destroyed by Bligh's orders. People talked about no man's property being safe and said, in dread and insecurity, 'my turn will be next'. Their grievances were damned by one who saw himself as immovable as Mount Ararat.[10]

Captain Anthony Fenn Kemp returned from Port Dalrymple to Sydney in August 1807. Those with whom he associated, including Wentworth, the Blaxlands and Dr Robert Townson, voiced their bitterness against Bligh's arbitrary behaviour. Pipes began to appear, one of which alluded to the mutiny on the *Bounty*. 'Oh tempora! Oh mores! Is there no CHRISTIAN in New South Wales to put a stop to the tyranny of the Governor?' Traducers spread stories about Bligh's cruelty, greed and corruption to blacken his character in the penal settlement and in London. Muckrakers said that this Caligula took counsel from a drunkard and from a snivelling ex-convict, that his language was obscene and that he visited a common whore. By October, the month in which Wentworth petitioned Castlereagh, a swell of indignation had arisen against the governor. With two ships in the harbour preparing to sail for London, several colonists put their complaints on paper. Elizabeth Macarthur told her friends at home that liberty had retired into the pathless wilds. Deputy-Commissary Robert Fitz spelt out his grievances to James Chapman. John Blaxland sent Banks a litany of personal complaints against Bligh. Lieutenant William Minchin informed King that he had never experienced such oppression as under the present governor. Johnston communicated with the military secretary, Lieutenant-Colonel Gordon, about Bligh's humiliating treatment of the soldiers under his command. Harris chronicled other ills. In writing to Piper on Norfolk Island, John Macarthur advised him that the corps was 'galloping into a state of warfare with the governor'. Back in England, Betsy Bligh learned of the mounting campaign to lay her husband low. She begged him to be cautious and to avoid pushing anyone to extremes.[11]

Harassed by no one more than John Macarthur, Bligh pushed him further than any other. Macarthur's extraordinary sensitivity and celerity of mind underlined his greater subversiveness. He provided the nucleus around which the governor's opponents formed. To each of the principal protagonists the stakes were all or nothing and the issue was

5 Nets of wrong and right

manifest: if Bligh could break Macarthur, he would succeed in imposing his authority on every inhabitant; if Macarthur could resist the governor, he would reduce him to a figurehead. In July 1807 Bligh depreciated the face value of a promissory note which Andrew Thompson had given Macarthur; in October the governor confiscated Macarthur's still; in December he impounded his schooner, the *Parramatta*, and in January 1808 he ordered constables to remove fencing from Macarthur's property on Church Hill. Whatever the subject of their differences, both men battled like leviathans. Bligh had proved in court the legality of his actions. Macarthur, however, considered himself the victim of the governor's vindictive will rather than the recipient of impartial law. In his view *rex* had become *lex* and wrongs cried out to be righted. It was therefore the citizen's responsibility to overthrow autocracy in order to safeguard person and property. Macarthur was no revolutionary in the mould of Paine or Robespierre, but a follower of Pym and Locke. The personal clash of Macarthur and Bligh took on an ideological dimension which papered over an economic contest between two would-be monopolists, the one advocating free-market forces, the other pedantically insisting on government control.[12]

In spite of the imbroglio, there was no danger of a rebellion so long as the military remained loyal to the governor. Bligh received a laudatory address on New Year's Day 1808 which bore 833 signatures. He wryly noted that John and Gregory Blaxland, Robert and John Townson, Garnham Blaxcell, Charles Grimes, Nicholas Bayly, Jamison and Wentworth had not affixed their names to it. Bligh's enemies were, by implication, Macarthur's allies. On 17 December 1807 Macarthur had been committed for trial on a charge of sedition. When the six regimental officers who sat on the criminal court sided with him on 25 January 1808, he had succeeded in a preconcerted plan to win the military to his side. Alarmed by rumours that Bligh intended to proceed against their officers for what he regarded as treason, the soldiers spoiled for a showdown. In Sydney at 3 o'clock on the afternoon of Tuesday 26 January, the twentieth anniversary of the foundation of the colony, an agitated group of soldiers and settlers paced back and forth between the barracks and the parade-ground. Wentworth was conspicuous among them, as were Bayly, the Blaxlands, Dr Townson and his brother, Jamison, Blaxcell and Lord. Whether or not he was privy to the intrigue, Johnston joined in a rapport with its strategists and was summoned from his Annandale estate where he was recuperating after falling from his gig. About 5 p.m. he arrived at the barracks. At Bayly's and Blaxcell's behest, he issued a warrant to release Macarthur from gaol. Some time later Macarthur entered the mess-room. There all was clamour and consternation. Johnston said, 'God's curse! What am I to do?' Macarthur drew up a requisition for Bligh's arrest, signed it, and left it for others to endorse. John Blaxland, James Mileham, Simeon Lord and Gregory Blaxland added their names immediately. Wentworth did not, preferring to await the outcome. Without any attempt to consult the governor, Johnston took on the leadership of the rebellion and became Macarthur's cat's-paw.[13]

Johnston ordered a call to arms. Some four hundred soldiers of the corps fell into line, fixed bayonets, unfurled their colours and marched from the parade-ground along High Street and up Bridge Street to Government House. Led by Johnston, whose right arm was in a sling and whose face was discoloured by bruises, accompanied by their officers with swords drawn and by the regimental band which played 'The British Grenadiers', and joined by a crowd of about two hundred onlookers, they had less than half a mile to tramp before they reached their destination. Jamison, the Blaxlands, Macarthur and his son Edward, Grimes and Dr Townson marched with them; Bayly and Blaxcell brought up the rear which was composed of stragglers who had not fallen in with the main body. Wentworth, no less a drummer, walked with this group. At 6.30 p.m. the soldiers met their comrades from the governor's guard who had loaded their muskets and kept the house under surveillance. United with one another, they stood orderly and at ease. At the gates they encountered their sole opposition when the governor's recently widowed daughter, Mary, brandished her parasol and cried out that they were rebels and traitors who intended to murder her father.

On entering Government House, Johnston, his officers, a small detachment of his men and nine of his civilian supporters found funk and flurry. Four of the guests who had dined with Bligh that afternoon—Griffin, Campbell, Palmer and Williamson—were promptly located, but the governor appeared to have vanished. While most of the intruders positioned themselves uneasily against the walls of the drawing-room, small parties were deployed to comb the residence and its grounds. Following an hour and a half of frustrating delay, it was past

8 o'clock when three of the soldiers raised a hullabaloo. They had collared Bligh in a room upstairs. It was later alleged that he had concealed himself under his steward's bed. His dishevelled appearance appeared to corroborate the story: cobwebs, feathers and fluff clung to the back of his coat, and dust covered its lapels and epaulettes. Apprehensive and distressed, the governor held Minchin's arm and walked with him down the flight of stairs. Johnston assured Bligh of his safety before requesting him to resign his authority and submit to arrest. The two shook hands. Having confiscated the governor's official papers and private letters, and stationed five sentinels at the house, the insurgents then departed, leaving the former governor alone, save for his daughter and the commissary's wife. During these proceedings Wentworth stayed with the crowd and the bulk of the troops at the gates. That night revolutionary committees began investigating the affairs of the late government. Again, Wentworth was uninvolved. He sympathized with the rebels, but had the canniness to keep in the wings and take no prominent part in the rebellion itself.[14]

After returning to Barrack Square, the soldiers shouted 'No tyranny', 'Johnston for ever' and gave three cheers. Buoyed up by all they had done, over the course of the next week they indulged in a frenzy of jubilation. Muskets and cannon volleyed in salute, sheep were roasted, liquor was distributed, bonfires lit the night in Sydney and Parramatta, and people signed their names to petitions that rejoiced in their deliverance. Bligh was burnt in effigy, ridiculed in a popular song called 'The Silly Old Man' and humiliated at taverns by signs that proclaimed 'The ever memorable 26th of January 1808'. Having huzzahed Macarthur's name throughout the town, his admirers resorted to bribery and intimidation to bend as many citizens as they could to their cause. Once more Wentworth chose to stay in the wings. Not a single colonist noticed his presence at the festivities or mentioned his participation in the committees which interrogated Bligh's officials. On the morning of 27 January he watched the inauguration of Johnston's administration. Lieutenant Minchin read a proclamation to the assembled throng. Informing them that peace had been restored and martial law discontinued, he congratulated the soldiers on their conduct and pledged that, henceforward, justice would be exercised with impartiality. Minchin also announced that Atkins had been removed as judge-advocate and Abbott appointed in his stead. All former magistrates had been dismissed; Kemp, Harris, Jamison, Grimes, Blaxcell, John Blaxland, Archibald Bell and Minchin were sworn in as their replacements. Bligh's chief advisers—Gore, Palmer, Campbell and Griffin—had been suspended from office and Bayly assumed the post of secretary to Johnston, who styled himself lieutenant-governor. Johnston invited every well-disposed inhabitant to attend church on the 31st to offer thanks to Almighty God for delivering them, without bloodshed, 'from the awful situation in which they stood before the memorable 26th'.[15]

Apart from attempting to validate the new order by rites and rituals, the junta tried to project a united front. As a sign of solidarity, colonists were invited or compelled to sign the requisition for the governor's arrest—after the event. Presented with the document, Wentworth saw only eleven names on it, the tenth being that of Charles Grimes who later swore that he had signed it once the coup was over. Some of the eleven were D'Arcy's friends, professional colleagues and those with whom he had business dealings. Most held positions in Johnston's government and could influence the bestowal of favours. While Wentworth had refrained from being directly involved in the rebellion, there were limits to his circumspection. At the barracks he had openly urged others on. Wishing to stand apart but unwilling to hazard the consequences of so doing, he added his name as the twelfth petitioner. Eventually, 152 signatures were gathered. Under pressure to demonstrate further commitment, Wentworth also endorsed an address of gratitude to Johnston. Dated 27 January, it thanked him for rescuing the officers and settlers 'from an order of things which threatened the destruction of all which men can hold dear'. Eighty-three people signed it, Wentworth being the twentieth. A further address, dated 30 January, was signed by sixty-six others, offering Johnston their backing. Many of them had pledged allegiance to Bligh on New Year's Day; they now recanted with an apology for having been misguided. If they had refused to sign the requisition or addresses, they would not only have caused offence but also have risked being victimized. Several settlers subsequently attested that they were coerced into signing by acts of intimidation, by the fear of losing their government servants, or by the threat of imprisonment.[16]

The leaders of the rebellion realized that the support of the general populace served only their immediate needs; convincing the British government of the probity of their actions was a greater challenge. They appreciated, too, the advantages to be gained by being first to make representations home. To this end, they kept Bligh a prisoner in Government House and convened a public meeting to appoint a delegate to go to England to plead their case. On the evening of 8 February Wentworth attended a gathering where he sat in company with Bayly, Blaxcell, John Blaxland, Minchin and others. Some days previously a considerable quantity of spirits had been landed. Primed by a generous supply of liquor, the crowd warmed to the occasion and the meeting grew noisy and disorderly. The assembly voted to present Johnston with a sword to the value of one hundred guineas, to congratulate the corps on arresting the governor, and to send Macarthur as a delegate to England to make His Majesty's ministers aware of the hardships which the colonists had endured under Bligh. Macarthur promised to work tirelessly in thus serving his fellows. Blaxcell proposed that money be raised by voluntary contribution to assist Macarthur in his undertaking. Lord, Kable and Underwood pledged £500 between them, Bayly, Blaxcell and the Blaxlands each promised £100, and twenty-four others agreed to donate sums ranging from £50 to five shillings. Wentworth gave nothing. For all the euphoria, the fund lapsed and Macarthur remained in New South Wales as colonial secretary.[17]

Although the 'janissaries' examined Bligh's public and private correspondence, they found nothing of substance to incriminate him or to justify their proceedings. In their malevolence they exacted revenge on the governor's advisers. William Gore was sentenced to seven years transportation to the coalmines at Newcastle; he was forced to leave his wife and four young children wholly dependent on his friends for support. George Crossley was also sentenced to a similar term at the same penal station. Henry Fulton was prohibited from performing the duties of his sacred office. A free settler, George Suttor, was gaoled for six months, and an ex-convict, James Belbin, was ordered to receive five hundred lashes, the former for refusing to acknowledge the legitimacy of the junta, the latter for providing succour to Bligh and Mary Putland. In contrast, the rebels gave their supporters trading perquisites, land grants and assigned convict servants. Unto those that had, it would be given. Wentworth soon reaped the first of his rewards.[18]

Under directions from Johnston, on 31 January Bayly sent Wentworth a copy of Bligh's letter to Windham in which the governor had censured him for employing convalescent convicts from the

The Wentworths

Parramatta hospital. Bayly advised Wentworth to proceed with whatever measures he thought appropriate. For the first time D'Arcy discovered the reasons for his dismissal. Stung by the contents of the documents, he took his cue from Macarthur who elected to be tried in the colony while Johnston held command. Although Macarthur had defied Bligh's orders, he used the proceedings in the criminal court on 2 February 1808 to vilify the governor. The trial was a sham. Macarthur was acquitted on all charges and chaired from the court. Wentworth chose to follow suit by requesting a court martial. His case was heard on 17 February before Captain Anthony Fenn Kemp, the president, Lieutenants William Moore, William Lawson, Thomas Laycock and Cadwallader Draffin, and the deputy judge-advocate, Charles Grimes. Wentworth was charged with taking government prisoners and assignees from the hospital for his own advantage. Bligh refused to recognize the court or to be represented at the proceedings. Griffin, Oakes and Beldon testified for the prosecution. Under cross-examination, Beldon admitted that it was customary for those in charge of the hospital to employ convalescent patients in their own homes or gardens. Wentworth addressed the bench. Jamison, Mileham, Rouse, George Mealmaker and Atkins gave evidence for the defence. The court honourably acquitted Wentworth and expressed its 'pointed disapprobation' of Bligh's conduct in 'taking private depositions against an officer, to be transmitted to His Majesty's Ministers, without allowing the party accused an opportunity to defend himself'. On 18 February Johnston published news of the acquittal in a Government and General Order. With his assistant-surgeonship restored, Wentworth informed his patron that the court martial had rescued him from the 'disgraceful situation' in which Bligh's 'frivolous' charges had so unjustly placed him. Grey twilight had given place to dawn.[19]

There were many who thought otherwise. Opponents of the new régime sent slanted accounts of the rebellion to England in an attempt to sway politicians' minds. Gore, Palmer, Fulton and Suttor joined with Bligh in endeavours to enlist the help of Banks, Wilberforce, Lord Darnley and Marsden so that their case might be put before the Colonial Office. To these upholders of constituted authority, the rebels were dupes of the fiend who had plotted the uprising, one whose ambition rendered him a contagion to all governors, the turbulent John Macarthur. They clamoured for his banishment, for the corps' removal

5 Nets of wrong and right

and for the full severity of the law to be wreaked upon the traitorous. Unless this course were adopted, New South Wales and Van Diemen's Land would continue at the mercy of a clique who enriched themselves, indulged their favourites, oppressed the poor and trampled on all vestiges of morality. Meanwhile, gripped by fear of repercussions, those who had supported Bligh's deposal—Macarthur, Bayly, Robert Townson, Abbott and Wentworth—collaborated with Johnston in forwarding their own version of events. They hoped that, through the intervention of such connexions as the Duke of Northumberland, Earl Fitzwilliam and Lord Uxbridge, the staff of the Colonial Office might be made sympathetic to their cause. Bligh had acted tyrannically by making his will the law. His malice had so distressed the inhabitants that a general insurrection had appeared imminent. Johnston had therefore been obliged to act in order to ensure Bligh's safety and to preserve the security of the settlement. Johnston deserved thanks rather than censure.[20]

That whimsical fellow, the botanist George Caley, stood beholden to neither party to the dispute. Some regarded him as silent and morose, some as flighty and cantankerous. He combined all these qualities and more. His study of nature had developed a peaceful side to his character which was apparent in the friendships he formed with Aborigines, but a string of amours with convict girls testified to his restlessness. When Caley reported on the coup of 1808 he harboured no wish to bend others to a purpose. He saw through the nets of wrong and right, and his observations were sharper for their impartiality. According to Caley, although Bligh had erred in judgement, he had generally meant well. His overbearing manner militated against his fitness for his post, but he had committed no crime to warrant his arrest. The rebels were carrion crows who preyed on the people; Macarthur was the chief instigator of the mischief and Johnston his puppet; the corps' posting had lasted far too long. If the penal colony had progressed, he thought it more by accident than design. Faction rent the community, liquor and land bought popularity, and artful ex-convicts got on while the deserving languished. No good would come until a middling rank emerged to fill the gap between the felons and the free. Looking to other gardens, Caley left New South Wales where rebellion had sown seeds of perpetual discontent.[21]

Greed and egotism prevented Wentworth from seeing life as Caley did. Never one to dwell on the wonders of the natural world, or on whether they were created by a divine hand, he fixed his mind on a narrower field in which devilry took human form. In April and May he informed Fitzwilliam that the rebellion had been provoked by Bligh's unjust measures and by his determination to violate the law. He claimed there was 'indubitable proof' that the governor had alienated Crown property for his private purposes. And he did not baulk at branding Bligh a coward: before his arrest he had hidden 'in a dark Closet between a Feather Bed and a Hair Mattress'. Nothing but his deposal 'could have saved the late Governor and his wicked advisers, at the head of whom was the notorious George Crossley, from falling Victim to an enraged People'. Johnston had answered the call of 'many of the Civil officers, and the whole of the Military, and great numbers of the most respectable inhabitants'. Wentworth's letters to Fitzwilliam supported the rebels' cause and echoed their language, but D'Arcy carefully removed himself from any participation in the events of the 'ever memorable 26th' to give the impression that he was but a spectator. At this stage his correspondence with his patron gave no hint that the enthusiasm of that day had begun to wane, and that jealousy, rivalry and distrust were dividing the alliance that had transferred power to Johnston.[22]

Major Johnston faced obstacles in his administration similar to those encountered by the governors who preceded him. Once the rebel officers and settlers resumed their agricultural and commercial enterprises, a number of those to whom he looked for support became his harshest critics. Almost from the day of Bligh's arrest, the Blaxland brothers made unreasonable demands, provoking Johnston to bemoan that, the more indulgences they were given, the more they were dissatisfied. Macarthur accused the officers of behaving 'scurvily' in that they would not rest content even if the government had given them 'the whole of the publick property'. Regarding Abbott as his worst detractor, he denounced Bayly as a 'violent oppositionist', considered Grimes a mischief-maker and had no confidence in Minchin. Aside from Kemp, Lawson and Draffin, and implicitly himself, Macarthur held that no man offered Johnston the least support. Much of the discontent stemmed from Macarthur's holding office as secretary to the colony and from the confidence that Johnston placed in him. To many, Macarthur was the virtual governor of the colony. On 18 February Wentworth had resumed his duties at the Parramatta hospital. He

5 Nets of wrong and right

received a letter, dated 26 April, which Johnston sent to seventeen members of his administration. The lieutenant-governor expressed concern at the prevailing discontent and charged anyone with a grievance against John Macarthur to come forward and state it openly. That day Wentworth and twelve others signed a letter of reply. Brief and cutting, it asserted that Johnston had the right to consult any individual he wished and that they would obey his orders, 'which is all they consider they have to do as officers serving under him'. The omission of any reference to Macarthur highlighted the tensions that had arisen. Confined in Government House, Bligh rejoiced to learn that those responsible for deposing him were 'divided and subdivided'.[23]

While some of the people who had overthrown Bligh squabbled and reproached one another, Wentworth focused more closely on his own concerns. The *Rose* anchored in Sydney Cove on 15 April, bringing word of the death of his colleague, James Thomson. The news raised D'Arcy's hopes of succeeding to the principal surgeonship. In May he asked Fitzwilliam to obtain a dormant commission for him so that, as senior assistant-surgeon, he could assume Jamison's office in the event of his death or departure. By September Wentworth's prospects brightened. His long-awaited leave of absence had arrived, but, because Jamison had also obtained permission to return to England, D'Arcy decided to stay in New South Wales. He knew that Jamison was unlikely to return, and D'Arcy had every reason to believe that he would be appointed to fill his place. Authorized by Johnston to take over Jamison's duties on 24 February 1809, Wentworth trusted that the home government would confirm him in the position. None the less, he was alert to the prospect of greater rewards. Under the terms of an agreement with Lord Camden's office, John Blaxland had undertaken to invest £6000 in the colony; in return, he was to receive a grant of 8000 acres and the use of eighty convicts, victualled and clothed by the government for eighteen months. Wentworth authorized Cookney to tender his resignation as surgeon if the secretary of war and the colonies agreed to grant him the same privileges on the same terms as Blaxland enjoyed. After 'eighteen years of faithful service', he believed he had some claim to this indulgence.

The year 1808 marked the 46th anniversary of Wentworth's birth. Thinking of William, who was about to turn eighteen, D'Arcy rejected all notions that he enter the army. From all the father had observed, heard and read, his son was mild in temper and in disposition, and ill suited to service in India. He urged Fitzwilliam to procure the post of provost marshal or vendue master for William, and was confident that his education would equip him for either situation. Wentworth had finally determined that his eldest son should return to New South Wales. As for 15-year-old D'Arcy, who showed every promise of being a 'fine, active young man', Wentworth sought Fitzwilliam's help in securing his appointment as a naval midshipman or as a cadet in the East India Company. D'Arcy and John were still with Mr Midgley, and William with Dr Crombie. Cookney attended to their needs and wants. In July 1809 he gave D'Arcy a fishing-rod and six bottles of port; the costs were £1 2s 8d and £1 10s respectively. In William's final year at Dr Crombie's institution (when the fees had risen to about sixty guineas per annum), Cookney increased his pocket-money to two shillings and sixpence a week, bought him a watch for £7 17s 6d and retained de Roufigny to tutor him in French. After the young man had left the Greenwich school, he gave him a gun, powder and shot, and a case in which to keep them; the bill came to £12 15s. Thirteen-year-old John appears to have received no present, other than one guinea. The expenses that Cookney incurred for grooming the boys as prospective gentlemen were duly debited against their father's account.[24]

Lieutenant-Colonel Joseph Foveaux sailed from England in the *Sinclair* and reached Sydney on 28 July 1808. His arrival shed no light on the British government's attitude to the rebellion, and his conduct infuriated Bligh and those loyal to him. Within twenty-four hours Foveaux assumed command as Johnston's senior in rank. Within another two days he publicly stated that it was beyond his authority to judge between Johnston and Bligh. Within five weeks he wrote to Castlereagh, taking the side of the rebels. Foveaux was pleasant in manner, handsome, if corpulent, in appearance, forceful in character and quite the man of business. He dispensed with the services of John Macarthur as colonial secretary, endeavoured to reduce expenditure, tried to cleanse the administration of the commissariat and improved public works. For all that, he was desperately anxious to wash his hands of the mess he had inherited from Johnston. To that end he wrote to his superior, Lieutenant-Colonel Paterson, at Port Dalrymple, urging him to come to Sydney. Paterson was in no hurry and thanked God that he lived at such a distance from headquarters. Foveaux and Paterson

5 Nets of wrong and right

were not alone in their misgivings. Bligh's presence in the colony served as a constant reminder of the rebels' deeds. Fears intensified that His Majesty's ministers would disapprove of the events of 26 January. Abbott and John Blaxland had second thoughts about their role in the uprising and were alarmed at its possible repercussions. Settlers like Thomas Arndell began to defect from the rebels' ranks. Others waited with foreboding for the home government to call them to account. By September Wentworth felt that, irrespective of Bligh's notorious nature and his flagrant actions, the Colonial Office would not sanction the rebellion lest other colonies saw it as a precedent and destroyed the peace and prosperity of the mother country. He wrote again to Fitzwilliam, seeking to distance himself—even farther—from the military. Had Bligh heeded his advice, Wentworth belatedly argued, there would have been no uprising. On the other hand, he now reluctantly admitted, the lamentable truth was that no individual in the British nation could govern the colony in opposition to the whims and caprices of the New South Wales Corps (designated the 102nd Regiment in 1809). It would be useless to expect any peace so long as its officers and men were allowed to remain.[25]

First tidings of the upheaval in Sydney Town reached London on 12 September 1808. Three days later the press ran brief announcements, but the news attracted little notice among the public and excited only minor attention in the departments of state. Young Edward Macarthur complained that ministers were too preoccupied with the international crisis to inform themselves fully about the situation in New South Wales, but he reported that the staff in the Colonial Office were averse to the measures which the rebels had taken. The undersecretary in that office was Edward Cooke. A son of a provost of King's College, Cambridge, he had administrative ability and an unaccommodating bent which made him a person of reckoning; with a preference for old ways, he was a foe to rebellion, whatever its hue. His chief, Viscount Castlereagh, the 2nd Marquis of Londonderry, was thirty-nine in 1808. Irish and to the purple born, he was tall, cold and feared, and never ruffled by the people's voice. Neither Castlereagh nor Cooke could ignore the extraordinary convulsion of 26 January 1808. The revolution in France in 1789, the mutinies at Spithead and the Nore in 1797, and the rebellion in Ireland in 1798 had seared them with antipathy towards any uprising. Within a month of obtaining information about the insurrection in New South Wales, they decided to have the corps recalled and agreed that the regiment which replaced it should serve there for only a limited term. Appreciating the awkwardness of the situation if Bligh were reinstated, Castlereagh wanted a military officer to succeed him. Soldiers, he expected, would be more inclined to obey one who wore their own cloth. Irked by insubordination, the secretary of state insisted that a new governor should re-establish order, quash every sign of tumult, rectify abuses and institute firm rule. It was also paramount that justice be seen to be done. Castlereagh and Cooke publicly supported Bligh. They later issued instructions that he be formally restored to nominal office for twenty-four hours, that Macarthur be tried before the criminal court in the colony and that Johnston return under arrest to be court-martialled; the members of the rebel government were to receive no salaries, all their transactions were to be annulled and the officials they had displaced were to resume their posts. On 10 November 1808 Castlereagh informed Fitzwilliam that it was difficult to foresee how other individuals would be affected by the part they may have borne in the rebellion. As he did not know whether Wentworth was in any degree involved, he decided to defer any decision about his future until more information became available.[26]

Unaware of these developments, Foveaux handed over the government to Paterson on 9 January 1809. While loyalists continued to undermine the rebel administration by denying its legitimacy and refusing to attend the muster, Wentworth cultivated his friendship with Foveaux. He also ingratiated himself with Paterson and his wife Elizabeth, 'a good, cosy, Scotch lass . . . fit for a soldier's wife'. Paterson distributed 'the Loaves and Fishes' among his favourites, only to find that the recipients of such largesse grew more envious of one another. Bligh stubbornly refused to leave the colony until March. In that month he boarded H.M.S. *Porpoise*. Rather than returning to England, on the 12th he proclaimed the New South Wales Corps to be in a state of rebellion, and named its officers and fifteen other colonists, including Wentworth, as suspected mutineers. Powerless, he then sailed for Van Diemen's Land, his passion thirsting for revenge on those who had participated in the abomination that had laid him low and tossed him like a cork on the ocean. As time passed, an increasing number of those—like Wentworth—who had supported the rebellion began to pretend that they had had nothing to do with it. Despite the animosity which existed between Johnston and John Blaxland, and between Macarthur and Foveaux, Wentworth managed to remain on amiable terms with all four. Macarthur and Blaxland sailed for England in March and September respectively. In recommending them to Lord Fitzwilliam, D'Arcy referred to the former as 'my most respected friend' and to the latter as 'a very respectable gentleman'. Through Cookney, Wentworth also sent Macarthur news of his wife, Elizabeth, and of the health of their eldest daughter who bore her mother's name.[27]

Wentworth had received a goodly share of the rebels' spoils. On 23 July 1808 Johnston granted him 270 acres in the Parramatta district and gave him twenty-two cattle. He obtained 500 acres in the same region from Foveaux on 3 December. From Paterson he received 100 acres at Liberty Plains on 11 April 1809, and three grants in the Parramatta district: 240 acres on 20 May, 12 acres on 29 September and 750 acres on 18 October. The grants totalled 1872 acres, of which 'Pat' had given 1102. By late 1809 Henry Fulton asserted that the usurpers had wantonly diminished the government herds and distributed most of the good land within fifty miles of the capital. Untroubled by public loss when it entailed his personal gain, Wentworth sought to emulate John Blaxland and become a man of property. The land he had acquired before 1808, and that granted by Johnston, Foveaux and Paterson, bolstered his ambitions. He again importuned his patron to obtain a grant for him identical to that given to Blaxland; he told him unctuously that he had given the name of Fitzwilliam Place to one of his properties at Parramatta; he repeated his wish to retire from the public service and to be independent for life; and he revealed his desire to leave 'the Name of Wentworth as great and respected as any in this Country'.[28]

Another struggle lay ahead. All who had benefited from the rebel administrations realized that their legal entitlement to land grants and other indulgences rested on the British government's decisions. Rumours of Brigadier-General Miles Nightingall's appointment as governor and of the imminent arrival of a detachment of the 73rd Regiment foreshadowed the end of an interregnum. With change impending, those who had received land grants in 1808–09 concentrated on improving their properties in an attempt to retain ownership. They hoped that the new governor would choose to confirm their grants rather than having to reimburse them for the expenses they had incurred. Wentworth claimed to have spent over seven thousand guineas in purchasing land and livestock, in erecting buildings and in developing his properties in other ways. Part of that sum was invested in his recent grants. That a senior assistant-surgeon on an annual salary of £182 10s could make such an outlay indicated either that Wentworth was a liar or that he had continued his trading activities—directly and indirectly—in spirits. Resolved to retain his land, he dreamed of founding a dynasty. He wanted to ensure his sons' prosperity and cherished 'unbounded affection' towards the three of them, but William was his favourite, and his heir. In September 1809 Cookney paid Captain Brooks £105 for William's passage to the colony. He gave the young man £35 to spend himself, paid his optician's account, shook hands in fond farewell and sent him by coach to Portsmouth. On 4 October the native son embarked for Port Jackson. Almost seven years had passed since he had last seen his father.[29]

Following months of delay, during which Castlereagh's decisiveness had been somewhat vitiated in its aim, on 8 May 1809 Lieutenant-Colonel Lachlan Macquarie was appointed to govern New South Wales. His commission enabled him to act with unrivalled authority over half a continent and its surrounding seas. Issued at the Court of St James on 9 May, his instructions amplified the powers conferred by his commission. In Macquarie's case, apart from minor particulars of names and dates, both his commission and principal instructions were practically verbatim repetitions of those handed to his predecessor, a remarkable circumstance given that a rebellion had occurred and that a military officer was legitimately to head the New South Wales government for the first time. Multifarious in their range, Macquarie's instructions catalogued his duties without apportioning priorities. For all their detail, they lacked pivot. Precisely how he was to reconcile the competing thrusts of economic *laissez-faire* and social control, and to adjudicate between the interests of the prisoners and the free, was left entirely to him. He was given an unfettered hand to exercise his capacities and to settle issues on the spot. A change of personnel, rather than of policies, it was thought, should settle matters. On 1 November Castlereagh and Cooke vacated the Colonial Office for Lord Liverpool and Charles Jenkinson who were even more uninterested in the penal colony than the men they had succeeded. Macquarie was to arrive in an unfamiliar land and send his dispatches to people who knew him by name alone

5 Nets of wrong and right

and with whom he was entirely unfamiliar. Whether he would follow his orders literally, or adapt and modify them to exigency, awaited resolution. He had scope for interpretation: to allocate emphasis and find nuance, to initiate policies himself, even to defer, block or abandon what his masters wished. Whether he would stand alone, or be governed, remained to be seen.[30]

Four of Castlereagh's orders directly affected Wentworth. First, Macquarie was instructed to relax the regulations on the import of spirits, but to impose a duty that would bring the importers' costs to about sixteen shillings a gallon. Secondly, he was to regard all the trials and investigations conducted during Johnston's administration as having no legal standing. Thirdly, he was to treat all grants of land, leases and livestock authorized by Johnston, Foveaux and Paterson as invalid; he was permitted, however, to exercise discretion in ratifying grants in his own name, provided he saw no objections to them. Finally, Castlereagh had reached a conclusion about Wentworth's dismissal as assistant-surgeon. The secretary of state wrote to him on 13 May conceding that Bligh had acted improperly, but, in view of the steps which Wentworth had subsequently taken to vindicate his cause, he declined to reinstate him. By implication, Macquarie was to acquaint himself with the case and pass final judgement. On 28 December the *Dromedary* entered Port Jackson's heads and bore Macquarie up the harbour, its water as smooth as a millpond. At 10 a.m. on the last day of the year the governor elect set foot on his territory.[31]

6

To catch a thief

'you have all your life been evading the laws, and very frequently breaking the peace; do you think this has qualified you peculiarly for being a guardian of the laws?' Sir Terence replied, 'yes, sure, set a thief to catch a thief is no bad maxim.'

Maria Edgeworth, *The Absentee*

On Monday 1 January 1810 the soldiers of the 73rd Regiment disembarked and marched from Sydney Cove to the parade-ground in Barrack Square where they formed serried ranks with the officers and men of the 102nd, and stood uncomfortably to attention in the glare and murmur of a summer noon. At 12.30 that afternoon Deputy Judge-Advocate Ellis Bent, shaded by an umbrella, read the governor's commission with due form and solemnity to the troops and assembled inhabitants. Macquarie then addressed his fellow citizens and fellow soldiers. In a short speech, delivered with particular energy, he told them of his intention to exercise authority justly and impartially; he hoped that harmony would replace dissension, that the upper ranks in society would set an example to the lower orders and that no European would molest the Aborigines; he concluded with an assurance that whosoever was honest, sober and industrious—whether free settler or convict—would ever find in him a friend and protector. Inspired by all he had seen and heard of the David come among them, the Reverend William Cowper preached a sermon in St Phillip's on the first Sunday of the new year, taking as his text 1 Samuel, chapter xvi, verse 12: 'Arise, anoint him; for this *is* he'.[1]

6 To catch a thief

The David whom Cowper beheld had arrived in a prison-colony of 10 452 souls, with a further 1321 in the dependency of Van Diemen's Land and 177 on Norfolk Island. The European population of New South Wales was composed of 5511 men, 2200 women and 2721 children. Its social hierarchy ran from the senior military and civil officers at the top, through the free settlers and emancipists to the convicts at its base. Numerous gradations and nuances existed within this pyramid, but it was the military who wielded power and loomed conspicuous in their uniforms and numbers. With a total strength of 1416, they comprised 13.5 per cent of the inhabitants, even more than the 1283 convicts who were victualled from the government stores. Macquarie had to cope with the results of the River Hawkesbury's floods in the previous year which ruined crops and left only 7615 acres under tillage, forcing the market price of wheat to £1 3s 1d per bushel and beef to 1s 6d per lb in January 1810. He had to come to terms with the violence endemic in a community which had placed George Prideaux Harris under arrest when he protested at the treatment of a female convict who had been tied to a cart-tail and flogged until she fainted; he also had to contend with the callousness of people who joked about a drunk whose nose had been chewed off by pigs while he lay unconscious in a street. Flushed with enthusiasm, Macquarie knew next to nothing of such matters.[2]

From Barrack Square the officials repaired to Government House where John Thomas Campbell, Macquarie's secretary, read a proclamation in which the British government passed judgement on the events of 26 January 1808:

> His Majesty having felt the utmost Regret and Displeasure on Account of the late Tumultuous Proceedings in this His Colony, and the Mutinous Conduct of certain persons therein towards his late representative, William Bligh . . .

This announcement, published in the *Sydney Gazette* on 7 January, occasioned rejoicing among Bligh's supporters and anxiety among his enemies. A second proclamation, printed in the same edition, demonstrated the home government's determination not to condone the rebel administrations. Every official appointment conferred by Johnston,

[127]

Foveaux and Paterson, and all their grants of land, livestock and leases, were declared null and void; the trials and investigations conducted since Bligh's deposal were also deemed to be unlawful. This promulgation effectively cancelled Wentworth's appointment as principal surgeon, his land grants and his exoneration on the charge of professional misconduct. At the outset, D'Arcy may well have viewed Macquarie's arrival as, at best, a mixed blessing.[3]

Wentworth quickly learned, however, that Macquarie's actions were at variance with the spirit of the proclamations. On 14 January the governor published another notice in the *Sydney Gazette*, granting indemnity from prosecution to all magistrates, gaolers and constables who had served the rebel administration. To the farmer, George Suttor, and others like him who had suffered by showing loyalty to Bligh after his deposal, it appeared that their new ruler's third proclamation had neutralized the previous two. To the men of the 73rd, it seemed strange that the governor allowed the 102nd to live in barracks in Sydney, but had ordered his own regiment to camp three miles away at Grose Farm where their staple was bread and potatoes. Despite their want of political acumen and despite the seediness of their private lives, Johnston and Foveaux enjoyed Macquarie's company; in spite of his alcoholism, Paterson resided as a guest at Government House where his wife took comfort in the way that the dames of the 102nd outshone in taste and fashion the women of the 73rd. If Macquarie were poised to cleanse the Augean Stables of Botany Bay, he was, from the beginning, indulgent to his brother officers in the New South Wales Corps. He eventually endorsed the bills they had drawn on the Treasury, induced 377 soldiers from the 102nd Regiment's complement of 697 to remain in the penal colony and showed partiality to their de facto leader, Foveaux. Wentworth was to benefit from his friendship with Foveaux when the lieutenant-colonel made representations on his behalf to the governor.[4]

Having been installed in office, Macquarie relied on Foveaux to acquaint him with conditions in New South Wales and the character of those who lived there. Foveaux respected the governor, coveted his favour and hoped—with his backing—to be exculpated for not having reinstated Bligh. For his part, Macquarie found Foveaux indispensable. He wrote that he was the only person to whom he felt obliged for assistance and candid information on assuming his command; he considered him the most qualified administrator he had ever met for improving an infant colony and recommended his appointment as lieutenant-governor of Van Diemen's Land; he valued his relish for regularity, his judgement and his understanding; moreover, he intended to follow his example to the utmost. Bligh returned to Sydney on 17 January to find the rebels garrisoning the town and their leaders the confidants of a successor who was unable and unwilling to reinstate him as governor for one day. The cannon salutes and other marks of honour paid to Bligh did not muffle the hoots of the populace nor dull his pain. He railed in a boisterous and frustrated manner, and was deeply hurt when his daughter, Mary, a headstrong young woman whose revealing dresses had shocked the more decorous members of society, decided against accompanying him home to England and married Maurice O'Connell, the lieutenant-governor. Indifferent to Bligh's plight, Macquarie described him as an obnoxious tyrant who was universally detested. His rages confirmed Macquarie's inclination to side with Bligh's opponents and to take counsel from them. People said that it was only natural that he should so do.[5]

Born on 31 January 1761 on the Hebridean islet of Ulva, the son of a poor tenant farmer, Macquarie had joined the army in 1776, served in the Americas, India, Egypt and Europe, and slowly risen from ensign to lieutenant-colonel. He weighed about 14 stone, and had sandy-grey hair and a brick-red complexion. In 1807 he had married Elizabeth Henrietta Campbell, a fellow Scot; their only daughter died in the following year. Macquarie had lived, travelled and undergone hardships in four continents, developing a rule-of-thumb manner that put stress on authority and discipline, on industry and perseverance, on routine and attention to detail. These facets had neither stifled his creativity nor robbed him of flexibility. Notions of order and symmetry guided his mind, stamped his plans and endorsed his deeds. He saw things as suddenly, manifestly and imperatively right. Yet, for all his insistence on system, he was thin-skinned and highly strung. Competing thrusts of respect and resentment, humility and vanity, generosity and meanness, aggression and obstinacy, recklessness and caution were rooted in him. Deeper still lay other traits: on some occasions he could be rattled, inconsistent and sceptical, on others temporizing and equivocal. He retained an inner cave, not an emptiness, that sighed for recognition and reward. Subject at times to whim and impulse, he made his mind up fast on meeting people and seldom modified or changed his opinion of them; he was less a man for abstractions than for relationships. In 1810 Macquarie turned forty-nine. He was one year older than D'Arcy Wentworth and had no patron.

In affirming his authority, Macquarie was buttressed by his personal entourage, by a disciplined regiment and by a man-of-war anchored off Garden Island, all of which served as caveats against disloyalty. Although his sympathy with certain individuals from the rebel faction accorded with that of the majority of the inhabitants of Sydney, he continued staunch in his conviction that none of Bligh's actions had warranted the proceedings taken against him. Macquarie's actions in reinstating William Gore, Bligh's provost marshal, reinforced the general view that he wanted to conciliate, to reconcile, to be the friend of all and the foe of no one. His manner of treating others created a common impression that he was a good, well meaning, humane and kindly disposed man who raised people's spirits and brought them hope of a better future. Much in the way of an improving landlord intent on developing a personal estate, the governor introduced a currency in silver coinage, promoted agriculture, trade and manufacturing, opened a new market-place, built schools and orphanages, established townships, cautiously encouraged exploration and inland settlement, embarked on an ambitious programme of public works and endeavoured to treat the convicts leniently. He had grasped the chance not only to rule the penal settlements, but to forward their progress and to transform the lives of those who resided in them. In many areas of government Macquarie's practices bore strong resemblances to those of his predecessors; the key differences were in their efficiency and higher cost. Despite the poor harvest of 1810, the caterpillar plagues in 1810 and 1812, the severe drought of 1813–14, the collapsed retail market in 1811 and the commercial depression for three years from 1812, he took pride in his success. Prices paid by the government for wheat and meat were to be reduced to 10 shillings a bushel and 7d per lb in 1815. By that year cattle numbered 25 239 and sheep 62 476, double their figures for 1810, and the area under crop had grown to 19 404 acres.[6]

Macquarie wrote to Castlereagh on 30 April 1810, spelling out an issue on which he differed markedly from the governors before him:

> I have, nevertheless, taken upon myself to adopt a new Line of Conduct, Conceiving that Emancipation, when United with

Rectitude and long-tried good Conduct, should lead a Man back to that Rank in Society which he had forfeited, and do away, in so far as the Case will admit, All Retrospect of former bad Conduct.

This principle was to be the foundation of what he would call his emancipist policy: that a convict, on the expiry or remission of his sentence, provided he were well behaved, ought to be treated as if he had never transgressed the law and should possess the same rights as a free man. A number of influences drove him in this direction, among them his personal sympathy with the downtrodden, his familiarity with the antislavery rhetoric of William Wilberforce, and his cardinal Christian principles, shared by Elizabeth, which were imbued with the themes of atonement, absolution and redemption. Foveaux, too, played a role, in suggesting that Macquarie bring forward the emancipists as much as possible and in warning him what to expect from designing settlers like Samuel Marsden who delighted in sowing seeds of discord and insubordination. The governor was grateful for intelligence about the inhabitants who were utter strangers to him and availed himself of those whom Foveaux recommended as trustworthy and useful. Macquarie's ready acceptance of this advice staggered Bligh and later led Macarthur to blame Foveaux for disseminating a mist of artifice and falsehood. Whether devious or not, Foveaux's counsel accorded with, or was tailored to suit, Macquarie's own impulses and prepossessions.

Practical considerations underlay Macquarie's adoption of an emancipist policy. He found relatively few free settlers with either the time or the wish to involve themselves in administration; on the other hand, a number of the emancipists seemed able and willing to support him. To a pragmatic man who wanted to get things done, their competence and acumen counted for more than their background or morals. There also were less altruistic motives behind his intent. Those he elevated considered themselves bound to him by no ordinary ties of gratitude and were consequently little disposed to check or thwart his plans. By choosing as his associates those people over whom their transportation and his benevolence had given him power, he placed them at his mercy. As he had raised them, so he could reduce them—or so he thought. While he regarded his actions as humane, they were also convenient. His desire for subordination strengthened the autocracy of his government and made his counsellors satellites to his planet. Some of the exclusives considered him a leveller set on abolishing distinctions in society, but their assessment was wide of the truth. Macquarie had never rid himself of the idea that material possessions were signs of character and success. His favourites were not the struggling ex-convict farmers; more often than not, the opulent emancipists attracted his notice and attained high office.[7]

On 20 February 1810 Macquarie instructed Wentworth to continue in the post of principal surgeon (on a salary of £365 per year) until the opinions of His Majesty's ministers were known. The order was published four days later in the *Sydney Gazette*, immediately beneath a proclamation in which the governor described cohabitation among the lower classes as scandalous to religion and decency. Macquarie subsequently informed Castlereagh that Wentworth was a gentleman of considerable professional abilities who was attentive to his patients and amply qualified to head the colony's medical establishment. By March 1810 the governor had told D'Arcy of his intention to recommend that the secretary of state should prevent Jamison from returning to New South Wales in his former office. With his surgeonship temporarily secured, Wentworth submitted a memorial to Macquarie in which he stated that he owned 119 horned cattle, 27 horses and about 400 sheep, and estimated that he had spent over £3200 in improving his properties. He affirmed his long-term commitment to the colony's development and maintained that the land he had been granted by Johnston, Foveaux and Paterson was, to some extent, in recognition of his contribution over twenty years as a landholder.[8]

To bolster his cause, Wentworth wrote to his patron on 17 March. His letter was to be delivered by Foveaux, whom D'Arcy recommended to Fitzwilliam as a man of reputation, honour and integrity. Wentworth asked that Fitzwilliam speak with Castlereagh's successor at the Colonial Office with the aims of securing his appointment as principal surgeon and obtaining approval for him to retain the 1872 acres granted to him by the rebel administrators. He explained that, although the grants had been invalidated, Macquarie had decided against cancelling them without further instructions from home. Once more D'Arcy avowed that he would prefer being a settler with the privileges which John Blaxland enjoyed to serving as principal surgeon. He referred to his changing fortunes, to the happy period at last arrived when he might enjoy a little tranquillity and to having received marked attention from Governor Macquarie, a gentleman whose conduct towards all ranks and persons excited almost universal approbation. Promising to send Fitzwilliam a black cockatoo and a number of parrots, he again deferentially assured him of his profound respect.[9]

Further marks of attention followed. On 31 March Macquarie announced that duties and fees collected in the port of Sydney and throughout New South Wales would be deposited in the 'police fund'. That day Wentworth was appointed its treasurer. While Macquarie regarded the post as an honorary one, Wentworth anticipated that it would be a situation 'of some profit'. On 7 April the governor made him one of the three commissioners for the turnpike road to be built from Sydney to the Hawkesbury; D'Arcy replaced Marsden and sat with Simeon Lord and Andrew Thompson. Regarding Wentworth as belonging to the emancipist class, Macquarie invited four of its representatives to dine with him at Government House—Wentworth, the principal surgeon, Redfern, the acting assistant-surgeon, Thompson, an 'opulent' farmer, and Lord, an 'opulent' merchant. Macquarie thought that they had conducted themselves with propriety and shown their willingness at all times to 'come forward in the most liberal manner' to assist the government. By April he planned to appoint Wentworth and Lord justices of the peace for the town and district of Sydney, and did so on 17 May. In this capacity Wentworth sat on the bench every Saturday with his fellow magistrates and with Ellis Bent.[10]

Meantime, in response to a request from Bligh's supporters who wished to frame an address of gratitude to their former governor, Gore convened a public meeting which was held in the market-place on 11 April. Wentworth, Bayly, Lord, Kable, Underwood, Blaxcell, Gregory Blaxland, Lawson and Kemp attended, bringing their servants and dependants to augment the opposition. Gore asked the assembled throng whether any of them had intended to massacre Bligh if Johnston had not placed him under arrest. A general cry of 'No! No! there was no such intention' went up from the crowd. Wentworth shouted, 'What, man! do you think we are going to put a rope round our own necks?' Gore called the meeting to order. Fulton enraged a section of the audience by denouncing the events of 26 January 1808. Pandemonium broke out. Amid the jeers and heckles of the rebels, the loyalists signed the address and withdrew. Bligh's enemies then took charge and attempted to put forward counter resolutions, but Gore refused to proceed. Macquarie directed him to reconvene the meeting. Shortly after 3 p.m. the rebels unanimously resolved that the earlier gathering had been calculated to provoke and revive enmity. They affirmed their determination to carry into full effect Macquarie's proclamation of 1 January 1810 which advocated that harmony and unity be restored to the colony. Tensions continued until 12 May when Bligh and his entourage—including Palmer, Robert Campbell, Fulton, Gore and Suttor—and Paterson and the remnants of the New South Wales Corps sailed for England. There Johnston was cashiered, Macarthur endured 'exile' until 1817 and many of the women and children of the regiment perished in an epidemic of measles. The Colonial Office's staff resumed their near apathy about what went on in New South Wales and Macquarie was left to get on with governing.[11]

Three months after reaching the colony, Ellis Bent concluded that its limited society was not worth 'six lines of a letter'. In that isolated and compressed community in which he was marooned, the daily rubs and jars of coexistence repeatedly created degrees of friction that were magnified out of all proportion. Petty jealousies, minor disputes and confidential denigrations led to persistent annoyance, constant resentment and enduring enmity. Wentworth's sudden rise to prominence and his apparent omnicompetence made him the more loathed, feared and watched by those who had cause to distrust him. Fulton wrote to Elizabeth Bligh, describing Wentworth as a former highwayman; Joseph Arnold told his brother that D'Arcy had bought 4000 gallons of rum at two shillings a gallon in Rio de Janeiro and sold it in Sydney at an 'enormous price'; Marsden sent letters to friends in England, implying that the newly appointed magistrate lived in a state of licentiousness. Worried lest such rumours gain wider credence and currency, Cookney urged Fitzwilliam to correct the prevailing idea that Wentworth had been sent to New South Wales as a convict. In the penal settlement D'Arcy's detractors prudently confined their aspersions to personal correspondence and private conversation, whether referring to his criminal past, his practices as a merchant or his private life. Through it all there was one recurrent theme: Wentworth remained a menace. Although he was a justice of the peace, in the eyes of his critics he was no gentleman.[12]

The homecoming on 17 March 1810 of D'Arcy's first-born, William, had elated his father and given him a steadfast ally. William was now aged nineteen, of middle height and solid build, with broad shoulders and a shock of auburn hair. Rugged and bedraggled in appearance, he was both intransigent and impulsive by nature, and of a mind to find a field for his considerable talents and to make his value felt. He soon became a familiar man about town where he seemed something of a Gulliver in Lilliput. In England he had received an education appropriate for a gentleman and been told that he was a scion of the Whig aristocracy, but he found that his father was not admitted to the homes of the self-styled gentry of New South Wales. Rumour had it that this affront to D'Arcy's aspirations stemmed from his domestic situation. The details of his appearances at the Old Bailey were not widely known in the colony and he continued to conceal much of his past from his sons. By circumstance and by choice, his main associates were emancipists. William knew that his father was slighted. The knowledge kindled his spite and bred in him a determination to redress the indignity by attacking the pretensions of the exclusives, the very families whose regard and esteem he most deeply coveted. D'Arcy's hope that, with Fitzwilliam's and Foveaux's backing, William might become acting provost marshal was to be realized on 26 October 1811 when Macquarie appointed him to the post. He held it for twelve months until Gore's return. D'Arcy then unsuccessfully sought for his son the position of collector of customs or that of vendue master, both of which brought an income of some £500 a year, vastly more than the salary of £91 5s paid to the provost marshal. On 25 August 1812 Macquarie granted William 1750 acres adjoining the Nepean River and Bringelly Creek in the district of Camden. He named his property Vermont, cultivated his land, ran sheep and bred cattle. In D'Arcy's view there was no young man in New South Wales with purer morals than his son, nor any who had given more general satisfaction. William rode Gig, his father's gelding, to victory in the Hyde Park races in 1810, served on a committee which drew up an address to the governor in 1813 congratulating him on the third anniversary of his arrival, and indicated his affinity with social outcasts by standing as a witness at Simeon Lord's marriage in 1814. Among his friends he numbered Redfern, George Johnston, the colonel's illegitimate son, and James Meehan, the deputy-surveyor and a former convict, whom he accompanied on some minor expeditions. He also wrote verse. In one poem he lamented unrequited love:

No more, no more can night impart
One hour to cheer my drooping heart,
Or e'er again the peace renew,
Its constant beat is still for you.
My restless soul still far will flee,
And, sighing, roam in search of thee.

In another, which took the form of a pipe, he lampooned the Macarthur family, implicitly contrasting the barbarian ancestry of the staymaker with the distinguished background of the Wentworths.[13]

William's brothers remained in England where D'Arcy grew into a high-spirited youth. By mid-1810 he was, in Cookney's estimation, 'doing no good' for himself. After Cookney had contemplated the options of placing him in the East India Company, in the military academy at Woolwich or in the commissariat, Fitzwilliam secured him an ensigncy in the 73rd Regiment in February 1811. Before D'Arcy embarked for New South Wales in May, Cookney paid on his behalf the sum of £88 17s to a woman named Miss Lindwood. D'Arcy was eighteen when he reached Sydney in September. Cookney advised Wentworth that the young man would need an annual allowance of £100, over and above his salary, to maintain himself as an officer. In 1812 Wentworth's account with Cookney was £402 in arrears. The costs of providing for his third son increased as John approached man's estate. Mild in manner and agreeable in disposition, John took his learning well. With Fitzwilliam's assistance, a post was found for him as a midshipman in the Royal Navy and in 1814, at the age of nineteen, he served in the *Royal Oak*, the flagship of Rear-Admiral (Sir) Pulteney Malcolm. John had met his cousin, Martha, a daughter of D'Arcy's brother, William. Despite writing regularly to D'Arcy, William complained that he had not heard from him since 1807. In July 1813 William again penned news from Ireland. William's son, Robert, had recently died; old Dr Patton was still in the land of the living, as were D'Arcy's sisters who sent their affection. One month later, in dispatching the merchandise Wentworth had requested, Cookney tetchily informed him of the difficulties he had encountered in forwarding the hose, hats, boots, cloth and lace he wanted. Cookney's son, Charles, a schoolmate of D'Arcy's son, William, had died in the East Indies and

Mrs Cookney was distraught. There is no evidence in Dr Wentworth's extensive archives that he conveyed condolences, either to his brother or to his agent.[14]

A notice had appeared in the *Sydney Gazette* on 28 April 1810 advising its readers that Mary Ann Macneal had absented herself without provocation from her husband's house and abandoned her infant son. Macneal threatened to prosecute anyone who harboured his wife and disclaimed any debts that might be incurred in her name. He later accused Wentworth of seducing his wife and enticing her to forsake her family. Mary Ann Lawes had come to New South Wales in the *Lady Madeleine Sinclair* in 1806 as a 13-year-old free woman and servant to the Gores. Ann, as she was known, married Macneal in 1808 and was seventeen when she deserted him for Wentworth. D'Arcy tried to minimize open scandal by screening his private life from public view. He attended functions at Government House either alone or accompanied by one of his sons by Catherine Crowley. Maria Ainslie remained with him and lived at Home Bush; Ann shared his homes in Sydney and at Parramatta. Ann and D'Arcy were to have eight children, the first of whom was born on 7 November 1810: their names were George (1810–51), Martha (1813?–47), Sophia (1816–78), Robert Charles (b.1818?), Charles John (1819–54), Mary Ann (1820?–70), Katherine (1825–98) and D'Arcy Charles (1828–66). Three years older than his 'stepmother' and twenty years older than his eldest half-brother, William eventually became 'almost a second father to the younger children'.[15]

There was one woman, however, whom Dr Wentworth found disagreeable, the more so after his son, D'Arcy, reached Sydney on 29 September 1811 to begin duty in the 73rd. That lady was Bligh's daughter, Mary O'Connell, the wife of the regiment's commander. Once created, the resentment between Wentworth and Mrs O'Connell was implacable. Each regarded the other's interference as unkindly meant. Convinced that Mary sought revenge for the rebuke which Castlereagh had delivered to her father for suspending him as assistant-surgeon in July 1807, Wentworth feared that she was so incensed at his son's appointment as to prevail on her husband to write to the Duke of York to have young D'Arcy removed from the 73rd. Wentworth had no evidence for this fear, only a propensity to believe in the malignancy of his enemies. Yet in November 1811 he begged Fitzwilliam to intervene, exhorting him to save his son's career from the 'malicious disposition of a base and artful Woman'. He described O'Connell as a weak man, contrasting him with Macquarie whose 'conduct to me and my family since the first day of his arrival has been one continued act of kindness'. Fitzwilliam was on amicable terms with Earl Bathurst, the new secretary of state for war and the colonies, and saw no reason for anxiety. In October 1812 Cookney relayed his lordship's assurances that Mrs O'Connell would not prejudice young D'Arcy's career and that he needed to attend only to his good behaviour to ensure success.[16]

In November and December 1810 Macquarie bestowed additional favours on Wentworth. With his partners Alexander Riley and Garnham Blaxcell, Wentworth contracted to build a general hospital in Sydney to cater for up to two hundred patients. The main section was to be 289 feet long and 28 feet wide, comprising two storeys, 38 feet in combined height, flanked by surgeons' quarters, with verandahs and a surrounding stone wall. It was to be set on seven acres on the eastern ridge of the town. The contractors' proposal not only freed the Crown from much of the expense involved in erecting the building, but envisaged that the government would accrue a revenue of £6750 in three years. The indenture was signed on 6 November. Work was to begin on or before 1 May 1811 and to be completed by 1 May 1814. Optimistically, the cost was estimated at £18 212. Under the terms of the agreement the contractors were permitted—over a three-year span—to import 45 000 gallons of spirits (on which they paid a duty of three shillings per gallon) and allowed to sell it in whatever manner they thought most advantageous; they were granted the labour of twenty male convicts, the use of twenty draught bullocks and the choice of eighty oxen for slaughter. Riley's younger brother, Edward, acted as the contractors' agent in Calcutta. Macquarie undertook to prohibit the import of any other spirits, with the exception of that required by the government, that involved in fulfilling existing contracts and that occasionally brought as cargo in visiting ships. In the event of default the contractors were bound to forfeit £10 000, but Macquarie was confident that Wentworth's rectitude of conduct and zealous attention would ensure that the terms were duly and faithfully executed. Wentworth was far wealthier than either Riley or Blaxcell. Without him the scheme would have been impossible. From Macquarie's standpoint

6 To catch a thief

it was a great bargain; from that of his detractors it created an undeserved and undesirable monopoly.[17]

Six months and six days previously, on 30 April 1810, Macquarie had written to Viscount Castlereagh advocating the unrestricted landing of spirits in New South Wales under a duty of 3 to 4 shillings per gallon. The measures he took on 6 November in regard to the 'Rum Hospital' constituted a volte-face. Although Lord Liverpool did not cancel the contract, he rebuked Macquarie for the embarrassment it occasioned: he saw it as interfering with freedom of trade, and as encouraging smuggling and illegal distilling; he expressed his concern about the effects that the contract would have on merchants who had already taken out licences to export spirits to the penal colony; and he also envisaged that the contractors themselves might have grounds for complaint if their anticipated monopoly proved more imaginary than real. Refusing to countenance the proposal, Liverpool left it to Macquarie's discretion to adopt measures that would do justice to all parties involved. Because the undertaking required a substantial outlay, Wentworth drew a set of bills on his account with Cookney, directing him to sell his Consols if he had insufficient funds. In August 1811 Cookney informed Wentworth that his account was in arrears and advised him against soliciting aid from Fitzwilliam who had already advanced £210 on his behalf. On 5 February 1812 Cookney drew Fitzwilliam's attention to Wentworth's precarious finances. Fitzwilliam advanced £300 to cover Wentworth's bills.[18]

One example of the darker elements in Wentworth's character was shown in his treatment of William Mansell. At Mansell's instigation, Assistant-Surgeon William Evans had been confined in gaol for a debt of £34 3s 6d. On 21 November 1810 Wentworth intervened on Evans's behalf, offering to liquidate the debt at £2 per month. He swore that he would destroy Mansell's reputation if he refused the offer, and said that he would place the matter before a bench of magistrates and have Evans discharged without paying a shilling of the debt. Rather than being intimidated, Mansell remained resolute. Three days later Wentworth visited Mansell at his home where he made out a promissory note for the amount and demanded that Mansell accept it. Wentworth then warned Mansell that if he or his family ever required medical attention it would be refused by Redfern, Evans and himself; he also threatened to persuade the doctors in the 73rd Regiment to deny him professional assistance. Having reiterated his determination to ruin Mansell, Wentworth stormed from the house, told the provost marshal that he had honoured the debt and proceeded to have his colleague released from prison. On 6 December, in a petition to the governor, Mansell complained of Wentworth's behaviour. The incident did not deter Macquarie from offering Wentworth another senior appointment.[19]

As part of his policy of reform, the governor initiated a programme to reorganize the police in Sydney. He had found the system for preserving the safety of property and person to be defective. The streets often presented scenes of rioting, drunkenness and other forms of excess, while robbery, burglary and assault frequently occurred. Accordingly, he asked Ellis Bent to frame a new code of police regulations which came into operation on 1 January 1811. Sydney was divided into five districts, each with a watch-house, a chief constable and six constables in ordinary, each armed with a cutlass and a rattle to sound the alarm. To head this establishment, under the appellation of superintendent of police, Macquarie chose D'Arcy Wentworth. His appointment was promulgated on 29 December 1810. In justifying his selection, Macquarie referred to Wentworth's assiduity and indefatigability, and to his long residence in the colony which had equipped him with a thorough knowledge of the nature of the inhabitants. Without fully appreciating the irony of his action, the governor had charged an erstwhile highwayman with the maintenance of law and order. He had set a thief to catch a thief. Wentworth volunteered to perform the duties without remuneration, but the governor recommended that he receive a salary of £200 a year, which was approved, retrospectively, on 3 February 1814. Grandeur filled the governor's vision, but inconsistency dogged his steps. While he reduced the number of public houses from seventy-five to twenty in an effort to stem dissipation, profligacy and crime, his hospital indenture abetted the increased consumption of spirits by giving a vested interest and a financial incentive in their sale to three contractors, one of whom, as superintendent of police, was charged with combating the outcome of drunkenness.[20]

Located at the hub of Sydney, Wentworth's house provided both a home and a business headquarters, combining as it did a shop and store. It was situated on the edge of The Rocks, close by the wharf and warehouses, and in the immediate vicinity of the barracks, the old hospital, the gaol, and the stocks and pillory. Near by stood the church of St Phillip, not far from the Jolly Sailor and Black Dog inns. From George Street it was only a ten-minute uphill walk along Bridge Street to Government House. If Wentworth's busy schedule too often impinged on his medical obligations to the populace at large, it did not preclude his attendance on the governor. The bond between governor and surgeon strengthened, for Macquarie increasingly took Wentworth into his confidence as a leading officer in his administration, as his family doctor and as his friend. D'Arcy provided medicine to relieve Mrs Macquarie from her spasms; when the governor was ill, it was Wentworth who was summoned to his bedside. In Egypt in 1802 Dr James McGrigor had treated Macquarie with mercury for a form of venereal disease. In London, in 1803 and in 1804, Dr Everard Home performed surgical operations on him 'of a very delicate nature', probably involving the insertion of a needle through his urethra to the perineum to relieve the suppression of urine. In New South Wales strain and overwork brought Macquarie to the edge of breakdown: at various stages he suffered from stomach-aches, biliousness, bowel complaints, dysentery and fever, and showed symptoms of resurgent syphilis. The debt of a patient to a doctor is immeasurable, the more so when the doctor is a confidant. The governor thought highly of Wentworth's medical attentions, as did the governor's lady. Macquarie mentioned his name in dispatches 'in the most distinguished and honourable manner'; in reciprocation, Wentworth presented Elizabeth Macquarie with a gift of seven Norfolk Island pines from his Home Bush farm.[21]

Within twelve months of Macquarie's arrival, Wentworth had become a key figure in the colony's civil service. He held the posts of principal surgeon (confirmed May 1811), superintendent of police, treasurer of the police fund, magistrate, commissioner for the turnpike road and hospital contractor; the first two of these offices brought him a combined annual salary of £565, an equivalent income in itself to that enjoyed by England's lesser gentry. Fifty years old in 1812, prominent and affluent, he was so enveloped by his status that he could not comprehend why he was envied and reproached by settlers who thought that he had overreached himself in securing undue advantages. Purpose and energy were his chief talents, and he had his pride, though few regarded it. Propelled by the activity on which he thrived, he later undertook endless civic duties, whether promoting the erection of a court-house, involving himself in the protection of South Sea Islanders stranded in Sydney, or serving on a committee which aimed to educate and civilize the Aborigines. There were also responsibilities of a different order: he kept an eye on the interests of Sir John Jamison, stood surety for Simeon Lord, inquired into the theft of a convict's belongings by the master of a transport vessel, sought redress against a private soldier for impounding a cow and her calf, acted as a professional referee, helped Mrs Jammond, the wife of an exiled purser, and sent two Rosehill parakeets to Considen in England for a lady friend who was 'fond of birds since she has not been blessed with any progeny'.[22]

As well as fag, there was fun. Wentworth found release from business through horse-racing and gambling, two of his favourite recreations. Sydney's races, first held in the week beginning 15 October 1810, continued each year until 1816 when the revelry and carousing degenerated into fights and riots. For seven years D'Arcy participated in the festivities. He cheered in 1810 when his bay gelding, Gig, defeated Commissary William Broughton's black gelding, Jerry, over three heats, netting him 120 guineas; and he proved a good loser in 1811 when Brigade-Major Thomas Cleaveland's horse, Scratch, beat Gig after three laps of the one-mile course. On another occasion he wagered one hundred guineas with Simeon Lord on the outcome of a single race. Gala balls were held during race-week, attended by the civil and military officers, and graced by the beauty and fashion of the colony. Enlivened by music, and with food and drink in abundance, the merry-making lasted well into the early hours of the morning.[23]

In 1813 Wentworth reaped added prestige and felicity through the achievement of his son, William. Invited to accompany Gregory Blaxland and 'Ironbark' Lawson, William had joined an expedition to cross the Blue Mountains. The three men, accompanied by four servants, five dogs, and four horses laden with provisions and ammunition, set off on 11 May. After enduring severe hardships which sapped their strength, on 31 May they achieved their goal and looked down on the plains to the west which resembled an arcady. By 6 June they had returned to their homes. William's journal of the journey contained only prosaic entries, but the majesty of the occasion was not lost on him and he would later write:

6 To catch a thief

> The boundless champaign burst upon our sight,
> Till nearer seen the beauteous landscape grew,
> Op'ning like Canaan on rapt Israel's view.

The news was greeted with caution in official circles and with relish by the graziers. After eight months had elapsed, on 12 February 1814, in recognition of their conquest of the barrier that separated the coastlands from the interior, Macquarie presented each of the explorers with a grant of one thousand acres in the newly discovered country. In July he commissioned William Cox to supervise the construction of a 101-mile road over the ranges to a place that would be known as Bathurst, beyond which a fertile hinterland stretched as far as the eye could see, with grass sufficient to support the livestock of the colony for the next thirty years. Reflecting on the opening up of 'a second Promised Land', D'Arcy Wentworth claimed the lion's share of the credit for the child he loved surpassingly. He boasted to Fitzwilliam that the feat had been achieved 'by the spirited and indefatigable Exertions of my son William & two other Gentlemen who at their own Expense undertook & compleated the arduous (& before often attempted) Enterprize'.[24]

Another spur to enterprise had come on 18 October 1811 when Macquarie re-granted the 1872 acres which D'Arcy Wentworth had nominally surrendered in the previous year, as well as approving title to his Home Bush estate which had grown to 990 acres. Mindful that, under the certainty of heaven, nothing is certain, Wentworth again fixed his course to hoard a worldly trove. In matters of income, property and possessions, he was a nabob, grounded in the significance of all sums great and small. Beyond his official duties, he supervised the management of his lands and expanded his holdings by judicious purchases in the districts of Sydney, Parramatta, North Harbour, Broken Bay, Toongabbie, Prospect, Windsor, on the Nepean, at Illawarra, and at Bringelly and Cook. In 1814 he bought 3345 acres (2065 from Ellis Bent, 700 from David Bowen and 580 from Frederick Jones); in 1817 he purchased 4280 acres in one lot from Gregory Blaxland. Grants of 950 acres in 1812, 1000 and 1200 acres in 1816, and of 300 and 350 acres in 1818 and 1819 respectively, further augmented Wentworth's stature as a man of property. From his first 60-acre farm on Norfolk Island in 1792, he had acquired 13 637 acres in New South Wales by 1817, more than the entire area of Norfolk Island. In 1818 he held

20 000 acres, none of it west of the coastal plains, and was the largest landowner in Australia. Two years later he owned 30 000 acres; among his nearest rivals were Sir John Jamison with 11 206 acres, John Macarthur with 9600, John Blaxland with 6850, and Marsden, Cox and Charles Throsby, with 4500, 4000 and 2520 respectively. By 1821 Wentworth's holdings included grants of 11 142 acres, of which Macquarie had granted 9130 acres since 1816. At the time of his death D'Arcy owned 34 145 acres, more than 53 square miles of the colony. Such was the conclusion of such a beginning.[25]

Untempted by the prospect of grazing sheep on the lands west of the Blue Mountains, Wentworth preferred to raise livestock for local sale rather than producing wool for export. By November 1818 he owned 950 horned cattle, 600 sheep, 96 horses and 20 hogs. From his farms he supplied beef, lamb, mutton and pork to the commissariat, to private markets in Sydney and the outlying areas, and to the captains of ships sailing from Port Jackson. The commissariat was fairly reliable in its demand for meat and was a ready source of Treasury bills, virtually the equivalent of sterling currency. Wentworth supplied it with 2000 lb of fresh meat in 1813, 6000 in 1815 and 12 000 in 1817; the figures increased to 18 000 lb in 1818 and to 53 000 in 1820; in one single month of 1827 he sold 1650 cattle for slaughter at a time when prices ranged between £10 and £12 a head. In 1814 he had bought a slaughterhouse at Cockle Bay for £325, enabling him to remove the middleman. This abattoir received his cattle, sheep, pigs and goats, and supplemented his income by the sale of such ancillary products as hides, bones and tallow. His entrepreneurial spirit also led him to breed quality saddle-horses and cattle, and to earn money from stud fees, particularly for his stallions Jack, Galloway and the Arab, Hector. Furthermore, he grew fruit and vegetables for sale, and by 1822 was producing honey from his bee-hives. Apart from engaging in the spirits trade, he imported and retailed general merchandise, set up as a rentier and operated as a money-lender. He discounted bills of exchange and lent sums of up to £600 at 8 to 12 per cent interest, taking a mortgage on land or other property as security. Appointed a director of the Bank of New South Wales—which opened on 8 April 1817 and used the house of the emancipist businesswoman, Mary Reibey, in Macquarie Place as its premises—he privately undercut the bank's commission on money exchanges by 1 per cent in 1818. Not until 1820 did he open a separate account for the police fund, preferring to conduct a substantial flow of its transactions through his personal account. Opportunities abounded for drawing, temporarily, on the public fund for his private purposes, though these advantages were regarded as comparable with the perquisites expected by army paymasters, customs officers and commissary-generals.[26]

Throughout the years from 1811 to 1816 Riley, Blaxcell and Wentworth attempted to exact better terms than those stipulated in the contract for building the general hospital. In late March 1812 they met the governor to resolve their difficulties. Macquarie made concessions, allowing them to buy an additional 10 000 gallons of spirits, extending the time for its disposal by six months and offering them moderate grants of land if the increase in their livestock were found to warrant it. That year the contractors endeavoured to lower the projected height of the building, to decrease the number of supporting pillars and to modify the roof. Sometimes Macquarie acquiesced, sometimes he stood firm. Exchanges between governor and contractors grew strained. On 29 December, with only half the hospital erected, Wentworth and his partners accused the government of subverting the agreement and threatened legal action. On 11 January 1813 they notified Macquarie of their intention to lay their grievances before His Majesty's ministers. Macquarie was jolted into calling a conference on 10 February. He listened to them in silence, knowing that any attempt to argue with them or vindicate his behaviour would be counterproductive. Only then did he give up the point, permitting them to land an extra 5000 gallons and granting another six months for its sale. An uneasy lull followed. In March the governor sent instructions to the contractors for a series of alterations and additions to the building. When they dismissed his suggestions as requiring sheer ornamentation he was exasperated. In May he proposed to relinquish the agreement unless they finished the hospital in an appropriate style. On this angry note, correspondence ceased, but construction continued. The building was completed on 3 March 1816 and occupied on 8 April. Wentworth moved into the principal surgeon's quarters. Francis Greenway, the government architect, recommended that the builders be fined for the delay and for defects in their work. Bickering and complaints persisted until 1820 before the contract was fulfilled. During these years the scale of the project was ridiculed by those who saw the grandiose plan as creating palaces for

The Wentworths

the medical staff and as being more suited to a West Indian community. The amount of spirits imported by the contractors increased by 33 per cent, from 45 000 to 60 000 gallons, as did the time they had to market it, from three years to four; and the building took twenty-two months longer than projected before it was used. Estimates of what the contractors realized varied immensely. Henry Kitchen, a private architect, exaggerated wildly in reckoning their profit at £140 000. Blaxcell maintained that he had actually made a loss. A later historian, H. P. Barker, calculated that £32 000 was outlaid on the building and about £36 000 on the spirits (including the duty), a total of £68 000; Barker also computed that the gross return from the sale of spirits was £89 000 and that the net profit was about £21 000. If the last figure is averaged over the five years from 1811 to 1816 and divided equally between the three principals, each may have earned as much as £1400 per annum. Blaxcell fell into financial difficulties, fled his creditors on 9 April 1817 and died in Batavia on 3 October; from being Macquarie's friend, Riley turned into an inveterate enemy and left the colony on 22 December that year; Wentworth alone of the partners remained close to the governor.[27]

Although Wentworth's primary duty lay with the medical establishment, he had little time and less inclination to give it more than passing attention. The old hospital in Major's Row, at The Rocks near Dawes' Point, was allowed to fall into a dilapidated state. When the new hospital in Macquarie Street was occupied, Wentworth visited the wards spasmodically, mostly as a consultant. He delegated his responsibilities to Redfern, the assistant-surgeon, who, because he conducted an extensive private practice and was a landowner in his own right, delegated several of them in turn to his subordinates, among them Henry Cowper. Wardsmen and nurses were usually convicts, rough and negligent in their treatment, and dissolute in their habits. Behind the façade the hospital hid its shame. The patients' diet was inadequate, sanitation was poor, and the misappropriation or theft of drugs, blankets, sheets and provisions was common. Hospitals at the outstations, as at Parramatta, provided inadequate accommodation for the sick in buildings that lay unrepaired for years; their supplies of medicine, candles, oil, bedding and cooking utensils were irregular and insufficient. Wentworth's problems were caused as much by his own neglect as by the shortage of trained and reliable staff.[28]

6 To catch a thief

He showed more zeal, however, as chief police magistrate in Sydney. With a jurisdiction inferior to that of the criminal and civil courts, and to the various benches of magistrates, Wentworth sat alone and dispensed summary justice. Day by day he presided over hearings at which queues of convicts filed sullenly before him charged with theft, drunkenness, unruly conduct, absence from work, abusive language, or with being rogues and vagabonds; the more serious offences included assault, highway robbery, fraud and buggery; now and again prisoners came of their own volition to complain about the poor quality of their rations or unfair treatment; sometimes he even tried free settlers. Lesser offenders were sentenced to serve in the gaol gang for periods ranging from one day to one year. Those found guilty of major crimes received fifty lashes or were banished to Newcastle for terms of up to three years. Free settlers were fined or bound over to keep the peace. Wentworth spared female convicts the pain and humiliation of the triangles, and usually sentenced them to be confined in the Female Factory at Parramatta or to be transported to the Coal River, depending on the nature of their offences. Given the callous and seamy side of life in a penal colony, his judgements on the bench were sound and the sentences he handed down were not excessive; indeed, a number of settlers thought his punishments erred on the side of leniency. On one occasion his persevering inquiries in 1814 saved two innocent men from the gallows. In that year Blaxcell privately condemned Wentworth's direction of the police as being 'dreadful in the extreme'. Peter Cunningham, too, criticized Wentworth's inability to exercise a rigorous surveillance over his department from his headquarters at the corner of George and Bridge streets. Yet, since constables were drawn mainly from the convict class and their remuneration was poor, Macquarie's efforts to maintain law and order had—under Wentworth's supervision—materially reduced the crime rate and his methods were as good as those in any English town. For all that, Wentworth's business interests did impinge on his duties to the community. John Harris was not the only person to be offended by the sight of the superintendent of police 'standing at the door of his Large Store & receiving the money for the Spirits that were sold there'. Wentworth was reluctant to convict those brought before him on charges of selling spirits without a licence or of running a disorderly public house. Aided by Robert Lathrop Murray, his principal clerk in the Police Office and a close friend, he treated them with partiality. When John Harris remonstrated with Wentworth about such matters, the businessman allegedly replied: 'it was good for trade; and good for the Police fund'. To Wentworth, there was no conflict of interest between his official position and his private concerns.[29]

Neither did he feel any qualms in gaining access to convict labour for his own purposes. A fugitive from the Coal River, who had previously worked for Wentworth and won his approval, appeared before a bench of magistrates. Feigning anger, Wentworth declared that the scoundrel would forget a flogging by the morrow and vowed that he would learn a better lesson if he were assigned to him. The felon was taken to Wentworth's farm where he bragged: 'I was by that night at sundown eating and drinking the best there was in the huts at Homebush ... you heard tell how all the doctor's men live ... Never got one lash the whole five years I was with him'. While the old lag regarded his master's action as motivated by affection, Wentworth had gained an able and proven labourer. Whether employing convalescents from the Parramatta hospital or refugees from the courtroom, he merged self-interest with a concern for those he had befriended. He allowed some of his former employees to set up farms at peppercorn rents and was indulgent to transportees recommended to his care. None the less, he was willing to subordinate humanitarian concerns to commercial profit. In January 1814 he entered into an agreement with his son William, Blaxcell, Riley, Captain William Campbell and Philip Goodenough, master of the *Cumberland*, to procure a valuable cargo of sandalwood to the east of the Friendly Islands in the South Pacific. To recover from a pulmonary disease, William joined the schooner as supercargo. At Rarotonga the behaviour of the crew led to violence. One of the islanders was killed and William narrowly escaped death while attempting to save a sailor. After more Europeans were slain, and the captain's mistress was abducted and murdered, William helped to bring the ship safely to Sydney, displaying the knowledge he had gained on his earlier voyage from England and no mean mathematical skill. On reading a report of the episode in the *Sydney Gazette*, Marsden called a meeting of the Philanthropic Society and pressed for an inquiry. D'Arcy Wentworth, Blaxcell, Riley and their fellow traders quashed his request and quietly buried the incident. In other cases Wentworth did not baulk at inquiries, even those involving litigation. In October 1810 he launched a successful suit against the firm of Kable & Underwood for £51 14s 7d; in court again in January 1811, he recovered £43 and costs from Thomas Wheeler; and in April 1813 he was awarded £182 3s 10d against Joseph Underwood. Concerned by the extent to which his civil officials were engaged in trade, Macquarie twice sought Bathurst's views on the subject. On 4 December 1815 the secretary of state gave his opinion decidedly, authorizing him to dismiss them from their posts. The governor chose to disregard this advice in the case of D'Arcy Wentworth whose business transactions continued unabated. Next year William counselled his father against anticipating that a future governor would turn a blind eye to his enterprises.[30]

By July 1813 Macquarie's patience with the soldiers in the 73rd had finally snapped. Complaining of their insubordination, he requested the regiment's recall. A detachment which included Lieutenant D'Arcy Wentworth left the colony on 17 January 1814 bound for Ceylon. There, young D'Arcy cursed the heat, the jungle fever and the endless drill, but was moved to send affectionate wishes for his father's welfare and happiness. In March and April the remainder of the corps sailed from New South Wales. They were replaced by the 46th under Lieutenant-Colonel George Molle, the new lieutenant-governor. Some inhabitants could not be so easily removed, and such individuals as Robert Townson and the Blaxland brothers continued to harry the governor. Moreover, Ellis Bent, who had worked indefatigably in assisting the government, turned against Macquarie in late 1813. Aged thirty, a balding, bespectacled, pallid and heavy man who suffered from bouts of rheumatism and pleurisy, Bent appeared grave and preoccupied. He was not one to ask for favours, or to cringe and flatter. Consequently, he believed, there were several people who exerted more influence at Government House than he. On 16 December 1813 Macquarie confronted Bent about his moodiness. Bent said that, by not building a suitable court-house in Sydney, Macquarie had shown a lack of consideration for the station of the deputy judge-advocate. From this day their relationship rapidly deteriorated as Bent set out to oppose and irritate the governor.[31]

The arrival in Sydney Cove on 28 July 1814 of Jeffery Bent presaged an escalation of the feud. Wizened, angular, officious and conceited, he was a melancholy and sensitive bachelor, two years older than his brother. Jeffery came as judge of the Supreme Court and was not a man to be crossed. Sworn in on 12 August, he refused to open his court, not least because the town had no premises he deemed suitable. When Macquarie allocated two wards of the general hospital for a courtroom and chambers, Bent informed him that he preferred the detached north wing, the very building the governor had set aside for the principal surgeon's residence. Resenting the precedence given to Wentworth, Bent wrote on 15 October to Henry Goulburn, the under-secretary at the Colonial Office. He argued that, in holding the comfort of the principal surgeon above the due and solemn administration of justice, the governor had degraded the office, the character and the person of His Majesty's judges in the colony. In December Bent again made representations to Macquarie which led to a compromise whereby the judge was allowed to use two rooms in the north wing. Although Wentworth had not directly offended Bent, the squabble over accommodation had a personal edge. Bent's opposition to Macquarie's policies was assured, as was his animosity towards Wentworth.[32]

Following numerous delays, Bent finally agreed to open the Supreme Court on 1 May 1815. Macquarie felt satisfied that his presence in Sydney was no longer required and sought release by making a trip across the Blue Mountains to see the country that William Wentworth had discovered. Symbolic of his total trust, on 24 April the governor left his only son, 1-year-old Lachlan, in the care of D'Arcy Wentworth, entreating him to send a dragoon if the child became ill during his parents' anticipated four-week absence. Next day he and Elizabeth set off by carriage, accompanied by a suite of ten gentlemen and a retinue of forty servants. On 7 May Macquarie named the site of the town of Bathurst. He considered that there was peace and plenty in his land, that his people improved in manners and in morals, that the immense continent would eventually become one of the greatest colonies in the British Empire, and that his own name would not be forgotten. In the shelter of his Sydney home Wentworth had heard that the Colonial Office was far from satisfied with Macquarie's conduct. Schooled by experience to read a turning vane, he realized that the governor's tenure was uncertain and had asked Fitzwilliam to be prepared to nominate a successor. As tokens of his esteem for his English patron, he sent him a pair of black swans, together with a collection of topazes of great size and beauty, and told him that he had named two of his estates Wentworth Park and Elmsall Place in remembrance of the family from which he was descended.[33]

7

The greatest burden

> The greatest burden is the past
>
> John le Carré, *The Russia House*

The year 1815 proved seminal to the future of Britain and Australia. With the allied victory at Waterloo, Bonaparte was crushed, the Napoleonic Wars terminated and an epoch ended. On the other side of the earth Major-General Lachlan Macquarie drew closer to the meridian in his colonial government. He had crossed the Blue Mountains and seen a countryside that beckoned countless pastoralists. In that year at Cockle Bay he also inaugurated John Dickson's mills which harnessed the power of a steam-engine to saw timber and grind grain. The industrial revolution had reached the antipodes. 1815 marked the twenty-fifth year since D'Arcy Wentworth had first set foot in Sydney. The European population of New South Wales totalled 12 911, while that of Van Diemen's Land stood at 1933. Six years later the figures had increased to 29 783 on the mainland and 7185 in the island dependency. From 1810 to 1821 the combined population of New South Wales and Van Diemen's Land more than trebled. During the last six years of Macquarie's administration almost as many people came to live in New South Wales as in its previous twenty-seven years of British settlement. By 1821 there were 1489 free settlers, 1884 native-born, 6891 ex-convicts, 12 235 convicts and 7284 children in the penal colony. Males numbered 21 453 and females 8330: the overall sex ratio approached three to one, though among the prisoners the men exceeded the women by almost thirteen to one. The arrival of so many convicts in so short a time placed additional burdens on the governor, stretched the resources of his gaol and posed problems which became too large for one man to handle.[1]

Other matters beset Macquarie in 1815. He had returned to Sydney on the afternoon of 19 May and was almost immediately embroiled in wordy warfare in which a principle of great moment would be shaped and canvassed. Intimations of this row had begun much earlier, like the advance creaking of rigging in a storm. For almost five years Ellis Bent had reluctantly permitted ex-convicts to act as agents in the civil courts because there were no free attorneys in the settlement; he was even prepared to countenance respectable emancipists serving as jurors. Yet he resented the military nature of his commission and thought that the words enjoining him to follow the governor's orders eroded his legal independence. By 1814 his views on the status of the judiciary *vis-à-vis* the executive had helped to estrange him from Macquarie. The arrival of Jeffery Bent exacerbated the bitterness. He initially refused to open the Supreme Court on the ground that there was no free solicitor in the colony. On 11 April 1815 Macquarie received a petition from George Crossley, an expiree, and from Edward Eagar, a conditionally pardoned convict, praying to be allowed to practise as barristers. The governor's support for them earned Bent's blistering rebuke that his interference amounted to an attempt to bias the court. On 11 May Bent refused to sit in the presence of emancipist attorneys and adjourned the Supreme Court until the opinion of His Majesty's government was known. In a concerted effort at a policy of exclusion, Ellis Bent adopted in the Governor's Court the principle for which his brother was contending so inflexibly.[2]

To the Bents the rule of law was imperilled. They conscientiously believed in the concept of an independent judiciary and in the governor being subject to English law. Their stand against emancipist attorneys was based on precedents in British legal decisions. In the absence of any elected legislature or an independent press, the courts functioned as a forum for legitimizing the governor's authority or the challenges to it. Revealingly, the manoeuvres centred on the emancipist policy, with one group seeking to preserve its privileges and the other endeavouring to shed the convict taint. To Macquarie the principle of *rex* versus *lex* was just as patent as it was to the Bents. By resisting his authority, they were, in his view, guilty of insubordination. They had raised a faction to oppose the measures of his government. Their efforts were fraught with dangerous consequences, for the issue did not rest with a few ex-convict attorneys. The two illiberal brothers wished to exclude emancipists from all places of trust and consequence, as well as from respectable company. A surrender to them would wound seven-eighths of the inhabitants. Open dissension between Macquarie and the Bents over the dictum that reformation should qualify ex-convicts for readmission into society provoked passions that warped the judgement of both parties. The point at issue provided the node for a mass of criticism of Macquarie's administration, both in New South Wales and in London.[3]

On 1 July 1815 Jeffery Bent wrote a letter to Lord Bathurst. In it he launched a withering attack on the three ex-convicts who wanted to practise as barristers in his court. He condemned Crossley as a perjurer, Eagar as deceitful and George Chartres, who was employed as one of Wentworth's clerks, as guilty of misconduct. Furthermore, Bent poured scorn on the four magistrates nominated by the governor to assist him in the Supreme Court. He denounced Lord as an ex-convict, Broughton as a man of inferior rank and Riley as a merchant who had benefited from the spirits monopoly; in the main, they were ignorant of the law and lacked impartiality. The gravamen of his charge against the fourth magistrate, D'Arcy Wentworth, was that he had come to New South Wales under degraded circumstances and was still not welcome in polite society. On 1 July Ellis Bent also wrote to Lord Bathurst, repeating his complaint that the comfort of the judges had been subordinated to the convenience of the principal surgeon. Mr Wentworth was to be afforded a residence at the hospital 'far beyond what his rank' entitled him to expect and 'such as must tend to promote jealousy in the minds of other officers' in the colony. Ellis Bent shared his home in Sydney with his brother. Their cave of Adullam lay only a stone's throw from Government House.[4]

Macquarie's enemies gravitated towards the Bents and formed a party which was intent on maligning his emancipist policy. In April 1810 the Reverend Samuel Marsden had refused to sit with Lord and Thompson as trustees of the turnpike road. Arguing that any association with the immoral would denigrate his sacred functions, he wrote to the godly in England and exposed the character of the emancipist magistrates. By 1815 he had gained the support of a group of sympathizers in London, including a few members of parliament. At one official reception in Sydney, Lieutenant Archibald Bell was peeved when Mrs Macquarie passed him by and held out her hand to former convicts. Before their arrival in New South Wales the officers of the 46th Regiment had agreed to exclude ex-convicts from their society. Joseph Arnold, no admirer of Macquarie, thought it preposterous that the governor invited emancipists to his table when the military refused to admit them to their mess. Arnold spent much of his time with Sir John Jamison who shared his views about 'the very impolitick levelling measures of this Government', the 'mortifying' state of the magistracy, and the police magistrate who had once been a notorious highwayman 'on Finchley Common and Hounslow Heath'. Others knew that, in appearing before a select committee of the House of Commons in February 1812, Bligh had said that Wentworth had been transported for highway robbery and that his conduct in the colony was far from exemplary. In impugning Macquarie's most cherished policy, the exclusives resurrected the history of one of his favourites. Wentworth's greatest burden was his past. Both a brake and a goad, it had, from 1790, held him back and spurred him forward.[5]

Like the Bents, on 1 July Macquarie also wrote to Lord Bathurst. He stated that it was impossible for him to work in amity with the two judges and offered to resign unless the Colonial Office removed them from New South Wales. Next day he wrote to his brother, Charles, telling him that, as he had been the patron and champion of all meritorious persons who had been convicts, he could never desert them. D'Arcy Wentworth was quick to defend the governor. In a series of letters he informed Fitzwilliam that the Bents had defied Macquarie's authority, and that their conduct towards him had been indecorous and violent in the extreme. The irreconcilable hostility between the governor and the judges, he went on, had drawn many others into the vortex of their disputes; the animosity had led to the emergence of a party which aimed to find fault with every aspect of Macquarie's conduct, thereby shattering the harmony that had existed in the colony. Impressed with Macquarie for effecting more improvements than all his predecessors, Wentworth asked Fitzwilliam to counteract the rancour of those who were agitating for the governor's recall. In D'Arcy's opinion nothing short of the Bents' removal would restore equilibrium. Wentworth knew that 'the faction' wanted Molle to become governor and feared that, if he did, he would dismiss him from his posts. Were

7 The greatest burden

there to be a change of governor, D'Arcy again suggested that Fitzwilliam should nominate one of his friends for the office. Finally, he referred to Bligh's malice in stating that he had been transported: it would be helpful if his noble patron clarified the matter to Lord Bathurst's satisfaction and arranged for someone to expose the vile falsehood by speaking in the House of Commons.[6]

In August 1815 Jeffery Bent wrote two letters to Macquarie which resulted in another row. Bent informed the governor that the tolls levied on the turnpike road were illegal and that he had no intention of paying them. Macquarie replied to the first letter by stating that it was worthy only of his contempt; he answered the second by declining all further written correspondence with its author, except in regard to public duty. On 31 August and 5 September the judge successively abused two gatekeepers, Patrick Cullen and Michael Wyer, threatened to have them gaoled and went his way without paying the toll. Early on the morning of 6 September Cullen and Wyer called on Wentworth and filed formal complaints against Bent. When Wentworth accidentally met the judge in the street outside his home he told him of the charges and tried to reach an understanding. Bent turned angrily on him and rejected the attempt at compromise. Wentworth then issued a summons for Bent to appear before him at 11 a.m. on the 9th to answer the complaints. Outraged at this presumption, Bent rejected the idea that he was amenable to any criminal jurisdiction in the colony, castigated Wentworth for failing to designate him by his title, accused him of exceeding the bounds of his office and told him that he would ignore the summons. In Bent's absence, Wentworth heard the case, found him guilty as charged and fined him forty shillings. A copy of the proceedings was sent to Macquarie who that day issued a Government and General Order announcing that an officer of very high rank in the civil service had refused to pay the toll. Although the order did not name Bent, it was common knowledge that Macquarie was referring to him. The notice enjoined the gatekeepers to call for police assistance if anyone used force or violence to avoid payment.[7]

Stung by this public admonition, Bent wrote a studied letter to Macquarie on 2 October, hectoring the governor for treating him as an officer under his command rather than as a judge with a commission that rendered him independent. Bent also took the opportunity to lambaste Wentworth for his ignorance of the law in proceeding against him with such haste and indecency. Macquarie responded by stating that Bent's letter was disrespectful—like all his earlier correspondence—and warranted no particular reply. On 4 November, while his brother Ellis lay dying, Jeffery Bent took up his pen again to draw Lord Bathurst's attention to his differences with Macquarie. In accusing the governor of mismanagement, he used Wentworth's toings and froings to exemplify how disreputable individuals gained key posts in the administration and how they abused their positions of privilege. Bent again rehearsed the circumstances under which Wentworth had come to New South Wales and again alluded to his social ostracism. What was more, the judge asserted:

> his Medical Duties are almost entirely neglected; He is an improper Person to be at the Head of Police, from his Ignorance of the Law, and from the Fact of his being one of the Principal Dealers in Spirits . . . His Clerk is a transported Attorney of bad Character, and is also a Publican . . . Mr Wentworth has the principal control over the Licences and the Public Houses; and the whole conduct of Office by no means gives satisfaction to the Public.

Unmoved by Bent's arguments, in April 1816 Lord Bathurst recalled the judges; although he censured their methods, he did not condemn their opinions. Ellis Bent had died on 10 November 1815, leaving a wife and five children without provision. His death gave Marsden an opportunity to inveigh against the government in a funeral panegyric which Macquarie considered blasphemous. Embittered and vengeful, the clergyman struggled to affirm the independent status of the church in the colonial establishment. His efforts reinforced his alliance with Jeffery Bent, who remained in Sydney until May 1817, continually harassing Macquarie, promoting the cause of his enemies and giving a focus to disquiet. Frederick Garling acted as deputy judge-advocate from November 1815 until John Wylde superseded him in October 1816; the Supreme Court was closed for about two years before Barron Field commenced proceedings on 1 May 1817.[8]

There were grounds for Jeffery Bent's disquiet. Wentworth's numerous activities left scant time for his medical duties. Even though he bore responsibility for hospitals in the outlying settlements, he rarely

7 The greatest burden

visited them. He attended patients in the Sydney hospital infrequently, usually at night. In so far as he concerned himself, on and off, with the general hospital, it was only to the extent of rectifying structural faults in the building and other defects of workmanship. The central block comprised four large wards and little else: no rooms for the nurses and attendants adjoined the wards; there were no water-closets save those in an outhouse at the rear of the hospital; no drains existed to carry away medical waste; and insufficient water was provided by the solitary well within the precinct. Yet it was a lofty and spacious building, constructed largely of stone, with verandahs and windows, upstairs and down, to admit light and air. From time to time the principal surgeon was beset by requests from the outstations for provisions of one sort or another. Erratic supplies from England hindered his ability to comply, as did the failings of certain members of his staff. For two years Thomas Parmeter, surgeon of the lunatic asylum at Castle Hill, quarrelled with its superintendent, George Suttor. Dr Parmeter was accused of misappropriating soap intended for the inmates. Suttor, in turn, was charged with using the lunatics as labourers on his farm at Baulkham Hills. In January 1819 an inquiry found both men guilty of neglect. James Morisset, the commandant at Newcastle, was frustrated by the lack of medicines at his outpost. Wentworth instructed Redfern to supply them, but his apprentice, Cowper, overlooked the request by carelessness or inadvertence. By June 1819 the governor was compelled to comment on the 'unwarranted inattention' displayed by certain officers in the medical department under Wentworth's direction. In regretting the sad truth that Redfern was the only individual at the Sydney hospital on whom he could rely, Wentworth passed tacit judgement on the rest of the staff for whom he was ultimately accountable. To his credit, he conscientiously investigated the complaints of various convicts about ill-treatment on their voyage from England; he undertook special inquiries into the mortality of convicts in the transport, *General Hewitt*, in 1814, and into the shooting of prisoners in the *Chapman* in 1817; by February 1818 he planned to inoculate all the colony's children against smallpox; he suggested that, on their admission to hospital, patients should be supplied with an entire change of clothing in the interests of cleanliness; and he advocated attaching a salary to the posts of clerk, overseer and matron at the general hospital to attract better people. All too often, however, his initiatives lapsed, mainly because he did not follow them through. His plan for victualling hospital patients exemplified his ways. In March 1817 he proposed to supplement their weekly allowances of fresh meat, unground wheat and sugar by introducing a diet which would include bread, tea, salt, milk and vegetables, according to the needs of each patient. The proposal was approved by the Colonial Office on 3 July 1818. Authorized by Macquarie to implement the change on 1 January 1819, Wentworth did nothing. His successor was to introduce the new system in November that year, within a fortnight of taking office.[9]

Between 1815 and 1819 Wentworth was only slightly more dedicated as superintendent of police than as principal surgeon. Bushrangers roamed the settlement and an alarming number of robberies occurred between Sydney and Parramatta. It was Macquarie, rather than Wentworth, who intervened. On 3 September 1817 he advised the colonists to travel only by day on the road that linked those towns and ordered constables to patrol the route every night. Seven months later, in an effort to improve the efficiency of the police by enlisting suitable men and retaining their services, Wentworth and Judge-Advocate Wylde jointly recommended that constables should be given a reasonable salary. They suggested that district constables be paid £20 per annum and petty constables £10, with an additional allowance of coal, slops and shoes in lieu of the existing ration. Reform was slow. By 1820, when there were fifty-seven policemen in Sydney, district constables received £15 a year and an allowance of one and a half rations weekly; petty constables received no salary, but were allowed one and a half rations as well as a double issue of slops. The listlessness with which Wentworth pressed the interests of the police force contrasted with the vigour he brought to his private concerns, whether as agriculturalist, supplier of the commissariat, retailer, money-lender or litigant. In February 1816 he bought £1235 worth of merchandise from the ship, *Ocean*; that month he donated five guineas for the 'Relief of the Sufferers at the memorable and glorious Battle of Waterloo'. In 1817, the year in which he lodged lawsuits against Daniel Cubitt, Lawrence Butler, Patrick Hogan, Edward Hall and William Broughton, he purchased 874 gallons of spirits for £861; in 1818 he bought a further 5271 gallons for £1701, and sought damages in court against John Laurie, John Horsley and Thomas Gilberthorpe.[10]

7 The greatest burden

Wentworth found a modicum of time for executive-work on the Philanthropic Society (from 1813) and the Native Institution (from 1814), and joined the committee of the Auxiliary Bible Society in March 1817. On the 28th he dined with twenty-eight guests at Government House to celebrate the third birthday of Macquarie's son. He continued to treat young Lachlan, who was a frail child. To relieve spasms in the boy's eyes, on 15 October Wentworth and Redfern blistered the back of his neck and gave him a purgative; sleep and his mother's solicitations countered the doctors' treatment and allowed him to recover. In his Irish home D'Arcy's brother, William, fretted over his 22-year-old son. On 3 May 1816 he asked Wentworth to use his influence to find a situation in the colony for the young man, who had failed in business in Dublin. William related other family news: three of their four sisters were well, two had large families and lived near Portadown, but he feared that their second eldest sister, Dorothy, had died in America, for he had not heard from her for some years. Underlining the point, he reminded D'Arcy that he had received only one letter from him. On 9 September 1817 William's wayward son, Charles, wrote to his uncle D'Arcy from Madras where he was employed as a writer in the mayor's office. Confessing that his father had no knowledge of his whereabouts, he begged Wentworth to help him obtain a passage to New South Wales. He concluded by stating that he would be happy to hear from one of whom 'my father has always spoken in the highest terms'. Wentworth's brother's and nephew's entreaties went unanswered. D'Arcy exhibited little emotional attachment to his wider kin or to the country of his birth.[11]

By 1815 Wentworth had five children of his own—his sons by Catherine Crowley, and a son and daughter by Ann Lawes, aged four and one respectively. Young D'Arcy was stationed with the lst Battalion of the 73rd Regiment at Kandy in Ceylon. Anxious to gain a captaincy, he wrote to his father in August and September, asking him to prompt Cookney to jog Fitzwilliam's memory. D'Arcy had received £200 in prize-money from a bloodless campaign, but the British soldiers had discovered none of the fabled gold belonging to a captured king. Declaring that he would prefer being shut up in gaol to remaining on 'this abominable island', D'Arcy sent his love to Maria Ainslie but made no reference to Ann Lawes. On 30 January 1816 his brother,

John, returned to Sydney. Within two months he was invited to Government House, in the company of his father who was determined that John should settle on the land. Macquarie granted him 700 acres at Bringelly on 18 January 1817. William Wentworth disagreed with the course that D'Arcy intended for John. Appreciating that he was accustomed to the hustle and bustle of the navy, and convinced that he would never cope with 'the seclusion and monotony of country life', William suggested that John should manage their father's mercantile affairs in Sydney. Nothing came of the proposal. D'Arcy refused to delegate the management of his business affairs to anyone, not even the emancipist agents who did his hack work and prided themselves on being his cronies. John remained restless at Bringelly and kept hankering for the sea.[12]

William's own future was far from certain. By June 1815 D'Arcy had decided that his eldest son was unsuited to farming and that his talents equipped him for something more elevated. To further his career, as well as to enable him to throw off the cough that had persisted since the Blue Mountains crossing, D'Arcy decided that William should sail for England. Early in 1816 William leased his land. With Macquarie's assistance he obtained a berth in the colonial brig, *Emu*. In the hope of securing Fitzwilliam's patronage for his son, D'Arcy sent him another pair of swans and offered to forward a collection of insects and seeds, if his lordship wanted them; as a gift for her ladyship, William carried a king parrot that whistled and talked. D'Arcy wanted William to obtain a commission in the Guards or to be appointed vendue master in the colony. William preferred to enter the law and could not understand why D'Arcy was so averse to the pursuit for which his inclination and acquirements had particularly fitted him. None the less, he was prepared to sacrifice his wishes to his father's. When news reached Sydney of the peace that followed Waterloo, D'Arcy changed his mind about William's prospects in the army. He permitted his son to study law, allowing him 250 guineas a year and a further 100 guineas for clothes and other necessities. William sailed from Sydney in late March and arrived in Hobart on 12 April. Although he attended a ball and supper at Government House, and dined at Edward Lord's home, it was the debauchery in the town that struck him most. In May the *Emu* anchored in King George's Sound off the south-western tip of the continent. The crew invited a number of Aborigines on board. Observing

7 The greatest burden

their ferocity and independence, William was moved to remark how little they knew of the nature of society and its obligations, to reflect that man came into the world without innate feelings, and to conclude that conscience was an acquired attribute. After encountering a gale which carried away her topmasts, the ship reached Simon's Bay on 5 August. There, for fourteen hours, she was lashed by a storm: while two Catholics fell to their knees and invoked the intercession of the Virgin Mary, William called on all the fortitude he possessed. The vessel ran aground near Simon's Town. When it was evident that it would take two months to carry out repairs, he travelled overland to Cape Town, intending to take another ship to England. He judged the town to be pretty, but found the people inhospitable and was obliged to pay £1 a day to stay at a boarding-house. In consideration of their father's many kindnesses to him and his brothers, he spent £40 on cloth for gowns for Cookney's daughters. He thought, too, of his family and friends in New South Wales, hoped that the governor and his well-wishers had dished Molle, Bent and their rascally faction, sent remembrances to his brother, John, and to poor Maria Ainslie, and consigned two boxes of raisins and almonds to his father for Christmas. For £36 he obtained a passage in the frigate, *Revolutionaire*. On the ten-week voyage he messed with her gunroom officers before landing at Plymouth on 27 November.[13]

From mid-1815 Dr Joseph Arnold found Macquarie vastly altered, as if a frost had penetrated his being. Edward Robarts discerned a similar iciness that probably stemmed from the governor's sense of persecution. Beleaguered by those who wished to injure his reputation and who crouched to pounce on any fault, Macquarie was goaded into a series of decisions that were both rash and miscalculated. Foremost among his unsettlers was the Reverend Benjamin Vale. On 23 February 1816 Vale seized the American schooner, *Traveller*, at anchor in Port Jackson, and claimed her as a lawful prize under the British Navigation Acts. Backed by the opinion of his solicitor, William Henry Moore, Vale had previously consulted Jeffery Bent about the legality of his action. Vale was arrested, court-martialled, found guilty of subversive conduct and sentenced to be publicly reprimanded; Moore's salary and rations were suspended; and the governor privately accused Bent of inciting rebellion. In the same vein of striking out at troublemakers, Macquarie castigated emancipist farmers for their sloth, withheld allowances from ships' captains who incurred his wrath, deported the meddling Catholic priest, Jeremiah O'Flynn, and sent detachments on punitive expeditions against the Aborigines. By this time he sorely needed a candid friend.[14]

During April 1816 Macquarie decided to enforce an order against trespass in the Government Domain. His intention was to deter people from using the park for improper purposes, and to prevent damage to the shrubs and saplings. Dissatisfied with Wentworth's leniency in merely cautioning those who had ignored the regulation, the governor directed two constables to conceal themselves in the grounds and to arrest anyone, male or female, bond or free, who entered the Domain. At 9 a.m. on 18 April Daniel Read, an ex-convict stonemason, scaled the wall. He was apprehended and placed in gaol. One hour later, while walking near the general hospital, William Blake, a blacksmith who had come to the colony as a free man, was seized with the urge 'to do his business', and, for decency's sake, there being women present, sought privacy in the park. He was arrested and imprisoned. At 7.30 a.m. on the 19th William Henshall, a silversmith whose sentence had expired, was stopped in the Domain by Constable John Wilbow and taken into custody. That morning Daniel Cubitt, the gaoler, reported to Macquarie. The governor issued an order directing the trespassers to receive twenty-five lashes each. Cubitt showed the order to Wentworth who immediately realized the foolhardiness of Macquarie's action and knew that it would play into the hands of his adversaries. Although he felt inclined to suppress the directive, Wentworth did not intervene. That the governor had encroached on his authority troubled him far less than the thought that Macquarie might mistake his interference for reproof. Wentworth stood aside, abrogating his responsibilities as magistrate, superintendent of police and friend.[15]

Cubitt summoned the public hangman, who flogged the three men. Riley described Macquarie's action as 'an unguarded measure, condemned and lamented by his best friends'. The governor's enemies capitalized on the incident. Determined that an account of what had happened should reach England, Bent took separate depositions on the 22nd from Henshall, Read and Blake. In the ensuing weeks Vale and Moore drew up a petition to the House of Commons and presented it to Bent. Considering it 'mimminy pimminy' and 'not half severe enough', he rewrote the document. The memorial raised a number of grievances, some of them exaggerated, but the sensational issue of the summary floggings formed its centre-piece. Those who believed in the principle that a British subject should not be punished without charge or trial were invited to sign the petition at Moore's house, as was anyone who harboured a grudge against the governor. Vale left Sydney for London in June, taking the memorial with him. Macquarie damned Moore for laying malicious charges against him and for forging signatures to the petition; of those who had legitimately signed the document, he dismissed George Williams from his post with the *Sydney Gazette*, and withheld land grants from Samuel Terry, Gustavus Low and Moore's brother, Thomas. Wentworth followed suit. He refused to license three publicans—Rose, Thompson and Armytage—because they had signed the petition. To Wentworth, it was not a question of rights but of obligations: whereas Macquarie had pardoned Rose and given him land, Rose had responded with base ingratitude. Wentworth allowed his partisanship to blur his judgement.[16]

Attempting to unite the inhabitants in a common cause, Macquarie called a meeting of magistrates, merchants and gentlemen to be held at Judge-Advocate Wylde's chambers on 22 November 1816. Wentworth and Molle were two of the fourteen who attended. Reflecting the divisions among them, they began by discussing the state of the currency, the local medium of exchange which was discounted against sterling. The words 'currency' and 'sterling' were beginning to take on wider connotations, the former being applied to the native-born and the latter to the free immigrants. Those present at the meeting agreed on the desirability of establishing the immediate circulation of sterling alone. In an attempt to overcome a drastic shortage of notes and coins, they resolved to adopt Macquarie's proposal to establish a colonial bank which would be incorporated as a joint-stock company. On 5 December forty-six individuals took shares in the Bank of New South Wales; Wentworth bought six at £50 each and his son, John, purchased two. Edward Eagar bought ten shares, anticipating that, with Macquarie's backing, he would be appointed a director. Within a fortnight a committee of fifteen was elected to formulate regulations for the institution. While most committee-members had no objection to conditionally pardoned convicts being shareholders, only a minority—including Wentworth and Redfern—supported the proposition that they should be eligible to stand for the board. Under the terms of Article

7 of the bank's charter anyone who was not absolutely and unconditionally free was excluded from serving as a director. Seven founding directors were then elected by ballot—Wentworth, Harris, Robert Jenkins, Thomas Wylde, Riley, Redfern and the chairman, J. T. Campbell. Plainly ruffled, the governor accepted the majority decision and later granted Eagar an absolute pardon as compensation for his disappointment. Macquarie palpably hurt the exclusives by announcing Bent's recall on 11 December 1816, but, when he held a dinner and ball on 18 January 1817 at Government House to celebrate the anniversary of Queen Charlotte's birth, 40 of the 155 invited guests declined to attend. The rifts in society were entrenched.[17]

Twelve thousand miles away, British parliamentary interest in New South Wales developed slowly. From 1810 colonial topics, when they did not empty the House of Commons, formed the stuff of intermittent debates. In 1816, with the temper of the country unfriendly to the ministry, the Whigs received welcome ammunition to assail the government on a subject far from the political forefront. The issue brought together diverse elements critical of the administration, among them theoretical Benthamites, radical Tories, humanitarians, economists and country back-benchers ever alert for means of reducing taxes. On 5 April Henry Grey Bennet led the debate on the offenders' transportation bill. Armed by Macquarie's traducers, he had a perfect stick with which to beat the ministry. Some of his criticism was formidably specialist, organized and effective; much was fanatical and inaccurate, biased and out of date; all was potentially destructive. The impact of his argument was felt and remembered, especially when he pointed to the costs of the prison-settlements and contended that, despite the exorbitant financial outlay, transportation had failed to punish, deter or reform. Bennet's view was largely shared by senior civil servants in the Home Office and the Treasury who were determined, in a postwar aftermath of economic and social dislocation, to give effect to the government's policies of repression and retrenchment. They hounded their colleagues in the Colonial Office with allegations of Macquarie's leniency and extravagance. From 1816 to 1821 Britain sent 13 103 convicts to New South Wales and 2993 to Van Diemen's Land; the number who landed in Sydney averaged 2184 annually, three times as many as in the years from 1810 to 1815. British expenditure on the penal colonies amounted to £1 842 000 in 1816–21, 53 per cent more than in 1810–15. As the cost mounted, the momentum of protest quickened, embarrassing Lord Bathurst and shaking his confidence in Macquarie.[18]

Having landed at Plymouth, William Wentworth made his way to London and to a reassuring fringe of political influence. He began on familiar ground. The Cookneys welcomed him and he stayed with them at Castle Street for more than two months. From this base he wrote to Fitzwilliam on 18 December 1816. Professing to have given mature consideration to his future, William asked for guidance as to the vocation he should follow, specifically, whether he should enter the Bar or the Church. He enclosed a letter from his father to Fitzwilliam, and awaited her ladyship's directions in regard to the parrot he had brought from New South Wales. Fitzwilliam replied on Christmas Day, tersely informing William that 'the bent of your own mind, & the acquirements you have already made, must lead to your decision . . . but that determination must be your own'. In offering no advice, Fitzwilliam gave sage counsel. William should do what he thought best. Twenty-one days later, on 15 January 1817, William wrote again to Fitzwilliam to tell him that he had resolved to study law:

> It is, my Lord, by no means my intention . . . to abandon the Country that gave me birth. I am sensible of the sacred claims which it has upon me—claims which in its present despised state and indigent situation I should blush ever to be supposed capable of neglecting. In withdrawing myself, therefore, for a time from that country I am actuated by a desire of better qualifying myself for the performance of those duties, that my birth has imposed.

By acquainting himself 'with all the excellence of the British Constitution', he trusted 'at some future period, to advocate successfully the right of my country to a participation in its advantages'. He entertained, as he put it, the proud hope that, by the excellence of his services in the law, he would be considered not unworthy of the name of Fitzwilliam.[19]

Aged twenty-six, the native son had begun to conceive of his destiny on a grand scale and to embrace an undertaking that matched his ambition. His letter, however, showed that he wanted some time to be footloose and that he was prepared to stoop to matters of pelf. With no university degree, he knew that he had to be enrolled at one of the Inns of Court for five years and to spend at least twelve terms to qualify as a barrister. By his reckoning, that left more than a year to fill. He was tempted to take his doctors' advice and make a return voyage to Sydney. On the other hand, if he remained in London, his father would have to pay even more for his upkeep. In a veiled appeal for Fitzwilliam's assistance, he disingenuously maintained that, to support him, D'Arcy would subject himself to privations when his advanced years entitled him to comfort. There was an alternative. He sent Fitzwilliam the draft of a letter he planned to forward to Lord Bathurst. It was an application for the post of vendue master in the colony. William was confident that, were he to obtain the office, Macquarie would appoint a deputy to do the work (he had in mind his brother, John), allowing him leave of absence and a share of the commissions. Taken by the young man's frankness and touched by his aspirations, Fitzwilliam commended his choice of profession; he saw nothing in the submission to Bathurst but what was proper, and invited Wentworth to call on him at his home in the city.[20]

So bidden, he went. Fitzwilliam, who was not a man for words, received him graciously on two occasions and indicated his willingness to serve his needs, in moderation. William gave him a specimen of iron ore from Van Diemen's Land and a colonial almanac; he subsequently advised D'Arcy to send some Cape Barren geese and to continue, by such little attentions, to retain his lordship's favour. While pacing up and down the polished floors, or walking along the galleries lined with portraits of his own and other people's ancestors, or sitting on the satin-covered chairs, or exchanging pleasantries under the candelabra, William seemed to have gained limited entrée to a sphere of privilege. On 5 February 1817 he paid £33 8s to enrol at the Middle Temple; the past cast its shadow when he stated that he was the son of D'Arcy Wentworth, Esquire, of New South Wales. He had decided against going to Christ Church or Oriel College because, as he told his father, he already regarded himself as a better classical scholar than nine out of ten graduates. Furthermore, he lacked the means to mix with the nobility at Oxford and would therefore be treated as one of the vulgars—and that was a fate he did not propose to endure. By frequently calling on the Macarthurs, the very family he had previously lampooned, William set about achieving another scheme for his own aggrandisement.

7 The greatest burden

Macarthur received him kindly, as did his 22-year-old son, John, who had studied at Cambridge and would soon be admitted to the Bar. Their meetings rekindled William's hope—which he had long and secretly cherished—of marrying Macarthur's eldest surviving daughter, Elizabeth. In broaching the subject to D'Arcy, William envisaged a dynastic alliance that would contribute to 'the future respectability and grandeur of our family'. Macarthur was by no means as favourably disposed to the union as the ardent suitor imagined. Elizabeth's and William's fathers had only suspended their personal acrimony in mutual opposition to Bligh. The proposed match was so imprudent as to be folly.[21]

Cookney, as practical as ever, realized that, although William was not extravagant, he would find it difficult to live on his allowance and would have insufficient money to pay his fees, furnish his chambers and buy his books. D'Arcy was still in debt to Fitzwilliam, to the sum of £244. William took rooms at No. 22, The Terrace, Pimlico, opposite a riding-school, the sight of which prompted him to ask his father for an additional £50 a year to keep a horse. He began to roister by night with his fellow students, to read Byron's poetry and to attend chapel on Sundays at the Middle Temple. As winter gave way to spring, he remained characteristically restless. His father had sent him a copy of the Vale–Moore petition and detailed the intrigues of those who produced it. On Saturday 8 March Bennet gave notice in *The Times* of his intention to table the petition in the Commons. Bennet had inspected Newgate prison where he saw 9-year-olds confined with incorrigible lags, observed women stupefying themselves to be rid of all reflection, and heard the desperation of those who cried at the gratings as they begged with spoons tied to the ends of poles. The experience stung him to wage a crusade against the penal system in general and transportation in particular. William wrote to Bennet on the 10th, offering to refute many of the allegations in the petition which had led to calumnies being levelled against Macquarie. That night, before reading Wentworth's letter, Bennet spoke in the House. He complained of the colony's unjust laws and the governor's oppression. Wentworth sat in the visitors' gallery and heard it all. Next day he received an invitation to visit Bennet. The two men had a long conversation. Detained by the civility of Mr Bennet, whose inquiries were most minute, Wentworth told him that those who had signed the petition were, in the main, 'publicans and shopkeepers of the convict description' who lived by preying on the vitals of the settlers. While he was unable to refute a number of charges stemming from events that had occurred after he left the colony, he gave his opinions decidedly and felt confident that he had convinced Bennet of the probity of Macquarie's character. The governor had warm friends in Castlereagh and the Duke of York, and there was no whisper of his removal. Moreover, given the postwar depression, with its drastic reduction in public expenditure, catastrophic falls in demand, and galloping unemployment, politicians were disposed to put everything of minor importance to one side, or so Wentworth thought. Behind the scenes Lord Bathurst was moved to action. On 23 April he wrote to Viscount Sidmouth, secretary of state at the Home Office, suggesting that a commission of inquiry should be held into the administration of New South Wales. A fortnight earlier Macarthur had sailed for the colony. Wentworth, whose application for the post of vendue master had been turned down, proffered his services to explore the fifth continent from its eastern extremity to its western—in return for an appropriate grant of land; on the 24th Bathurst politely declined the proposal. William then decided to journey abroad, as John Macarthur junior had done, and to stay in France and Switzerland for the remainder of the year. He said that he wanted to study his law books, to acquire greater proficiency in French and other fashionable accomplishments so requisite to a successful career, to gain relief from the pains in his chest, and to live more frugally. Before he sailed he lent £20 to William Bucknell, his cousin Martha's husband; William had been twice bankrupted and Martha was expecting their fourth child. On the 28th, the day Wentworth left London, he sent gifts to his father and brother, John. It was to Paris he travelled, on pleasure bent.[22]

Back in Sydney, William's family and friends were involved in a row for which he was responsible. Before leaving for England he had passed his idle hours by composing a number of pipes, replete with allusions to Horace, Milton and Pope. One of them ridiculed Riley, another lampooned the officers of the 46th Regiment and a third gibbeted Molle. William left the poems in the keeping of his brother, John, and their accomplice, young George Johnston. In order to conceal the authorship, John and George agreed to distribute the verses long after William had left the colony. William knew that Molle had slighted

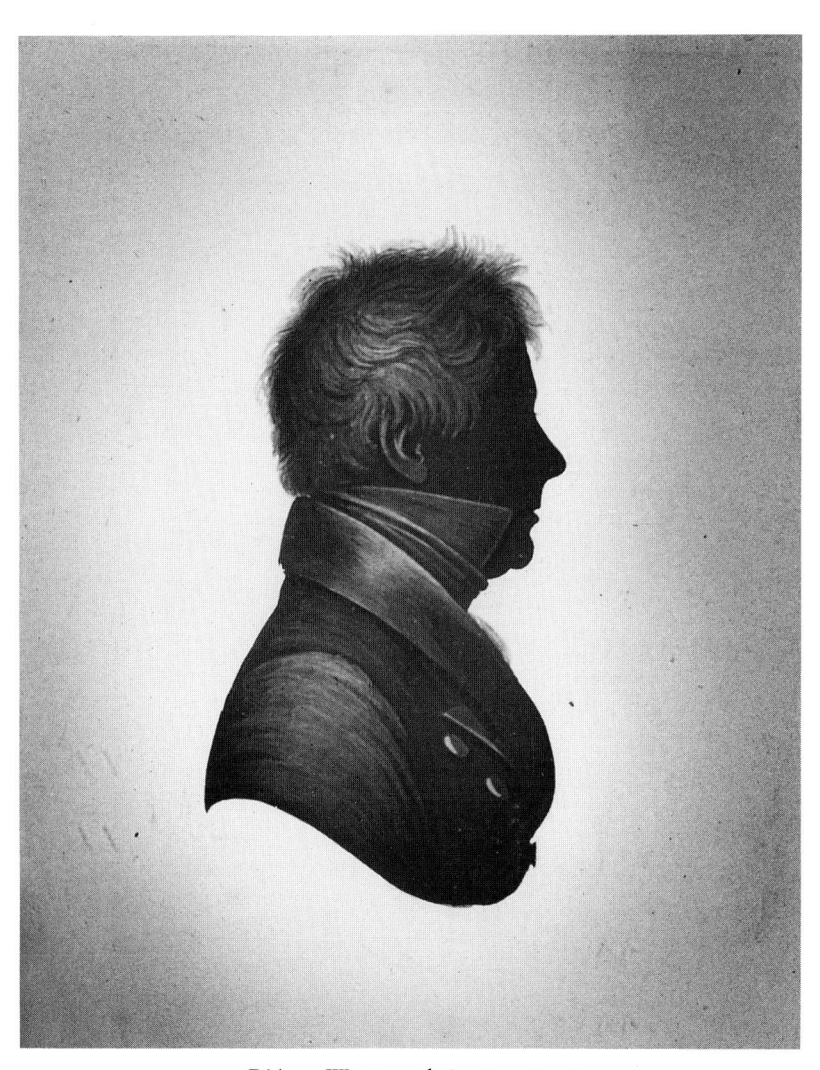

D'Arcy Wentworth (1762–1827)

William Charles Wentworth (1790–1872)

Sarah Wentworth, née Cox (1805–80)

D'ARCY WENTWORTH'S FAMILY

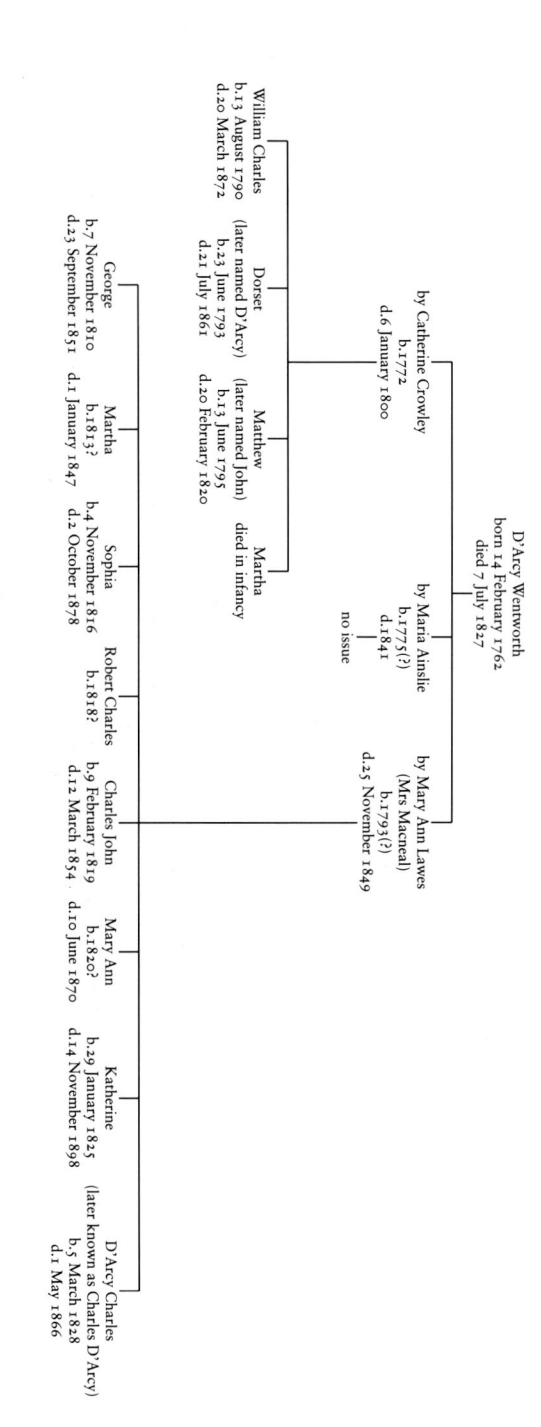

D'Arcy Wentworth
born 14 February 1762
died 7 July 1827

by Catherine Crowley
b.1772
d.6 January 1800

- William Charles
  b.13 August 1790
  d.20 March 1872
- Dorset (later named D'Arcy)
  b.23 June 1793
  d.21 July 1861
- Matthew (later named John)
  b.13 June 1795
  d.20 February 1820
- Martha died in infancy

by Maria Ainslie
b.1775(?)
d.1841
no issue

by Mary Ann Lawes (Mrs Macneal)
b.1793(?)
d.25 November 1849

- George
  b.7 November 1810
  d.23 September 1851
- Martha
  b.1813?
  d.1 January 1847
- Sophia
  b.4 November 1816
  d.2 October 1878
- Robert Charles
  b.1818?
- Charles John
  b.9 February 1819
  d.12 March 1854
- Mary Ann
  b.1820?
  d.10 June 1870
- Katherine
  b.29 January 1825
  d.14 November 1898
- D'Arcy Charles (later known as Charles D'Arcy)
  b.5 March 1828
  d.1 May 1866

7 The greatest burden

D'Arcy. Seeing himself as his father's avenger, he used the pipes as a means of reversing the indignity. His satire targeting Molle was vicious, wily, clever, and very funny. The pipe-maker tilted at Molle's haughtiness and bravado, as well as at his *bons mots* and style of dancing; the lieutenant-governor was depicted as Macquarie's secret foe, the insidious spring propelling the 46th Regiment to oppose the governor; the work ended with a damnation:

> Of all the mongrels, that to wit lay claim,
> The basest bred, that e'er prophan'd the name!
> And now farewell thou dirty, grov'ling M-ll-
> Go with thy namesake burrow in thy hole.

Molle was affronted. As he sought to unmask his traducer, his agitation excited public curiosity and copies multiplied to meet the demand. The officers of the 46th raised £200 as a reward for information about the pipe; Macquarie offered to pardon any convict who could help in revealing its origins. In spite of the inducements, the author's identity remained a mystery and Molle's anger turned to rage. Following prolonged inquiries, suspicion finally fell on Robert Lathrop Murray, D'Arcy Wentworth's clerk. Wylde directed him to appear before a bench of magistrates on 11 June 1817 to answer a complaint lodged by Molle and his ally, Riley. Wentworth was subpoenaed to give evidence. D'Arcy knew William all too well, detected his hand in the verse and called him to account. William admitted his part in the business. Although he professed sorrow for quitting the colony without confiding in his father, he remained unrepentant about the pipe. At the hearing D'Arcy made his knowledge public, avowing that he had ascertained the fact after the event. Molle grasped his hand and thanked him, but the officers of the 46th seized the opportunity to vindicate their stand against Macquarie's emancipist policy. They pronounced that the libels came 'from the Pen of Men so much Our Inferiors in Rank and Situation, that We know them not but among that promiscuous Class, which (with Pride we Speak it) have been ever excluded from intercourse with us'. Goaded by Captain Edward Sanderson, within a fortnight Molle made it clear that he would prosecute Dr Wentworth for gross disrespect and contempt in aiding and abetting the writing and publishing of scurrilous libels. For weeks nothing happened.

The Wentworths

Wentworth deliberately brought things to a head on 6 September by writing a letter that insulted Molle. Three days later Molle placed him under close arrest. On the 15th he was brought before a court martial. What ensued was an anticlimax. Wylde announced that Wentworth, as a civil officer, was not subject to military jurisdiction. The court dissolved. Lieutenant-Colonel James Erskine's 48th Regiment replaced the 46th and Molle boarded the *Matilda* on 20 September, bound for India. Next day Macquarie congratulated Wentworth on a complete victory over his vindictive enemy. Worried that the whole affair might be canvassed in England, Wentworth wrote to Fitzwilliam, requesting that his side of the story be made known to Lord Bathurst.[23]

Throughout 1817 Macquarie received a number of dispatches from the Colonial Office which disparaged his conduct; one of them deprecated his actions in penalizing those who had signed the Vale-Moore petition and another reinstated Moore. Instead of anticipating reproval, the governor had expected Bathurst to send him a list of Vale's and Moore's co-signatories so that he might prosecute them in New South Wales for criminal libel. Towards the end of the year Macquarie concluded that his opponents had succeeded in prejudicing the minds of His Majesty's ministers against him. On 1 December he sent a confidential letter to the secretary of state in which he formally tendered his resignation. He took exception to Bathurst's reprimands and wrote at length of the evil-minded men who had destroyed his lordship's confidence in him. To this letter he appended the names of twelve settlers whom he labelled as 'discontented', 'intriguing' or 'vindictive'. Samuel Marsden headed the list. Incensed with the clergyman for funnelling every scrap of nasty rumour, Macquarie summoned him to Government House on 8 January 1818 and, in the presence of three witnesses, accused him of treachery and of heading a seditious, low cabal. Marsden was infuriated rather than humbled. He continued his campaign to discredit the governor by attacking Wentworth. In February he wrote to William Wilberforce, trying to raise a fuss over the state of the hospital at Parramatta. He alleged that the building lacked a room in which to place the dead and that, before their burial, corpses lay side by side with live patients; he asserted that the institution was a place of want and wretchedness where the sick lacked such necessities as rice, sugar and tea; and he condemned the vice and debauchery which had turned the hospital into 'an infamous brothel'.

7 The greatest burden

The inference was obvious: Wentworth had failed in his responsibilities as principal surgeon. On 28 March the *Sydney Gazette* carried a report of the parson's dismissal from the magistracy.[24]

Pressure intensified for a royal commission into what went on in New South Wales. Benjamin Vale wrote to Bathurst on 16 April 1818 censuring Macquarie's emancipist policy: 'The general plan pursued under the present government is not to raise the convict to the rank of the free settler but to degrade the free settler to the rank of a convict'. He also maintained that Wentworth was duplicitous, both in the amount of spirits he distributed to the prisoners and in acquitting felons who had committed nefarious crimes. Jeffery Bent added his salvo by informing Bathurst that Macquarie had appointed a notorious highwayman and a convicted criminal to the Supreme Court. Although Bent did not name Wentworth and Lord, Bathurst knew the identity of those to whom he alluded. On 5 June, in presenting the report of the select committee on police, Bennet told members of the House of Commons that transportation was ineffectual in preventing crime and that the system needed to be changed immediately. In the same month the Marquis of Lansdowne drew attention in the House of Lords to evidence that the number of crimes committed in Britain had trebled since 1808; only one in eight of those convicted of capital offences was executed, the situation of convicts in the penal settlements (formerly akin to slavery) had softened and transportation was no longer regarded with dread. By 1818 New South Wales provided staple fare for politicians who clamoured for investigations into the state of the gaols, the criminal laws, and the transport vessels. The antipodean outpost gave rise to books and pamphlets, and later to their reviewers' barbs. In its explosive propensity, Botany Bay furnished lobbyists with a cause, whether they defended Marsden, Bent, Vale or the Domain trespassers. Henry, the third Earl Bathurst, rode the wake of these protests. Those who judged Bathurst by the shell alone saw him as an old, stumped-up Tory, the last man in England to wear a pig-tail, a sceptic averse to Benthamite verve, a trifler, unambitious and unattractive. In fact there was far more to him. His appearance and manner disguised a serious, astute and tolerant mind. Graced with command of temper and insight into human nature, he considered himself the guardian of his appointees' reputations and defended them vigilantly. At the same time he knew that no governor was beyond reproach. Bathurst's reliable deputy, Henry

The Wentworths

Goulburn, retained a conservative mould that made him as wary of colonial ballyhoo as of democracy. Bearing a similar stamp, Bathurst and Goulburn discounted many complaints from Sydney as cavil and paid little heed to conspirators who purported to be spokesmen for the aggrieved. Yet they were unable to ignore representations from government departments and members of parliament: this constituted disapproval of a different dimension. A commission of inquiry would help them to evaluate the *raison d'être* of New South Wales and ultimately to decide whether it should be a gaol or a colony.[25]

D'Arcy turned fifty-six in 1818. All too suddenly, it seemed, the colonists began to refer to him as 'old Doctor Wentworth'. For more than twelve months he had planned to retire to Home Bush and live there with Ann Lawes. Their union had lasted eight years and she had borne four of his children, all of whom were given his surname. Unlike Catherine Crowley and Ann Lawes, who were seventeen when D'Arcy began his liaisons with them, Maria Ainslie was twenty-nine when she accompanied Wentworth to Norfolk Island in 1804. By 1818 she was forty-three. He had in mind to move her from Home Bush to a cottage he owned in Sydney. His son, John, took offence at the proposal, refused to speak to Ann and swore that he would not remain under the same roof as she. Father and son fell out. John sought counsel from his eldest brother, William, who replied in a private letter on 26 May. While he sympathized with John's intention to leave if D'Arcy installed Ann at Home Bush, he thought that their father would pause and reflect before taking such a step. Whereas William showed affection for Maria, he regarded 25-year-old Ann as an opportunist, 'who for the single sake of ameliorating her condition . . . has abandoned her child, her husband . . . burst asunder alike the ties of nature as of Society and stigmatised herself by the violation of every duty'. He described his father as being 'long past the prime of life when he could have been expected to inspire Love', and trusted that he would have his eyes opened 'to the folly & disgrace of his conduct . . . In any other person I should reprobate such a miserable infatuation—in him I can only pity and forgive it. How lamentable that a man otherwise possessed of the finest feelings & the most comprehensive judgement should be insensible alike of the Censure of the World and the Duplicity of the Siren who charms him'. William hoped that the recent attacks on D'Arcy's name would 'convince him of his error, and suggest to him, before it is too late, the bitter anguish that will sadden his last moments . . . surrounded by a Set of Harpies, impatiently waiting for his last sigh to Seize and Pillage the fruits of a life of Industry & Exertion'. He exhorted John not to abandon D'Arcy.

> Now that his health is evidently on the decline, return the cares and trouble he bestowed on us . . . do not incur the remorse of having failed in the discharge of your duties towards him . . . After all he has been in every other respect a good and indulgent father; forget therefore his weaknesses; be the stay of his declining years and repay him . . . for all the kindness and solicitude he has ever manifested for our common welfare.

Children are merciless in their reproach. Although William's words evinced a measure of compassion, he and his brother overlooked the stability of the relationship between D'Arcy and Ann, as well as the ties that united them. Less experienced in the complexities of life, and blind to any standards but their own, William and John could not understand their father's sexual drives. In was not that Ann had enchanted, enamoured or enslaved D'Arcy; she served his needs, and did so contentedly and unquestioningly. With a determination that matched his sensuality, old Dr Wentworth took Ann to Home Bush and sent Maria to Sydney. At the age of twenty-three John quit his father's house and again went to sea.[26]

That D'Arcy Wentworth wanted to set his domestic affairs in order was indicative of something more. His health had been declining for some time and worsened in 1818. Sickness brought with it intimations of his own mortality. On 5 May he wrote a letter to Macquarie, enclosing a memorial to Bathurst in which he tendered his resignation as principal surgeon and superintendent of police. Wentworth referred to his advancing age and his increasing infirmity, attributing the latter to the dedication with which he had carried out his duties. After twenty-eight years service he wished 'to pass the remainder of his Days in the bosom of his Family'. He therefore sought Bathurst's permission to retire from public life, on half-pay or with an appropriate pension. To strengthen his case, he informed Bathurst that more than £100 000 had passed through his hands as treasurer of the police fund; he had held that office for eight years without receiving one penny in remuneration. In forwarding the memorial, Macquarie praised Wentworth for his zeal, vigilance and integrity, and for the honourable, just and humane manner with which he had executed his responsibilities. Wentworth also secured Fitzwilliam's support. Despite this patronage, Bathurst told Fitzwilliam in December that he would not have hesitated to grant Wentworth an allowance except for the fact that the Colonial Office had received a number of complaints to which the memorialist needed to respond. The governor recommended that Redfern should succeed Wentworth as principal surgeon. When James Bowman received the post, William Wentworth felt that the ministry had surrendered to the illiberal hue and cry raised in England against Macquarie for appointing emancipists to offices of trust and dignity.[27]

Meanwhile, in the spring of 1817 William Wentworth had taken a residence in Paris. Although he initially intended to venture to Switzerland and thence to Italy, he stayed in the capital for fifteen months. Influenced by the ideology, temper and frame of mind of the Regency, with its pace, levity and indulgence, its conspicuous consumption, restlessness and rapidity of change, he was also touched by the Romanticism that inspired the work of Byron, Scott, Cruikshank, Nash and Turner. Byron's poem, *The Corsair*, about a pirate who forced the world into the shape he willed, fired William's fantasies and filled his soul as wind in a sail. For a brief period he saw himself as a Byronic hero, standing above and outside conventional morality. Indulging in a life of gaiety and excess, he spent more money than was wise. In August Cookney advanced him £100. Stricken with rheumatic gout through the winter of 1817–18, William was compelled by his doctors' fees to borrow more. By March 1818 he was £225 in debt. Like *Childe Harold*, he grew sated and disillusioned with pleasure-seeking. The disease may have been a blessing in disguise for it confined him indoors. Early in 1818 he adopted an idea previously suggested by John Macarthur junior and began to write a pamphlet on New South Wales. He spent three hours each day reading law and devoted most of his remaining time to examining the past and present state of the colony. This study, and the discipline and effort it entailed, buttressed his belief in the Whig tradition, in British political institutions and in the value the Augustans placed on duty, integrity and responsibility. As his pamphlet developed into a book, the tension between his romantic nature and the classical restraints of law and politics found an outlet.

7 The greatest burden

His motives in writing the treatise were both pure and base. He saw himself as an instrument for securing a free constitution for his country; he also thirsted for revenge against Bligh who would 'curse the hour' that he wantonly made an enemy of D'Arcy.[28]

By mid-1818 William was desperately short of funds. When his creditors dunned him, he appealed to Fitzwilliam, expecting a happy outcome. The outcome was anything but happy. Fitzwilliam, who had opposed the Paris venture from the start, refused to lend him money. Wentworth then asked John Macarthur junior to remit a promissory note for £250 to Paris. The result was 'an unpleasant correspondence', copies of which were sent to their respective fathers. By hook or by crook Wentworth made his way to England early in August 1818. Convinced that Paris was 'a vile hole compared with London', he took a room in the Hungerford Coffee House. He collected a letter which came from Sydney and bore the handwriting of old John Macarthur. He opened it immediately. It informed him, in hurtful terms, that he could not marry his daughter, Elizabeth. In that instant Wentworth determined to 'pay him off in his own coin' and to damn young John Macarthur as 'a complete chip off the old block'. Wentworth's good opinion, once lost, was lost forever. In a moment of wounded pride, he resolved to marry another lady of whom he had written:

> Why Jane, oh why, thou glory of thy kind
> Supreme in loveliness, and grace, and mind,
> Why was I doomed to see thee peerless shine,
> To know thee faultless, yet not call thee mine? . . .
> Those easy manners, that pure native vein,
> Flow of mind, which others ne'er attain;
> That sportive wit, that revels unconfined,
> Delights, reproves, yet leaves no sting behind . . .
> Relentless charmer, I must love thee still.

After vowing that he would not rest happy until he had made her altogether his, he then decided against this precipitate action. Alexander Riley was another to whom he turned for money, even though Riley had parted from D'Arcy on unfriendly terms, not least because of William's pipe deriding him as 'Cacomanus'. On 25 August William apologized to Riley for writing the pipe. It had originally been his intention to satirize Marsden; that Riley's name replaced the clergyman's was due, he said, to chance rather than design. Whatever sympathy Riley might have had for the young man was dissipated when William swore that he would never alter his opinion of Molle, whom he was prepared to challenge to a duel. The experience of successively begging from Fitzwilliam, Macarthur and Riley was humiliating and caused William to admonish his father: 'I hope you will in future take care that I need not the assistance of any man'. Cookney finally helped him. He paid £100 for Wentworth's fees at the Middle Temple where he began his course in the Michaelmas term. William took chambers in Elm Court at £30 per annum; the price for the fixtures and furnishings was two hundred guineas. On top of this sum, he asked his father for £500 to obtain a good library. Each morning and night he worked for two hours on his book, and filled the interval by reading law and attending the courts. While Wentworth kept his first term, Bathurst chose John Thomas Bigge, a barrister-at-law of the Inner Temple, to conduct the commission of inquiry into the penal colonies of New South Wales and Van Diemen's Land.[29]

8

What one is

One's past is what one is

Oscar Wilde, *An Ideal Husband*

Almost eight months elapsed between September 1818 when Bigge was selected as commissioner and 30 April 1819 when he left England for New South Wales. In the interim he received the Colonial Office's briefings and a clear indication of the trend of parliamentary thought on the antipodean prisons. Early in the new year Bennet stridently attacked Macquarie's administration in a *Letter to Viscount Sidmouth*. Drawing on information provided by Marsden and Bent, Bennet pressed the case for establishing a legislative council to restrain the governor from exercising arbitrary power. In his 138-page pamphlet he accused Macquarie of engaging in a wicked experiment to build a general hospital by exploiting the colonists' avidity for spirits; he argued that it would have been better to provide accommodation for the female convicts at Parramatta than a palace in Sydney for the principal surgeon; and, in debunking the governor's emancipist policy, he cited the example of D'Arcy Wentworth and alleged that, although this individual had been transported for highway robbery, he had been elevated to the magistracy and appointed superintendent of police. No man, he submitted, was fit to sit on the bench if he could be openly reproached for having committed a criminal offence. Wounded by the public revelation that his father had been a convict, William was meteoric in his response. His initial impulse was to avenge his father by ensuring that the author of the infamous calumny should pay for it with his blood. Calmer counsel persuaded him to speak with Bennet instead of challenging him to a duel. So, one bitter day in February 1819, Wentworth was admitted to Bennet's study where he berated him with a torrent of words. Bennet responded with an awkwardness of manner, symptomatic of his forbearance and his nervousness. Startled by the uncouth talk of being forced to wash away the foul stain with his blood, Bennet 'changed colour, and showed other signs of agitation'. When at last he was allowed to speak, he offered to atone for any libel he might have published, but said that he based his account of D'Arcy's conviction on information he had received about his appearance at the Old Bailey. This final disclosure made William realize how little he knew of his father's past.[1]

The two men parted to check their respective sources. Through a communication with Lord Fitzwilliam, Bennet found that he was in error in assuming that Wentworth had been convicted. From Cookney, William learned that D'Arcy had indeed been arraigned at the bar of justice on a criminal charge. Given William's craving for fame and fortune, and his self-confidence and éclat, the discovery was at once cathartic and a defining moment. He had to come to terms with what he was, with the stigma on his family name, and with the innuendoes about his father that circulated in New South Wales. Although shocked, bewildered and disillusioned, he responded as his father's son and directed his anger at D'Arcy's detractors: they would be punished for his humiliation and pain. First he wrote to Bennet, acknowledging the truth of the allegation that D'Arcy had faced a charge of highway robbery; but, he added, his father had been acquitted, and no one had the right to draw any other conclusion than that he was innocent of the crime imputed to him. He concluded his letter with his own interpretation of why D'Arcy had gone to Norfolk Island:

> Descended from a long unsullied race of illustrious progenitors He felt that the Glory of his Ancestry was in some degree tarnished by the mere imputation that had been cast on his Character and He sought by a voluntary exile to a far distant clime to efface for ever the recollection of an unjust accusation—Vain Hope!

Bennet acknowledged William's letter and thanked him for the 'fresh and becoming manner' with which he had communicated the results of his investigation. In a gust of passion William informed his father that 'you have to thank that dark villain Samuel Marsden (Heaven requite him one day or other according to his deserts) for this most unpleasant occurrence'. As for Bennet, he would compel that 'prying slanderer'—who was too intimately connected with Methodists and missionaries—to make 'the most public and ample reparation'. This Mr Bennet undertook to do. On 18 February, while William sat in the visitors' gallery, Bennet introduced a motion in the House of Commons for the appointment of a committee to inquire into the management of the hulks, the transportation system and the government of New South Wales. He used this opportunity to tell his fellow members that the gentleman he had mentioned in his pamphlet was not a convict, and that he had conducted himself with the utmost propriety throughout his residence in the colony. Castlereagh acknowledged Bennet's admission and warned him to be more circumspect. Bennet stopped the sale of the first edition of his pamphlet, and, in the second edition, included an apology for and a correction of the libel contained in the first. There, for Bennet, the matter ended, but not for Wentworth. Knowledge of his father's past forced him to shelve his embryonic plan to lead the free settlers in a movement for self-government, but it so galvanized his ambition that he confided to D'Arcy: 'I will not suffer myself to be outstripped by any competitor and I will finally create for myself a reputation which shall reflect a splendour on all who are related to me'.

He also confided his views on other matters. His father's pension was delayed, due no doubt to charges brought against him by Molle; D'Arcy would be well advised to rely on Macquarie's generosity rather than that of the Colonial Office. William was pained that Redfern was not to succeed D'Arcy as principal surgeon, especially since he had set his heart on so doing. Young D'Arcy was ill and despondent; having again missed out on a company, he was thinking of resigning from the army unless his father gave him the means to purchase a captaincy. And, as for himself, William maintained that he existed by constant self-denial. He was spending, each year, £40 on rent, 12 guineas on a laundress, £20 on washing, £10 on firewood and candles, and £50 ('most moderate') on clothing. He asked that his allowance be increased by £100 per annum, backdated to 1 January 1818, and 'For God's sake do not neglect sending me money for the purchase of a library'.[2]

As winter gave way to spring, William's health was never better. He took an active interest in the proceedings of the select committee of the House of Commons which, on 22 March 1819, began its investigations into the state of the gaols. Because its members included Bennet and 'that old woman Wilberforce', he kept a vigilant eye for any sullying of his father's reputation. Bennet subjected Bigge, whom Wentworth then regarded as 'a very clever man', to a series of 'dominating' visits and ensured that he received copies of the evidence taken by the gaols committee, particularly when it turned its attention to New South Wales. The committee examined nine witnesses about conditions in the penal colony, among them Riley (who made eight appearances), Bent and John Macarthur junior. Wentworth was not called to give evidence, though he had expected to be asked. The committee's report was tabled later in the year. It made no reference to Dr Wentworth. Nor was there anything about him in the evidence that could be construed as derogatory, though some witnesses had cast aspersions on the state of the colony's hospitals. None the less, the appendix to the published report contained two letters which Bent had sent from Sydney to Lord Bathurst. Together, they contained damning indictments of D'Arcy's character and professionalism.

The first letter referred to the degraded circumstances under which D'Arcy had left England; the second accused him of neglecting his medical duties and of being an unsuitable person to head the police force because of his ignorance of the law and his trading interests in spirits. Once more William flew to D'Arcy's defence, shouting that he would either wipe out the stain with Bent's blood or shed the last drop of his own in the effort. It was his intention, he told D'Arcy, to chastise the cowardly assassin, thereby demonstrating that he had a proper feeling of the duty that a child owed to an affectionate father. By this stage William had acquired a name as a hothead. Prevailed on to adopt a moderate course, he sent Lord Bathurst a letter which gave Bent 'a complete trimming' for his malicious attack, and he asked that this letter be included in any future report of the gaols committee. Goulburn replied that it would be indecorous for the committee to receive such a submission, relying as it did on defiant invective. At Goulburn's request, he then wrote a more temperate refutation of Bent's allegations.[3]

On 4 May 1819 Messrs G. and W. B. Whittaker of Ave-Maria Lane, London, published a *Statistical, Historical, and Political Description of The Colony of New South Wales, and Its dependent Settlements in Van Diemen's Land*. Its author styled himself 'W. C.

Wentworth, Esq., a native of the colony'. The book had 466 pages; the text ran to some 100 000 words. After describing the physical, social, political and economic state of the penal settlements, Wentworth put forward proposals for reform. His argument was straightforward: whether administered by a 'monster' like Bligh, or by the 'humane and upright' Macquarie, the colony suffered because excessive power was concentrated in the person of the governor. His solution was clear: restrictions on trade should be removed, British emigration should be redirected from North America to Australia, and trial by jury and free government should be introduced. He advocated the establishment of a nominated legislative council and an elected legislative assembly. A 'just equipoise between the democratic and supreme powers of the state' was essential: the council was to resemble the House of Lords, repressing the 'licentiousness' of the masses and curbing the 'tyranny' of the governor. Freeholders with estates of 500 acres or more could stand for parliament. Those who possessed a 20-acre freehold would be eligible to vote in the country districts; those with a leasehold to the value of £5 per annum and those who paid house rent of £10 a year would be enabled to vote in the towns. In magnificent, if extravagant, language, Wentworth envisaged 'the day when oppression was hurled from the car in which it had driven triumphantly over prostrate justice, virtue and religion', and when the political and civil liberty that flowered under British institutions would take root in the land of 'the convicts' clanking chains'.[4]

It was with mixed feelings that Wentworth wrote the passages in his book which related to Macquarie. While grateful for the kindness that the governor had shown to his family, he did not want to be taxed with being one of his partisans. William told his father that he had heeded his injunction: 'Where I have not been able Conscientiously to speak in the Governor's favour, I have been silent. All that could be said in praise of His Administration, I have said'. He was worried by what had happened in the Commons on 23 March. In tabling William Blake's and George Williams's petitions, Henry Brougham charged Macquarie with inflicting punishments 'unknown to British law'. The governor's supporters—W. T. Money, William Manning, G. V. Hart and Charles Forbes—defended him in the House, but Wentworth regretted that Macquarie had so 'committed himself that none but the most corrupt parasite can attempt his vindication'. William forwarded copies of his book to his father, Redfern and Macquarie, and sent another to Lord Fitzwilliam. Sales were slow until a number of newspapers began to print extracts from the work.

In summer the Pons comet appeared over England. According to Wentworth, it had a 'terrible effect' on the atmosphere, making the heat in London 'unbearable' during August. Having holidayed with friends in Normandy, he returned to find that one thousand copies of his book, the entire run, had been cleared by late November and that Whittaker planned to publish a second edition in 1820. Wentworth had not sold the copyright; the 1819 edition was printed at his own cost. Recouping the £50 he had paid as his share of the publisher's outlay, he made a profit of £150. He opened the reviews with trepidation. In the *Edinburgh Review* Sydney Smith, 'the wisest of witty men, and the wittiest of wise men', quipped that 'a Botany Bay parliament would give rise to jokes'. The *Quarterly Review* was more sympathetic, but its reviewer concurred that it was premature to grant representative government to New South Wales while most of the population consisted of convicted felons. Macquarie read the book with 'interest' and thought it contained 'much useful information'. John Macarthur found it mischievous; he viewed any elected house as anathema and trusted that his son had no hand in the radical suggestion. D'Arcy Wentworth was not in favour of an elected government, and, among the leading ex-convicts, only Edward Eagar advocated a popular assembly. William remained undeterred by the reactions. Seeing himself as a champion of self-government, as a leader of the emancipist faction and as a prospective member of the legislative council, he was a man in a hurry.[5]

John Bigge was in no haste when he was rowed from the *John Barry* to Sydney's shore at midday on the hot, dusty and windy Sunday of 26 September 1819. Born to the gentry on 8 March 1780 at Long Benton, Northumberland, he was educated at Westminster School and Christ Church, Oxford. He was admitted to the Bar in 1806 and served (1814–18) as chief justice in Trinidad where the range of his experiences in a slave-owning community broadened his attitudes, sharpened his faculties and added to his self-assurance. His veneration of the law developed in him qualities of detachment and objectivity, and his talent and imagination were secured by his stability of character and his sense of propriety. Of middle height and spare in build, with a suggestion of the effeminate in his appearance, he had a sharp mind and a sardonic wit. In politics he leaned to the Whigs but admired George Canning. His official correspondence revealed little of the inner man, save that he was reticent about himself and that he was given to neatness, precision and elegant understatement. Ruled by reason and not emotion, by temperament he was unromantic, composed and aloof. When he spoke, his words were studied and measured, their soft tone conveying their own warning; when he acted, he was guarded. With steely strength, he was endowed with tenacity and a shrewd perception of his fellows. In many ways he was the antithesis of Macquarie, and of the Wentworths—both father and son.[6]

Within a month of Bigge's arrival, Macquarie announced that Bowman was to succeed Wentworth as principal surgeon on 25 October. The *Sydney Gazette* carried a Government and General Order praising Wentworth for his honour and integrity, and the 'able, zealous, humane, and intelligent manner' in which he had conducted his duties for more than twenty-nine years. Through J. T. Campbell, Macquarie privately informed D'Arcy that he hoped his 'long, faithful and meritorious services' would be adequately rewarded with a pension, once he had given a satisfactory answer to the Victualling Board's query about the whereabouts of certain stores. Expecting that his retirement would be complete as soon as he shed the post of superintendent of police, Wentworth anticipated seeing more of his friends, especially the Macquaries, and making greater use of the goods Cookney had recently sent him—a set of ivory-handled cutlery, some gold-rimmed spectacles and a pair of comfortable slippers.[7]

One day after Bowman took up his duties, Bigge was able to observe Wentworth's conduct as a magistrate. Robert Lathrop Murray, a former military officer of noble descent who had been transported for seven years for bigamy, had been appointed assistant-superintendent of police and was one of the few people admitted to Wentworth's domestic circle, both in Sydney and at Home Bush. He ate at D'Arcy's table, knew Maria Ainslie and called Ann Lawes by the familiar name 'Nancy'. Some time in 1818 Elizabeth Crook had lodged a complaint against Murray for his alleged part in the abduction of her 15-year-old daughter, Emma, who had been taken from the colony on board Captain Howard's ship, *Daphne*. In handling the complaint, Wentworth and Murray behaved like amoral brutes, ridiculing Crook and dismissing her charge. She later appealed to the governor who referred the matter to a bench of magistrates. On 26 October 1819 Wylde, Lord, Harris and Wentworth officiated at the hearing. Murray denied any complicity and swore that Howard and Emma had willingly cohabited; furthermore, he declared that the girl was a prostitute and that her mother lived off her earnings. Despite his assertions, Lord, Harris and Wylde found him guilty of being an accessory to the abduction; Wentworth declined to give any opinion. To avoid being dismissed from the Police Office, Murray resigned. Wentworth helped him to set up near Hobart Town where Murray named his country house after him. They kept in touch. Murray called himself 'your old follower' and declared 'I can never forget all I owe you'.[8]

Loyalty to a friend led Macquarie to experience the first of his disagreements with Bigge. It lasted fifty days, from 30 October to 19 December. The governor had promised Redfern a magistracy to alleviate his disappointment at not succeeding Wentworth as principal surgeon. Bowman, who had arrived with Bigge in the *John Barry*, soon quarrelled with Redfern over arrangements in the general hospital; adding insult to injury, he said that the commissioner would ensure that no future magistrates came from the ranks of the emancipists. On 26 October, two days after Redfern had resigned as assistant-surgeon, Macquarie took steps to carry out his promise. Rejecting Bigge's cautionary advice, the governor avowed that, if he did not appoint Redfern, it would afford a triumph to those turbulent malcontents who had opposed his emancipist policy and who were endeavouring to prejudice the commissioner. Bigge contended that the faithful discharge of an assistant-surgeon's duties constituted no special claim to the magistracy; he also thought that Redfern was too intimate with the governor and wielded excessive influence over him. When Macquarie asserted that he preferred surrendering his government to Bigge rather than incurring the reproach that he was controlled by the commissioner on such an important measure, Bigge kept his sentiments about the appointment silent and awaited the verdict of his superiors in London. Within a year Bathurst ordered Macquarie to terminate Redfern's magistracy.[9]

Like Bigge, Wentworth expected news from London. In October 1819 he learned that his pension had been held over. Contrary to William's suspicions, Bathurst had not been influenced by any complaint from Molle. The delay was occasioned by the Victualling Board which, in 1818, had notified the Colonial Office of its dissatisfaction

8 What one is

with certain anomalies in the way D'Arcy had accounted for a number of crates of lime juice that had been delivered to him for medical purposes. Knowing that lime juice was commonly added to rum to make the drink more palatable, Wentworth had sold the contents of the crates and purported to have used the proceeds to buy other articles for the hospitals. While he fretted that Bigge might report unfavourably, he was chided by William for believing that 'such a paltry matter' could hinder the granting of his pension. D'Arcy's fears were well founded. Although William anticipated that a pension of £200 per annum, drawn on the police fund, would soon be paid, the Victualling Board continued to seek a satisfactory explanation until as late as 1823. The pension was never granted because Wentworth chose not to forward any full or satisfactory explanation. His resignation as superintendent of police occurred in this context. On 31 March 1820 a Government and General Order informed the public that William Minchin was to succeed Wentworth as superintendent on 1 April. In that notice Macquarie proclaimed his unqualified approbation of Wentworth's steady, upright, able and impartial conduct in discharging his arduous duties, with equal credit to himself and benefit to the community, for more than nine years. At the age of fifty-eight D'Arcy moved permanently to Home Bush to enjoy the fruits of retirement. He advertised his George Street store for lease and briefly acted as a magistrate at Parramatta. Yet he was vexed by one word the governor had used in the promulgation.[10]

Macquarie had publicly thanked him for the services he had 'gratuitously' rendered as treasurer of the police fund. Wentworth was taken aback. Over the next fifteen days governor and treasurer exchanged thirteen letters in their tussle for advantage. On 31 March Wentworth made it plain that he had never intended to execute the duties of treasurer of the police fund without compensation. Declaring that his predecessors, Harris and Thomas Jamison, had been allowed a percentage of the money they handled, he stated his willingness to lay his case before the lieutenant-governor, the judges or the commissioner of inquiry. Macquarie was stunned. His first actions were to recall the General Order and to issue a new one which omitted all reference to gratuitous services. He then informed Wentworth that, as he had neither promised nor contemplated paying him any salary, he was unable to make any reimbursement without reference to Lord Bathurst.

The governor offered to support Wentworth if he prepared a memorial to the secretary of state. Wentworth responded coldly to this proposal, reminding Macquarie that the Colonial Office had treated him shabbily in regard to his pension. On 5 April Macquarie wrote that he understood Wentworth's reluctance to appeal to His Majesty's ministers and proposed a compensatory grant of 2000 acres. Declining this offer, Wentworth threatened to keep 2.5 per cent of the money he had recently received as treasurer. Macquarie countered by expressing his bewilderment that Wentworth had waited so long without seeking remuneration; he had thought that D'Arcy shared his understanding that the offices of superintendent of police and treasurer of the police fund were combined, and that the salary of the former took into account the duties of the latter. In reply, Wentworth pointed out that the situations he held were quite distinct, and that he had been appointed treasurer nine months before he was made superintendent. By 7 April he decided that an appeal *ad misericordiam* was best. He told Macquarie that he was mortified at unintentionally offending him and that he would sacrifice his interests, and those of his family, to conform to the governor's wishes. Avowing affection, he threw himself upon His Excellency's sense of justice. On the 11th Macquarie yielded, informing Wentworth that he would accept responsibility for paying him £100 per annum for each of his ten years service. That afternoon Wentworth accepted the offer. On the 15th Macquarie issued a warrant authorizing Wentworth to pay himself £1000 and to charge the amount to the police fund. This done, on 1 June Minchin became treasurer.[11]

Meanwhile Bigge had begun his investigation. Because he thought that the inhabitants would reveal more without the trappings of solemnity, he declined being appointed a justice of the peace, arguing that the necessity of giving evidence on oath might restrain some of his witnesses whereas others had so little respect for an adjuration that they would swear to a lie. Proceeding in a manner that displayed a pattern only in retrospect, the commissioner's course meandered and turned back on itself. In the seventeen months he spent in the penal settlements he interviewed most of the free settlers, some fifty emancipists and hundreds of convicts, accumulating over 15 000 pages of material of which the minutes of the oral evidence comprised about 30 per cent. Equally prepared to humble the self-regarding and to take notice of the meek, he was a skilful cross-examiner who knew how to unearth inefficiency and corruption. He started by looking at weaknesses in Macquarie's administration, and, as time passed, sought ways to set them right. In October and November 1819 he conducted his first formal interviews by examining George Druitt, the chief engineer, William Hutchinson, the principal superintendent of convicts, and D'Arcy Wentworth, the superintendent of police. Each of these men exposed defects in the penal system. Anxious to transfer to the governor responsibility for any mismanagement in their own departments, Macquarie's own officials and intimates emerged as his most damaging critics.[12]

Bigge interviewed Wentworth four times on matters pertaining to the police, on 10, 16, 19 and 23 November. In an attempt to gain an overview of the establishment, the commissioner inquired into the structure and daily operations of the police, and the procedures for issuing warrants, inflicting punishments, and granting and revoking publicans' licences. Wentworth recommended that, although complaints of misconduct were seldom laid against his constables, the police should receive higher salaries to attract better men to their ranks. Priding himself on his knowledge of the character and whereabouts of those prisoners who were permitted to live outside the barracks, he referred to two flash houses, run by Margaret Waples and William Welsh, which furnished him with means of gathering information about the criminal underworld. To curtail the convicts' access to liquor, he recommended that prisoners should not be paid for work performed in their own time, that they should be compelled to wear a distinctive uniform, and that penalties should be imposed on publicans and settlers who sold spirits to them. He had no qualms about having refused to renew the licences of Rose, Thompson and Armytage as a reprisal for signing the Vale–Moore petition. While he regretted Macquarie's action in flogging the Domain trespassers, he pointed out that Blake was a notorious receiver, that Henshall was suspected of coining and that the Domain had become a hiding-place for stolen goods.[13]

Other colonists were critical of the way the police functioned under D'Arcy Wentworth. As Bigge's inquiries continued, he interviewed William Cox, John Harris, Robert Cartwright, Judge Barron Field and John Wylde. Cox told him that the system which had operated before Wentworth's appointment was more effective in reducing crime. Harris agreed with Cox and indicated that, during Wentworth's term as police magistrate, floggings were more frequent, but were less dreaded because they were less severe. Cartwright suggested paying the police magistrate a salary commensurate with his rank to discourage him from spending undue time on his private interests. Wylde alleged that Wentworth was reluctant either to bring to trial or to convict persons accused of selling spirits without a licence; in contrast, Field attested that he found Wentworth useful and competent on the bench. Harris divulged the extent of Wentworth's involvement in the liquor trade and spoke of his casual attitude to disorderly public houses. In regard to D'Arcy's social standing, Wylde testified that he was generally considered in the same light as those belonging to the convict class and that he rarely mixed in society. Harris stressed that Wentworth came to the colony as a free man, but agreed with Wylde that he seldom mixed in polite circles.[14]

More than seven months passed before Bigge interviewed Wentworth about the state of the colony's hospitals. In that time the commissioner took evidence from at least seven different members of the medical staff, ranging from three assistant-surgeons to an orderly, an overseer, a clerk and a doctor's apprentice. He listened intently while 19-year-old Henry Cowper catalogued instances of neglect and irresponsibility within the medical establishment. The young man disclosed that Wentworth rarely attended the general hospital and that Redfern worked there only in the mornings; he also alleged that Redfern spent periods of a month or more on his farm and took medicine from the hospital for his private practice. Cowper referred to the 'intermingling' of male and female patients, and said that some of them exchanged their rations for spirits; he told Bigge that, owing to a number of robberies and escapes, the windows of the hospital were kept locked. In his opinion the nurses were often intoxicated, medicine was incorrectly administered, hospital records were irregularly kept, and meals were prepared and cooked in the wards. On occasions the stench was so foul as to cause vomiting and to deter Redfern from his rounds. A decisive majority of assistant-surgeons supported Cowper's testimony. James Hunter had seen nurses throw raw meat to the patients, dirty bandages kicked under the beds, and pans unemptied of evacuations. Conditions were even worse in hospitals at the outstations where the staff spoke of dirt and overcrowding, complained of the want of medicine and supplies, and maintained that Wentworth did not heed their requisitions.[15]

8 What one is

If Bigge were disposed to regard the principal surgeon as an ineffective hospital administrator, his interview with Wentworth did nothing to dispel the impression. Wentworth admitted that meals were cooked in the wards of the general hospital, but excused this practice on the grounds that one kitchen was used as a store and the other as a mortuary. Although he had been consulted about the plans of the hospital, he attributed the lack of indoor water-closets and a 'Dead House' to an oversight on his part. On the other hand, he thought that Macquarie's decision to give one room to the artist, John William Lewin, and four to the courts had stretched the hospital's resources. Wentworth agreed that the doors of the lower wards lacked locks, but said that it was common knowledge that the female patients were syphilitics and this deterred the males from sexual intercourse. Bigge had learned of critical shortages in medical supplies and of the haphazard supervision of hospital stores. Taxed about a quantity of Glauber's salts that had lain hidden for three years beneath a pile of bedding in a storeroom, Wentworth replied that it had 'escaped our observation'. It had not occurred to him to install shelves in the room. Robust in his defence when questioned about the crates of lime juice, he told Bigge that, with the governor's permission, he had sold the surplus privately and at public auction, using the proceeds to buy several articles for the hospital and to pay for the cartage of goods from the wharves. He was less prepared to justify Redfern's conduct in absenting himself from his official situation to conduct his private practice and in procuring supplies from the general hospital for his own dispensary. In contrast to the way he ran his business affairs, as principal surgeon Wentworth habitually delegated responsibility to his subordinates; he was rarely inclined to monitor their performance. Rightly or wrongly, Bigge treated Wentworth as a public official rather than a free settler and never cross-examined him about his activities in trade or agriculture.[16]

By the spring of 1820 D'Arcy Wentworth had regained his health, but still felt tired and dispirited, partly due to some disquieting accounts of his patron. At a public meeting in York in 1819 Lord Fitzwilliam had censured those responsible for the Peterloo massacre. The Tory government reacted by dismissing him from the lord-lieutenancy of the West Riding and he was roughly treated by the conservative press, especially the *Morning Post*. Not only did Fitzwilliam fall from political favour. At the age of seventy-two he fell ill with influenza and almost died. His recuperation was protracted. For six weeks he was unable to walk, a severe restraint on one who was fond of exercise. In July 1820 William happily informed his father of Fitzwilliam's recovery, adding that the king parrot had become a great favourite of Lady Fitzwilliam who took it everywhere and prided herself on owning the handsomest bird in England. In the same letter he imparted the cheerful news that he had heard from his brother, John, and expected to be reunited with him in London. Their uncle, William, encouraged the widow, Elizabeth Crothers, a neighbour at Portadown, to solicit D'Arcy's patronage. She asked D'Arcy to protect her son, John, who had been 'led astray by bad company' in England and transported for seven years to New South Wales: 'he has left me heart broken and I never cease thinking of him'. The plea was unavailing. Early in October 1820 D'Arcy learned of his own son's death. After leaving Sydney in 1819 in the *General Stewart*, John Wentworth had sailed to Batavia. There he had a disagreement with the transport's master and took a passage for England in the *Borneo*. Her captain, J. C. Ross, appointed him chief officer. Stricken with yellow fever, John died on 20 February 1820 and was buried at sea with the rites of the Church of England. He was twenty-four years old. Ross took John's effects to England and delivered them to William. Among them was a hookah which John had bought as a present for his father. On 5 October Elizabeth Macquarie wrote to Dr Wentworth to tell him that she knew the agony of losing a child and how it placed a parent beyond mortal aid. She chose not to intrude on his sorrow. That day Macquarie visited D'Arcy to convey his condolences. Wentworth left no record of his grief, save for a letter to Cookney, written nine months later, in which he broke the 'melancholy' news of the death of his 'dear son'.[17]

Unaware of Wentworth's loss, Bigge re-examined him in November about the evidence he had previously given and requested that he submit his accounts, both for the police fund and for transactions at the general hospital. On 25 January 1821 the commissioner informed him that a number of colonists had commented on his conduct as a magistrate and as treasurer of the police fund; Bigge thought it only right that he should have an opportunity to answer their allegations. Wentworth replied on the following day. His six-point response was succinct. He admitted selling spirits from his George Street store, but asked how else could the contractors have built a hospital which cost, by his estimation, £40 000. He flatly denied having said that the sale of spirits was good for trade and good for the police fund. He could not agree that public houses were disorderly during the period of the hospital contract; after all, liquor cost more at that time than in subsequent years. He repudiated the charge that he had discounted bills at a lower rate of interest than the Bank of New South Wales, of which he was a director, yet added the rider that he was in no way precluded from using his own money as he thought fit. He acknowledged that he had issued promissory notes while he was treasurer of the police fund, but vouched that his action benefited the settlers and gave general satisfaction. Finally, he asserted that he had repeatedly urged the governor to allow him to place the balance of the police fund in the bank instead of keeping it at his home. He concluded by thanking Bigge for his candour. Whatever their differences, Bigge and Wentworth treated each other with civility.[18]

Conversely, Redfern accused the commissioner of resorting to the methods of a Spanish inquisitor and of endeavouring, in the course of their interview, to goad him into a breach of good manners. He also alleged that Bigge had demeaned himself by questioning 'common strumpets in the streets of Sydney' about 'the character of Mr Wentworth and myself'. And he damned Bigge's friend, Bowman, for transforming the general hospital into the slaughterhouse of New South Wales. To Redfern, Bowman's sole achievement lay in the employment he provided for coffin-makers, gravediggers and chaplains. In comparison with Redfern, Macquarie exercised restraint when he replied, on 4 February, to sixty-three charges which Bigge had referred to him. Some of them related to the management of the medical establishment. The governor defended Wentworth, but was not prepared to shoulder all the blame for his shortcomings. Macquarie agreed that supervision of the building of the general hospital was not as thorough as it should have been and that several rooms essential in a hospital had escaped consideration, but he regarded these oversights as venial. From his own inspections, the colony's hospitals seemed to be in a satisfactory condition and the patients appeared to be treated humanely. As for dietary practices, and the loss or misappropriation of medicines and supplies, such points of duty rested with and depended upon the honour of the surgeons in charge. The governor's replies were those of an exhausted man who found solace in having achieved much, no matter what his tormentors said.[19]

Four days later, on Thursday 8 February, Bigge embarked for England in the *Dromedary*, the same ship that had brought Macquarie to New South Wales. On 26 March, after holding office for less than a year, Minchin died suddenly. Convinced that there was no other suitable person to discharge his duties, Macquarie again asked Wentworth to accept the posts of superintendent of police and treasurer of the police fund. The salaries were £200 and £100 per annum respectively. Wentworth agreed, on the understanding that he could resign, should he so wish, when a new governor arrived. He was gratified by the way Macquarie behaved on this occasion and told Cookney, with no little hyperbole, that his appointment was 'hailed with genuine Acclamation by the whole Colony'. Robert Lathrop Murray wrote to Wentworth from Hobart Town, soliciting his old post as assistant-superintendent. Wentworth declined his services. The *Sydney Gazette* announced Wentworth's appointment on 31 March. Almost immediately he was ordered to suppress bushranging on the Parramatta and Liverpool roads; although soldiers were detached to support his constables, he was unable to end robbery on the king's highways. Closer to home, on the night of 9 May a successful break-out occurred at the Sydney gaol. James Erskine, the lieutenant-governor, told Wentworth to ensure that there would be no repetition of the event. Notwithstanding his precautions, a second break-out took place on the morning of 7 July. A bench of magistrates found that the gaol was badly in need of extensions and repairs, and that there were insufficient irons to secure the inmates.[20]

In the succeeding months Wentworth's friends, Redfern and Eagar, prepared to sail for England. On 23 January 1821 Redfern had chaired a meeting at which the emancipated colonists decided to draw up a petition seeking the full restoration of civil rights for any convict who had received an absolute or conditional pardon. It was signed by 1368 emancipists—one-sixth of their total number. Wentworth did not participate in the campaign. A fund was raised to defray the expenses of sending two delegates to present the petition to the secretary of state and to reinforce its plea in person. Chosen by the emancipists as their representatives, Redfern and Eagar carried letters of introduction from Macquarie to Lord Bathurst. They also bore their grievances against Commissioner Bigge. In 1815 Eagar had married Jemima McDuel, the 19-year-old illegitimate daughter of John McDuel and Margaret Maloney; by 1820 Edward and Jemima had three children. In 1819

Eagar had served as secretary to the committee which drew up a petition to the Prince Regent advocating the introduction of trial by jury. That year he wrote a long letter to Bigge recommending constitutional reform, but the commissioner did not invite him to elaborate on his submission. In April 1820 Field ruled that Eagar could not bring an action in court on the ground that he was a convict attaint. Fired by their ideals and nourished by their grievances, Redfern and Eagar left Sydney in the *Duchess of York* on 27 October 1821.[21]

An old regime was yielding place to a new. On 7 November Sir Thomas Brisbane, the governor elect, landed in Sydney. Frederick Goulburn, the new colonial secretary, impressed Brisbane with his principles of political economy while Macquarie was absent on a tour of the northern settlements. Returning to headquarters on the 21st, Macquarie met his successor walking in the Domain. He hoped to spend three months acquainting Brisbane with his policies before transferring the government to him, but Sir Thomas would have none of that and was sworn in on 1 December. Sir John Jamison and Wentworth convened a meeting on the 7th to frame addresses from the inhabitants to their past and present governors. Due to a lack of unanimity, it was resolved that the addresses would bear the words 'the undersigned' magistrates, chaplains, civil officers and landowners, rather than purporting to come from the community as a whole. Wentworth proposed that Macquarie be presented with a gold cup, to the value of five hundred guineas. The money was raised by individual subscriptions of £1. On the 15th Wentworth presented the address to Macquarie. It expressed appreciation for all he had done to promote the welfare and development of the colony. Under his auspices 265 public buildings and works had been completed. By 1821 there were 72 998 cattle and 121 875 sheep in New South Wales, almost a threefold and a twofold increase respectively since 1815; the land under crop had grown by 66 per cent to 32 273 acres; farmers and graziers held 95 637 acres in 1810, 208 547 in 1815 and 381 467 in 1821; by 1821 the price paid by government for meat had fallen to 5 pence per lb and wheat had stabilized at 10 shillings per bushel. On 31 January 1821 the governor had written to Wentworth in familiar terms: 'This being *my Birth-Day*, your friend Mrs Macquarie insists on your coming to dine with us *today* at 6 o'clock . . . and we will take no excuse'. In the following year Wentworth was one of a select group invited to celebrate Macquarie's

The Wentworths

61st birthday. Before relinquishing office, Macquarie granted Wentworth 3150 acres and paid £1500 on behalf of the government for a house he owned in Sydney. On Tuesday 12 February 1822 the Macquaries boarded the *Surrey*. Detained by contrary winds, the vessel cleared Port Jackson's heads on the 15th. The family took one last look at the country that had been their home. Young Lachlan wept and his parents came close to tears. Convinced that it was necessary to preserve the public purse by making the colony provide for itself, the governors who succeeded Macquarie adopted different ways of doing things. New South Wales outgrew its place in an imperial pattern of which it was a subordinate piece.[22]

After returning to England in July 1821, Bigge took twenty months to write his reports. The first, on 'the State of the Colony', was submitted to the House of Commons on 19 June 1822; the second, concerning the 'Judicial Establishments', was tabled on 21 February 1823; the third, about 'Agriculture and Trade', was presented on 13 March that year. Running to 186, 90 and 112 pages respectively, the reports totalled over 300 000 words and constituted the most thorough account of the penal colonies in the years from 1810 to 1821. For the most part Bigge's judgements were accurate and fair, given his brief. On many major topics of his inquiry there was agreement among his witnesses, particularly on the subjects of economy and agriculture; on matters where opinion was divided, such as the elevation of emancipists and trial by jury, he was circumscribed by the attitude of British administrators and by his own prejudices; where he was legitimately puzzled, as on the need for a legislative council, he remained reserved and did not create any blueprint for sweeping reform. The reports were plain in style and straightforward in treatment, but poise and authority informed Bigge's words when he discussed the significance of his investigations and made recommendations for change. Overall, he presented guarded suggestions for the governance of New South Wales in a period which would see its gradual evolution from a gaol to a colony.[23]

There were points on which Bigge and Macquarie concurred. Both saw New South Wales as a gaol and as a colony, but they disagreed on how to reconcile the one with the other. To Bigge, the transition from a penal to a free society depended on an independent landed gentry; to Macquarie, the ex-convicts and the native-born comprised the principal agents of change, under his guiding hand. The emancipist issue gave focus to their fundamental ideas on human nature. Bigge's views on good and evil were influenced by what he saw as a need for retribution and discrimination; Macquarie's beliefs made greater allowance for compassion and grace. With his Whiggish leanings, mechanistic utilitarianism and rational approach, the commissioner represented a new type of individualism, strongly inclined towards austerity and free enterprise; with his philanthropic Toryism, as well as his organic and emotional approach, the governor favoured autocratic but paternalistic control of communities, whether a clan, a regiment or an imperial state. These features deepened their difference from a personal to an ideological level.[24]

In essence, the commissioner argued that New South Wales and Van Diemen's Land were capable of continuing to receive convicts, and of punishing and reforming them. Whereas Macquarie believed in leniency, Bigge recommended the maintenance of vigour to render transportation an effective deterrent to crime in Britain. He saw the same randomness that pervaded the governor's distribution of pardons exhibited in his promotion of ex-convicts to positions of authority: by showing partiality to emancipists, Macquarie had violated the feelings of the free population, and the immoral lives of some of the recipients of his favour had lowered public respect for the offices they filled. Bigge criticized, *pari passu*, Macquarie's building programme, dismissing it as unjustifiable in its expense to the Crown and as inefficacious in reforming those it employed. He recommended that government should instead retain only a minimum number of convicts to undertake works of immediate utility; most prisoners should be dispersed to the country areas and the worst sent to secondary penal stations remote from the mass of the people. From the theme of human error Bigge turned to the opportunities offered by the new land. The light which he threw on the penal colony's future was refracted through the prism of his own bias. While he admitted that only a small proportion of the exclusives had fulfilled his expectations, he supported a controlled extension of settlement by encouraging a nascent economy in which men of capital would rear sheep and export fine wool to England. In return for government assistance through land grants and convict servants, the pastoralists had a duty to superintend the labour and the conduct of their assignees. Throughout his reports the commissioner's praise of Macquarie was niggardly. He made insufficient allowance for the unreliability of the subordinates with whom Macquarie had to work and for his difficulties in governing during a time of extraordinary growth. For all that, Bigge did propose a scheme which reconciled punishment with profit. By yoking severity to savings, he convinced his masters that they had found an improvement on the practices of a governor who had been guided by motives of humanity rather than by reason.[25]

Wentworth received passing notice in the commissioner's first report. Citing D'Arcy's testimony that the urge to obtain spirits drove convicts to crime and that their conduct would improve only if they were forbidden access to liquor, Bigge added—parenthetically and pointedly—that Wentworth had 'considerable experience on this subject'. The report censured Redfern for misappropriating government medical supplies for use in his private dispensary, but cleared Wentworth on this score. Nevertheless, Bigge stated that, for several years, Wentworth had neither prohibited nor commented on Redfern's theft of public property. Finally, Bigge remarked on Wentworth's forbearance in inflicting corporal punishment and noted his opinion that prisoners dreaded solitary confinement more than the lash. In his second report the commissioner asserted, without naming Wentworth, that certain magistrates were involved in the sale of spirits; their vested interests made them reluctant to reduce the number of licensed public houses and led them to thwart the prosecution of unlicensed retailers:

> In a community wherein it was of the utmost importance that the exercise of magisterial authority should be placed above the suspicion of being actuated by personal motives, it was certainly unfortunate . . . that any of the magistrates should have had, or should now possess an interest in the extended use of a commodity, which they knew to be the cause of mischief to the colony, in proportion as it was the cause of profit to themselves.

Convinced that drunkenness was a further cause of crime, Bigge reproved the police for failing to enforce the closing-hours of public houses and the 9 p.m. curfew on assigned servants. Although he found that law and order was maintained in the streets of Sydney, other than at The Rocks, he considered many of the petty constables to be inefficient, inattentive or inebriated, largely because of their low pay and the lack of supervision by the chief constables and the assistant-superintendent. The commissioner suggested that a person experienced in police work in London should be appointed to head the department, on a salary of £500 per year, and that the police fund should be independently administered by a colonial treasurer. Bigge's third report listed Wentworth among the colony's seven largest proprietors of sheep and cattle, and as one of the main beneficiaries of land grants. While praising his diligence as treasurer of the police fund, Bigge regretted that the receipts had never been audited; he also made it clear that, although Wentworth had advanced as much as £3500 of his own money when the fund was in debit, he had been reimbursed, with interest, by bills drawn on the Treasury. Bigge was more critical of Wentworth's supervision of the medical establishment, though only by inference. He deplored the neglect in keeping records of patients treated and medicines prescribed; he condemned the damage, loss and embezzlement of hospital stores; and he found that there was inadequate provision for diet and cleanliness. Referring specifically to the general hospital, he attested that it was overcrowded, with beds only two feet apart and ninety patients in wards designed to accommodate half that number, and he regretted the want of simple precautions to separate male and female patients. As for the building itself, he attributed its flaws to the grandiosity of Macquarie's plan and to the shortage of skilled workmen.[26]

Whereas Bigge treated Wentworth leniently in his published reports, he was harsher in his private correspondence. The commissioner's confidential letters, sent to Lord Bathurst on 9 September 1822 and 7 February 1823, reflected on the character and reputation of some of the highest officials in the colony, among them Macquarie, Marsden and Wentworth. Resurrecting D'Arcy's appearances at the Old Bailey in 1787 and 1789, Bigge stated that, on the latter occasion, Wentworth was acquitted on evidence which left 'a very strong presumption of Guilt'. Although the nature and number of the charges brought against him were not well known in the colony where he was 'much trusted by Individuals of all Classes', he was commonly denominated an emancipist. Moreover, the circumstances of Wentworth's private life afforded cause for 'serious reproach'. In Sydney and Parramatta he lived 'in a state of concubinage' with 'the wife of a free person'; at Home Bush he lived with 'another female'. Ann Lawes had given birth to 'several' of his children, as had Catherine Crowley, his mistress on Norfolk Island.

The Wentworths

As a consequence, Bigge continued, Mr Wentworth rarely mixed in polite circles in New South Wales—though 'he has always been distinguished by propriety of demeanour when invited to partake of it'—and 'has been observed to shun rather than court attention'. The commissioner felt bound to state that he had received no information to impeach Wentworth's conduct as superintendent of police. He did comment, however, on his open involvement in the sale of spirits during and after the term of the hospital contract, on his reluctance to convict unlicensed vendors and on his influence in encouraging them to act 'with impunity'. In sum, Bigge judged that, as police magistrate, Wentworth had not administered justice impartially. Turning to his conduct as principal surgeon, Bigge found little that deserved praise or censure. He remarked on Wentworth's limited medical experience and added that the hospitals in New South Wales had 'not afforded the means of improving it'. In superintending the medical department in Sydney, Parramatta and Windsor, he had shown 'little activity' and was disposed to spend more time on his other concerns. The standard method of victualling patients which he had long allowed and which Bowman immediately terminated was 'at variance with all known principles of medical treatment'. Bigge hesitated to blame Wentworth for the dilapidated condition of some hospitals since his requests for assistance had met with little co-operation from the officers in charge of public works. Surprised by D'Arcy's reluctance to inform the Victualling Board about precisely what he had done with the cases of lime juice, Bigge thought that his behaviour, in this instance as in others, although not incorrect, left a lot to be desired.[27]

Copies of Bigge's first report reached Sydney in November 1822 on a day when Brisbane was at Camden with John Macarthur watching the sheep-shearing. The *Sydney Gazette* gave less space to announcing the report's arrival than to news that a monster snake had been seen two miles from Liverpool. According to the newspaper's editor, Robert Howe, great men trembled as they read the report. Their apprehension was unwarranted. Simeon Lord displayed a copy at his home for the perusal of those who had contributed to Eagar's and Redfern's mission, but a lack of subscribers prevented a local printing of the report. The novel, *My Landlord*, proved more popular. While the *Sydney Gazette* predicted that a number of colonists would complain of the obloquy that Bigge had cast on their characters, Wentworth took the publication in his stride. He was similarly unmoved in October 1823 when copies of the second and third reports reached New South Wales. Young John Macarthur told his mother that the reports were candid and fearless, but defective in arrangement and clogged with detail; none the less, he was confident that Bigge's recommendations would improve colonial society and increase the standing of men of property. John's father, who was furious with Bigge for suggesting that the emancipist, Richard Fitzgerald, was admitted to the Macarthur family circle, thought that the commissioner had been imposed upon and was too fond of gossip.[28]

Robert Peel expressed Home Office approval of the commissioner's findings, as did his colleagues in the Treasury. The senior staff at the Colonial Office held Bigge's report in such esteem as to use it almost as a text. Bathurst was convinced that Brisbane's objectives should be to enforce rigorous control, severe discipline and unremitting labour upon the convicts, and to end the appointment of emancipists to high positions of trust. By restoring to transportation its punitive purpose, Bathurst effectively ditched the measures that Macquarie had adopted and the principles to which he had adhered. From 1822 the Colonial Office took further steps to create in Sydney an administration independent of the governor's influence and to curb the costs of the colony. With the aim of checking gubernatorial power, Bathurst instructed James Stephen and Francis Forbes to draft a bill 'for the better Administration of Justice' in New South Wales (4 Geo.IV, c.96). The bill provided for a legislative council of between five and seven members, appointed by the Crown, and for trial by a jury of twelve colonists in civil cases, where both plaintiff and defendant agreed to this procedure. Beyond civil service and parliamentary circles, Bigge's reports were favourably received, for the most part. James Losh, a Whig, found them duller than they need have been, but considered them a valuable addition to colonial literature. Sydney Smith deemed the first report to be the product of an honest, sensible and respectable man who had done his duty to the public.[29]

When Macquarie, Redfern, Eagar and William Wentworth read those passages that touched on them, they behaved as men maligned. Macquarie wrote a defence of his administration in answer to Bigge's 'false, vindictive and malicious report'. Redfern's rage was unseemly, as befitted a bully. He indicted Bigge for libel and summoned Robert Wilmot Horton, the new under-secretary at the Colonial Office, to appear before a grand jury at Clerkenwell. Eagar sent Lord Bathurst a 119-page letter in which he rebutted Bigge's assertions about the emancipists and levelled 'charges of a very grave nature' against the commissioner. Forming an alliance with a 16-year-old girl, Ellen Gorman, who bore her first child by him in 1823, Eagar decided to remain in London and continue his lobbying. In July 1822 Wentworth, still his intemperate self, challenged Bigge to a duel for stating that he was the author of the pipes attacking Molle. Wilmot Horton placed Wentworth under police restraint, an action which added to his fury and made it more difficult for Bigge to come to terms with him. Responding to William's insistence that D'Arcy had prefaced his revelation of the pipe-maker's identity with the words 'he had reason to believe', Bigge admitted that he may have drawn an unjust conclusion about William's culpability and offered to publish an explanation in the London press. In the face of William's further protest, the commissioner then agreed to delete the offending passage before his first report was tabled in the House of Lords and to insert an apology in his second report. Despite Bigge's conciliatory attitude, the native son remembered his wounds.[30]

William saw Redfern and Eagar frequently during the latter half of 1822, especially in July, August and November when Macquarie was based in London. The currency lad and the two emancipists fixed themselves as constellations to his shattered sphere. Elizabeth Macquarie's affection for the long-haired and ungainly William grew to admiration on learning that he would remain loyal to her husband and champion the emancipist cause. Wentworth had slowly gravitated in this direction. Rebuffed by the Macarthurs, father and son, and stung by what Bennet, Bent and Bigge had published, he had been compelled to accept what he was—the illegitimate son of a father who had been tried for highway robbery and a mother who had been a convict. His father had always stuck by him. In return he would stand by his father, and his father's friends. After leaving Paris in 1818, William had resumed his course at the Middle Temple, completed his pleading and conveyancing, and been called to the Bar on 8 February 1822. His chambers at 1 Garden Court, Temple, were on the fourth floor and the flights of stairs deterred prospective clients. With few friends, he found business slow and was delighted that his brother, Lieutenant D'Arcy of the 73rd, took leave in London. William had a thoughtful side to his nature, as evident in the presents he sent home: for the Reverend Henry Fulton a set of grammar books; for Maria Ainslie some linen, two dozen pairs of stockings, a few bonnets and a number of gown pieces, all of good quality, though not too fine lest she hoard rather than wear them. He also had romantic longings and gave them rein. In 1820 Wentworth told Riley that he was betrothed to 'a young lady of good family and tolerable fortune'. She was 'an orphan' and lived 'with her maternal uncle' who was averse to the match. William asked Riley for a character reference. This Riley declined to give, and the engagement was broken. Three years later Wentworth wrote a love poem to a Miss Taylor on her birthday:

> But when the wild flowers bloom again
> When shines thy natal star
> Where—Bella—, what shall I be then?
> From thee a wanderer far . . .
>
> Still will I pray kind Providence
> Its choicest gifts to send,
> And bless with health, peace, competence
> My kindest, truest friend.[31]

Assisted by a gift of money from Dr Redfern and a subsequent loan of £250 from Lord Fitzwilliam, on 27 February 1823 Wentworth entered Peterhouse, Cambridge's oldest college. There was, he told his father, a certain prestige in having been at university. In signing the admissions book, however, he concealed the past and gave neither his age nor his father's name. At thirty-two William was much older than most of the undergraduates. Thirty-five of the commoners roomed in Peterhouse under the charge of five dons who specialized in classics, history and literature. Founded in 1284 by the Bishop of Ely, Peterhouse had received large endowments from the Fitzwilliam family. The college was rooted in things celestial and terrestrial. Outside its entrance ran Trumpington Street which became the London Road; to the west of Peterhouse, by the river, lay Little St Mary's Lane, with its landing-place, taverns and whorehouses; Market Hill was situated a quarter of a mile to the north; in spring daffodils bloomed in the deer-park leading south to Coe Fen. While reading law, Wentworth lived in Burrough's Building, and had a bedroom, a study and a keeping-room.

Meals were served in the dining-hall in front of a Tudor fireplace. The Perne Library housed every book he needed. Since daily religious observance was compulsory, he walked past the lawn in Old Court to the early-seventeenth-century chapel where, above the altar, Bernard Van Linge's stained-glass window depicted the crucifixion and its theme of redemption.[32]

Aiming to achieve more in a month than John Macarthur junior had done in four years at Cambridge, Wentworth submitted a 443-line poem for the chancellor's medal. The subject that year was Australasia and he was awarded second place from twenty-five entrants. His poem was dedicated to Macquarie. In the preface Wentworth referred to the former governor as his patron: Macquarie had presided over the colony and promoted its growth with the solicitude of a parent; his zeal, wisdom and humanity had enhaloed him as a philanthropist; those who impugned his administration had vented the calumnies of their fleeting day. Though Macquarie's services might be underrated in Britain, the preface continued, they would live in the minds of Australians; though his material achievements might perish, the fruit of his principles would descend to posterity. Intent on redressing the injustice done to Macquarie, Wentworth vowed to discharge his obligation to one who had been his foster-father. From the past his poem turned to the future, to the day when Australasia would rise to gladden her parent's heart by becoming a 'new Britannia in another world'. On 18 March, after the Colonial Office had rejected his application for the post of attorney-general in New South Wales, William informed his father that he would return to the colony 'only as an individual'. He had made up his mind 'to hold no situation under Government. As a mere private person I feel that I might lead the colony; but as a servant of the Governor, I could only conform to his whims, which would neither suit my tastes, nor principles'. Before his first term ended, he had decided to forge a political career in his homeland and to use the emancipists' grievances as a rallying point for constitutional reform.[33]

On 21 July 1823 Lord Fitzwilliam, whose wife had died in the previous year, married Louisa, widow of Lord Ponsonby and daughter of the 3rd Viscount Molesworth. Fitzwilliam was seventy-five years old. That summer the New South Wales bill was debated in the Commons. Wentworth sat with Eagar in the visitors' gallery and heard two great men of the age participate. Sir James Mackintosh presented the emancipists' petition and spoke forcefully, though unavailingly, for the recognition of their claims. Canning successfully proposed that the bill's duration be limited to five years so that the case for wider changes could then be reconsidered. Mightily impressed, Wentworth rekindled his hopes for reform in his native land. In late 1823 he collaborated with Eagar on the third edition of his history which they planned to use as a vehicle for their views, both on Bigge's reports and on the New South Wales Act. Wentworth persuaded Robert Wardell, a barrister of the Middle Temple, editor of the London newspaper, the *Statesman*, and a boon companion, to try his hand in Sydney. Accompanied by John Mackaness, the sheriff designate, Dr and Mrs Redfern, and Wardell and his mother, in February 1824 the currency lad sailed from England in the *Alfred* for the land of his birth.[34]

9

Life's little day

Swift to its close ebbs out life's little day;
Earth's joys grow dim, its glories pass away

Henry Lyte, 'Abide with me'

Sir Thomas Brisbane grew restive in New South Wales from December 1821 to August 1822 when he was little more than a caretaker governor. Subsequently instructed to implement Bigge's recommendations to the letter, he embraced Frederick Goulburn's ideas of political economy, threw the penal settlement on its own resources and boasted that he had saved the government up to £100 000 by 1824. Brisbane regarded the colony as a machine which, once put in order and regularly propelled, would run so smoothly that he could relinquish management of day-to-day affairs to the colonial secretary and his team of civil servants. Happiest in retirement at Parramatta with his family and his astronomical pursuits, Sir Thomas was gentlemanly, reserved and absent. He did his best to avoid intimacy with Macquarie's cabal of emancipists who, he privately confided, had destroyed the fabric of social order and helped to create the worst community on earth. Under Brisbane's governorship several of Macquarie's most bitter critics—Bowman, John and Hannibal Macarthur, Marsden and Goulburn—gained political ascendancy and the influence it endowed. In Van Diemen's Land Lieutenant-Governor Arthur took over from William Sorell on 14 May 1824 and tried to mould an effective gaol by introducing sets of meticulous and impersonal rules. His penchant for prayer distanced him from *hoi polloi* as effectively as did Brisbane's sylvan retreat.[1]

9 Life's little day

D'Arcy Wentworth continued to serve Brisbane as superintendent of police and treasurer of the police fund, on a combined salary of £300 per annum. The change in governors had little impact on his daily duties. His office received numerous complaints which ranged from irritation at stray dogs to annoyance at the harpies who congregated on street corners. Wentworth investigated misdemeanours, such as the selling of underweight bread, and serious crimes, including brutal murders. Hardly a night passed, according to one correspondent in the *Sydney Gazette*, without a burglary being committed in the town. Although their wages had been augmented, gaolers, constables and watchmen were often dismissed for drunkenness or neglect. By 1825 the colony's police numbered 259 (of whom 82 were based in Sydney), a ratio of one policeman to every 120 inhabitants. Bushrangers still posed a major problem and rewards for their capture rose from £1 per head in December 1821 to £5 in March 1825. By April 1824 William Balcombe had been installed as colonial treasurer (on a salary of £1200 per annum), allowing Wentworth to shed his supervision of the police fund. Within two months D'Arcy wrote to Brisbane threatening to resign unless he received an increased salary as superintendent of police. He was prevailed on to retain office at the existing rate.[2]

A foundation member (from 1822) of the Agricultural Society of New South Wales and of its offshoot, the Agricultural Stock Club, Wentworth joined the Sydney Turf Club in 1825, even though the exclusives predominated in all three organizations. He continued as a director of the Bank of New South Wales until January 1825, was re-elected to the board in the following year and succeeded Captain Piper as president in January 1827. Brisbane treated Wentworth with measured cordiality and invited him to dine at Government House on at least two occasions, in November 1822 and July 1824; D'Arcy also attended a dinner of welcome for Francis Forbes, the new chief justice, in March 1824. From 1821 to 1824 Wentworth remained a commissioner of the turnpike road and a committee-member of the Native Institution. Having donated £10 towards the building of a Catholic chapel in Sydney and supported Father John Therry's appeal for a government subsidy, on 17 March 1827 'D'Arcy Wentworth of Armagh' chaired a dinner at Cumming's Hotel in honour of St Patrick at which forty merry-makers, Protestant and Catholic, toasted the patron saint with glasses brimful of Irish whisky. Late in life Wentworth steadily began to gain popularity. While he found the experience as gratifying as it was novel, he was not distracted from pursuing more tangible rewards. In 1820 he had transferred the capital from his remaining trading interests to pastoral activities. After applying unsuccessfully in 1823 for a grant of land at Bathurst on which to run sheep, he concentrated on expanding his cattle holdings, especially in the Illawarra, and continued to profit by supplying the commissariat.[3]

Mary Ann and Katherine, Wentworth's sixth and seventh children by Ann Lawes, were born in 1820 and 1825 respectively, enlarging the little commonwealth at Home Bush and adding to the dense context of its bondings. With more forbearance than rapport, D'Arcy's youngest sister, Mary Anne, sent news from Ireland of his extended family on 6 May 1822. She had read William's book and applauded his talents and abilities, but she wanted nothing from D'Arcy: 'thank God, we have secured a competency for ourselves'. Her brother, William, wrote to Wentworth on 15 January 1824 to say that he had seen young D'Arcy march through Dublin with a division of the 73rd. William's daughter, Martha, planned to emigrate with her husband, William Bucknell, a jeweller and watchmaker, and her father asked Wentworth to help her settle in the colony. From friends in Portadown came tidings of unrest and famine, of Dr Patton's death, and of other countrymen who had embarked for New South Wales, either as free emigrants or as convicts. Cookney wrote from London, recommending his son, George, and his brother-in-law, Mr James, to Wentworth's protection. There were also letters from friends in Australia. Warren Kerr, at Port Macquarie, expressed gratitude for Wentworth's support. Undeterred by receiving scarcely any replies to his correspondence, Robert Lathrop Murray wrote copiously from Hobart Town, twice a year on average. He sent Wentworth a box of cigars; he told him that Governor Arthur was a 'wretched reptile' who surrounded himself with Methodists and prayed 'four times a day'; and he asked D'Arcy to employ a particular convict who was 'sober, honest, active, and obedient and humble and willing, but a great fool & dreadfully stupid'.[4]

Wentworth's duties as a magistrate ran the gamut from matters that were whispered to those that roared. He heard the appeal of William Pritchard whose fiancée, Eleanor Leach, had been sentenced to the Parramatta Factory for absconding from her master's home;

9 Life's little day

because their marriage banns had been published and Eleanor was 'in the family way', Pritchard begged D'Arcy to remit her sentence. A far more weighty issue occupied Wentworth and his fellow magistrates in 1824. The clauses of the New South Wales Act which affected judicial establishments had been embodied in a Charter of Justice. Promulgated in Sydney on 17 May, the charter provided for Courts of Quarter Sessions, but made no specific mention of juries. Saxe Bannister, the attorney-general, considered that these civil courts could not function without juries and advised Brisbane to establish them. On 4 August, in representing the views of the magistrates, Wentworth and John Oxley expressed doubt as to the legality of instituting trial by jury beyond the jurisdiction of the Supreme Court. On the 26th Wentworth chaired a meeting of eight Sydney magistrates. They were divided on the question, and sought written opinions from Bannister and the solicitor-general, John Stephen. Furnished with their conflicting views, the magistrates appealed to the governor who referred the question to the Supreme Court. Chief Justice Forbes determined the issue on 14 October by upholding Bannister's contention. The magistrates were then invited to draw up lists of prospective jurors. In 1819 Wentworth had thought that the colony was not 'ripe' for the introduction of trial by jury; he had therefore refused to sign Eagar's petition. Persuaded by his son, William, in August 1824 D'Arcy made it known that he supported the measure. While he declined an invitation to chair the first Court of Quarter Sessions, he did so only on the ground of ill health. He was aged sixty-two.[5]

William Wentworth was greeted as a hero by the *Sydney Gazette*, the currency lads and lasses, and the supporters of the emancipist party when he returned to Sydney in July 1824. Almost thirty-four years old, sensitive and highly strung, ambitious and self-confident, he knew exactly what he wanted and would stop at nothing to achieve his goal— to become the most powerful man in New South Wales. He was endowed with the same ruthlessness and much of the unremitting drive that characterized his father; he was intensely patriotic and revealed that his love of Australia was the 'master passion' of his life; and he had high principles, though he was willing to sacrifice them to expediency. Donning the mantle of a tribune of the people, he turned to the emancipists, the native-born and the small settlers, and planned to advocate their cause, perhaps less for its own sake than to further his political ends. Yet he was still a bundle of contradictions and acted in ways that bewildered his supporters. The man who was capable of enunciating in Augustan phrases his vision for the colony's future could also resort to the language of a vindictive brat. At one moment he prided himself on his connexion with the English aristocracy; at another he bragged of how he would defang 'that yellow snake', John Macarthur, or take revenge on 'that dark villain', Samuel Marsden. With his dishevelled hair, inturned eye, grating voice and clumsy walk, William was an unprepossessing figure. His enemies described him as 'an ungentlemanlike fellow' who was bound to offend grossly. His close friends formed a hard-drinking set, among them Wardell, Mackaness, Dr Henry Grattan Douglass, Bannister, Stephen and his sons, John and Francis, and the emancipists, Redfern and Dr William Bland. Gossip had it that they held carousals, enlivened by radical talk, pipe-writing and bawdy conversation, in a house in Castlereagh Street. Wentworth was placed under military restraint on three occasions for being drunk and disorderly. It seemed that his prodigality and wanton passions were diverting him from a higher course.[6]

On 25 August, barely a month after Wentworth had stepped ashore from the *Alfred*, the Legislative Council began its initial session. In the absence of Lieutenant-Governor William Stewart who was yet to arrive in the colony, the other four members—Forbes, the chief justice, Goulburn, the colonial secretary, Bowman, the principal surgeon, and Oxley, the surveyor general—adjourned the meeting for want of business. Wentworth was offended by the composition of the council and saw it as 'a wretched mongrel substitute' for the institution he had envisaged. On 10 September, in his first appearance on the stage of public life, he spoke for nearly two hours in the Supreme Court when he and Wardell were admitted to practise as barristers and solicitors. They soon became the leading advocates in the court and had no equals among the government's law officers. William rented offices and rooms in Macquarie Place, employed two clerks and took a junior partner, Charles Chambers. Working in Equity, conveyancing, and civil and criminal law, the firm received a gross income of £3108 between August 1825 and June 1826. Wentworth made net profits of £869 in 1825 and £1384 in 1826. Although he was no quixotic lawyer, he frequently found himself short of money.[7]

9 Life's little day

To advance their campaign for the rights of emancipists, trial by jury and self-government, on 14 October Wentworth and Wardell launched a weekly newspaper, the *Australian*. It was both a vehicle for their political views and a means of attracting followers. The first issue told readers that a free press was the most legitimate and strongest weapon that could be employed against nepotism, tyranny and oppression. Wardell, who had brought the press and plant from England, looked after the day-to-day running of the newspaper and wrote most of the copy. Wentworth contributed some editorials and paid more than £4000 in 1824-25 as his share of the capital and running costs; income from the accumulated profits on the lease of his properties was limited and he was forced to borrow from his father. Costing one shilling, the *Australian* comprised four pages, with up to four columns of editorial comment, much of it critical of the administration and the exclusives. Within a year the proprietors revelled in the knowledge that the *Australian*'s circulation approached the *Sydney Gazette*'s. Wardell's and Wentworth's audacity in publishing without official permission forced Brisbane to acquiesce and to discontinue government censorship of the *Gazette*. Lord Bathurst thought that freedom of the press would prove 'highly dangerous' in a penal colony; Barron Field saw it as comparable with producing a radical newspaper in Newgate; and the exclusives prophesied that it would leave New South Wales at the mercy of 'freebooters and pirates'. On 24 October 1824 lists of those deemed eligible to serve as jurors were fixed to the doors of Sydney's churches: the name of every person who had come to the colony as a prisoner was omitted. Wentworth used the courtroom and the columns of the *Australian* as platforms to challenge this decision. The conjunction of the roles of barrister and journalist was liable to abuse, but it cemented his solidarity with the emancipists. Socially ostracized and excluded from political power, the ex-convicts and their children constituted one-half of the population. Their former leaders—Redfern, Terry, Hutchinson and Lord—acknowledged Wentworth's dominance. In December he became a director of the Bank of New South Wales. Following his election, rancour between the exclusives and emancipists on the board so intensified that the exclusives established a rival institution, the Bank of Australia, in 1826. Henry Dumaresq, who was to fight a duel with Wardell but later befriend him, regarded Wentworth as 'the demagogue of this country—the champion of the convict classes to which he belongs . . . a man of immoral life and lowest origins'.[8]

News of Macquarie's death had reached the colony in October 1824. John Thomas Campbell and D'Arcy Wentworth invited friends of the late governor to meet at Campbell's house at noon on 5 November to discuss ways of showing respect. As a result of that meeting, at 10 a.m. on Sunday 14 November many of the citizens of Sydney assembled at the court-house in Castlereagh Street. Led by seven mutes, they marched in solemn procession to St Phillip's where the Reverend William Cowper preached a sermon on the text of Isaiah, chapter LX, verse 1: 'Arise, shine, for thy light is come'. The new administration was not officially represented at the service; none of the exclusives chose to attend; and the principal surgeon forbade the tolling of the bell in St James's lest it disturb the sick in the general hospital. William Wentworth was one of the mourners who filed from St Phillip's. On 11 November, in the *Australian*, he had marked the death of Lord Byron:

> The wayward Harold, with his eye of pride,
> The outlaw'd Conrad, Juan's soul of mirth,
> Liv'd each his life intense, and early died.

In the same issue he gave greater space to an obituary in which he praised Macquarie for elevating the emancipists and restoring their self-esteem; he declared that his excesses were 'the errors of the system—not of the man'; and he concluded with the words of the bards who sorrowed over Cú Chulainn's tomb:

> Peace to thy soul, in thy cave,
> Chief of the Isle of Mist.

In eulogizing Macquarie, Wentworth intentionally chose the image of a Celtic warrior and portended a battle to come. From a mythical past he was forging a weapon for the future. On the night of 26 January 1825 a party of emancipists and native-born, eighty in all, met at Mrs Hill's Hyde Park tavern to celebrate the thirty-seventh anniversary of the foundation of the colony. Wentworth was their president and Redfern his deputy. Among many toasts, they drank to the memory of Macquarie, to a house of assembly, to freedom of the press, to trial by

9 Life's little day

jury and to the currency lasses. They sang songs till the early hours of the morning. During the exuberance, the laughter and the shouting, Michael Robinson called on them to drink the toast, 'The land, boys, we live in'. The radical emancipists had their cause; in Wentworth they had found their leader; in Macquarie, their revived hero.[9]

About this time copies of the third edition of Wentworth's book reached New South Wales. The emancipists hailed its author as their historian and their advocate. In this edition, which Eagar had largely revised, Wentworth recommended constitutional reform, representative government, a free press and complete trial by jury. The two-volume work, entitled a *Statistical Account of the British Settlements in Australasia*, ran to 891 pages and was dedicated to Sir James Mackintosh. Wentworth used his book to criticize Commissioner Bigge's reports and the New South Wales Act of 1823 which stemmed from them. He denounced Bigge for having violated the truth in his 'nauseous' reports, and for 'raking together all the dirt and filth, all the scandal, calumnies and lies that were ever circulated in the colony'. For those who had never read the reports, Wentworth depicted Bigge as a blight on the colony, a prejudiced and narrow-souled inquisitor, an official puppet, an accredited spy, and a tool of the exclusives. Furthermore, Bigge was damned for increasing the punishment of convicts and removing their freedom to marry, for curtailing land grants to the native-born and for depriving the emancipists of their jury rights. Wentworth had politicized the past by depicting Macquarie's era as a golden age which had been terminated by Bigge and Bathurst, and interred by Brisbane and Goulburn. Issuing a catchcry for a campaign, his book urged the colonists to petition the Crown and parliament for their right to a voice in the legislature. From these heights Wentworth stooped to vent his animosity against Marsden by accusing him of hypocrisy and cruelty. Marsden found a soul mate in Archdeacon Thomas Hobbes Scott, Bigge's erstwhile secretary, who arrived in May 1825 and winced at being lampooned in the *Australian* as his 'Venerability'.[10]

That month Sarah Cox, the 20-year-old daughter of two ex-convicts, brought a breach of promise action in the Supreme Court against John Paine, a sea captain who traded between Sydney and Van Diemen's Land. Paine had proposed to Sarah in 1822 and been accepted, but he later courted Miss Redmond, daughter of a wealthy emancipist, before paying suit to a widow, Mrs William Laverton. When scandal began to circulate, Sarah accused Paine of 'injuring her reputation'. Asserting that she was a respectable girl who 'kept good company and was never out late at night', she took him to court. Wardell acted for Paine; William Wentworth represented Sarah. The jury awarded her £100 damages plus costs. By that stage she was two months pregnant with Wentworth's child. In 1790 Sarah's father, Francis Cox (1745–1831), had been convicted of burglary and sentenced to seven years transportation; his destitute wife, Margaret, and their three sons and infant daughter remained in Shropshire, surviving largely on poor relief. Cox set up as a blacksmith in Sydney in 1797. Sarah's mother was Frances Morton (1767–1847). Tried in Middlesex in 1795 on a charge of stealing, Fanny was transported for the term of her natural life and reached Sydney in April 1796. She was found guilty of theft in 1798 and charged with using abusive language in 1799. About this time she formed an association with Cox; though they never married, she was referred to as his 'wife'. Fanny and Francis were to have five children: James (born in 1800, died before 1810), Sarah (1805–80), Elizabeth (1807–44), Mary Maria (1809–85) and Henrietta (1812–92). Their home was a modest cottage by the waterfront on Sydney Cove, adjoining the workshop where Cox specialized as a ship and anchor smith. In 1803 he was acquitted on a charge of receiving stolen goods. Found guilty of selling 80 lb of government lead in 1809, he served twelve months at the Coal River. During that year his family lived on a farm at Parramatta. Cox re-established his smithing business in 1810. Largely in response to pressure from his eldest son, John, who served as a private with the 73rd in New South Wales in 1810–14, Francis agreed to make a regular provision for his wife and family in England. From 1823 he leased land near Phillip and Bent streets on which he built two cottages; in his late seventies he continued to work as a smithy.

Sarah received a rudimentary education and learned to read and write, but her 'sentences were rarely punctuated' and her spelling was 'erratic'. At sixteen she was apprenticed to Mrs Elizabeth Foster, a milliner and free immigrant. The native-born Sarah, an illegitimate daughter of twice-convicted parents, had never been admitted to genteel society and her moral character was blemished. In mid-1825 Wentworth took her six miles from Sydney along the Parramatta road

9 Life's little day

to the privacy of Petersham, an estate he rented. Their daughter, Thomasine (Timmie), was born there on 18 December. She was baptized at St James's Church, Sydney, on 15 January 1826, the child out of wedlock of 'Sarah Cox and W. C. Wentworth'. In September Wentworth bought Petersham from Captain Piper, paying £1500 for the 295-acre farm, with its house, orchard and grazing paddocks. He stayed with Sarah at weekends and spent the rest of the week in Sydney. In his absence she had the company of several servants. A serene and practical woman, with raven hair, a high forehead, searching eyes, tight lips and a full figure, she was strikingly attractive. Wentworth was to find in her a stabilizing influence and to write of her:

> For I must love thee, love thee on,
> Till life's remotest latest minute;
> And when the light of life is gone,
> Thou'll find its lamp had *thee* within it.[11]

Meantime, in May 1825 Sir Thomas Brisbane received news that stunned him. He had repeatedly told the Colonial Office that he had transformed the penal colony by cutting costs, eliminating peculation, restricting pardons, diminishing crime and elevating morals. What he had not told his superiors was that he usually spent one day a week on business in Sydney and the other six at Parramatta where he found time to observe twelve thousand stars. In moments of despair he felt that an angel sent from heaven could not succeed in ruling so strangely constituted a society as that which came to be known as Bottomless Bay. Allegations of Brisbane's negligence reached Downing Street, as did reports that he had fallen out with Frederick Goulburn. On 29 and 30 December 1824 Lord Bathurst wrote letters recalling both of them. In public Brisbane responded with a becoming grace. He cordially accepted his dismissal, if thereby the public interest would benefit; he referred with pride to his achievements; and he held out a forgiving hand to Goulburn. In private correspondence Brisbane wrote that, in place of the thicket of thorns he had encountered, he would leave a bed of roses to his successor, Lieutenant-General Ralph Darling, whose salary was higher than his own. Sir Thomas's vanity was piqued. From May 1825 he endeavoured to boost his reputation in the colony. He hoped to enlist the support of 'the general voice of the Inhabitants' and to assure his patron, the Duke of Wellington, that he had been unjustly recalled.[12]

As well as being a significant month in the lives of Sarah Cox, Scott and Brisbane, May 1825 saw D'Arcy Wentworth's resignation as superintendent of police and presiding magistrate. Nine of his fellow justices of the peace presented him with a valedictory address acknowledging 'the kind, considerate and deliberate manner' with which he had instructed them, and the 'humane', 'firm and impartial spirit' which had characterized his decisions on the bench. They expressed their good will towards him and trusted that his successor would tread in his 'official' steps. Overlooking the deliberate emphasis on his public role, their colonial elder made a dignified reply and retired to the domesticity of Home Bush. On the 19th of that month Captain Francis Nicholas Rossi commenced duty as superintendent of police. He was paid £600 per annum, three times what Wentworth had received. In a matter of months Rossi reorganized the Sydney police in line with London's Bow Street office. Able and conscientious, he kept a strict surveillance over his constables, but was continually hampered by inadequate funds and poor recruits. Although his supervision was limited to the police in Sydney, he felt the weight of his duties and, in 1827, was temporarily appointed to a less arduous post as acting-collector of customs.[13]

So readily did Brisbane court the people's voice that the *Australian* began to extol his virtues. It portrayed him as one who had facilitated the transition from a gaol to a colony by granting the inhabitants a free press and a limited form of trial by jury. On 21 October more than a hundred people attended a public meeting at the court-house to frame a farewell address to their governor. Alexander Berry, an ally of the exclusives, presented a draft to the gathering. Wentworth brushed it aside as 'too lukewarm, too inadequate', a 'mere milk and water' production. After lauding Macquarie and Brisbane, he launched an attack on the exclusives, 'the yellow snakes of the colony'. They misled Commissioner Bigge; they employed clandestine tactics; and they opposed liberty. Although the exclusives were powerful, he would deprive them of their venom and their fangs. Wentworth then put forward his own address which proclaimed the necessity of introducing 'two fundamental principles of the British Constitution', trial by jury in its fullest extent and taxation by representation. He advocated the establishment of a house of assembly of 'at least one hundred Members'. Wardell objected to parts of Wentworth's proposal, but it was carried 'triumphantly' to prolonged applause. Five delegates—D'Arcy and William Wentworth, Thomas Raine, J. Brown and Daniel Cooper —were elected to deliver the address to the governor. In the presence of his senior staff, Brisbane received them at Government House and accepted the address. The governor told them that public approval of his administration was of 'peculiar value and importance' to him. He went on to state that popular institutions of the parent country could be introduced with advantage in New South Wales and that he would promote the colonists' claims for an extension of their civil rights when he returned to England. Wentworth was convinced that he had achieved all he usefully could from the *Australian* and severed his connexion with that newspaper. Henceforward he intended to use public meetings and petitions as the major means of conducting his personal crusade. The *Sydney Gazette* dubbed him the 'Australian Counsellor'.[14]

John Macarthur rallied opposition to Wentworth's wild ideas. In Macarthur's opinion the meeting on 21 October had not only inflamed 'the worst passions of the lower orders', but excited 'a spirit of animosity' towards the upper classes and 'contempt' for all legitimate authority. To dispel any impression that Wentworth's address had universal support, the exclusives drew up a petition, secured sixty-one signatures and forwarded it to Lord Bathurst. The petition contained three major recommendations: the creation of an Executive Council; increasing the Legislative Council to fifteen members chosen by the Crown from the most respectable landholders and merchants in the colony; and extending trial by jury, provided that jurors were selected on the same principles as in England. As a means of helping Bathurst appreciate the nature of the pro-convict group, Macarthur sent some brief character sketches of their leaders. He depicted them as criminals, debtors, publicans, shopkeepers, slave-traders, adventurers and Jews; against the names of D'Arcy and William Wentworth he wrote 'too well known to require a description'. At this time the exclusives proposed to honour Brisbane with a farewell dinner to which no emancipist would be invited. Brisbane tried to persuade his prospective hosts to extend the list of guests, but they remained obdurate and cancelled the occasion. Capitalizing on this political blunder, William Wentworth, Raine and Cooper arranged another dinner for the governor. Brisbane accepted their invitation. Held on the night of 7 November at Nash's Inn,

Parramatta, the farewell proved an outstanding success. With D'Arcy Wentworth as president and the governor seated at his right hand, a hundred guests ate and drank at tables arranged in the shape of a horseshoe. Conviviality and good humour prevailed. When D'Arcy was forced by illness to retire from the chair, William assumed his place. Acknowledging that he was proud to be the son of such a worthy man, he described his father as an 'upright and zealous friend of liberty'. Toasts were drunk to the king, to the prosperity of Australia and to the memory of Phillip and Macquarie. In proposing the toast to Brisbane, William referred to the many benefits that the colony had received from his hand. On 1 December Brisbane sailed for England in the *Mary Hope*. He called at the Colonial Office where he was rebuked for having injudiciously encouraged demands for trial by jury and representative government.[15]

Darling was sworn in as the seventh governor of New South Wales on 20 December 1825. He was fifty-three years old and had served with the army in the West Indies, at the Horse Guards in London, and in Spain. Posted to Mauritius as military commander in 1819, he was acting-governor of that island in 1819–20 and 1823. His concept of government was one of military simplicity: it entailed the unquestioning allegiance of his subordinates and the strictest adherence to regulations. Honourable, dignified and exact, Darling was also forbidding, humourless and pedantic. He lacked ease and frankness, and commanded respect without winning affection. Before he reached Sydney he had written a dispatch indicating his wish to adopt an even-handed approach in dealing with a community which comprised such 'jarring and discordant Members':

> It is quite clear that the Emancipists . . . have gained an ascendancy . . . These people will not be *put down*, or rather *kept down* by the old Settlers who are comparatively few in number . . . In making this observation, I distinctly disclaim even the most remote wish of inducing, much less urging a familiar intercourse with Men, who have forfeited their Claim to good character; still I can discover no just or reasonable ground for treating the Emancipists, as a Body, with indiscriminate contumely, which I apprehend has too generally been the practice of the old Settlers, or making them feel that reformation is unavailing.

9 Life's little day

He had therefore determined to govern 'for the benefit of the Colony at large, without any view of becoming popular with any Party'.[16]

At his inauguration Darling expressed the hope that each and every individual would find that justice was administered impartially under his administration; and in his first proclamation he invited all and sundry to adopt a spirit of concord. In the beginning he acted as a mediator and conciliator, seeking to promote 'peace and good fellowship'. To that end he received William Wentworth at Government House with 'courtesy and attention'. Wentworth acknowledged that Darling treated him with 'hospitality and respect'. Yet there were signs that the two could never come to terms. Darling quickly discerned Wentworth's hostility towards him, but was mystified as to the cause. In part it stemmed from personal dislike. The governor had married late in life, at the age of forty-five. His wife Elizabeth, née Dumaresq, was twenty-six years younger than he. Eliza knew Ralph's endearing traits as a husband and father, though these qualities were rarely demonstrated beyond their family circle. In public Darling was icy, formal and unbending. 'Everything about him was meticulous and neat'. 'His nose was sharp, his eyelids heavy', 'his fingers delicate' and his nails carefully pared. His 'face bore little expression', except for a suggestion of assurance and a trace of superciliousness or disdain. Composed, thorough, decisive and extremely hard working, he introduced reforms to centralize the public departments, over which he kept careful watch. Darling was less urbane than Brisbane and as obstinate as Macquarie; his mind lacked flexibility and subtlety; he was easily hurt and had a vindictive streak. It did not take him long to dismiss Wentworth as 'a vulgar, illbred fellow, utterly unconscious of the Common Civilities, due from one Gentleman to another. Besides, he aims at leading the Emancipists, and appears to have taken his stand in opposition to the Government'. When the Bucknells arrived in Sydney, Darling sneered at the shabbiness of Wentworth's 'noble' relations.[17]

In a proclamation, gazetted on 20 December 1825, Darling announced that the Legislative Council was to be expanded to include three civilian members—John Macarthur, Robert Campbell and Charles Throsby—besides the lieutenant-governor, the chief justice, the archdeacon and the colonial secretary; he also announced the establishment of an Executive Council consisting of the men who held these four offices: Stewart, Forbes, Scott and Alexander McLeay. Wentworth felt slighted at being omitted from the council. He was indignant at the inclusion of Scott and infuriated by the selection of Macarthur. As for McLeay, the more Wentworth came to know of the colonial secretary the less he liked him. McLeay was a Scot, a Tory, a former secretary of the Transport Board, a distinguished entomologist and a fellow of the Royal Society. In Wentworth's eyes he was a pensioner, a sinecurist and a lickspittle who knew nothing about the colony. What probably offended Wentworth most was that McLeay understood Darling's values and served him dutifully by working twelve hours a day. Another sign of new directions occurred towards the end of the year with the arrival in Sydney of Robert Dawson, the agent for the Australian Agricultural Company. In the *York* and the *Brothers* he brought 720 sheep, Durham bulls, horses, plants and servants. As a return for its investment of £1 million capital, the company was to receive large areas of land in New South Wales on which to rear flocks of sheep of the finest and purest breed. Its principals, James Macarthur, James Bowman and Hannibal Macarthur, invited many prominent citizens to become shareholders. The emancipists were purposely excluded. Wentworth disapproved of the venture from the start and condemned it as a monopoly dominated by the Macarthurs and their connexions.[18]

On 22 December 1825 fourteen colonists, headed by D'Arcy Wentworth, requested the sheriff, John Mackaness, to convene a public meeting to prepare an address of welcome to Governor Darling. Held at the court-house from noon on the stormy Thursday of 12 January 1826, and attended by 120 people, the meeting was orchestrated to shatter Darling's hopes of concord. William Wentworth gave notice that he was prepared to oppose the administration if it failed to meet popular expectations. As soon as the meeting came to order he grasped the initiative by insisting that whatever address were framed it should not be a panegyric. There was no point, he argued, in bestowing praise before it was merited. He acknowledged that changes had recently taken place with the establishment of an Executive Council and the enlargement of the Legislative Council, but contended that these developments merely favoured 'a certain party'. 'Hear, hear!', his listeners responded. Sensing an opportunity to use the native-born in his vendetta against the Macarthurs, he told the currency lads that they were unfairly treated because the free immigrants were being granted all the good land in the colony. The remedy was clear-cut: they must put

9 Life's little day

down the faction that kept them in vassalage. He then read a draft address which emphasized the need for an elected assembly and unlimited trial by jury. The danger of deferring a people's legislature, he continued, exacerbated those internal dissensions which had disturbed the community ever since the arrival of Commissioner Bigge. Led on by passions he had aroused in the crowd, he proceeded to savage the Australian Agricultural Company, though he refrained from referring to the concentration of wealth in the hands of the few. Finally, he indulged in some vulgar abuse of Darling for his unpopularity in Mauritius and regretted to inform his audience that His Excellency was officially connected to the Tory party. The meeting endorsed the address and appointed a deputation of fifteen to present it to the governor. On the 19th William and D'Arcy Wentworth, Robert Lowe, Redfern, Lawson, Terry, Raine, Lord, Cooper, Hutchinson, Edward Smith Hall, James Underwood, John Connell, William Walker and R. C. Pritchett repaired to Government House. Darling received them with his characteristic *sang-froid*. Although he was offended by what he had heard of the conduct of the meeting, he studiously abstained from committing himself and gave no intimation of his views. His reply was a model of dignity: 'Gentlemen, I receive, as I ought, the address which you have been pleased to present to me, conveying the assurance of your loyal and constitutional allegiance to His Majesty'. 'You are aware', he went on,

> that I have not yet had an opportunity of forming an opinion on the points to which you have adverted. I must, therefore, abstain from making any observations in reply. But I shall not fail to put His Majesty's Ministers in possession of your sentiments as now communicated to me, and you may be assured they will receive every due consideration.

The governor declared that his 'exertions for the prosperity and happiness of all classes of the Inhabitants' would be 'stimulated not less by inclination than by a sense of public duty'. Darling's personal view was that the colony was still in its infancy and by no means prepared for such an institution as a Legislative Assembly.[19]

Seven days later, on the hot summer evening of 26 January, William Wentworth presided at a dinner to celebrate the thirty-eighth anniversary of the colony's foundation. Redfern was again his deputy. Almost a hundred guests assembled at Mrs Hill's tavern and remained long into the night. Once more they did as Wentworth bid them. They gave three cheers for King George IV, the Duke of York and the army, the Duke of Clarence and the navy, the Duke of Sussex and the rest of the royal family, and for the health of their present governor. They toasted their heroes, Phillip, Macquarie and Brisbane; they toasted freedom of the press, trial by jury and a house of assembly; they toasted the currency lads and lasses; and they toasted the fleece and plough, and the trade and commerce of New South Wales. Buoyed up by liquor and laughter, they raised their glasses and shouted, 'Hail, Australia'. Wentworth made three short speeches and cracked some jokes about the members of the Legislative Council. At appropriate intervals the band of the Buffs played marches, airs and reels; the music became louder and more out of tune as midnight came and went. By the time the revellers dispersed they had deluded themselves that all that stood between them and their dreams of liberty were that martinet, the governor, or 'that pompous "Venerability", the archdeacon, or that efficient clerk, McLeay, or that madman, John Macarthur'.[20]

One 30-year-old, native-born Australian was based in Scotland, far from the madding crowd. That man was William's brother, D'Arcy. In 1823, owing to difficulties with his commanding officer, he had unsuccessfully sought a transfer to another regiment. He remained with the 73rd and was appointed deputy judge-advocate in charge of courts martial. Next year, acting on Fitzwilliam's advice, he drew a bill on his father for £1100 to buy a company; the balance of the purchase-money was to come from the sale of his lieutenancy. Fitzwilliam asked Wentworth to honour the bill. On 16 August 1824 D'Arcy informed his father that he had encountered numerous disappointments in the army and had no wish to be subjected to more. He hoped that his father would provide the money to enable him to secure a captaincy, and that he would increase his allowance from £50 to £100 a year. Most of Lieutenant Wentworth's peers had 'something handsome besides their pay'; some owned a horse and gig; and all of them enjoyed 'many little comforts and amusements' which D'Arcy could ill afford. If he were successful in obtaining a company, he planned to try to enter the Royal Military College at Sandhurst: 'I shall fag hard whilst there and have little doubt of getting such certificates as will entitle me to . . . staff attention'. On 20 May 1825, in a letter to William, D'Arcy disclosed his good fortune in gaining a promotion without purchase. He trusted that their father 'would no longer evince that apathy and negligence which has hitherto so unfortunately marked his conduct towards me'. Having heard rumours that his regiment was about to be posted to the West Indies, Captain Wentworth was toying with the idea of exchanging with an officer in India or entering the cavalry.

By the end of the northern winter of 1826 young D'Arcy received the news for which he had waited eighteen months. On the last day of February he wrote to his father, thanking him for his liberality in meeting the £1100 bill. He told him that he had used £100 of this amount to pay off his debts. If his father were prepared to send additional money, he would be able to purchase a commission as major. This higher rank would increase his pay and add to his respectability. He assured his father that he had conducted himself 'in a manner deserving the great name I am proud to bear'. Despite such upright conduct, he had drunk a 'bitter draught' to 'the dregs' and could find no cause to which to ascribe 'the determined silence you have for some years (I may say since the time I left New South Wales) maintained towards me'. His father had said that D'Arcy seldom wrote to him. D'Arcy protested—rather too much—that the opposite was the truth.

At St Cuthbert's parish church, Princes Street, Edinburgh, on 27 April 1826 Captain D'Arcy Wentworth married Elizabeth Macpherson, the third daughter of the late Major Charles Macpherson, barrackmaster general for Scotland, and his wife, Margaret. Before their nuptials D'Arcy and Eliza signed a matrimonial contract. Both parties agreed to share D'Arcy's assets to the value of £6000; any surplus was to be 'at his own absolute and exclusive disposal'. D'Arcy consented to educate any children of the marriage and to bequeath to Eliza, should she survive him, 'all the household furniture, linen and plate'. Eliza brought her husband a dowry of £800 and undertook to give him whatever she might inherit from her mother. The bride's brothers, Duncan, a captain in the 24th Regiment, and George, an assistant-surgeon with the East India Company, pledged themselves to look after her interests. D'Arcy and Elizabeth were married for thirty-five years. They remained childless.[21]

Like the prodigal in the parable, who wasted his substance on riotous living but ate of the fatted calf, William was Dr Wentworth's

The Wentworths

favoured son. Little by little, by perceptible and accumulating degrees, D'Arcy came to see in his first-born a bolder and enviable version of himself. There was something singular about William. After converting his father to his causes, he exploited D'Arcy's links with the emancipists and his standing in the wider community. In no way daunted by how unfledged, unpolished and uncommitted the emancipists were, the Australian Counsellor reinvigorated them as a party and seized the political running. The exclusives retaliated by exerting pressure on Governor Darling. Archdeacon Scott railed against the press for mocking church and state, and for sowing the seeds of vice and discord. To counter the forces of evil and anarchy, he made it known that the Church of England was to receive large areas of land in New South Wales and Van Diemen's Land which would provide the wealth for its missions of salvation and social order. When Scott was satirized in the *Australian* he asked Darling for redress. On 29 April 1826 John Macarthur, by then sick in body and mind, importuned the governor to institute legal action against Robert Howe for libelling him in the *Sydney Gazette*. Darling stood firm. Believing that Scott had no judgement and would never be respected, and that Macarthur was intemperate, factious and turbulent, the governor declined to intervene, though he was pressed to do so by such alarmists as Oxley and Bowman. The law, Darling said, lay open to Scott and Macarthur, as it did to any individual who wished to institute his own proceedings. Samuel Marsden's reprisal took the form of a 92-page pamphlet, *An answer to certain calumnies in the late Governor Macquarie's pamphlet, and the third edition of Mr Wentworth's Account of Australasia*. In it he set out why he had opposed Macquarie's measures to reduce bond and free to one common level. Fulminating against his detractors, the clergyman denied that he trafficked in spirits, that he lusted for material comforts and that he was a severe magistrate. By the Reverend Marsden's own lights, he was strict, but never severe. Bathurst judged that Marsden's vehemence was as little suited to his advanced age as it was to the profession to which he belonged. In August the secretary of state directed Darling to caution him accordingly. By the following month Darling was immersed in his work, reforming the public service and publishing new regulations for the granting and purchase of land. He was convinced that those he governed were—in the main—quiet, orderly and apparently well disposed, that his administration could confidently hold its ground and that things would go on 'peaceably and pleasantly'. In Darling's opinion the government 'never stood higher than at present in public estimation'.[22]

Within sixty days Darling received a rude awakening. The advent of the *Australian* had liberated the colony's newspaper press, giving impetus to and providing outlets for political disaffection. Wardell's wit and gusto, and his lucid, if prolix, style, were appreciated by his readers. Under his editorship the *Australian* continued to needle the government, the exclusives and the Church of England in the person of the archdeacon. In May 1821 Robert Howe had succeeded his father, George, as editor of the *Sydney Gazette*. The son of a convict, Robert married a currency lass, Ann Bird. Family ties bound him to the emancipists and native-born, but he was sober and religious in outlook, and reluctant to take a political side. Although he was disturbed by William Wentworth's forcing tactics, Howe gravitated towards an anti-exclusivist stance and promoted the idea of a legislative assembly. He adopted the words, 'ADVANCE AUSTRALIA' as the motto for the *Gazette* and from 11 February 1826 flanked the imprint with a kangaroo and emu. His newspaper was published twice a week from October 1825 and for a brief period in 1827 as a daily. By that year its circulation ran to six hundred copies. On 19 May 1826 another newspaper, the *Monitor*, was launched in Sydney. Priced at one shilling, this eight-page weekly was edited by Edward Smith Hall. He had come to the colony as a lay missionary in 1811, failed as a farmer and taken a post with the mercantile firm, Jones & Riley; Hall's wife died in childbirth in August 1826, leaving him with a son and seven daughters to rear. The *Monitor*'s masthead bore a glaring eye and the words 'Nothing Extenuate Nor Set Down Aught In Malice'. In the first issue Hall promised to use the language of sense and moderation. By espousing the cause of the poor, he was driven to expose the barbarity of the convict system and its corrupt officials; that step taken, he was drawn to support the liberties of the people and to condemn Darling's intractability. On 5 April 1827 the *Gleaner* appeared. Published weekly, costing ninepence and with a circulation of two hundred, its editor was Dr Laurence Hynes Halloran, an Anglican clergyman and schoolmaster who had been transported in 1819 for forgery. Halloran affirmed that the *Gleaner* would be conducted on the principle '*salus populi suprema lex*' and that his newspaper would consider the public good as the primary object of its labours. Pro-emancipist, but calmer in tone than the *Monitor* and the *Australian*, the *Gleaner* opposed oppression, but upheld the necessity of subordination, deference and submission in society. It often defended Archdeacon Scott. The *Gleaner* folded in less than six months, ceasing publication on 29 September. Before its demise, John Macarthur complained of 'four newspapers . . . all in the convict interest and the editors all desperate radicals alike, shameless and ill-principled'. As early as August 1826 Darling's attorney-general officially informed him that the *Monitor* had published seditious material and that the *Australian* had libelled officers in the king's service.[23]

Two privates in the 57th Regiment, Joseph Sudds and Patrick Thompson, brought matters to a crisis, though the pair were mere pawns in the ensuing manoeuvres. Between 8 p.m. and 9 p.m. on 20 September 1826 Sudds and Thompson stole twelve yards of calico from Michael Napthali's shop in York Street, Sydney, in the hope of being convicted and dismissed from the army. After their arrest they confessed that they had intended to start a new life by settling in the colony. Shocked by this admission, and by the fear that other soldiers might follow their example, Darling learned that a Court of Quarter Sessions had sentenced them to be transported to a secondary penal station for seven years. The governor was unsatisfied with this sentence and altered it to seven years hard labour in chains on the public roads. At 11 a.m. on 22 November the two men were brought before a parade at the barracks to be drummed out of the regiment. They were stripped of their uniforms and clad in convicts' yellow slops. Their legs were clamped in iron rings, and an iron collar with protruding bars was fastened around their necks; chains linked the collar to the leg-irons. Darling had personally designed these instruments of punishment which weighed 14 lb and were more than three times heavier than the fetters and chains worn by prisoners in the road gangs. While the regimental band played 'The Rogue's March', Sudds and Thompson were escorted to the barracks gates, handed over to the constabulary and sent to gaol. Sudds, who had been ill for a fortnight, died on the 27th. Thompson was taken to Lapstone Hill where he toiled in a road gang. Nine days later he was imprisoned in the hulk, *Phoenix*.[24]

The press responded swiftly. On 29 November the *Australian* charged Darling with torture and with exceeding his powers in changing the sentence imposed on Sudds and Thompson. Through the

9 Life's little day

Monitor, Hall endorsed Wardell's view and cited Darling's actions as 'proof of the defectiveness of autocratic government which required to be curbed by the grant of trial by jury and a legislative assembly'. Howe pursued a more cautious and trimming line; the *Sydney Gazette* ultimately sided with the governor. By 20 December Wardell had inspected the irons and conceded that they were 'not calculated to inflict torture'. The *Australian* also acknowledged that the surgeon and medical staff, rather than Darling, were to blame for Sudds's death. Towards the year's end the criticism showed signs of dissipating. Yet there was one prominent colonist who refused to forget what had happened. On 15 December William Wentworth wrote to Lord Bathurst, informing him that the incident had aroused a 'feeling of horror among all classes except the immediate dependants of Governor Darling'. Submitting that Sudds and Thompson had been subjected to a punishment that constituted a 'high misdemeanour in law', he called for Darling's impeachment. Wentworth knew that the New South Wales Act of 1823 was soon to be reviewed. It would help his cause if he could discredit the existing form of government. In addition to threatening to have the case of Sudds and Thompson raised in the House of Commons, he endeavoured to rally public support in the colony for a petition in favour of constitutional reform. Darling realized that Wentworth was engaging in a prolonged campaign:

> Mr Wentworth speaks, as he wrote when Compiling his Book, of the Independence of the Colony, and compares it to the situation formerly of America and the probability of its being driven, as America was, to shake off the Yoke. In short, he is anxious to become the 'Man of the People'; and he seems to think that the best means of accomplishing this is by insulting the Government.

Dumaresq recognized that the death of Sudds had provided Wentworth with a 'political lever', enabling him to thrust his 'pretensions before parliament'. And Forbes saw how Wentworth intended to use the episode both as a 'War Cry' and a 'political juggle'.[25]

As a result of Wentworth's agitation, on 16 January 1827 twenty-four colonists, headed by Sir John Jamison and an ailing D'Arcy Wentworth, requested the sheriff to convene a public meeting on Friday the 26th. The crowd in the court-house cheered when William

The Wentworths

Wentworth rose to speak. He informed them that they had assembled to consider the propriety of petitioning the king and both houses of parliament to grant two great constitutional privileges, trial by jury and taxation by representation. In a loud, clear voice Hall read Wentworth's proposed petition. It affirmed that the people's competency for trial by jury had been established by two years experience in the Courts of Quarter Sessions; it maintained that four-fifths of the inhabitants had been excluded from the right to serve as jurors; it prayed for a legislative assembly of no fewer than one hundred members to give the colonists a voice in the management of their interests; it recommended that those who owned one thousand acres or more should be permitted to stand for election, and that £10 householders and £10 leaseholders be enfranchised. After some observations by Jamison, Gregory Blaxland, D'Arcy Wentworth and Wardell, William Wentworth moved that the petition be adopted. Jamison seconded the motion. It was carried unanimously by 'the Voice of Australia'. Darling forwarded the petition to England. He dismissed the proposal for an assembly as 'totally inadmissible' and expressed concern over the growing influence of the 'Radicals'. In an attempt to discredit William Wentworth, the governor described him as 'the natural son of a Highwayman and a convict'. Forbes was more liberal in his response to the petition. He thought it contained 'many truths . . . the voice of the public will be heard, and, if it is not permitted to speak through the medium of a house of assembly, it will seek such other channels of proclaiming itself as cannot be closed'.[26]

Disturbed by these developments, Darling took up a suggestion made by Lord Bathurst in July 1825 that the government should license the newspapers as a means of restraining them. The difficulty was that no legislation could be passed by the Legislative Council unless the chief justice certified that it accorded with English law. The time had passed when governor and chief justice saw eye to eye; by 1827 Darling knew that Forbes had become a drinking partner of William Wentworth and Wardell. On 11 April the governor submitted the drafts of two bills to the Legislative Council: one was to license newspapers and increase the penalties for publishing blasphemous or seditious libel; the other was to impose a stamp duty on the press. In Forbes's absence the Executive Council endorsed the bills. Although the chief justice had serious reservations, Darling was adamant that the legislation should be passed. The first bill was enacted, uncertified and without the licensing clauses, on 27 April as 8 Geo.IV, no.2. Following further debate, the second bill became law on 3 May. Late in that month Forbes spelt out in dignified and measured language why he had withheld his approval. The real object of the bills, he contended, was to cripple or destroy the circulation of the newspapers; as such, the legislation was repugnant to the principle of freedom of the press. He refused to certify the licensing sections of the former bill and to approve the amount of four pence specified as stamp duty in the latter. Darling had the humiliation of having to rescind the Act, 8 Geo.IV, no.3, on 31 May. The *Australian* and the *Monitor* exalted Forbes as their idol, but the chief justice's protracted silence had undermined the governor. Forbes incurred Darling's displeasure and was to suffer for it.[27]

In the early months of 1827 D'Arcy Wentworth was troubled by the actions of a man who had reason to detest him. After losing his wife to Wentworth in 1810, James Macneal had spent many years in Van Diemen's Land. He returned to Sydney to find that Ann was cohabiting 'with her base seducer', and had 'several children, now living with herself at a farm of his called *Home Bush*'. In October 1824 Macneal sought redress against Wentworth for alienating the affections of his wife, an act 'persevered in, and well known to the world'. Wentworth had occasioned him 'great injury' and frustrated 'his hopes in life'. Intent on instituting a prosecution, Macneal submitted a petition to Bannister, the attorney-general, but was advised that Wentworth could not be indicted on a criminal charge. In August 1825 Macneal chose to bring a civil proceeding for the restoration of his wife. Owing to his poverty, he sought legal assistance. George Allen, a solicitor, a pious member of the Methodist Society and a free immigrant, initially agreed to act in his interests and, on 1 February 1827, filed a suit against Wentworth for £1500 damages. When Macneal was unable to pay Allen's fees, the lawyer deserted him. The case was tried on 22 March. Wentworth was summoned to appear, but the ill-fated Macneal, with no barrister to represent him, was non-suited and the court dismissed the case.[28]

Almost as if there were a certain circularity to life, D'Arcy Wentworth was reminded not only of his comparatively recent past but also of his distant origins. He received a letter from one he had befriended, David Masiere of County Armagh, who referred to 'the days of Auld Lang Syne' when D'Arcy was famous as a fisherman on the river-banks at Tanderagee and Portadown; Masiere gave him a rod, reel, line and flies, and sent best wishes for his health. Wentworth had been ill for months and his strength was failing. He also received a letter from his sister, Martha. She reproved him for not replying to her earlier correspondence and concluded that he had either forgotten his friends in Ireland or that they were beneath his owning them as relations. Martha told him that he was very near to his eternal state. 'You are fast going down the stream of time into the great ocean of eternity. The pleasure of sin will therefore soon be gone . . . old age or weakness will prevent [you] taking pleasure in the world, or in gratification of unlawful desires.' She urged her brother to 'be deeply humbled for your past sins . . . the sins of your youth as well as those of advanced years'. Prompted 'by nothing but love', Martha prayed daily for D'Arcy's salvation. Although she felt 'unwanted', she asked him to believe that she was still his affectionate sister. On 5 July D'Arcy signed a complex will which was witnessed by Redfern, and by Wentworth's servants, Patrick O'Donnell, Thomas Harpur and John Gow. D'Arcy Wentworth died of pneumonia early on the winter morning of Saturday 7 July 1827 at Home Bush. He was sixty-five. William sat by his father to the end, fathomed the sorrows of his aged face and felt the enormity of being alone.[29]

10

Of graves and epitaphs

> Let's talk of graves, of worms, and epitaphs . . .
> Let's choose executors and talk of wills
>
> Shakespeare, *Richard II*, Act 3, scene ii

At 1 o'clock on the wet and dismal afternoon of Monday 9 July 1827 some 150 people, including magistrates, merchants and members of the Bar, assembled at Home Bush; fifty came on horseback and the remainder arrived in forty carriages and gigs. Draped in black cloth, the coffin that contained all that was mortal of D'Arcy Wentworth was placed in a hearse, drawn by four horses. The cortège made its way to St John's, Parramatta, where a large number of tradesmen and common people had gathered. Redfern and four mutes led the procession into the church. William Wentworth and his half-brother, George, were the chief mourners. On the occasion of a funeral, enmity can be suspended, if not forgotten. Samuel Marsden, no friend of the Wentworths, conducted the service according to the rites of the Church of England and read those immortal lines, 'We brought nothing into this world, and it is certain that we can carry nothing out . . . verily every man living is altogether vanity . . . Man that is born of a woman hath but a short time to live . . . He cometh up, and is cut down, like a flower'. Marsden also recited the words which summed up D'Arcy's earthly pilgrimage, 'My heart was hot within me'. The eldest son, who loved his father boundlessly, shed tears, as did the woman whom D'Arcy had loved and whose child quickened within her. After the hearse was driven to the nearby cemetery, the coffin was borne to the graveside by eight of Wentworth's servants. Piper, 'Ironbark' Lawson and Campbell walked as pallbearers on one side, Harris, Brooks and Throsby on the other. D'Arcy Wentworth's body was committed to the earth of his adopted country. One hundred of those present then adjourned to Walker's Inn. With Mackaness and Lawson seated in places of honour at either end of the table, a cold collation was served. The guests drank a single toast, and that in silence, to 'the memory of our departed friend'.[1]

William Wentworth had arranged for the remains of his mother, Catherine Crowley, to be removed from a contiguous grave and buried with those of his father. He set in place a simple tombstone on which was chiselled: 'Here lie the Mortal Remains of D'Arcy Wentworth Esquire . . . Also of Catherine his Wife'. The inscription included their years of death and an estimate of their age. William added one further line, 'An honest man the noblest work of God'. Whether he had been struck by Alexander Pope's couplet,

> A wit's a feather, and a chief a rod;
> An honest man's the noblest work of God

or by the words of Robert Burns,

> Princes and lords are but the breath of kings,
> 'An honest man's the noblest work of God',

William retained an idealized image of his father. The ardency of his love for the man who had planted ambition in his heart, and given him the means to fulfil it, made him determined to transmit his impression of D'Arcy—unreal as it was—to his contemporaries and to posterity.[2]

All four editors of the colony's newspapers were disposed to accord with William Wentworth's intent. Three of them—Howe, Hall and Wardell—had, in differing degrees, fallen under his sway; none of them had intimate knowledge of D'Arcy's career before 1810; and, as a body, the editors were inclined to concentrate on the last three years of his life, the period with which they were most familiar. The *Sydney Gazette* published its eulogy on 9 July. According to Howe, Wentworth had:

> studiously devoted the best part of his eventful life in this country to the service of its public. During the length of time he was in the

Medical Department, whether as Subordinate or Principal Medical Officer, a single complaint was never known to have been preferred against him. As Minister of Police, to the duties of which post he gave his nights as well as days, the whole Colony can bear testimony to the value of his talents, zeal and usefulness. In the exercise of his Magisterial functions he aimed at informality and no judicial character could exceed in that particular. Though decidedly what the world would term a Ministerial character, nevertheless he was never known meanly to subserve the interests of any party. He was loyal from principle, and indefatigable in his public career, from a desire of being useful to his King and Country; indeed he might be viewed as a Patriot, in whom were blended the political virtues of loyalty and independence.

On the 10th the *Monitor* waxed panegyrical. Hall declared that Wentworth's death was 'a *national loss*'. On a feature page, enclosed in black borders, the *Monitor* referred to him as:

> a lover of freedom; a consistent steady friend of the people; a kind and liberal master; a just and humane Magistrate; a steady friend; and an honest man. Mr Wentworth's talents were not brilliant, but they were very solid. To a great measure of prudence and caution, he joined a stern love of independence. He was a lover of liberty on whom the people *could rely*. He was one of the greatest land-holders in the Colony, and perhaps the wealthiest man. But he considered his possessions as calling upon him the more to support the true welfare of the people by maintaining their rights. Therefore, whenever the Colonists wanted a friend to address the King, the Parliament, or the Governor, Mr Wentworth never shrank from the station allotted to him by Providence. He felt that by his wealth, talents, and experience, he was the natural protector of the people's rights. He was therefore a steady attendant on all public conventions of the Colonists, and the first to place his name at the head of a Requisition to the Sheriff, when grievances required to be redressed.

Two days later the *Monitor* added, 'Mr Wentworth had the art of maintaining his own opinion ... without making any enemies'. In the

The Wentworths

Australian on 11 July Wardell used William Wentworth's account of D'Arcy's lineage to trace the fortunes of the Fitzwilliam and Strafford families in England and Ireland. D'Arcy's father was described not as an innkeeper but as 'a country gentleman of moderate income'. Emphasizing the approbation Dr Wentworth had received on retiring from his various offices, Wardell concluded:

> As a medical practitioner, Mr Wentworth was distinguished for the tenderness with which he treated his patients of every degree ... He was peculiarly skilful in treating the diseases of children ... As an able, upright and impartial Magistrate, Mr Wentworth's merits are too well remembered by all classes of the community to need repetition here. As a man, his manly and independent principles—his high integrity—his moderation—his urbanity—his public and private virtues could not fail to endear him to his friends and fellow citizens, and to excite throughout the Colony the liveliest feelings of regret at his demise ... It might, without great exaggeration, be said of him ... 'He is the only person I have ever known, whom all his countrymen agree in praising'.

Halloran followed suit on 14 July. In paying tribute to D'Arcy Wentworth, the *Gleaner* reported that he had filled the important offices of assistant and principal surgeon, superintendent of police, treasurer of the police fund and senior magistrate:

> In these high, and confidential, but arduous employments, it was his singular good fortune, by his moderation and integrity, to conciliate the esteem of each successive Administration ... without ... compromising his claim to popular respect ... In private life Mr Wentworth was warm-hearted, frank, friendly, and affectionate, and his memory will be long cherished by his family and connexions with the sincerest regard.

Such eulogies became the stuff of legend.[3]

Two people in England had a rather different perspective. In 1828 Lady Frances, Lord Fitzwilliam's second sister, broke the news of Wentworth's death to her brother, William. 'All you did for him has not been thrown away. He has left four widows. The rest of the history is as good as it is wonderful. The provision for his eldest son is beyond belief—in money £150 000 and 4000 acres'. D'Arcy's 'nine younger children are provided for out of the rest of the property. Best of all he died in a very high situation in the law, Chief Justice or something like it, and with a character unimpeached in his situation!' She had received this account, partly garbled and partly accurate, from young D'Arcy. The 4th Earl Fitzwilliam died on 8 February 1833 at the age of eighty-four and was succeeded by his only son, Charles. In July 1834 Cookney wrote from Castle Street to the 5th Earl, making yet another endeavour to serve the Wentworths' interests. He began the letter with his version of part of the family history.

> I presume your Lordship recollects a Mr D'Arcy Wentworth who went through Your Lordship's Father's Interest to New South Wales. He had two sons by the first woman he lived with, one named 'William Charles' and the other 'D'Arcy', and a host by other women. William Charles now flourishes as a counsel in Sydney. D'Arcy went into the Army and has always conducted himself well. He is now senior captain in the 63rd Regiment of Foot.

Cookney asked whether Fitzwilliam would lend young D'Arcy £1400 so that he could purchase a majority. D'Arcy was prepared to repay £955 as soon as possible and the balance over two years. In August 1834 the new earl minuted the letter: 'Agreed to provide £1400'.[4]

The Sydney newspapers and William Wentworth erred in their panegyrics, no less than did Lady Fitzwilliam and Cookney who saw little more in D'Arcy Wentworth than a womanizing Croesus. None of their accounts really explained why he was as he was. If his sister, Martha, were to be believed, D'Arcy left Ireland in 1785 under something of a cloud. In London he strayed from his profession, formed dangerous liaisons and was tried four times on nine separate charges of highway robbery. That he lacked strength of character was further shown on his voyage from England. The colony to which he sailed in the *Neptune* had a European population of only 591 in 1790; it increased sixtyfold to about 35 000 by 1827. During his career Dr Wentworth served under six different governors and saw the seventh installed. To colonists with a history of British settlement of less than four decades, he seemed to have been in New South Wales from time out of mind. At Queenborough, on Norfolk Island, Wentworth seized virtually every opportunity that came his way; while he served as acting assistant-surgeon and superintendent of convicts, he ventured into farming, and importing and exporting. In New South Wales he made money as a trader, retailer, grazier, agriculturalist, rentier, builder, banker and money-lender, as well as the salaries he drew as a government official. His retrospective allowance of £100 a year as treasurer of the police fund, with his salaries of £365 as principal surgeon and £200 as superintendent of police, meant that he received £665 per annum between 1811 and 1819, a considerable sum, though his successors in those three offices were paid a total of £2010 in 1825.[5]

Settlers in any pioneering community, especially a penal one, need to be tough to survive and ruthless to prosper, the more so if they are placed in a remote outpost, on the margin of the margins. D'Arcy Wentworth reached Norfolk Island with little, if any, knowledge of agriculture or of the management of convicts. What he did possess was ambition, a capacity for hard work, and business acumen. Pushed by a desire to succeed, he blotted out his past and used his medical skill, drive, aggression, personal charm and family connexions to win favour, promotion and indulgences. In New South Wales under Governor Hunter he expanded his trading activities and his landholdings, only to find that his achievements aroused envy. During King's term of office Wentworth marked time. Impetuous and insecure, frustrated and disappointed, he found further grounds to reinforce his belief that a private fortune was a buffer against every adversary and most adversities. Under Bligh he suffered anxiety and humiliation. He retaliated by allying himself with those who brought about the governor's downfall. Wentworth exploited Macquarie's good will and weakness to his own material advantage, and grew in self-assurance, despite the prejudice and jealousy of his enemies. With Brisbane he was initially more circumspect, but gradually began to be politically assertive, a characteristic that intensified under Darling. For thirty-seven years in a frontier society Wentworth demonstrated the opportunism of a man of enterprise in an age of conflict and competition. Prepared to be underhand and unscrupulous, he dealt in spirits, employed unauthorised convict labour, acted litigiously, and speculated in sandalwood, hospital building, land and livestock. These activities were much to the detriment of his public duties. Resourceful and persevering, he was above all a survivor, and one who prospered.

Perhaps Wentworth's most prominent characteristic was his acquisitiveness, a feature of highwaymen. He steadily amassed wealth and was not too particular as to how he did so. Money, however, could not buy him admittance to the ranks of the free settlers. That did not disturb him unduly. He acquiesced in his exclusion from polite society and made his closest friends among the emancipists. His ambition encompassed the next generation. For the most part, he avoided challenging the caste divisions in New South Wales society because he was reluctant to draw attention to circumstances which might damage the prospects of the son for whom he cherished great expectations. His public support for the emancipists' political campaigns in 1824–27 was largely in response to William's urgings and to his own desire to forward his son's ambitions. D'Arcy Wentworth was usually prepared to live and let live. A Whig in his political leanings and an Anglican in his nominal religious allegiance, he was not a man for books and found letter-writing a chore. He showed no interest in music and art. It was the real and the practical, rather than the abstract or the aesthetic, that attracted him. He enjoyed horse-racing, gambling and fishing, was careful in his dress and appearance, and liked to dine well. As a magistrate he was tolerant and humane, certainly in comparison with his fellow justices. He did lose his temper, but, in contrast to many of his landowning contemporaries, he was generally affable and good-natured as a master, and even kind-hearted on occasions. He was well liked and relatively popular, mainly because he never lost the common touch.[6]

Wentworth had twelve children, three sons and a daughter by Catherine Crowley, four sons and four daughters by Ann Lawes. Little evidence survives of his relationship with his second family, of whom the eldest child was sixteen and the youngest only two at the time of their father's death. The twelfth child, D'Arcy Charles (later known as Charles D'Arcy), was born on 5 March 1828. As one who had been indulged in his own childhood and boyhood, Wentworth doted on the little ones, all the more as he grew older. He lavished affection on William, his first-born son and heir. D'Arcy and John recognized that William was their father's favourite and seem to have accommodated themselves to what was widely regarded as the natural order of things.

The Wentworths

Their respect for their father was sorely tested when John was caught up in the row involving Ann Lawes and Maria Ainslie, and when D'Arcy felt that his father continually overlooked opportunities to assist his promotion in the army. In his last will and testament Wentworth provided generously for all his children; he was aware of the importance of their schooling, though he was not overly impressed with the advantages of an English education. If he took his sons into his confidence, it was only to a limited degree: to none of them did he voluntarily reveal that he had been tried for highway robbery. Even less is known of D'Arcy Wentworth as a 'husband'. It is clear that his affection for Catherine grew to something more, that his passion for Ann remained intense, and that he liked Maria, before he placed her in the wings. In her own will, signed on 15 April 1841, Maria Ainslie asked, in vain, that her remains be buried in D'Arcy's grave. Wentworth had known numerous women, among them Mary Wilkinson, Mrs Wilson, Mary Ginders, Catherine Crowley, Maria Ainslie and Ann Lawes. In his view women existed to serve his needs; they had no right to question. At the same time, he knew how to please a woman, not least by his sense of humour, attention and generosity. Whether because of a previous marriage in Ireland or England, or some innate reluctance on his part, he never married in New South Wales. He was aware that his domestic situation in the colony could not be officially condoned and he submitted to a measure of ostracism in order to avoid publicity, partly for his family's sake.

D'Arcy had stipulated that John Thomas Campbell, William Lawson, William Redfern and William Wentworth should be the executors of his will. They were asked to hold in trust all his property, subject to a number of provisions. Maria Ainslie, whom he designated his 'housekeeper', received a lump sum of £200 and an allowance of £3 per week for the remainder of her life, irrespective of whether she stayed in the colony or left it. She was also permitted to live rent-free in the cottage in George Street until she died, when the property was to pass to D'Arcy. Dr Wentworth's 'dear friend', Ann Lawes, 'the mother of seven of my children', was allowed to 'occupy and possess' the 1205-acre Home Bush estate, and to have use of all the household furniture, linen, plate and china, as well as the carriages, carts and horses; in the event of her death, the property was to pass to John. Of the younger children, George and Martha were jointly bequeathed, as tenants in common, the Elmsall Park estate at Bringelly, some 8515 acres; John received the 2280-acre South Creek estate, as well as 130 acres in the vicinity of Home Bush; Katherine was given the estates at Broken Bay, North Harbour and Duck River, in all about 1905 acres; Martha, Sophia, Robert, Mary Ann and Katherine were granted equal shares in the property at Illawarra, 13 050 acres or thereabouts, and in the 130 acres their father owned at Liverpool. Of the elder children, D'Arcy inherited the 2850-acre Fitzwilliam estate at Toongabbie and an additional 100 acres at Duck River Bridge. To William, his father left 3947 acres in the District of Cook, the house and grounds (31 acres) at Parramatta, two acres at Cockle Bay, the lease on a block of land in Sydney (valued at £5000), and D'Arcy's favourite curricle and harness. In all, he willed 34 145 acres to his beneficiaries. Dr Wentworth's remaining possessions —whether bank stock, money, securities, horses, cattle or sheep—were to be divided into ten equal shares, one for each of his children and one for Ann Lawes. The personalty was not to be delivered over to them until they attained the age of twenty-one, or on the day they married, whichever happened first. Probate was granted on 22 May 1828.[7]

There were a number of interesting features to the will. First, Wentworth showed caution in appointing four executors, rather than giving sole responsibility to William. Secondly, D'Arcy stipulated that none of his estate was to benefit the issue of any of his legatees unless they were 'lawfully begotten by my said children in Holy Wedlock'. If any of his children died, that child's property was to descend to his or her sons and daughters in order of primogeniture, males being preferred to females. If any of his children died without issue, that child's property was to revert to the eldest surviving sibling and to descend to his or her heirs. Moreover, he enjoined that none of his children should marry without the written consent of the trustees. Wentworth directed that his younger children should be sent to the best schools in the colony, and he appointed his trustees as guardians of his under-aged children. Finally, he left no curio to Fitzwilliam and made no provision for Cookney, although he owed obligations to both of them; he gave nothing to his poor relations in Ireland and nothing to any of his servants or tenants. In that sense he thought only of his immediate family and was as self-centred in death as he had been in life. In January 1827 it was estimated that Wentworth had an income of more than £23 000 a year from the land he rented and from the sale of his livestock. The figure was exaggerated, but it suggested the extent of his wealth. A month after his death a thousand cattle from his estates were advertised for sale by contract at ten guineas a head.[8]

On 13 August 1827 William Wentworth turned thirty-seven. He was one of the richest men in the colony. With 1000 acres in the Bathurst district, 1750 near Camden, 3947 at Cook, and smaller holdings at Parramatta, Petersham, Cockle Bay and in Sydney, he owned a total of 7025 acres. The only blood relation who was an executor of his father's estate, he had the major say in managing D'Arcy's properties, herds and money. By this stage Wentworth's daughter, Timmie, was approaching her second birthday and Sarah was again pregnant. A son, William Charles (Willie), was born on 26 December 1827 and baptized in St Phillip's in January 1828. The infant's surname was registered as Cox. Timmie and her brother were as devoted to their father as he was indulgent towards them. Wentworth had a second family to care for. As principal guardian to his eight younger half-brothers and half-sisters, he took his responsibilities seriously, watched over the children, and paid for their clothing and schooling. William employed George to manage their father's properties. The family was an extended one. Sarah's brother-in-law, William Todhunter—a clerk in the commissary's office who had married her younger sister, Elizabeth, in 1825— acted as Wentworth's agent in business matters. Martha Bucknell frequently travelled from her home at Newtown to visit her cousins.[9]

Wealth was one instrument that would enable William Wentworth to realize his aspirations and climb to the summit of New South Wales politics. With his schooling, legal training and terms at university, he had the additional advantage of being one of the best-educated men in the colony. His other resources came from within— ambition, energy, pertinacity and pride, all of which stamped him as his father's son. In June 1827 William paid £1500 to buy the 105-acre Vaucluse estate and its 'genteel dwelling house'. This single-storey stone home had eight rooms, with stables, a detached kitchen, a dairy, an orchard and gardens. Overlooking a bay, not far from South Head, Vaucluse lay about six miles east of Sydney. The cottage had been built in 1803 by Sir Henry Browne Hayes who had been transported for abducting an heiress. He named his 'rustic little paradise' after Petrarch's home in the south of France. From 1804 the estate had been leased by Hayes's friend, Samuel Breakwell. Occupied in 1812–14 by Lieutenant-Colonel and Mrs O'Connell, the house remained empty until February 1822 when Captain Piper bought it for £425. He held the property for five years before it was auctioned to meet his creditors' demands. William took Sarah to Vaucluse in November 1827 and sold Petersham to Wardell. Within fourteen months Wentworth had extended his new estate by acquiring an adjoining 410 acres. Renovations began in mid-1828 to transform Vaucluse House into an 'elegant château'. The architect, George Cookney, was commissioned to design a suite of outbuildings, among them new stables and a coach-house. Barracks were erected for convict labourers. Before long a new dining-room and bedrooms were built on the western side of the house. On the east a winter sitting-room and a small drawing-room with French windows opened on to a wooden verandah. A new wing was added to the back of the house, with a large kitchen, scullery, larder, butler's pantry, dairy, a room for the housekeeper, domestic quarters for the servants, and a nursery or schoolroom on the first floor. The gardens were gradually improved by planting fruit trees, vegetables, herbs and flowers. Sheep, cattle and horses grazed in the adjacent paddocks. Inside the home, the windows were dressed with curtains and drapes, and the floors covered with carpets and rugs; fine furniture and paintings completed the adornment. The 'Australian Counsellor' had begun to surround himself with the worldly grandeur he had known in the houses of the great Whig families in England. [10]

Despite Alexander McLeay's opinion that Wentworth was 'an infamous Blackguard, and in every respect worthy of his birth . . . being the Son of an Irish Highwayman by a Convict Whore', the object of the colonial secretary's contempt had, by 1827, become a man of means and consequence. Wentworth well knew that a long struggle lay before him to bring the fundamental liberties of the British constitution to the penal colony of New South Wales. Aware that he was physically and politically distancing himself from the emancipists, the native-born and the small settlers, he set out to re-create the Britannia of the Fitzwilliams on the shores of Port Jackson. At Vaucluse he built a retreat where he sought escape and solace with his family. In due course, however, he learned the truth of the proverb, 'Who has neither fools nor beggars nor whores among his kindred, was born of a stroke of thunder'.[11]

Abbreviations

A.D.B.	*Australian Dictionary of Biography*
A.J.C.P.	Australian Joint Copying Project
A.O.N.S.W.	Archives Office of New South Wales
A.N.U.	Australian National University
B.L.	British Library
B.T.	Bonwick Transcripts
CO	Colonial Office
D.N.B.	*Dictionary of National Biography*
HO	Home Office
HoC	House of Commons
HoL	House of Lords
H.R.A.	*Historical Records of Australia*
H.R.N.S.W.	*Historical Records of New South Wales*
J.R.A.H.S.	*Journal of the Royal Australian Historical Society*
M.L.	Mitchell Library
N.L.A.	National Library of Australia
n.d.	no day, no date
n.n.	no name
N.R.O.	Northamptonshire Record Office
P.P.	*Parliamentary Papers*
P.R.O.	Public Record Office
R.S.S.S.	Research School of Social Sciences
T	Treasury
W.O.	War Office

Notes

1 FLAME-COLOURED TAFFETA

1 *Burke's Peerage and Baronetage*, London, 1904, pp. 616–17; K. C. W. Miles to J. Ritchie, 5 August 1994.
2 Ibid.; *The Times*, 30 July 1986; *Dictionary of National Biography*, London, 1964, vol. 7, pp. 235–6; Letters and Papers of the 4th Earl Fitzwilliam, see especially papers relating to estate matters, Wentworth Woodhouse Muniments, F70 to F106, Archives, Sheffield City Libraries; T. Davis, *Wentworth Woodhouse Visitors Guide*, Sheffield, 1979, esp. pp. 5 and 30; D. Hey, *Yorkshire* in the series *Buildings of Britain, 1550–1750*, Derby, 1981, pp. 104–8; J. Summerson, *Architecture in Britain 1530–1830*, Harmondsworth, 1953, p. 207; N. Pevsner, *The Buildings of England: Yorkshire—The West Riding*, Harmondsworth, 1959, pp. 531–7; *Archaeological Journal*, vol. 137, 1980, pp. 393–6; ibid., vol. 125, 1968, pp. 325–7; *Sydney Morning Herald, Good Weekend*, 14 September 1991.
3 D'Arcy Wentworth, Medical Notebook, Wentworth Papers, B196, f.112.
4 *D.N.B.*, vol. 20, pp. 1179–94; B. Burke, *A Genealogical History of the Dormant, Abeyant, Forfeited and Extinct Peerages of the British Empire*, London, 1962, pp. 575–7.
5 Wentworth Papers, Miscellaneous Material, MSS 8, M.L.; Wentworth family tree, n.d., Wentworth Papers, A754-1, ff.283–92; letters to D. Wentworth from his brothers and sisters, May 1816 to February 1826, ibid., A754-2, ff.296, 414–15, 418–19, 438–9 and 454–6; Kathleen Dermody, D'Arcy Wentworth, 1762–1827, Ph.D. thesis, Faculty of Arts, A.N.U., 1990, p. 9; D. E. Fifer, William

Notes: Chapter 1

Charles Wentworth in Colonial Politics to 1843, M.A. thesis, University of Sydney, 1983, p. 11; M. H. Ellis Papers, K21887, M.L.; *Australian Dictionary of Biography*, Melbourne, 1967, vol. 2, p. 579; M. H. Ellis, 'D'Arcy Wentworth', in *Australian Encyclopaedia*, Sydney, 1958, vol. 9, p. 235; K. C. W. Miles to J. Ritchie, 5 August 1994 and 13 February 1997.

[6] Ibid.; C. Coote, *Statistical Survey of the County of Armagh*, Dublin, 1804, pp. 130–3; M. A. Titmarsh (W. M. Thackeray), *Irish Sketch-Book*, London, 1843, pp. 217–19; S. Lewis, *A Topographical Dictionary of Ireland with Historical and Statistical Descriptions*, vol. 2, London, 1850, pp. 58–63, 423–4 and 505–6; A. Young, *A Tour in Ireland, 1776–1779*, London, 1892; W. Wilson, *The Post-Chaise Companion or Traveller's Guide Through Ireland*, Dublin, 1786, pp. 460, 486 and 527.

[7] Dermody, loc. cit., pp. 8–9.

[8] J. M. Flood, *Ireland: its Myths and Legends*, New York, 1970, pp. 1, 3, 7, 35–41, 56–70; A. and B. Rees, *Celtic Heritage*, London, 1961, pp. 83–4, 89–94, 300–1, 318–22 and 342–51; B. L. Picard, *Celtic Tales*, London, 1964; W. B. Yeats (ed.), *Fairy and Folk Tales of Ireland*, London, 1988; see also note 6 above.

[9] W. Wentworth to D. Wentworth, 12 July 1813 and 3 May 1816, ff.478–9 and 519–20; M. Overend to D. Wentworth, 6 May 1822, ff.601–2; M. Sinnamon to D. Wentworth, 8 May 1822, ff.597–9; J. Dawson to D. Wentworth, 13 May 1822, ff.604–6; L. Dobbin to D. Wentworth, 22 May 1822, ff.611–13; W. Wentworth to D. Wentworth, 15 January 1824, ff.618–20; M. Johnson to D. Wentworth, 3 February 1826, ff.629–31, Wentworth Papers, A754-2; W. Wentworth to D. Wentworth, 16 October 1807, ibid., A751, ff.222–3; Judge Blacker's MSS, vol. 3, AW81/4, f.130, M.L.; O. MacDonagh, *Jane Austen*, New Haven, 1991, pp. 97–128.

[10] J. Hill to D. Wentworth, 19 February 1822, Wentworth Papers, Miscellaneous Material, MSS 8/4, item 93.

[11] H. Kinkead to H. W. Keays Young, n.d., Wentworth Papers, Miscellaneous Material, MSS 8, item 73; L. Dobbin to D. Wentworth, 22 May 1822, Wentworth Papers, A754-2, ff.613–14; *Freeman's Journal*, 21 November 1778 and 17 February 1779.

[12] O. MacDonagh, *States of Mind*, London, 1983, pp. 1–33.

Notes: Chapter 1

[13] F. Hardy, *Memoirs of the Political and Private Life of James Caulfield, Earl of Charlemont*, London, 1812, vol. 1, pp. 184–7.

[14] H. Kinkead to H. W. Keays Young, n.d., Wentworth Papers, Miscellaneous Material, MSS 8/4, item 73, M.L.; L. Dobbin to D. Wentworth, 22 May 1822, Wentworth Papers, A754-2, ff.613–14; Dermody, loc. cit., pp. 11–13.

[15] *Freeman's Journal*, 6 and 12 March 1782; H. Grattan, *Miscellaneous Works of the Right Honourable Henry Grattan*, London, 1822, pp. 170–2.

[16] J. J. Auchmuty in *A.D.B.*, vol. 2, p. 579; W. B. Lynch, 'D'Arcy Wentworth', a 664-page typescript, held by the author, Randwick, New South Wales; Dermody, loc. cit., p. 15; T. Dawson's statement, 27 January 1786, D'Arcy Wentworth Miscellaneous Material, MSS 8/4, item 89; R. Sinclair to D. Wentworth, 20 November 1785, Wentworth Papers, A754-2, f.1; J. Archockey to D. Killican, 22 December 1785, ibid., ff.5–6; J. Villiers to D. Wentworth, 18 July and 16 November 1787, ibid., A751, ff.7–8 and 9; H. P. Barker, D'Arcy Wentworth, M.A. thesis, University of New England, 1971, p. 2.

[17] A. Patton to D. Wentworth, 30 November 1785, Wentworth Papers, A751, ff.1–3.

[18] J. Dawson to D. Wentworth, 11 June 1787, ibid., A751, f.5; J. Villiers to D. Wentworth, 18 July and 16 November 1787, ibid., ff.7–8 and 9; D'Arcy Wentworth, Medical Notebook, ibid., B196, f.112; F. B. Smith, *The People's Health*, London, 1979, pp. 249–94, 346, 357–8, 364–8 and 376; *A.D.B.*, vol. 2, p. 579; J. M. Adair, *Medical Cautions*, London, 1786, p. 165; C. M. H. Clark, *A History of Australia*, vol. 2, Melbourne, 1968, p. 41, footnote 2.

[19] H. J. Dyos (ed.), *Collins' Illustrated Atlas of London*, Leicester, 1973, plate 7; H. B. Wheatley, *London Past and Present*, London, 1891, reissued 1968, vol. 2, p. 620; I. McCalman, *Radical Underworld*, Cambridge, 1988, passim.

[20] Lord Sydney to Lords Commissioners of the Treasury, 18 August 1786, *Historical Records of New South Wales*, vol. 1, Part 2, pp. 14–20; P. Colquhoun, *Treatise on the Police of the Metropolis*, 7th edn, London, 1806; L. Radzinowicz, *A History of English Criminal Law and its Administration from 1750*, 3 vols, London, 1948–56; J. Ritchie, *Punishment and Profit*, Melbourne, 1970, p. 3.

Notes: Chapter 1

[21] B. Weinreb and C. Hibbert (eds), *The London Encyclopaedia*, London, 1983, pp. 231 and 709; Wheatley, op. cit., vol. 1, pp. 509–10, vol. 2, pp. 98–100; C. Knight (ed.), *London in the Eighteenth Century*, 6 vols, London, 1841–44, see especially vol. 3, ch. 67, and vol. 5, ch. 121; J. West, *The History of Tasmania*, (ed.) A. G. L. Shaw, Sydney, 1971, p. 341.

[22] Weinreb and Hibbert, op. cit., pp. 69–70 and 784.

[23] Agenda Books, Lent Assizes, Kent, 1787, ASSI 31/15, pp. 23–4, P.R.O.; Felony File, Lent Assizes, Kent, 1787, ASSI 35/227/5/PFF 3692, P.R.O.; *Kentish Gazette*, 16–19 January 1797.

[24] See note 23 above; Dermody, loc. cit., pp. 20–1; *Kentish Gazette*, 23–27 March 1787.

[25] J. White, *Journal of a Voyage to New South Wales*, Sydney, 1962, pp. 47 and 51; W. Tench, *A Narrative of the Expedition to Botany Bay*, London, 1789, p. 11; evidence of J. Harris to Commissioner Bigge, 16 August 1820, C.O.201/120, ff.157–9, copy in the Bonwick Transcripts of the Appendix to the Bigge Reports, B.T. Box 1, pp. 268–9.

[26] R. Sinclair to D. Wentworth, 20 November 1785, Wentworth Papers, A754-2, ff.290–1; J. Villiers to D. Wentworth, 18 July and 16 November 1787, ibid., A751, ff.12–13 and 15; Lord Fitzwilliam to W. C. Wentworth, 9 February 1821, ibid., A757, ff.6(b)–6(c); Dermody, loc. cit., pp. 18 and 31.

[27] *Old Bailey Session Papers*, 1787–1788, pp. 15–20, transcript in Macarthur Papers, Miscellaneous Manuscripts, 1787–1888, D185, vol. 109, ff.2–17, CY774; Weinreb and Hibbert, op. cit., p. 397.

[28] Macarthur Papers, D185, vol. 109, ff.18–28; *Old Bailey Session Papers*, op. cit., pp. 22–5.

[29] Ibid., pp. 15–20; *Daily Universal Register*, 30 November, 3 and 6 December 1787; *The Brewer Dictionary of Phrase and Fable*, Hertfordshire, 1986, pp. 97 and 740.

[30] *Daily Universal Register*, 1 and 6 December 1787.

[31] *Old Bailey Session Papers*, 1787–1788, pp. 17–18; Macarthur Papers, D185, vol. 109, ff.2–17.

[32] *Old Bailey Session Papers*, 1787–1788, pp. 22–5; Macarthur Papers, D185, vol. 109, ff.18–28.

Notes: Chapter 1

33 *Daily Universal Register*, 13 December 1787; P. Colquhoun, op. cit., pp. 4, 6 and 20; Ritchie, op. cit., p. 77; *Maidstone Journal*, 1 January 1788, as quoted in M. Flynn, *The Second Fleet*, Sydney, 1993, p. 602.

34 Blacker MSS, vol. 3, f.131; P. Colquhoun, op. cit., p. 95; 'A Student of the Inner Temple', *Criminal Recorder*, London, 1804, p. 118.

35 Evidence of J. P. Heywood, *Old Bailey Session Papers*, 1789–1790, p. 4; evidence of Thomas Little, ibid., 1787–88, pp. 16–17.

36 *Old Bailey Session Papers*, 1789–1790, p. 4; Macarthur Papers, vol. 109, ff.2–36.

37 J. C. Villiers to unnamed correspondent, 16 October 1789, HO42/15, X/LCC475.

38 *The Times*, 13 November 1789; Flynn, op. cit., p. 602.

39 *D.N.B.*, vol. 7, p. 236; *The Times*, 13, 17, 20 November and 1 December 1789.

40 *London Chronicle*, as quoted in Flynn, op. cit., p. 602.

41 Ibid., pp. 142–3; W. Wentworth to H. G. Bennet, 12 February 1819, Wentworth Papers, A756, ff.115–18; *D.N.B.*, vol. 7, pp. 907–8; J. Steven Watson, *The Reign of George III*, Oxford, 1964, p. 409; D. Hay et al., *Albion's Fatal Tree*, London, 1975, pp. 17–63.

42 *Old Bailey Session Papers*, 1789–1790, pp. 2–4.

43 Ibid., p. 4; *The Times*, 10 December 1789; Dermody, loc. cit., p. 31; Macarthur Papers, D185, vol. 109, ff.29–36; C. Cookney to Lord Fitzwilliam, n.d. July 1834, Wentworth Woodhouse Muniments, 1796–1834, FM4/747; *Australian Encyclopaedia*, vol. 9, p. 235; A.D.B., vol. 2, p. 580.

44 *The Times*, 12 and 15 December 1789.

45 C.O. 201/4, ff.169, 175 and 177; Remarks and Statement of the Proceedings of Donald Trail, Master of the *Neptune*, during his passage to Port Jackson, *Accounts and Papers relating to Convicts on Board the Hulks and those Transported to New South Wales*, London, 1792, pp. 62–3; Flynn, op. cit., pp. 29–31; Barker, loc. cit., pp. 4–5.

46 A.D.B., vol. 2, p. 581; Lord Fitzwilliam to W. C. Wentworth, 9 February 1821, Wentworth Papers, A757, ff.6(b)–6(c); C. Cookney to Lord Fitzwilliam, n.d. July 1834, Wentworth Woodhouse Muniments, FM4/747; C. Cookney to D. Wentworth, 17 December 1789, Wentworth Papers, A751, ff.11 and 12(a).

Notes: Chapters 1 and 2

47 Ibid.
48 J. Villiers to unnamed correspondent, 16 October 1789, HO42/15, X/LCC475; Macarthur Papers, vol. 109, f.36; evidence of J. Harris, 16 August 1820, B.T. Box 1, pp. 269–71; T. Hill to D. Wentworth, 16 January 1790, Wentworth Papers, A751, f.13.
49 Flynn, op. cit., pp. 31 and 37–42.
50 T. Hill to D. Wentworth, 16 January 1790, Wentworth Papers, A751, f.13.
51 Flynn, op. cit., p. 43; W. Wentworth to D. Wentworth, 15 January 1824, Wentworth Papers, A754-2, ff.618–20.

2 THE LIVING AND THE DEAD

1 M. Flynn, *The Second Fleet*, Sydney, 1993, pp. 16–23. For this chapter I have drawn heavily on Michael Flynn's book which combines meticulous scholarship, fine analysis and an eye for revealing detail.
2 J. Nicol, *The Life and Adventures of John Nicol*, Edinburgh, 1822, p. 119; L. F. Fitzhardinge (ed.), *Sydney's First Four Years*, Sydney, 1961, p. 170; *Historical Records of Australia*, Series 1, vol. 1, p. 203; D. Collins, *An Account of the English Colony in New South Wales*, (ed.) B. H. Fletcher, Sydney, 1975, vol. 1, p. 96; C. Bateson, *The Convict Ships, 1788–1868*, Glasgow, 1969, pp. 120–3; M. Gillen, *The Founders of Australia*, Sydney, 1989, p. 376; A.D.B., vol. 2, p. 506; H.R.N.S.W., vol. 1, Part 2, pp. 767–8; Flynn, op. cit., p. 727.
3 Ibid., pp. 24–5; Lord Sydney to the Lords of the Admiralty, 29 April 1789, H.R.N.S.W., vol. 1, Part 2, pp. 230–1; M. D. Nash (ed.), *The Last Voyage of the Guardian, Lieutenant Riou, Commander, 1789–1791*, Cape Town, 1990, p. 121; Bateson, op. cit., pp. 124–6; see also H.R.N.S.W., vol. 1, Part 2, pp. 438, 754–8 and 763–7.
4 Flynn, op. cit., pp. 32 and 43.
5 Ibid., pp. 26–9, 35, 42 and 75; E. Nepean to A. Phillip, 20 June 1789, H.R.A., 1, i, p. 123; W. Hill to S. Wathen, 26 July 1790, H.R.N.S.W., vol. 1, Part 2, p. 367; Collins, op. cit., vol. 1, p. lvi.
6 Flynn, op. cit., pp. 28 and 34.
7 Ibid., pp. 28–31 and 737; Sir G. Yonge to the Treasury, 20 May 1789, H.R.N.S.W., vol. 1, Part 2, pp. 232–3.
8 Ibid., vol. 2, p. 492; Flynn, op. cit., pp. 31–2 and 727.
9 Ibid., pp. 32–3.

Notes: Chapter 2

[10] Report of the Commissioners of His Majesty's Navy, Statement of H. Martin et al., 15 February 1792, and Remarks and Statement of the Proceedings of Donald Trail, *Accounts and Papers*, 1792, op. cit., p. 74; Mrs Macarthur's Journal, Macarthur Papers, A2906, vol. x, ff.1-10; *H.R.N.S.W.*, vol. 2, pp. 487-9; Dermody, D'Arcy Wentworth, pp. 35-6; Flynn, op. cit., pp. 33-4 and 61.

[11] Ibid., pp. 16, 66 and 728-33; C. M. H. Clark, *A History of Australia*, vol. 1, Melbourne, 1962, pp. 90-110; A. G. L. Shaw, *Convicts and the Colonies*, London, 1966, pp. 146-65; L. L. Robson, *The Convict Settlers of Australia*, Melbourne, 1965, pp. 29-85; J. B. Hirst, *Convict society and its enemies*, Sydney, 1983, pp. 7-27; S. Nicholas (ed.), *Convict Workers*, Sydney, 1988, pp. 3-24; R. Schlomowitz, 'Convict workers: a review article', in *Australian Economic History Review*, vol. 30, no. 2, September 1990, pp. 67-88.

[12] C. Liston, *Sarah Wentworth, Mistress of Vaucluse*, Sydney, 1988, p. 15; Flynn, op. cit., p. 229; C. M. H. Clark, op. cit., vol. 2, p. 41.

[13] Flynn, op. cit., pp. 35-7 and 332-3.

[14] Ibid., pp. 37-41; *H.R.N.S.W.*, vol. 2, pp. 487-9 and 491.

[15] Ibid., p. 489; *A.D.B.*, vol. 1, pp. 2-3 and 519-20, vol. 2, pp. 144-5, 153-4 and 536, vol. 5, p. 122; Flynn, op. cit., pp. 33, 35, 37, 43, 47, 108-11, 125, 229, 302, 320-1, 332-3, 411, 414-15, 457-8, 485, 575, 602 and 737.

[16] S. Macarthur Onslow (ed.), *Some Early Records of the Macarthurs of Camden*, Sydney, 1973, pp. 2-15 and 52; M. H. Ellis, *John Macarthur*, Sydney, 1955, pp. 6 and 16-26; H. King, *Elizabeth Macarthur and Her World*, Sydney, 1980, pp. 11-14; H. King, *Colonial Expatriates*, Sydney, 1989, pp. 7-8; *H.R.N.S.W.*, vol. 2, p. 489; Dermody, loc. cit., pp. 36-7 and 43; Mrs Macarthur's Journal, loc. cit., f.5; *Accounts and Papers*, 1792, op. cit., p. 77; J. Ritchie (ed.), *A Charge of Mutiny*, Canberra, 1988, p. xix; A. T. Atkinson, 'John Macarthur Before Australia Knew Him', *Journal of Australian Studies*, no. 4, June 1979, pp. 22-37, esp. p. 28; James Macarthur, 'Memorandum for life of the late John Macarthur, Esq.', n.d., Macarthur Papers, A2897, f.178; James Macarthur's memoir of his father (1853?), ibid., f.179; information re Macarthur's date of birth from Dr Margaret Steven, A.D.B., R.S.S.S., A.N.U., 14 March 1995.

Notes: Chapter 2

[17] Macarthur Onslow, op. cit., pp. 7–9, 11 and 17; Flynn, op. cit., p. 33.

[18] Ibid., pp. 46–7; Macarthur Onslow, op. cit., pp. 8–10 and 15; King, *Elizabeth Macarthur*, p. 12.

[19] Macarthur Onslow, op. cit., pp. 9–13 and 17–18; Flynn, op. cit., pp. 47–8.

[20] *Accounts and Papers*, 1792, op. cit., pp. 61 and 65–6; Collins, op. cit., vol. 1, p. 100; Macarthur Onslow, op. cit., p. 13; Bateson, op. cit., p. 129; Flynn, op. cit., pp. 43, 67 and 182–5; Dermody, loc. cit., p. 36.

[21] H.R.N.S.W., vol. 2, p. 493; Flynn, op. cit., pp. 43 and 59–60; Dermody, loc. cit., p. 37; West, op. cit., p. 347.

[22] *Accounts and Papers*, 1792, op. cit., p. 74; W. Gray to J. Shapcote, 13 April 1790, ibid., p. 66; J. Shapcote to Navy Board, 24 April 1790, ibid., p. 68; Macarthur Onslow, op. cit., pp. 13 and 19; H.R.N.S.W., vol. 1, Part 2, p. 366; ibid., vol. 2, p. 493; Flynn, op. cit., pp. 33 and 43–5; Dermody, loc. cit., p. 37.

[23] H.R.N.S.W., vol. 2, p. 366; Macarthur Onslow, op. cit., pp. 13–19; Flynn, op. cit., pp. 43 and 48.

[24] Macarthur Onslow, op. cit., p. 14; H.R.N.S.W., vol. 2, p. 367; Flynn, op. cit., pp. 44–5; Dermody, loc. cit., pp. 37–8.

[25] Collins, op. cit., vol. 1, p. 99; *Accounts and Papers*, 1792, op. cit., p. 63; Macarthur Onslow, op. cit., pp. 14 and 40; H.R.N.S.W., vol. 2, p. 367; Dermody, loc. cit., p. 41; Ellis, *Macarthur*, p. 25; Flynn, op. cit., pp. 45 and 48; King, *Elizabeth Macarthur*, pp. 14–15.

[26] *Accounts and Papers*, 1792, op. cit., pp. 70–1 and 73–7; H.R.N.S.W., vol. 1, Part 2, p. 367; Macarthur Onslow, op. cit., p. 14; Dermody, loc. cit., pp. 38–9; Flynn, op. cit., pp. 45–6 and 69.

[27] Collins, op. cit., vol. 1, p. 99; H.R.N.S.W., vol. 1, Part 2, pp. 353 and 367; J. Cobley, *Sydney Cove 1789–1790*, Sydney, 1980, pp. 224–33; Flynn, op. cit., pp. v, 46, 302 and 734; Bateson, op. cit., pp. 115–16, 126–7 and 129.

[28] *Morning Chronicle*, 4 August 1791; Collins, op. cit., vol. 1, p. 99; H.R.N.S.W., vol. 1, Part 2, pp. 387–8; ibid., vol. 2, p. 768; Bateson, op. cit., pp. 128–30; Flynn, op. cit., pp. 49–53.

[29] H.R.A., 1, i, pp. 188–9; Collins, op. cit., vol. 1, pp. 100, 147, 310, 317–18 and 385–6; H.R.N.S.W., vol. 1, Part 2, pp. 366–8; Flynn, op. cit., pp. 136–7 and 332–3; A.D.B., vol. 2, p. 398.

Notes: Chapters 2 and 3

[30] *H.R.A.*, 1, i, pp. 330–1 and 334; Bateson, op. cit., pp. 130–1; Flynn, op. cit., pp. 52, 54–60 and 75; C. M. H. Clark, op. cit., vol. 1, p. 128.

[31] Flynn, op. cit., pp. 61–82 and 576–8; Shaw, *Convicts and the Colonies*, p. 111.

[32] An Officer, *An Authentic Journal of the Expedition under Commodore Phillips to Botany Bay*, London, 1789; An Officer just returned in the Prince of Wales, *An Authentic and Interesting Narrative of the Late Expedition to Botany Bay*, London, 1789; An Officer of the Late Expedition to Botany Bay, *An Authentic and Interesting Narrative*, Aberdeen, 1789, facsimile series 12, Sydney, 1978; A. Phillip, *The Voyage of Governor Phillip to Botany Bay*, London, 1789; Tench, *A Narrative of the Expedition to Botany Bay*; J. White, *Journal of a Voyage to New South Wales*, London, 1790; Macarthur Onslow, op. cit., p. 3; Ellis, *Macarthur*, p. 30; C. M. H. Clark, op. cit, vol. 1, pp. 113–18; King, *Elizabeth Macarthur*, pp. 15–19.

[33] Ellis, *Macarthur*, pp. 11 and 27–35; *H.R.N.S.W.*, vol. 1, Part 2, pp. 369–70; Flynn, op. cit., p. 51; Dermody, loc. cit., pp. 43–5; G. Mackaness (ed.), *Some Letters of the Reverend Richard Johnson*, Sydney, 1954, p. 35; Cobley, op. cit., passim; King, *Elizabeth Macarthur*, p. 16; Macarthur Onslow, op. cit., p. 27.

[34] Collins, op. cit., vol. 1, p. 106. For a novelist's insight, see E. Dark, *Storm of Time*, Sydney, 1948, p. 146.

[35] A. Phillip to P. G. King, 3 January and 30 November 1792, P. G. King's Letterbook, Norfolk Island, 1788–1799, C187, ff.83 and 128, M.L.; Collins, op. cit., vol. 1, pp. 106 and 556; Cobley, op. cit., p. 263; Flynn, op. cit., p. 51; Dermody, loc. cit., pp. 47 and 51; H. J. Rumsey, *The Pioneers of Sydney Cove*, Sydney, 1937, p. 39.

3 REMEMBER NOT PAST YEARS

[1] M. Hoare, *Norfolk Island*, Brisbane, 1969, pp. 1–2 and 5; R. Wright, *The Forgotten Generation of Norfolk Island and Van Diemen's Land*, Sydney, 1986, pp. 3 and 5.

[2] *H.R.A.*, 1, i, p. 13; J. Cook, *A Voyage Towards the South Pole, and Round the World Performed in His Majesty's Ships the Resolution and Adventure in the Years 1772, 1773, 1774 and 1775*, London,

Notes: Chapter 3

1777, vol. 2, pp. 147–9; Hoare, op. cit., pp. 3–4 and 8; Wright, op. cit., pp. 6–9; *A.D.B.*, vol. 2, pp. 55–6 and 60.

[3] P. G. King, *The Journal of Philip Gidley King, Lieutenant, R.N., 1787–1790* (reproduction of MS, Safe 1/16, M.L.), Sydney, 1980, pp. 40–2, 44, 87 and 103–5; G. B. Worgan, *Journal of a First Fleet Surgeon*, Sydney, 1978, p. 38; A. Bowes Smyth, *The Journal of Arthur Bowes Smyth*, Sydney, 1979, p. 65; Wright, op. cit., pp. 10–11 and 52; Hoare, op. cit., pp. 15–17; *H.R.N.S.W.*, vol. 2, p. 759.

[4] *A.D.B.*, vol. 2, pp. 397–8; Hoare, op. cit., pp. 18–19; Wright, op. cit., pp. 11–14; M. L. Treadgold, *Bounteous Bestowal: The Economic History of Norfolk Island*, Canberra, 1988.

[5] Wright, op. cit., pp. 63–4; Hoare, op. cit., pp. 20–1.

[6] W. Bradley, *A Voyage to New South Wales 1786–1792*, facsimile edition, Sydney, 1969, pp. 193–7 and 210; J. Hunter, *An Historical Journal of the Transactions at Port Jackson and Norfolk Island*, London, 1793, pp. 188 and 190; R. Clark, *The Journal and Letters of Lt. Ralph Clark 1787–1792*, Sydney, 1981, pp. 156–8; C. A. Liston, 'William Charles Wentworth—The Formative Years 1810–1824', *Journal of the Royal Australian Historical Society*, vol. 62, part 1, June 1976, p. 20; Liston, *Sarah Wentworth*, p. 21; A. C. V. Melbourne, *William Charles Wentworth*, Brisbane, 1934, p. 6; Barker, *D'Arcy Wentworth*, pp. 7–10; Fifer, *William Charles Wentworth*, p. 14; Norfolk Island Victualling Book (compiled, apparently, from 1792), A1958, pp. 1(b), 16 and 75(a), M.L.; D. Wentworth to Lord Fitzwilliam, 30 November 1811, Wentworth Woodhouse Muniments, F114/52; W. Wentworth to Lord Fitzwilliam, 18 December 1816, Fitzwilliam MSS, 85/38, ff.1–3, Northamptonshire Record Office, Wootton Hall Park, Northampton; Affidavits of E. L. Wentworth and F. K. Reeve, items 81 and 83, D'Arcy Wentworth, Miscellaneous Material, MSS 8/4; C. M. H. Clark, *A History of Australia*, vol. 2, pp. 41–2; *A.D.B.*, vol. 2, p. 582.

[7] Bradley, op. cit., pp. 210–11; R. Clark, op. cit., p. 159; Hunter, op. cit., pp. 188–9.

[8] Ibid., p. 190; Bradley, op. cit., p. 211; Wright, op. cit., p. 14; Hoare, op. cit., p. 21.

[9] Hunter, op. cit., p. 400; R. Clark, op. cit., pp. 154, 162, 165, 169 and 287–8; Ross's proclamation, 26 March 1790, C.O.201/9, ff.4–6; D. Paine, *The Journal of Daniel Paine*, Sydney, 1983, p. 30; see also

Notes: Chapter 3

J. Grant to his mother, 2 May 1804, Grant Papers, MS 737, folder 14, f.7, N.L.A.; J. Holt, *The Memoirs of Joseph Holt*, London, n.d., vol. 2, pp. 70–4; *A.D.B.*, vol. 1, p. 568; Dermody, D'Arcy Wentworth, pp. 54–7.

[10] D. Considen to D. Wentworth, 24 February 1804, Wentworth Papers, A751, f.134, and CY699, ff.125–8; to J. Banks, 18 November 1788, *H.R.N.S.W.*, vol. 1, Part 2, p. 220; R. Clark, op. cit., pp. 142, 165 and 285; Bradley, op. cit., pp. 204–5; Hunter, op. cit., p. 196; King, op. cit., pp. 388–94; P. G. King, Description of Norfolk Island, 10 January 1791, C.O.201/9, f.354.

[11] D. Collins to D. Wentworth, 21 March 1791, Wentworth Papers, A754-2, ff.9, 11 and 293; R. Clark, op. cit., p. 184.

[12] Ibid., p. 180; D. Collins to D. Wentworth, 21 March 1791, Wentworth Papers, A754-2, f.293.

[13] Letter to W. Keays Young, 22 March 1883, Wentworth Papers, Miscellaneous Material, MSS 8/3; correspondence of 27 January and 5 February 1886, Wentworth Papers, A760, ff.439–48; Present State of His Majesty's Settlement on Norfolk Island, 18 October 1796, C.O. 201/18, ff.150–1; R. Clark, op. cit., passim; Wright, op. cit., p. 10; Dermody, loc. cit., p. 59; *A.D.B.*, vol. 1, pp. 225–6; P. Robinson, *The Women of Botany Bay*, Sydney, 1988, pp. 200–5; M. Flynn to J. Ritchie, 13 June 1994, with a typescript on Ralph Clark, held by the A.D.B., A.N.U.

[14] R. Clark, op. cit., pp. 192–3.

[15] Ibid., pp. 194, 199–200, 202, 208–9, 217, 219–20 and 296; *H.R.N.S.W.*, vol. 2, p. 32.

[16] R. Clark, op. cit., pp. 195–6 and 299; J. Easty, *Memorandum of the Transactions of a Voyage from England to Botany Bay 1787–1793*, Sydney, 1965, p. 105.

[17] P. G. King, Journal of Philip Gidley King while Lieutenant-Governor of Norfolk Island, 1791–1796, MS 70, f.4, N.L.A.; R. Clark, op. cit., pp. 217–19.

[18] Ibid., pp. 197, 202, 207 and 218.

[19] P. G. King, Journal, MS 70, f.4; P. G. King to E. Nepean, 23 November 1791, C.O. 201/9, f.49; *H.R.A.*, I, i, pp. 241–3; *A.D.B.*, vol. 2, p. 56; Wright, op. cit., p. 15.

[20] Ibid.; P. G. King to D. Wentworth, 10 December 1791, C.O. 201/9, f.59, and Wentworth Family Papers, 1796–1834, in Wentworth

Notes: Chapter 3

Woodhouse Muniments, F66/13 and FM/747; to A. Phillip, 29 December 1791, and to H. Dundas, 8 May 1792, King Letterbook, Norfolk Island, 1788–1799, C 187, ff.87–8 and 96, M.L.; W. C. Wentworth to H. G. Bennet, 12 February 1819, Wentworth Papers, A756, ff.115–16; Dermody, loc. cit., p. 65; *A.D.B.*, vol. 2, p. 398.

21 P. G. King to Lord Grenville, 29 December 1791, C.O. 201/9, f.107; Watercolour sketch of Wentworth's house, in R. Jones, 'Recollections of 13 Years Residence at Norfolk Island', Safe 1/2d, M.L.; *H.R.N.S.W.*, vol. 1, Part 2, p. 179; Collins, *An Account*, vol. 1, p. 18; Phillip, *Voyage*, pp. 95–6.

22 A. Phillip to P. G. King, 3 January 1792, King Letterbook, C 187, f.83; P. G. King, Journal, MS 70, f.21; P. G. King, A Journal of Transactions on Norfolk Island, 4 November 1791 to 6 November 1794, A1687, f.66, M.L., and C.O. 201/10, f.282; P. G. King to E. Nepean, 23 November 1791, C.O. 201/9, f.50; to J. Banks, 24 May 1793, Joseph Banks Collection, MS 9/94a, N.L.A.; R. Clark, op. cit., p. 178; Wright, op. cit., p. 15.

23 J. McMahon, *Fragments of the Early History of Australia 1788–1812*, Melbourne, 1913, p. 59; Dermody, loc. cit., p. 72; Wright, op. cit., pp. 24–8 and 35–47; Hoare, op. cit., pp. 9, 11, 22.

24 P. G. King to E. Nepean, 9 March and 8 May 1792, C.O. 201/9, ff.95 and 160; *Advertiser*, 20 January 1792, see Bonwick Transcripts, Biography, vol. 4, A 2000-4, f.1106; *Annual Register*, 1792, p. 26; P. G. King, Journal of Transactions, A1687, ff.152 and 427–8; *H.R.N.S.W.*, vol. 2, pp. 19 and 83.

25 Hunter, op. cit., p. 579; A. Phillip to P. G. King, 30 November 1792, and P. G. King to D. Collins, 12 July 1795, King Letterbook, C 187, ff.128 and 291, M.L.; P. G. King to E. Nepean, 4 March 1793, C.O.201/9, f.198.

26 Lord Fitzwilliam to D. Wentworth, 24 June 1793, Wentworth Papers, A754-2, ff.13–15; D. Collins to D. Wentworth, 18 October 1793, ibid., A751, CY699, f.17.

27 Hoare, op. cit., pp. 21–5; Wright, op. cit., pp. 15, 18–23 and 52; *A.D.B.*, vol. 2, p. 56.

28 W. N. Chapman to his mother, 5 May 1792, W. N. Chapman Letters, 1791–1838, A1974, ff.21–2, M.L.; P. G. King, Journal of Transactions, A1687, ff.152 and 427–8, M.L.; *H.R.N.S.W.*, vol. 6, p. 321; *A.D.B.*, vol. 2, p. 57; Dermody, loc. cit., pp. 72–3; *D.N.B.*,

vol. 7, p. 236; Letters and Papers of the 4th Earl Fitzwilliam, especially those of 1794–95, F 1 to 31; R. F. Foster, *The Oxford History of Ireland*, Oxford, 1989, p. 150; R. F. Foster, *Modern Ireland 1600–1972*, London, 1989, pp. 263-4.

[29] P. G. King, Journal, MS 70, ff.81-5, 88-9, 145, 154 and 169-70, N.L.A.; copy of vouchers for payment of swine flesh, 3 April to 30 July 1794, C.O. 201/10, f.238; list of bills issued by Z. Clark, 30 January to 10 May 1794, ibid., f.226; P. G. King to Lord Fitzwilliam, 19 February 1796, Wentworth Woodhouse Muniments, FM4/747; voucher for payment of wheat, 23 November 1795, Banks Papers, Brabourne Collection, A78-6, vol. 7, f.4, M.L.; Norfolk Island Victualling Book, A1958, ff.80(b) and 83(a), M.L.; K. C. W. Miles to J. Ritchie, 5 August 1994.

[30] W. N. Chapman, Letters, A1974, f.23; P. G. King, Journal, MS 70, ff.93-4 and 222-4; Account Book, Wentworth Papers, A754-2, ff.19-22, 34-5, 46-65 and 540; J. S. Cumpston, *Shipping Arrivals and Departures, Sydney, 1788–1825*, Canberra, 1964, p. 3.

[31] P. G. King, Journal, MS 70, ff.181, 207 and 209-10.

[32] Ibid., f.83; *H.R.N.S.W.*, vol. 2, pp. 103-10 and 135-73; Wright, op. cit., p. 61; Hoare, op. cit., p. 23.

[33] P. G. King to D. Collins, 12 July 1795, King Letterbook, C187, f.291; D. Collins to P. G. King, 17 October 1795, ibid., ff.294 and 303.

[34] D. Wentworth to Lord Fitzwilliam, 23 January 1796, Wentworth Woodhouse Muniments, FM4/737; Dermody, loc. cit., pp. 82-3.

[35] P. G. King to Lord Fitzwilliam, 19 February 1796, Wentworth Woodhouse Muniments, FM4/737; Norfolk Island Victualling Book, loc. cit., ff.1(b), 60(a), 75(a), 80(b) and 83(a); Collins, op. cit., vol. 1, p. 384.

4 SMILE AT THE RISING SUN

[1] J. Hunter to J. Banks, 12 October 1795 and 20 August 1796, Governor Hunter's Letters, 1795–1802, A1787, ff.1-4 and 16, M.L.; Cumpston, *Shipping Arrivals*, pp. 30-1.

[2] Ritchie (ed.), *A Charge of Mutiny*, pp. xiii–xiv.

[3] For this paragraph I have drawn on two papers by N. G. Butlin, 'Yo, Ho, Ho And How Many Bottles of Rum?', in *Australian Economic History Review*, 23, no. 1, March 1983, pp. 1-27, and his

Notes: Chapter 4

provisional draft, 'Property Rights, Wealth and Markets in a Gaol Economy', Department of Economic History, R.S.S.S., A.N.U., 1985; P. Statham (ed.), *A Colonial Regiment: New Sources Relating to the New South Wales Corps, 1789–1810*, Canberra, 1992; R. J. Craig and S. A. Jenkins, 'The Cox and Greenwood ledger of the New South Wales Corps 1801–1805: The account of Captain John Macarthur', in *J.R.A.H.S.*, vol. 82, part 2, December 1996, pp. 138–52.

[4] D. Wentworth to Lord Fitzwilliam, 1 May and 10 September 1796, Wentworth Woodhouse Muniments, F114/8 and 9; Hunter's statement, n.d. 1798, Wentworth Papers, A751, f.27; *H.R.N.S.W.*, vol. 3, pp. 43–4 and 74; C.O.201/13, ff.19 and 73; *A.D.B.*, vol. 1, pp. 566–72; C. M. H. Clark, *A History of Australia*, vol. 1, pp. 142–3.

[5] P. G. King to D. Wentworth, 16 April 1796, Wentworth Papers, A754-2, f.314; D. Wentworth to Lord Fitzwilliam, 1 May 1796, Wentworth Woodhouse Muniments, F114/8.

[6] Ibid.

[7] D. Wentworth to C. Cookney, shopping list, 1796, Wentworth Papers, A751, ff.25–8; to Lord Fitzwilliam, 10 September 1796, Wentworth Woodhouse Muniments, F114/9.

[8] Collins, *An Account*, vol. 1, p. 308; J. Hunter to J. Banks, 12 October 1795 and 30 March 1797, Governor Hunter's Letters, 1788–1802, A1787, ff.1–4 and 19–23; R. Atkins, Journal, entry of 6 June 1794, Atkins Papers, MS4039 (NK37), f.52, N.L.A.; G. Suttor, 'Sketch of Events in New South Wales, 1800–1820', C783, f.5, M.L.; J. Hunter, *Governor Hunter's Remarks on the Causes of the Colonial Expense of the Establishment of New South Wales*, London, 1802, pp. 20–7; G. Mackaness (ed.), *Letters of Richard Johnson*, p. 7; Paine, *Journal*, p. 23; R. Murray, 'The Britannia Journal of Robert Murray, Port Jackson, New South Wales, 1792–1794', in *J.R.A.H.S.*, vol. 60, part 2, June 1974, p. 80.

[9] Balmain Papers, 1751–1869, A2022, f.4, M.L.; J. R. Elder (ed.), *The Letters and Journals of Samuel Marsden, 1765–1838*, Dunedin, 1932, p. 33; W. Paterson, to J. Banks, 20 February 1800, Banks Papers, A82, vol. 19, ff.123–4, M.L.; Dermody, *D'Arcy Wentworth*, p. 93, f.n.25. Wentworth's salary as assistant–surgeon was five shillings a day, £91 5s per annum, see D. Wentworth, Accounts, Wentworth Papers, A754-2, f.540; P. Statham, "Of Officers and

Notes: Chapter 4

Men in N.S.W., 1788–1800', provisional paper delivered to a seminar in the Economic History Department, R.S.S.S., A.N.U., 6 November 1987, Appendix, p. 23.

[10] Paine, op. cit., p. 23; V. Ross (ed.), *The Everingham Letterbook*, Wamberal, 1985, pp. 40–5; R. Atkins, Journal, entry of 10 January 1795, loc. cit., f.55; J. Grant to Lady Grant, 19 December 1794, Seafield Muniments, GD248/351/7, Scottish Record Office, A.J.C.P. M985–6; D. Mann, *The Present Picture of New South Wales*, London, 1811, p. 69.

[11] Evidence of M. Margarot, Report of the Select Committee on Transportation, House of Commons, *Parliamentary Papers*, ii, no. 341, 1812, Appendix 1, p. 53; T. F. Palmer Letters, 23 April 1796, MS761, f.9, N.L.A.; *H.R.N.S.W.*, vol. 3, pp. 19–22 and 430–2; *A.D.B.*, vol. 1, pp. 51 and 74.

[12] J. Hunter to J. Banks, 30 March 1797, Governor Hunter's Letters, 1795–1802, A1787, ff.22–3; J. Turnbull, *A voyage round the World in the Years 1800, 1801, 1802, 1803, and 1804*, Philadelphia, 1810, p. 363; M.L.; Elder, op. cit., p. 32; Dermody, loc. cit., p. 97, f.n.31.

[13] Court of Civil Jurisdiction, Rough Minutes of Proceedings and Related Case Papers, 1 July 1788–August 1801, 2/8147, ff.177–9, 181–4 and 189–90, A.O.N.S.W.; D. Wentworth, account with C. Cookney, Wentworth Papers, A754-2, f.539; D. Wentworth to Lord Fitzwilliam, 19 August 1797, Wentworth Woodhouse Muniments, F114/17; C. Cookney to Lord Fitzwilliam, 10 July 1798, ibid., FM4/747; C. H. Waller to D. Wentworth, 18 December 1798, Wentworth Papers, A751, ff.31–2; G. Lidwell to D. Wentworth, 20 April 1806, ibid., A754-2, ff.165–6.

[14] D. Wentworth to Lord Fitzwilliam, 19 August 1797, Wentworth Woodhouse Muniments, F114/17; C. Cookney to D. Wentworth, 17 and 30 August 1797, Wentworth Papers, A751, ff.23–5 and A754-2, ff.66–7; D. R. Hainsworth, *The Sydney Traders*, Melbourne, 1981, chs 1–2.

[15] Statham, loc. cit., p. 23; J. King to Lord Fitzwilliam, 3 August 1797, Wentworth Woodhouse Muniments, FM4/747; C. Cookney to D. Wentworth, 1 August 1798, Wentworth Papers, A754-2, ff.74–6; inventory, n.d. 1800, ibid., A751, f.55; wager, 29 November 1798, ibid., f.29; *H.R.N.S.W.*, vol. 3, pp. 300 and 356; Hunter's invitation, 21 December 1798, Wentworth Papers, A751, f.33.

Notes: Chapter 4

[16] *H.R.N.S.W.*, vol. 3, p. 672; ibid., vol. 4, p. 47; Despatches from Governors of New South Wales, Enclosures, 1836–7, A1267-14, M.L.; M. F. Peron, *A Voyage of Discovery to the Southern Hemisphere*, London, 1809, p. 282; Elder (ed.), op. cit., p. 8; R. J. Ryan, *Land Grants 1788–1809*, Sydney, 1974, pp. 121 and 129; W. Paterson to J. Banks, 28 November 1799, Banks Papers, A82, vol. 19, f.102, M.L.; Duke of Portland to J. Hunter, 5 November 1799, *H.R.N.S.W.*, vol. 2, pp. 506–12 and vol. 3, p. 738. Home Bush was later styled Home–bush and eventually Homebush.

[17] *H.R.N.S.W.*, vol. 3, p. 235; ibid., vol. 4, pp. 119–31, 185 and 861; J. Hunter to P. G. King, 4 October 1800, P. G. King, Letters Received and Other Papers, MSS 710, f.43, M.L.; E. Paterson to G. Johnston, 10 February and 3 October 1800, Elizabeth Paterson's Papers, Ap36/5–6, M.L.; Mann, op. cit., p. 5; C. M. H. Clark, op. cit., vol. 1, p. 170; *A.D.B.*, vol. 2, p. 519.

[18] D. Wentworth to Lord Fitzwilliam, 11 October 1800, Wentworth Woodhouse Muniments, F114/20; D. Wentworth to C. Cookney, n.d (probably October 1800), Wentworth Papers, A751, ff.107–9; *H.R.N.S.W.*, vol. 3, p. 231; M. Margarot's Journal, Rusden Papers, B1374, M.L.

[19] Copy of an extract of a letter from F. Grose to J. Foveaux, 25 June 1799, Wentworth Papers, A753, f.567; D. Wentworth to L. Macquarie, 8 September 1817, ibid., f.568; to n.n. (probably D. Considen), n.d., ibid., A752, ff.283–4; W. Kent to D. Wentworth, 2 May 1800, ibid., A751, f.50; Hunter, *Remarks*, p. 29; Hainsworth, op. cit., ch. 2.

[20] Inscription on vault, Wentworth Papers, A754-2, f.635; A. Campbell to D. Wentworth, 16 February 1800, Wentworth Papers, A751, ff.39–41; W. Kent to D. Wentworth, 2 May 1800, ibid., f.43; J. Hunter, letter of recommendation for D. Wentworth, 20 September 1800, Wentworth Woodhouse Muniments, FM4/747; C. Baxter (ed.), *Musters and Lists, New South Wales and Norfolk Island* (Australian Biographical and Genealogical Record), Sydney, 1988, see especially AHO21, p. 88, AJ124–5, p. 94, AD290, p. 40, and AC126, p. 28; Liston, *Sarah Wentworth*, p. 15; C. M. H. Clark, op. cit., vol. 2, p. 42; P. Yeend to C. Cunneen, 28 August 1993, copy held by the A.D.B.; P. Yeend to J. Ritchie, 3 August 1994; M. Flynn to J. Ritchie, 23 March 1994.

Notes: Chapter 4

[21] P. G. King to Under-Secretary King, 8 March 1799, P. G. King, Letterbook, 1797–1806, A2015, ff.29–34, M.L.; to the Duke of Portland, 29 April 1800, and to Under-Secretary King, 3 May 1800, *H.R.N.S.W.*, vol. 4, pp. 78 and 83; J. Hunter to P. G. King, 8 July 1800, ibid., pp. 171–2; P. G. King, On Spirits and Trade, September 1805, New South Wales, Colonial Secretary's Papers, MSS 681/2, f.245, M.L.; *H.R.N.S.W.*, vol. 4, pp. 139–40 and 170.

[22] Ibid., pp. 141–3 and 177.

[23] Ibid., pp. 202, 205, 497–8, 501 and 613; Mann, op. cit., pp. 7–8 and 65; S. Marsden to W. Wilberforce, 11 August 180(1 or 2), Hassall Correspondence, A1677-2, vol. 2, f.15, M.L.; Hunter, *Remarks*, p. 27.

[24] D. Wentworth to Lord Fitzwilliam, 11 October 1800, Wentworth Woodhouse Muniments, F114/20; to C. Cookney, n.d. (probably October 1800), Wentworth Papers, A751, ff.107–9; C. Cookney to J. Sullivan, 10 December 1802, ibid., A754-2, f.381; to D. Wentworth, ibid., ff.381–2; W. Balmain to D. Wentworth, 25 March 1803, ibid., A751, ff.113–14; A. J. King to D. Wentworth, 18 July 1804, ibid., ff.148–9; *H.R.N.S.W.*, vol. 4, p. 613.

[25] C. Cookney to D. Wentworth, 2 June 1801 and 8 February 1803, Wentworth Papers, A754-2, ff.368–9 and 381–2; Cookney's accounts with D. Wentworth, 26 January 1809, ibid., f.198; Lord Fitzwilliam to D. Wentworth, 30 July 1802, ibid., f.371.

[26] *H.R.N.S.W.*, vol. 4, p. 587; D. Wentworth to Lord Fitzwilliam, 23 August 1801 and 12 May 1803, Wentworth Woodhouse Muniments, F66/18 and F114/21; W. Balmain to D. Wentworth, 25 March 1803, Wentworth Papers, A751, ff.112–13.

[27] W. Paterson to J. Banks, 2 November 1801, New South Wales, Colonial Secretary's Papers, MSS 681/2, f.377; to Colonel Brownrigg, 11 March 1802, Banks Papers, A83, vol. 20, f.133; P. G. King to J. Banks, 21 July 1805, ibid., A78-6, vol. 7, f.271; *H.R.N.S.W.*, vol. 4, p. 612; J. Macarthur to J. Piper, 4 December 1801 and 8 September 1802, Piper Papers, A256, vol. 3, ff.463–5, and A254, vol. 1, f.25; W. Balmain to D. Wentworth, 25 March 1803, Wentworth Papers, A751, ff.105–12; *A.D.B.*, vol. 2, pp. 154–5 and 318.

[28] D. Wentworth to T. Jamison, 4 July 1802, New South Wales, Colonial Secretary's Papers regarding Norfolk Island, 1800–05, MSS

Notes: Chapter 4

681/3, f.13, M.L.; *H.R.N.S.W.*, vol. 4, p. 798; P. G. King to J. Foveaux, 9 August 1802, Governor King's Letter Book, A2015, f.254, M.L.; D. Wentworth to Lord Fitzwilliam, 12 May 1803, Wentworth Woodhouse Muniments, F114/21.

29 Turnbull, *A voyage*, p. 332; *H.R.N.S.W.*, vol. 5, pp. 126–9; P. G. King to D. Wentworth, 17 January 1803, Wentworth Papers, A751, f.105. According to Professor Iain McCalman of the Humanities Research Centre, A.N.U., the literary model for this pipe, and probably for others, was the work of Peter Pinder (John Wolcot).

30 W. N. Chapman to his sisters, 13 December 1800, Chapman Papers, A1974, f.78, M.L.; *H.R.N.S.W.*, vol. 4, p. 498; ibid., vol. 5, p. 143; G. Caley to J. Banks, 24 April 1803, Banks Papers, A79-1, f.122, M.L.; J. H. Tuckey, Papers, 1804, A2000-1, ff.42–3, M.L.; W. Balmain to D. Wentworth, 16 August 1802, Wentworth Papers, A754-2, f.378; D. Wentworth to Lord Hobart, 19 April 1803, ibid., A751, ff.119–22; Steven Watson, *Reign of George III*, p. 581; *A.D.B.*, vol. 2, p. 318.

31 The best discussion of Wentworth's dealings with Crossley is to be found in Dermody, loc. cit., pp. 127–34; see also *H.R.A.*, 1, i, pp. 581–95; C. M. H. Clark, op. cit., vol. 1, pp. 165–6; *A.D.B.*, vol. 1, pp. 262–3; A. R. Robinson to P. G. King, 31 December 1802, King Family Papers, A1976, vol. 1, ff.62–3; M. Flynn to J. Ritchie, 23 March 1994.

32 G. Chalmers to J. Banks, 10 (or 18?) May 1805, Banks Papers, A78-3, f.211a; J. Grant to his mother and sister, 2 April 1804, MS737, folder no. 14, ff.12 and 15, N.L.A.; Turnbull, op. cit., p. 351; Tuckey, loc. cit., f.7; Hainsworth, op. cit., p. 91; see also letters from S. Lord to D. Wentworth, reprinted from Equity Court papers, A.O.N.S.W., in D. R. Hainsworth, *Builders and Adventurers*, Melbourne, 1968, pp. 19–20; G. Howe to D. Wentworth, 16 November 1801, Wentworth Papers, A751, ff.82–3; *A.D.B.*, vol. 1, p. 558; Peron, op. cit., p. 282; D. Wentworth to T. Jamison, 1 January 1803, Wentworth Papers, Medical Stores, Hospital Returns, 1803–1820, A762; *Sydney Gazette*, 22 January 1804, p. 2; D. Wentworth to Lord Fitzwilliam, 12 May 1803, Wentworth Woodhouse Muniments, F114/21.

33 Ibid.; see entry under 'Wentworth' in T. D. Mutch, King's Musters, 1800–1802, A1443, M.L.; *H.R.N.S.W.*, vol. 4, p. 933; ibid., vol. 5, pp. 432–5; *Sydney Gazette*, 8 April 1804, p. 3.

Notes: Chapter 4

[34] D. Wentworth to W. Balmain, n.d. 1803, Wentworth Papers, A751, ff.117–20; C. Cookney to D. Wentworth, 31 October 1803, 13 April 1804 and 31 December 1805, ibid., A754-2, ff.130–2, 136–7 and 161–4; W. C. and D. Wentworth to D. Wentworth, 24 July 1804, ibid., A756, ff.1–3; P. Yeend to C. Cunneen, 26 August 1993, copy held by A.D.B.; P. Yeend to J. Ritchie, 3 August 1994; see also *A.D.B.*, vol. 1, p. 583.

[35] Holt, *Memoirs*, pp. 193–203; *H.R.N.S.W.*, vol. 5, pp. 345–57; P. G. King to D. Collins, 20 April 1804, King Letterbook, A2015, ff.302–3, M.L.; Mann, op. cit., pp. 13–14; E. Marsden to J. Piper, 14 April 1804, Piper Papers, A256, vol. 3, ff.545–56, M.L.; G. Mackaness (ed.), *Memoirs of George Suttor*, Sydney, 1948, p. 47; *Sydney Gazette*, 11 March 1804; D. Woodriff to 'whom it may concern', n.d., Woodriff Family Papers, 1803–65, MSS 613, part 1, M.L.; R. Connell, 'The Convict Rebellion of 1804', in *Melbourne Historical Journal*, vol. 5, 1965, pp. 27–37.

[36] *H.R.N.S.W.*, vol. 5, p. 300; D. Wentworth to unnamed correspondent, 14 May 1804, Wentworth Papers, A751, ff.151–3; to J. Savage, 14 August 1804, ibid., ff.142(b)–(e); P. G. King to J. Foveaux, 16 January 1804, King's Letterbook, A2015, f.367, M.L.; J. Foveaux to P. G. King, 16 June 1804, Colonel Foveaux's Letterbook, A1444, ff.81–2, M.L.; *A.D.B.*, vol. 1, pp. 52 and 408; T. Jamison to D. Wentworth, 14 April 1804, Wentworth Papers, A754-2, f.134; J. Piper's account with D. Wentworth, Piper Papers, A254, vol. 1, ff.29–31; New South Wales, Colonial Secretary's Papers regarding Norfolk Island, 1800–1805, MSS 681/3, ff.112, 201, 287 and 293, M.L.; Norfolk Island, Letters, papers and returns, 1794–1808, COD 412, ff.183, 193 and 199–200, COD 413, ff.279, 355 and 453, A.O.N.S.W.; D. Considen to D. Wentworth, 20 February 1804, Wentworth Papers, A751, ff.125–8; I. Clementson to D. Wentworth, 5 May 1804, ibid., ff.135–7; extract from parish register, St Giles in the Fields, 25 November 1803, ibid., f.123; C. Cookney to D. Wentworth, 11 June and 31 October 1803, ibid., A754-2, ff.126–8 and 130–2; D. Considen to D. Wentworth, 9 October 1806, ibid., f.427; D. Wentworth to unnamed correspondent, 14 May 1804, ibid., A751, f.153; Holt, op. cit., pp. 272–3.

[37] P. G. King to J. Foveaux, 31 May and 20 July 1804, King's Letterbook, A2015, ff.148–52, 394 and 425–6; A. J. King to D. Wentworth, 18 July 1804, Wentworth Papers, A751, ff.148–9;

Notes: Chapter 4

W. Balmain to D. Wentworth, 25 March 1803, ibid., ff.111–14; J. Mileham to D. Wentworth, 18 August 1804, ibid., ff.159–60; statement of facts on behalf of D. Wentworth, to Earl Camden, n.d., ibid., A754-2, ff.398–403; D. Wentworth to Lord Fitzwilliam, November 1806, Wentworth Woodhouse Muniments, F114/22.

[38] A.D.B., vol. 1, p. 408; D. Considen to D. Wentworth, 9 October 1806, Wentworth Papers, A754-2, ff.427–8; W. C. Wentworth to D. Wentworth, 11 August 1805, ibid., f.763; H.R.N.S.W., vol. 5, p. 550, and vol. 6, p. 80; Holt, op. cit., pp. 220–1, 225, 229–30 and 233–5; R. Jones, *Recollections.*, ff.3–5, 7–8 and 15–18; J. Mitchell, 'Norfolk Island, 1804 till 1809', in N. D. Stenhouse Papers, MSS 27, ff.2–3, M.L.; L. Davoren, *A New Song Made in New South Wales*, privately printed by G. Mackaness, Sydney, 1951, pp. 20–1; J. Grant to W. Cox, 21 October 1805, and copy of a 'Note to the Commandant of Norfolk Island', 26 March 1806, John Grant's Journal, MS 737, ff.45 and 66, N.L.A.; J. P. Perkins to C. Cunneen, 24 January 1994, with enclosures, Foveaux file, held by the A.D.B.

[39] H.R.N.S.W., vol. 5, p. 550; ibid., vol. 6, p. 204; Holt, op. cit., p. 231; Jones, loc. cit., ff.8 and 27–9; Mitchell, loc. cit., f.3; P. G. King to J. Piper, 6 January 1805, King's Letterbook, A2015, f.471, M.L.; C. Cookney to D. Wentworth, 31 December 1805, Wentworth Papers, A754-2, ff.417–18.

[40] C. Cookney's accounts of expenses on D. Wentworth's sons, 27 September 1803 to 15 July 1807, ibid., f.315 and passim; D. Considen to D. Wentworth, 26 February 1804, ibid., A751, ff.129–31; C. Cookney to D. Wentworth, n.d. 1804, ibid., A754-2, ff.136–7; to Lord Fitzwilliam, 25 December 1804, Wentworth Woodhouse Muniments, FM4/747; to D. Wentworth, 13 April and 19 June 1805, Wentworth Papers, A754-2, ff.148–50 and 152–3; D. Wentworth (jnr) to D. Wentworth, 4 July 1805, ibid., A755, ff.1(a)–1(b); W. C. Wentworth to D. Wentworth, 11 August 1805, ibid., A756, ff.1–3; C. Cookney to D. Wentworth, 27 September, 8 October and 31 December 1805, ibid., A754-2, ff.156–7, 161–4 and 431; D. Considen to D. Wentworth, 9 October 1806, ibid., ff.171–4; C. Cookney to D. Wentworth, 21 November 1806, ibid., ff.175–7; D. Wentworth to C. Cookney, 12 March 1806, ibid., A751, ff.167–167(a); H.R.N.S.W., vol. 5, p. 587; A.D.B., vol. 1, p. 583.

Notes: Chapters 4 and 5

[41] P. G. King to J. Piper, 24 February 1806, King's Letterbook, A2015, f.520, and New South Wales, Colonial Secretary's Papers regarding Norfolk Island, 1800–1805, MSS 681/4, f.21, M.L.; T. Jamison to D. Wentworth, 8 February 1806, Wentworth Papers, A751, f.163; D. Wentworth to C. Cookney, 12 March 1806, ibid., ff.167–167(a); D. Considen to D. Wentworth, 9 October 1806, ibid., A754-2, ff.171–4; C. Cookney to D. Wentworth, 21 November 1806, ibid., ff.175–7; *H.R.N.S.W.*, vol. 6, p. 80; J. Piper to P. G. King, 28 March 1806, N.S.W., Col. Secy's Papers, MSS 681/4, f.25; J. Piper to Commissioners of the Treasury, 30 March 1806, Wentworth Papers, A754-2, f.160.

5 Nets of wrong and right

[1] *Sydney Gazette*, 13 April, 4 May and 11 May 1806; *H.R.N.S.W.*, vol. 6, pp. 67, 81, 97, 113, 125 and 397; C. Cookney to D. Wentworth, 31 December 1805, Wentworth Papers, A754-2, ff.161–4; J. Macarthur to J. Piper, 6 April 1806, Piper Papers, A256, vol. 3, f.477; A. Serle to S. Marsden, 15 April 1805, Marsden Papers, A1992, f.26; S. Marsden to D. Wentworth, 12 July 1806, Wentworth Papers, A751, ff.169–70; Suttor, 'Sketch', C783, f.7; D. Wentworth to Lord Fitzwilliam, 4 November 1806, Wentworth Woodhouse Muniments, F114/22.

[2] Ibid.; D. Wentworth to C. Cookney, 18 October 1807, Wentworth Papers, A751, ff.237–40; Evidence of W. Bligh, Report of the Select Committee on Transportation, p. 45; Ritchie (ed.), *A Charge of Mutiny*, pp. 333–4; *A.D.B.*, vol. 2, pp. 60–1.

[3] *Sydney Gazette*, 17 August 1806; *H.R.N.S.W.*, vol. 6, pp. 165–6 and 188–92; copy of Hawkesbury Settlers' address, 30 August 1806, Wentworth Papers, A751, ff.171–80; *A.D.B.*, vol. 1, p. 290; ibid., vol. 2, p. 155.

[4] W. Bligh to J. Banks, 10 October and 5 November 1807, Banks Papers, A85, vol. 22, ff.193 and 261; *H.R.N.S.W.*, vol. 6, pp. 145–8, 231–2 and 343; *Sydney Gazette*, 17 August 1806; G. Mackaness, *The Life of Vice-Admiral William Bligh*, Sydney, 1951, p. 354; Dermody, *D'Arcy Wentworth*, p. 157; *A.D.B.*, vol. 1, pp. 118–20; ibid., vol. 2, pp. 309–10; Ritchie (ed.), *A Charge of Mutiny*, pp. xiv and xix; J. Ritchie, *Lachlan Macquarie*, Melbourne, 1986,

Notes: Chapter 5

pp. 102–3. War with France continued from 1793 until 1815, save for the peace that followed the Treaty of Amiens which only lasted from 27 March 1802 to 17 May 1803.

[5] C. Cookney's accounts of expenses on D. Wentworth's sons, 15 July 1807 to 9 May 1809, Wentworth Papers, A754-2, f.315 and passim; D. Wentworth (jnr) to D. Wentworth, 9 March 1807, ibid., A755, ff.1(e)–2(a); *Sydney Gazette*, 31 August 1806; Trial of John Stephens for theft at Parramatta, 29 August 1806, A.O.N.S.W., CCJ 5/1149, p. 289; *H.R.A.*, I, vi, pp. 163 and 167; *H.R.N.S.W.*, vol. 6, pp. 151, 162 and 231–2; C. Cookney to D. Wentworth, 21 November 1806, 10 June 1807, 14 November 1807 and 29 April 1808, Wentworth Papers, A754-2, ff.175–7, 181–2, 185–8 and 189–91; D. Considen to D. Wentworth, 9 October 1806, ibid., f.427; W. Redfern to D. Wentworth, 16 September 1807, ibid., A751, ff.201–3; Lt W. Wentworth to D. Wentworth, 16 October 1807, ibid., ff.205–7; Will of Maria Ainslie, 15 April 1841, and codicil, 25 November 1841, Probate Office, Series 1, no. 1311, A.O.N.S.W.; *A.D.B.*, vol. 1, p. 519; ibid., vol. 2, pp. 12–13, 19, 227 and 370; Wright, *Forgotten Generation*, p. 167; K. C. W. Miles to J. Ritchie, 5 August 1994; M. Flynn to J. Ritchie, 10 November 1994.

[6] *H.R.N.S.W.*, vol. 6, pp. 316–26; D. Wentworth, Address to the Court-Martial, 18 July 1807, Wentworth Papers, A751, ff.189–92; D. Wentworth to Lord Fitzwilliam, 18 July 1807, Wentworth Woodhouse Muniments, F114/32; H. V. Evatt, *Rum Rebellion*, Sydney, 1955, pp. 89–96; R. Fitzgerald and M. Hearn, *Bligh, Macarthur and the Rum Rebellion*, Kenthurst, 1988, pp. 77–8; Ritchie (ed.), *A Charge of Mutiny*, p. 160.

[7] *H.R.N.S.W.*, vol. 6, pp. 314–15 and 326–30; D. Wentworth to Lord Fitzwilliam, 17 October 1807, Wentworth Woodhouse Muniments, F114/23–24; to C. Cookney, 18 October 1807, Wentworth Papers, A751, ff.237–40; to J. Villiers, 18 October 1807, ibid., ff.227–30; W. Bligh to W. Windham, 31 October 1807, *H.R.A.*, I, vi, p. 143; *A.D.B.*, vol. 2, p. 598.

[8] *H.R.A.*, I, vi, pp. 188–90; *H.R.N.S.W.*, vol. 6, pp. 313–15 and 368–70; D. Wentworth to Lord Fitzwilliam, 17 October 1807, Wentworth Woodhouse Muniments, F114/23–24; Lord Fitzwilliam to Lord Castlereagh, 18 April 1808, ibid., F114/26; Castlereagh to Fitzwilliam, 25 April 1808, ibid., F114/27; C. Cookney to Lord

Notes: Chapter 5

Fitzwilliam, 9 April 1808, ibid., FM4/747; W. Bligh to Lord Fitzwilliam, 31 October 1807, ibid., FM4/747; C. Cookney to D. Wentworth, 14 June 1808, Wentworth Papers, A754-2, f.193; Ritchie (ed.), *A Charge of Mutiny*, pp. 160-1; Ritchie, *Macquarie*, p. 104.

9 *H.R.N.S.W.*, vol. 6, pp. 199, 253 and 400; E. Bligh to Mrs Bond, 14 September 1807, Elizabeth Bligh's Letters, MS 1016, M.L.; W. Bligh to J. Banks, 10 October 1807, Banks Papers, A85, vol. 22, ff.189-93; R. Hassall to unnamed correspondent, 8 September 1808, Hassall Papers, A859, ff.224-6, M.L.; S. Marsden to J. Banks, 28 September 1808, Banks Papers, A83, vol. 20, ff.305-6; M. Putland to E. Bligh, 10 October 1807, Bligh Correspondence, Safe 1/45, f.106, M.L.; *A.D.B.*, vol. 1, p. 308; ibid., vol. 2, p. 139.

10 Macarthur Onslow, *Early Records*, pp. 136-7; *H.R.A.*, I, vi, pp. 150 and 331; *H.R.N.S.W.*, vol. 6, pp. 275-8, 286-7, 305-6, 310, 339 and 343; Ritchie (ed.), *A Charge of Mutiny*, pp. xvi, 57, 180-1, 217, 229, 288-9, 294-5 and 328; *Sydney Gazette*, 26 July and 16 August 1807; W. Bligh to J. Banks, 5 November 1807, Banks Papers, A85, vol. 22, ff.262-3, M.L.; T. Jamison to G. Johnston, 14 February 1808, New South Wales, Colonial Secretary's Papers, 1799-1806, MSS 681/2, ff.225-6; Dermody, loc. cit., p. 184; *A.D.B.*, vol. 1, pp. 115-17; ibid., vol. 2, pp. 31, 129, 536-8 and 547-8.

11 J. Blaxland to J. Banks, 22 October 1807, Banks Papers, A83, vol. 20, ff.188-91, M.L.; E. Bligh to W. Bligh, 15 February 1808, Bligh Correspondence, Safe 1/45, f.123, M.L.; to J. Banks, 1 February 1808, Banks Papers, A78-5, ff.39-40, M.L.; J. Macarthur to J. Piper, 11 October 1807, Piper Papers, A256, vol. 3, f.482, M.L.; *H.R.N.S.W.*, vol. 6, pp. 305-6, 308-12, 331, 339, 342-9 and 652; Ritchie (ed.), *A Charge of Mutiny*, p. 217; Macarthur Onslow, op. cit., p. 137; Ritchie, *Macquarie*, p. 102; *A.D.B.*, vol. 1, p. 380; ibid., vol. 2, pp. 39 and 233.

12 *H.R.A.*, I, vi, pp. 307-10, 318-21 and 332-5; *H.R.N.S.W.*, vol. 6, pp. 335, 378, 413-14, 416-17, 485, 575-7 and 612; *Sydney Gazette*, 5 July 1807; Ritchie (ed.), *A Charge of Mutiny*, p. xv; Evatt, op. cit., pp. 86-8, 97-103 and 118-22; see also A. Atkinson, 'Jeremy Bentham and the Rum Rebellion', *J.R.A.H.S.*, vol. 64, part 1, June 1978, pp. 1-13, and 'The British Whigs and the Rum Rebellion', ibid., vol. 66, Part 2, September 1980, pp. 73-90.

Notes: Chapter 5

[13] *H.R.A.*, I, vi, pp. 208–13, 298–300, 312–14, 347–9, 371, 411, 420–1 and 424; *H.R.N.S.W.*, vol. 6, pp. 410–11, 434 and 554–5; W. Bligh to Lord Minto, 12 August 1808, Bligh Correspondence, Safe 1/45, f.146, M.L.; E. Abbott to P. G. King, 13 February and 4 April 1808, King Papers, A1976, ff.121(b to n), M.L.; C. Grimes to J. Piper, 20 December 1807, Piper Papers, A254, vol. 1, ff.115–16, M.L.; R. Hassall to unnamed correspondent, 8 September 1808, Hassall Papers, A859, ff.234–8, M.L.; G. Johnston to Duke of Northumberland, 16 December 1811, George Johnston's Letterbook, C474, ff.6–7, M.L.; Ritchie (ed.), *A Charge of Mutiny*, pp. xv, 148–9, 151–2, 205, 209, 220, 236, 267 and 301–3; Evatt, op. cit., p. 113; Mackaness, *Bligh*, pp. 394–419; *A.D.B.*, vol. 1, p. 487.

[14] Ritchie (ed.), *A Charge of Mutiny*, pp. vii–viii, 26, 84, 100, 106–7 and 109–11; W. Bligh, notes on the rebellion, June 1808, King Papers, A1976, vol. 1, ff.149–50, M.L.; W. Bligh to Lord Minto, 12 August 1808, and to Sir Edward Pellew, 15 August 1808, Bligh Correspondence, Safe 1/45, ff.147–8 and 163–8, M.L.; *H.R.A.*, I, vi, pp. 213 and 430–3; *H.R.N.S.W.*, vol. 6, pp. 556–9 and 615–19; J. Macarthur to E. Macarthur, 26 January 1808, Macarthur Papers, A2898, vol. 2, f.2, M.L.; Mackaness, *Bligh*, pp. 420–31; Barker, *D'Arcy Wentworth*, pp. 77–8.

[15] E. Abbott to P. G. King, 13 February 1808, King Papers, A1976, f.121(h), M.L.; G. Johnston to Colonel Gordon, 9 April 1808, DOC 61, M.L.; Ritchie (ed.), *A Charge of Mutiny*, pp. viii, 35, 80–1, 93, 109–10, 114–17, 121, 137, 155, 197–8 and 444–6; *H.R.N.S.W.*, vol. 6, pp. 453–4, 458 and 584.

[16] Ibid., pp. 412, 434–5, 454–5 and 458–9; Memorial of the Free Settlers to Viscount Castlereagh, 3 November 1808, Ab60/1, M.L.; Ritchie (ed.), *A Charge of Mutiny*, pp. 122–6, 133–5, 137–8, 285–7 and 354; Mackaness, *Bligh*, p. 415; Barker, loc. cit., pp. 76–7.

[17] *H.R.N.S.W.*, vol. 6, pp. 625–6; G. Caley to J. Banks, 28 October 1808, Banks Papers, A79-1, vol. 8, ff.190–1; E. Abbott to P. G. King, 13 February 1808, King Papers, A1996, f.121(g); Memorandum of the Proceedings of a Committee, 8 February 1808, The Rebellion, 1808, Miscellaneous Documents, Safe 1/41, ff.29–34, M.L.; Ritchie (ed.), *A Charge of Mutiny*, p. 300.

[18] Ibid., pp. viii–ix, 104 and 107; *H.R.N.S.W.*, vol. 6, pp. 459–60 and 672.

Notes: Chapter 5

[19] *H.R.A.*, 1, vi, pp. 188–90; *H.R.N.S.W.*, vol. 6, pp. 368–70, 459–60, 465–510 and 522–7; E. Abbott to P. G. King, 13 February 1808, King Papers, A1996, ff.121(f to i), M.L.; D. Wentworth to N. Bayly, 9 February 1808, Wentworth Woodhouse Muniments, FM4/747; to Lord Fitzwilliam, 12 April 1808, ibid., F114/33; Ritchie (ed.), *A Charge of Mutiny*, p. 334.

[20] Ritchie, *Macquarie*, pp. 103 and 251.

[21] Ibid., pp. 103–4 and 251.

[22] D. Wentworth to Lord Fitzwilliam, 12 April and 1 May 1808, Wentworth Woodhouse Muniments, F114/33 and 34.

[23] *H.R.N.S.W.*, vol. 6, pp. 527, 600–2, 626, 630, 665, 669 and 795; J. Macarthur to J. Piper, 24 May 1808, Piper Papers, A254, vol. 1, ff.138–9; Macarthur Onslow, op. cit., pp. 160–3.

[24] *Sydney Gazette*, 22 May 1808; D. Wentworth to Lord Fitzwilliam, 1 May, 8 and 12 September 1808, Wentworth Woodhouse Muniments, F114/34, 36 and 37; to C. Cookney, n.d. September 1808 and 14 October 1809, ibid., FM4/747; C. Cookney to D. Wentworth, 29 April 1808, Wentworth Papers, A754-2, ff.189–91; Cookney's accounts of expenses on D. Wentworth's sons, 18 August 1808 to 31 August 1809, ibid., ff.198, 315 and passim; D. Wentworth to J. Finucane, 1 September 1808, ibid., A751, ff.247–8; *H.R.N.S.W.*, vol. 5, pp. 678–9; ibid., vol. 7, p. 51; Ritchie (ed.), *A Charge of Mutiny*, p. 471; Dermody, loc. cit., p. 229.

[25] *Sydney Gazette*, 31 July 1808; *H.R.A.*, 1, vi, pp. 624 and 632–4; *H.R.N.S.W.*, vol. 6, pp. 532–3 and 701; ibid., vol. 7, p. 205; E. Abbott to P. G. King, 13 February 1808, King Papers, A1976, ff.121 (b to j); D. Wentworth to Lord Fitzwilliam, 8 and 12 September 1808, Wentworth Woodhouse Muniments, F114/36 and 37; W. Paterson to J. Banks, 29 September 1808, Banks Papers, A78-3, vol. 4, f.305; Ritchie (ed.), *A Charge of Mutiny*, pp. 244 and 322; C. M. H. Clark, *A History of Australia*, vol. 1, pp. 224–6; *A.D.B.*, vol. 1, p. 408; ibid., vol. 2, p. 318.

[26] Lord Castlereagh to Lord Fitzwilliam, 10 November 1808, Wentworth Woodhouse Muniments, F114/35; Macarthur Onslow, op. cit., pp. 167 and 169; Ritchie, *Macquarie*, pp. 104–7 and 251–3.

[27] *H.R.N.S.W.*, vol. 7, pp. 40 and 66; D. Wentworth to Lord Fitzwilliam, 12 September 1808, Wentworth Woodhouse Muniments, F114/37; to C. Cookney, n.d. September 1808 and

14 October 1809, ibid., FM4/747; E. Paterson to D. Wentworth, 4 September 1807, Wentworth Papers, A751, ff.197–9; H. Fulton to E. Bligh, n.d. 1809, Banks Papers, A78-5, ff.153–4, M.L.; W. Gore to E. Bligh, 6 October 1809, ibid., ff.167 and 185; G. Blaxcell to J. Macarthur, 2 May and 6 November 1809, Macarthur Papers, A2900, vol. 4, ff.8–12, M.L.; Macarthur Onslow, op. cit., pp. 192 and 194; Mackaness, *Bligh*, p. 489; *A.D.B.*, vol. 1, pp. 117 and 408–9; ibid., vol. 2, pp. 318–19.

[28] D. Wentworth to Lord Fitzwilliam, n.d. (probably October 1809), Wentworth Papers, A752, ff.280–1; to L. Macquarie, and to Lord Castlereagh, n.d. 1809, ibid., ff.5–7 and 11; to Lord Fitzwilliam, 14 October 1809 and 17 March 1810, Wentworth Woodhouse Muniments, F114/38 and F114/43; to C. Cookney, 14 October 1809, ibid., FM4/747; H. Fulton to E. Bligh, n.d., Banks Papers, A78-5, ff.162–3, M.L.; R. Hassall to unnamed correspondent, 8 September 1808, Hassall Papers, A859, f.249, M.L.; *H.R.A.*, I, vii, pp. 14 and 113–14; Ryan, *Land Grants*, pp. 191, 194, 198, 204, 215 and 290; Barker, loc. cit., p. 86.

[29] Cookney's accounts of expenses on D. Wentworth's sons, 1 September to 5 October 1809, Wentworth Papers, A754-2, f.315 and passim; C. Cookney to D. Wentworth, 25 November 1809, ibid., ff.205–7; *H.R.N.S.W.*, vol. 6, p. 233; W. Gore to E. Bligh, 6 October 1809, Banks Papers, A78-5, ff.185–6; H. Fulton to E. Bligh, n.d., ibid., ff.162–3; G. Blaxcell to J. Macarthur, 6 November 1809, Macarthur Papers, A2900, f.10; D. Wentworth to Lord Fitzwilliam, 17 March 1810, Wentworth Woodhouse Muniments, F114/43; to C. Cookney, n.d. September 1808 and 14 October 1809, ibid., FM4/747; to Lord Fitzwilliam, n.d. 1810, Wentworth Papers, A752, ff.9–12; to L. Macquarie, n.d. January 1810, ibid., ff.5–7; Dermody, loc. cit., p. 235.

[30] Ritchie, *Macquarie*, pp. 108–12 and 253–4.

[31] *H.R.N.S.W.*, vol. 7, pp. 142, 144–5 and 148–9.

6 To catch a thief

[1] Ritchie, *Macquarie*, p. 120.

[2] Ibid., pp. 121 and 255.

[3] *H.R.N.S.W.*, vol. 7, pp. 252 and 255–7; *Sydney Gazette*, 7 January 1810.

Notes: Chapter 6

⁴ Ibid., 14 January 1810; W. Bligh to E. Bligh, 8 March 1810, Bligh Papers, Safe 1/45, f.284, M.L.; D. Wentworth to Lord Fitzwilliam, 17 March 1810, Wentworth Woodhouse Muniments, F114/43, ff.1-8; L. Macquarie to D. Wentworth, n.d. (probably September 1817), Wentworth Papers, A753, ff.347-9(a), a copy of which is in the Wentworth Woodhouse Muniments, F114/59, ff.17-18; Mackaness (ed.), *Suttor Memoirs*, p. 50; Ritchie, *Macquarie*, pp. 121-2 and 255.

⁵ Ibid., p. 122, 134 and 259; Mackaness, *Bligh*, pp. 503-6 and 511; A.D.B., vol. 2, p. 295.

⁶ Ritchie, *Macquarie*, passim, but esp. pp. 92 and 112-13.

⁷ Ibid., pp. 132-6 and 258-60; Suttor, 'Sketch', C783, ff.20-1; J. Foveaux to D. Wentworth, 13 March 1811, Wentworth Papers, A752, ff.325-6; J. Macarthur to E. Macarthur, 21 April 1811, Macarthur Papers, A2898, ff.103-4; Report of the Select Committee on Transportation, pp. 36, 45 and 64; Macarthur Onslow, *Early Records*, pp. 215-16; Barker, *D'Arcy Wentworth*, p. 117; for a discussion of the origins of the terms 'emancipist' and 'exclusive' see C. A. Liston, New South Wales Under Governor Brisbane, 1821-1825, Ph.D. thesis, University of Sydney, 1980, pp. 410-14.

⁸ *Sydney Gazette*, 24 February 1810; *H.R.A.*, I, vii, pp. 255-6 and 327; *H.R.N.S.W.*, vol. 7, p. 365; D. Wentworth to Lord Fitzwilliam, 17 March 1810, Wentworth Woodhouse Muniments, F114/43, ff.1-8, and C. Cookney to Lord Fitzwilliam, 25 April 1810, ibid., FM4/747; L. Macquarie's replies to J. Bigge's queries, n.d., Wentworth Papers, A753, ff.347 and 350a; D. Wentworth, draft letter, n.d. 1810, ibid., A751, f.9; D. Wentworth to C. Cookney, 8 May 1810, ibid., A752, ff.15-18; L. Macquarie to Treasury officers, 28 July 1810, ibid., f.19; Memorial no. 329, 1810, Colonial Secretary Miscellaneous Papers, 4/1822, A.O.N.S.W.

⁹ D. Wentworth to Lord Fitzwilliam, n.d. 1810, Wentworth Papers, A752, ff.9-12, and 17 March 1810, Wentworth Woodhouse Muniments, F114/43, ff.1-8.

¹⁰ *H.R.A.*, I, vii, pp. 224, 276 and 809; *H.R.N.S.W.*, vol. 7, p. 381; D. Wentworth to C. Cookney, 8 May 1810, Wentworth Papers, A752, ff.15-18; *Sydney Gazette*, 31 March, 7 April and 19 May 1810; J. T. Campbell to D. Wentworth, 31 March 1810, New South Wales Colonial Secretary, Out Letters, 4/3490, f.160, A.O.N.S.W.; to D. Wentworth, 1 January 1811, Wentworth Papers, A752 (CY699),

Notes: Chapter 6

ff.29–33; Treasury Orders on the Police Fund, 1812–25, ibid., A763, ff.375–544; Barker, loc. cit., p. 95; J. McLaughlin, The Magistracy in New South Wales, 1788–1850, LL.M. thesis, University of Sydney, 1973, p. 142; C. H. Currey, *The Brothers Bent*, Sydney, 1968, p. 52.

[11] *H.R.A.*, I, vii, pp. 330 and 342; *H.R.N.S.W.*, vol. 7, p. 327; *Sydney Gazette*, 7 January and 7 April 1810; L. Macquarie to C. Forbes, 18 June 1810, Macquarie Papers, MS 202, letter no. 5, N.L.A.; W. Bligh to E. Bligh, 11 August 1810, Bligh Papers, Safe 1/45, f.299, M.L.; Ritchie (ed.), *A Charge of Mutiny*, pp. 101–4, 224–5 and 458–9; Ritchie, *Macquarie*, pp. 122 and 255; Mackaness, *Bligh*, pp. 504 and 513.

[12] E. Bent to his mother, 4 March and 25 October 1810, Bent Papers, MS195/2, ff.99 and 203, N.L.A.; H. Fulton to E. Bligh, n.d. 1809, Bligh Papers, Safe 1/45, f.280, M.L.; J. Arnold to his brother, 25 February to 25 October 1810, Joseph Arnold Correspondence, A1849-2, ff.3–4, M.L.; J. M. Good to S. Marsden, 25 December 1814, Marsden Papers, A1992, ff.177–8, M.L.; S. Marsden to W. Wilberforce, 27 July 1810, Hassall Family Correspondence, A1677-2, ff.23–4, M.L.; Evidence of A. Riley, Report of the Select Committee on the State of Gaols, House of Commons, *Parliamentary Papers*, vol. vii, no. 579, 1819, p. 55; C. Cookney to Lord Fitzwilliam, 9 June 1810, Wentworth Woodhouse Muniments, FM4/747.

[13] *H.R.A.*, I, vii, pp. 320 and 652; *H.R.N.S.W.*, vol. 7, pp. 365, 369 and 630; D. Wentworth to C. Cookney, 8 May 1810, Wentworth Papers, A752, ff.15–18; C. Cookney to D. Wentworth, 2 February 1811, ibid., A754-2, ff.217–19; D. Wentworth to Lord Fitzwilliam, 30 November 1811, Wentworth Woodhouse Muniments, F114/52; W. C. Wentworth to Lord Fitzwilliam, 7 May 1810 and 15 December 1811, ibid., F114/44 and 53; *Sydney Gazette*, 2 January 1813 and 26 February 1814; for the pipe about the Macarthurs, see Wentworth Papers, A4073, f.24; C. M. H. Clark, *A History of Australia*, vol. 2, pp. 42–3; *A.D.B.*, vol. 2, p. 583; Fifer, William Charles Wentworth, p. 25; Liston, 'William Charles Wentworth', p. 21; G. B. Barton, 'The Life and Times of William Charles Wentworth', clippings from the *Australian Star*, Sydney, 1898–99, provided by Father Brian Maher, St Vincent's parish church, Aranda, Canberra, and 56-page copy of same in M.L. at QA923.29/W479/2A1.

Notes: Chapter 6

[14] J. Macarthur to E. Macarthur, 3 May and 20 July 1810, Macarthur Papers, A2898, ff.45–51 and 57–64; W. Lawson to D. Wentworth, n.d. 1811, and A. Kemp to D. Wentworth, 13 March and 15 August 1811, Wentworth Papers, A752, ff.41–3, 55 and 67–9; L. Macquarie, Memoranda, 29 September 1811, Macquarie Papers, A772, f.43; Lord Fitzwilliam and C. Cookney to the Commander-in Chief, 19 February 1811, Wentworth Woodhouse Muniments, F114/47–8; H. Torrens to Lord Fitzwilliam, 26 February and 2 March 1811, ibid., F114/49–50; C. Cookney to Lord Fitzwilliam, 29 October 1810 and 26 December 1813, ibid., F114/45 and 56; C. Cookney to D. Wentworth, n.d. September 1810, 2 February 1811, 28 March 1811 and 16 January 1812, Wentworth Papers, A754-2, ff.213–15, 218, 221–3 and 229–31; C. Cookney to D. Wentworth, 17 August 1811, 16 January 1812, 6 December 1813 and 13 August 1814, ibid., A752, ff.71–3 and A754-2, ff.229–31, 247–8 and 253–5; J. Wentworth to W. C. Wentworth, 20 July 1813, ibid., A754-2, ff.239–41; F. Auber to D. Wentworth (jnr), 4 May 1811, ibid., A755, f.2(b); W. Wentworth to D. Wentworth, 12 July 1813, ibid., A754-2, ff.235–6; C. Cookney's accounts, July to August 1813, ibid., ff.243–4; *H.R.A.*, 4, i, pp. 146 and 789; *D.N.B.*, vol. 12, pp. 856–8.

[15] *H.R.N.S.W.*, vol. 6, p. 125; *Sydney Gazette*, 28 April 1810; J. Macneal to S. Bannister, 8 October 1824, and to the Governor in Council, August 1825, Colonial Secretary, In Letters, Bundle 25, Letters and Petitions, nos 1–27, ff.76–8, A.O.N.S.W.; *H.R.A.*, iv, 1, p. 789; evidence of J. Harris, CO201/120, f.158; L. Macquarie, Memoranda, A772, ff.66, 76, 83, 141a and 157; Liston, *Sarah Wentworth*, pp. 15–16 and 26; Mackaness, *Bligh*, p. 356; K. C. W. Miles to J. Ritchie, 10 January 1997.

[16] *Sydney Gazette*, 5 October 1811; D. Wentworth to Lord Fitzwilliam, 30 November 1811, Wentworth Woodhouse Muniments, F114/52; C. Cookney to Lord Fitzwilliam, 15 May 1812, ibid., F114/55; Bathurst to Fitzwilliam, 1 April 1814, ibid., F82/15; C. Cookney to D. Wentworth, 11 October 1812, Wentworth Papers, A763, f.15; *A.D.B.*, vol. 2, pp. 294–6.

[17] *H.R.A.*, 1, vii, pp. 384–5, 401–5 and 595–7; *H.R.N.S.W.*, vol. 7, pp. 449–53; Papers concerning the Sydney Hospital, 1810–17, Wentworth Papers, A761, ff.1–17 and 290–374; *Sydney Gazette*, 2

Notes: Chapter 6

November 1811; Barker, loc. cit., pp. 101–4 and 110–11; *A.D.B.*, vol. 2, pp. 381 and 581; Ritchie, *Macquarie*, p. 128; M. H. Ellis, 'Governor Macquarie and the "Rum" Hospital', in *J.R.A.H.S.*, vol. 32, part 5, 1946, pp. 273–93; Hainsworth, *Sydney Traders*, pp. 57 and 209–10.

[18] *H.R.A.*, I, vii, pp. 250 and 486–8; C. Cookney to Lord Fitzwilliam, 5 February 1812, Wentworth Woodhouse Muniments, F114/54; to D. Wentworth, 16 January 1812, Wentworth Papers, A754-2, ff.229–31; D. Wentworth's account with C. Cookney, ibid., ff.536–63; C. Cookney to D. Wentworth, 17 August 1811, ibid., A752, ff.71–2; Barker, loc. cit., pp. 100 and 115–16.

[19] Deposition of W. McIntosh, J. Johnston, G. Shaw and T. Storer, 30 November 1810, petition of W. Mansell, 6 December 1810, deposition of W. Mansell, 6 December 1810, Colonial Secretary, In Letters, 4/1725, ff.220–6, A.O.N.S.W.

[20] *H.R.N.S.W.*, vol. 7, pp. 476, 479–85 and 607; *H.R.A.*, I, viii, pp. 131, 311 and 597; *Sydney Gazette*, 29 December 1810 and 8 April 1815; Government and General Order, 8 April 1815, Wentworth Papers, A754-2, f.261; extract from a dispatch from Earl Bathurst to L. Macquarie, 3 February 1814, ibid., f.490; bill of exchange, 12 September 1810, ibid., A752, f.23; J. T. Campbell to D. Wentworth, 8 January 1811 and 10 April 1815, ibid., ff.29–30 and A754-2, f.265; D. Wentworth's salary as superintendent of police, 1811–1823, ibid., MS D1, ff.133, 141, 145, 153, 163, 171, 180, 200, 210, 214, 218–19, 223, 226 and 255; D. Wentworth to Lord Fitzwilliam, 30 June 1815, 83/23, f.2, N.R.O.; L. Macquarie, Memoranda, 1 January 1811, A772, f.30; Ritchie, *Macquarie*, pp. 124 and 128; Barker, loc. cit., pp. 105–7, 124 and 164.

[21] D. Wentworth to Lord Fitzwilliam, 30 November 1811, Wentworth Woodhouse Muniments, F114/52, and 15 October 1814, Fitzwilliam MSS, 82/54, ff.1–9, N.R.O.; L. Macquarie, Memoranda, 9 September 1812 and 28 June 1814, A772, pp. 46 and 80–1; B. Thomas, two maps, *Early Sydney, 1803–1810*, Sydney, 1979, and *Macquarie's Sydney*, Sydney, 1975, M.L.; undated notes by H. Macquarie and W. Redfern, Wentworth Papers, A4073, items 5 and 6, M.L.; D. Wentworth, Medical Book, 1810–1827, ibid., B196, ff.1–184; invitation to D. Wentworth to celebrate His Majesty's birthday at Government House, Sydney, n.d., ibid., A754-2, f.436; Ritchie, *Macquarie*, pp. 60, 161 and 179.

Notes: Chapter 6

[22] *Sydney Gazette*, 1 February 1812, 3 July and 11 December 1813; *H.R.A.*, i, 7, p. 362; *H.R.N.S.W.*, vol. 7, p. 540; Colonial Secretary, In Letters, 10 September 1814, 4/1730, ff.341–5, A.O.N.S.W.; L. Macquarie to D. Wentworth, 18 January 1812, Wentworth Papers, A754-2, f.233; D. Wentworth's commission as principal surgeon, 1 May 1811, ibid., f.225; C. Cookney to D. Wentworth, 17 August 1811, ibid., A752, ff.71–2; also letters to D. Wentworth from J. Jamison, 7 March 1811, S. Lord, 26 August 1812, D. Considen, 21 May 1812, L. Macquarie, 2 February 1815, a 'Poundkeeper', 10 June 1815, ibid., ff.4, 45, 48, 80, 87–90, 151, 355, 406–8 and 424.

[23] *Sydney Gazette*, 18 August and 20 October 1810, 17 August 1811, 22 and 29 August, and 4 September 1812; for the wager with Lord which bears no date, see Wentworth Papers, A752, f.367; L. Macquarie to D. Wentworth, 13 August 1816, ibid., A4073, f.4.

[24] W. Wentworth to Lord Bathurst, n.d. 1813, ibid., A756, f.77; W. Wentworth, Journal of an expedition across the Blue Mountains, May 11–June 6, 1813, ibid., Safe 1/22a and C122, M.L.; D. Wentworth to unnamed correspondent, fragment of an undated letter (possibly written on 28 June 1815), ibid., A752, ff.134–6; D. Wentworth to Lord Fitzwilliam, 30 June 1815, Fitzwilliam MSS, 83/23, ff.2–4, N.R.O.; J. A. Richards (ed.), *Blaxland-Lawson-Wentworth, 1813*, Hobart, 1979, esp. pp. 109–14; W. C. Wentworth, *Australasia*, London, 1823, p. 13; C. M. H. Clark, op. cit., vol. 1, p. 278, and vol. 2, pp. 43–4; Liston, 'William Charles Wentworth', p. 22; Ritchie, *Macquarie*, p. 127.

[25] *H.R.A.*, I, vii, pp. 310 and 436; ibid., I, x, pp. 565–6; CO201/123, items D36 and D62; C. M. H. Clark, op. cit., vol. 1, p. 384; Barker, loc. cit., pp. 97, 129–31, 186 and 219; MacDonagh, *Austen*, pp. 51 and 63; Dermody, loc. cit., p. 355; *A.D.B.*, vol. 2, p. 581.

[26] Ibid., pp. 373–4; Police Reports and Accounts, 1810–27, Wentworth Papers, MS D1; Police Fund Account, 1821–22, ibid., B149; D. Wentworth's Account Book, 1821–27, ibid., A759 and FM4/1223; M. Robinson to D. Wentworth, 20 January 1817, ibid., A753, ff.1–3; *Sydney Gazette*, 1 November 1822; *Australian*, 18 May 1827; Dermody, loc. cit., p. 355; Barker, loc. cit., pp. 99, 130–1, 187, 221–2, 270–1 and 316; R. F. Holder, *Bank of New South Wales: A History*, vol. 1, 1817–1893, Sydney, 1970, pp. 16, 18 and 43–5; Hainsworth, *Sydney Traders*, pp. 61–2; *A.D.B.*, vol. 2, pp. 373–4.

Notes: Chapter 6

[27] A. Riley to E. Riley, 18 February and 28 March 1812, 14 September 1813, Riley Papers, Safe 1/50, ff.21 and 27, and A107, f.43; Hospital contractors to L. Macquarie, 2, 4, 23 and 28 March, 18, 29 and 30 December 1812, 11 January and 4 February 1813, Wentworth Papers, A761, ff.26–9, 30, 34, 38–58, 60–4, 70–3, 78–9, 82 and 90; J. T. Campbell to the contractors, 21 December 1812, 10 February and 8 May 1813, ibid., ff.70–3, 84–6 and 98–100; Contractors to J. T. Campbell, 12 February 1813, ibid., f.88; L. Macquarie to the contractors, 26 March and 30 December 1812, CO201/124, ff.54–6 and Wentworth Papers, A761, f.74; Contractors to L. Macquarie, 4 May 1813, CO201/124, ff.78–82; L. Macquarie, Memoranda, 3 November 1813, A772, f.66; H. Macarthur to J. Macarthur, 4 July 1813, Macarthur Papers, A2901, ff.49–52; Holt, *Memoirs*, pp. 315–16; J. D. Lang, *An Historical and Statistical Account of New South Wales*, London, 1852, vol. 1, pp. 147–8; Barker, loc. cit., pp. 111–15, 118–23 and 155–6; for the best estimate of the costs of the hospital, see ibid., pp. 160–3; Ritchie, *Punishment and Profit*, p. 200; Dermody, loc. cit., pp. 263–70; *A.D.B.*, vol. 1, pp. 115 and 471; ibid., 2, p. 380. Wentworth guessed that the cost of the building was £40 000, see below, chapter 8, note 18.

[28] D. Wentworth's requisition for medicines, 12 August 1813, Wentworth Papers, A762, f.11; D. Wentworth's invoice for medicines, 21 November 1814, ibid., A752, f.137; L. Macquarie to D. Wentworth, 27 February 1815, ibid., ff.412–13; J. T. Campbell to D. Wentworth, 13 April 1815, ibid., f.149; W. Bland to D. Wentworth, 13 June 1815, ibid., f.155; M. O'Connell's report, 31 December 1813, CO201/124, ff.420–1; D. Wentworth to L. Macquarie, 15 January 1821, ibid., f.421; L. Macquarie to J. Bigge, 4 February 1821, ibid., f.444; evidence of W. Wakeman, CO201/124, f.64; Minutes of Proceedings, Bench of Magistrates, Sydney, entries for 25 August 1810, and 4 April and 2 May 1812, COD 233–4, A.O.N.S.W.; *A.D.B.*, vol. 2, pp. 369–70; Ritchie, *Punishment and Profit*, pp. 158–9.

[29] *H.R.A.*, i, vii, pp. 406–13, 666 and 720; ibid., 4, i, pp. 810–11; *H.R.N.S.W.*, vol. 7, pp. 479–85; *Sydney Gazette*, 5 June 1813, 28 May, 4 June, 29 June, 16 July, 30 July and 17 September 1814; Evidence of A. Riley and R. Jones, Report of the Select Committee on the State of the Gaols, pp. 56 and 147; I. Nicholls, Account Book and

Notes: Chapter 6

Diary, 1816–1819, MS3243, unfolioed, N.L.A.; Return of fines and punishments in the Police Office, Sydney, 8 May 1817 to 31 December 1820, CO201/121, ff.499, 503, 527, 540 and 554–5; Minutes of Proceedings, Bench of Magistrates, Sydney, COD 234; Evidence of J. Harris, J. Lara and J. Hodges, CO201/120, ff.159, 207 and 210; Evidence of A. Nash, CO201/121, f.54; Evidence of J. Blaxland, CO201/123, f.99; R. Jones to D. Wentworth, 12 March 1811, Wentworth Papers, A752, f.51; G. Blaxcell to J. Macarthur, 1 June 1814, Macarthur Papers, A2900, f.42; Dermody, loc. cit., pp. 271–5, 277–8, 293–6 and 360; *A.D.B.*, vol. 1, p. 268; ibid., 2, p. 273; P. Cunningham, *Two Years in New South Wales*, Adelaide, 1966, vol. 1, pp. 64–5; H. Golder, *High and Responsible Office*, Sydney, 1991, pp. 39 ff; J. McLaughlin, loc. cit., pp. 140–3; information from Dr J. M. Bennett, Mittagong, New South Wales, 11 April 1996.

[30] *H.R.A.*, 1, viii, pp. 58–9, 156 and 644; *Sydney Gazette*, 11 December 1813, 1 and 22 January 1814; I. Cornwall's land grant, 1 January 1810, Wentworth Papers, A752, ff.12–13; J. Foveaux to D. Wentworth, 13 March 1811, ibid., ff.53–4; Articles of agreement, January 1814, ibid., A752, ff.98–100; W. Wentworth to T. Moore, 4 June 1815, ibid., A756, ff.5–11; S. Marsden to J. Pratt, 26 October 1815, Marsden Papers, MS 55/35, Hocken Library, Dunedin, New Zealand; *Sydney Gazette*, 22 October 1814; A. Harris, *The Secrets of Alexander Harris*, Sydney, 1961, pp. 108–9; Barker, loc. cit., pp. 100, 127–8, 131–3 and 180–1; Fifer, loc. cit., p. 24; *A.D.B.*, vol. 2, p. 583; H. E. Maude and M. T. Crocombe, 'Rarotongan Sandalwood', in *Journal of the Polynesian Society*, vol. 71, no. 1, March 1962, pp. 32–53; Richards, op. cit., p. 187; Hainsworth, *Sydney Traders*, p. 176; Melbourne, *Wentworth*, p. 13.

[31] *H.R.A.*, 1, vii, pp. 552–3, 558–9 and 598; ibid., 1, viii, pp. 4, 124, 163 and 391–3; L. Macquarie to C. Macquarie, 31 August 1813, Macquarie Papers, MS 202, f.71, N.L.A.; D. Wentworth (jnr) to D. Wentworth, 3 July 1814, Wentworth Papers, A755, ff.3–6; Suttor, 'Sketch', C783, f.28; E. Bent to his mother, 27 July 1810, Bent Papers, MS 195/2, f.182, N.L.A.; Ritchie, *Macquarie*, p. 113; *A.D.B.*, vol. 1, p. 87; ibid., vol. 2, p. 243.

[32] *H.R.A.*, 1, vii, p. 777; ibid., 1, viii, pp. 293, 296, 300–1 and 381–3; ibid., 4, i, pp. 94, 106–7, 109–10, 111 and 114–16; J. H. Bent, Journal 1814, MS 195/3, ff.205–6, N.L.A.; Cunningham, op. cit.,

vol. 2, p. 121; Barker, loc. cit., pp. 136–42; Ritchie, *Macquarie*, p. 145; *A.D.B.*, vol. 1, p. 89.

[33] C. Cookney to Lord Fitzwilliam, 15 May 1812, Wentworth Woodhouse Muniments, F114/55; D. Wentworth to Lord Fitzwilliam, 15 October 1814, Fitzwilliam MSS, 82/54, ff.1–9, N.R.O.; L. Macquarie to D. Wentworth, 24 April 1815, Wentworth Papers, MSS 8/1; *A.D.B.*, vol. 1, p. 89.

7 THE GREATEST BURDEN

[1] D. Wentworth to unnamed correspondent, 28 June 1815, Wentworth Papers, A752, f.136; Ritchie, *Macquarie*, pp. 144–5 and 262.

[2] Currey, *Brothers Bent*, pp. 104–12; *A.D.B.*, vol. 1, pp. 218–19, 263 and 343; Ritchie, *Macquarie*, pp. 145–6.

[3] Ibid., pp. 146–7.

[4] *H.R.A.*, 4, i, pp. 135, 144, 146–7 and 153.

[5] Report of the Select Committee on Transportation, House of Commons, *Parliamentary Papers*, ii, no. 341, 1812, p. 45; D. Wentworth to Lord Fitzwilliam, 15 October 1814, Fitzwilliam MSS, 82/54, ff.1–9, N.R.O.; A. Bell's and J. Blaxland's evidence to Commissioner Bigge, C.O. 201/123, ff.62 and 99; J. Arnold, Journal, C720, ff.382–4 and 391–6, M.L.; *H.R.A.*, 1, ix, p. 445; J. Good to S. Marsden, 25 December 1814, Marsden Papers, A1992, f.180; Ritchie, *Macquarie*, p. 147; *A.D.B.*, vol. 1, pp. 78–80; ibid., vol. 2, p. 11.

[6] *H.R.A.*, 1, viii, p. 621; L. Macquarie to C. Macquarie, 2 July 1815, Macquarie Papers, MS 202, ff.110–13, N.L.A.; D. Wentworth to Lord Fitzwilliam, 15 October 1814, 30 June 1815 and 23 March 1816, Fitzwilliam MSS, 82/54, ff.1–9, 83/23, ff.1–10, and 84/15, ff.1–6, N.R.O.

[7] *H.R.A.*, 1, ix, pp. 3–22; depositions of P. Cullen, M. Wyer and S. Hockley, 6 and 7 September 1815, Colonial Secretary, In Letters, 4/1733, ff.30–3, A.O.N.S.W.; D. Wentworth to L. Macquarie, 9 September 1815, ibid., ff.27–9; to J. Bent, 7 September 1815, ibid., ff.34–5; J. Bent to D. Wentworth, 8 September 1815, ibid., f.36; D. Wentworth's findings, 9 September 1815, ibid., f.37; copy of Government and General Order, 9 September 1815, in Wentworth Papers, A752, ff.431–3.

Notes: Chapter 7

[8] H.R.A., 1, ix, pp. 22–5; ibid., 4, i, pp. 162–70, esp. p. 168; J. Bent to L. Macquarie, 2 October 1815, Colonial Secretary, In Letters, 4/1733, ff.39–44, A.O.N.S.W.; L. Macquarie to J. Bent, 2 October 1815, ibid., f.47; J. Bent to Lord Bathurst, 1 July and 4 November 1815, Report of the Select Committee on the State of Gaols, pp. 440 and 448; Ritchie, *Macquarie*, pp. 146–8; A.D.B., vol. 1, p. 90.

[9] H.R.A., 1, ix, pp. 258–63 and 810–11; *Sydney Gazette*, 28 February 1818; evidence of Assistant-Surgeon R. W. Owen, 15 April 1820, Appendix to Commissioner Bigge's reports, B.T. Box 6, p. 2464; J. T. Campbell to hospital contractors, 27 March, 12 April, 18 and 24 June 1816, C.O.201/124, ff.340–4; report of committee on the hospital building, March 1816, ibid., ff.391–2; G. Suttor to D. Wentworth, 3 February 1818, ibid., ff.140–1; D. Wentworth to J. T. Campbell, 27 May 1819, ibid., ff.355–6; J. Arnold, Journal, C720, ff.398–400; correspondence between T. Parmeter, L. Macquarie and D. Wentworth, 3 June 1816 to 3 February 1819, Wentworth Papers, A753, ff.601–4, 612 and 714; D. Wentworth to L. Macquarie, 13 February 1818, Colonial Secretary, In Letters, 4/1740, ff.79–80, A.O.N.S.W.; H. Macarthur to L. Macquarie, 16 January 1819, ibid., 4/1742, f.65; J. T. Campbell to D. Wentworth, 1 December 1818 and 1 June 1819, Wentworth Papers, A753, ff.215–17, and A762, ff.41–3; Report of the Commissioner of Inquiry on the State of Agriculture and Trade in the Colony of New South Wales, House of Commons, *Parliamentary Papers*, x, no. 136, 1823, p. 109; D. Wentworth to L. Macquarie, 20 and 28 March 1817, Wentworth Papers, A753, ff.7–9, and Colonial Secretary, In Letters, 4/1737, ff.231–3; L. Macquarie to D. Wentworth, 2 and 17 April 1816, Wentworth Papers, A752, ff.181 and 189; Barker, *D'Arcy Wentworth* pp. 205–10; A.D.B., vol. 2, pp. 260, 499 and 581.

[10] J. Wylde and D. Wentworth to L. Macquarie, 18 April 1818, Colonial Secretary, In Letters, 4/1740, ff.132–4; L. Macquarie's memorandum, 25 July 1816, Wentworth Papers, A752, f.221; *Sydney Gazette*, 3 February 1816; W. C. Wentworth, *A Statistical, Historical, and Political Description of the Colony of New South Wales*, London, 1820, p. 257; Barker, loc. cit., pp. 172, 174, 185–6, 224–5 and 241; Report of the Commissioner of Inquiry into the State of the Colony of New South Wales, House of Commons,

Notes: Chapter 7

Parliamentary Papers, xx, no. 448, 1822, pp. 106–7; Report of the Commissioner of Inquiry on the Judicial Establishments of New South Wales, and Van Diemen's Land, House of Commons, *Parliamentary Papers*, x, no. 33, 1823, pp. 70–1.

[11] W. Wentworth to D. Wentworth, 3 May 1816, Wentworth Papers, A754-2, ff.295–6; C. W. Wentworth to D. Wentworth, 9 September 1817, ibid., ff.291–2; L. Macquarie, Memoranda, 28 March, 15 and 19 October 1817, A772, ff.95, 136–7 and 138; *New South Wales Almanac*, 1817, p. 28; *Sydney Gazette*, 5 February 1816 and 15 March 1817; Barker, loc. cit., pp. 183 and 188. The Philanthropic Society was initially known as The New South Wales Society for affording Protection to the Natives of the South Sea Islands, and promoting their Civilization.

[12] H.R.A., 1, ix, p. 56; ibid., 1, x, p. 566; D. Wentworth (jnr) to D. Wentworth, n.d. August and 8 September 1815, Wentworth Papers, A755, ff.11–17 and 19–22; W. Wentworth to D. Wentworth, 16 August 1816, ibid., A756, ff.31–6; D. Wentworth to Lord Fitzwilliam, 23 March 1816, Fitzwilliam MSS, 84/15, f.1, N.R.O.; L. Macquarie, Memoranda, 28 March 1815, A772, f.95.

[13] H.R.A., 1, ix, p. 62; *Sydney Gazette*, 25 March 1816; D. Wentworth to Lord Fitzwilliam, 30 June 1815 and 23 March 1816, Fitzwilliam MSS, 83/23, ff.1–10, and 84/15, ff.1–6, N.R.O.; D. Wentworth to unnamed correspondent, n.d. 1816, Wentworth Papers, A752, ff.257–9; to W. Wentworth, 6 April 1816, ibid., ff.187–8; L. Macquarie to D. Wentworth, 13 January 1816, ibid., A754-2, f.273; W. Wentworth to D. Wentworth, 9, 11, 12 and 14 April 1816, ibid., A756, ff.13–16, and CY700, ff.775–9; W. Wentworth to D. Wentworth, 16 and 21 August, 27 November 1816, and 7 February 1817, ibid., A756, ff.21–36, 37–9 and 45–8; J. Macarthur to E. Macarthur, 9 December 1816, Macarthur Papers, A2898, f.333(b); Melbourne, *Wentworth*, pp. 15–16.

[14] H.R.A., 4, i, pp. 186–8 and 192–5; ibid., 1, ix, pp. 42–8; L. Macquarie to C. Macquarie, Macquarie Papers, MS 202, ff.108–10, N.L.A.; J. Arnold, Journal, C720, ff.373–406; C. Throsby to D. Wentworth, 5 April 1816, Wentworth Papers, A752, ff.447–50; G. Dening (ed.), *The Marquesan Journal of Edward Roberts, 1797–1824*, Canberra, 1974, pp. 215–16; Ritchie, *Macquarie*, pp. 152 and 262; A.D.B., vol. 2, pp. 255–6 and 550.

Notes: Chapter 7

[15] *H.R.A.*, 1, ix, pp. 732–6; ibid., 4, i, pp. 208–11; Appendix to Commissioner Bigge's reports, C.O. 201/121, ff.26–7, 41–2 and 46–7; Bigge, Judicial Establishments, pp. 75–6; M. H. Ellis, *Lachlan Macquarie*, Sydney, 1958, pp. 340–3.

[16] *H.R.A.*, 4, i, pp. 208–11 and 847–8; ibid., 1, ix, pp. 329–31 and 333–5; C. Thompson to L. Macquarie, 29 January 1821, C.O. 201/119, ff.422–3; evidence of D. Wentworth, ibid., ff.17–19; Report of the Select Committee on the State of Gaols, pp. 59, 122 and 145–6; Ritchie, *Punishment and Profit*, pp. 79 and 191; *A.D.B.*, vol. 2, pp. 256 and 550.

[17] *H.R.A.*, 1, ix, pp. 218–35 and 861–3; ibid., 4, i, p. 788; *Sydney Gazette*, 30 November and 7 December 1816, 8 February, 22 March and 5 April 1817; Bigge, State of the Colony, pp. 150–2; L. Macquarie, Diary, 11 December 1816 and 18 January 1817, A773, ff.73 and 81; Government and General Order, 11 December 1816, Wentworth Papers, A752 (CY699), f.243; J. T. Campbell to D. Wentworth, 19 November 1816, ibid., f.235; evidence of J. Wylde, 27 September 1820, B.T. Box 7, pp. 2884–6; Barker, loc. cit., pp. 177–9; Holder, *Bank of New South Wales*, pp. 11–18; *A.D.B.*, vol. 1, p. 343; W. S. Ramson (ed.), *The Australian National Dictionary*, Melbourne, 1988, pp. 186–7 and 632.

[18] Ritchie, *Macquarie*, pp. 153–5; Ritchie, *Punishment and Profit*, pp. 16–29; J. J. Eddy, *Britain and the Australian Colonies 1818–1831*, Oxford, 1969, pp. 50–3.

[19] J. Macarthur to E. Macarthur, 9 December 1816, Macarthur Papers, A2898, f.333(b); W. Wentworth to D. Wentworth, 27 November 1816, Wentworth Papers, A756, f.45; to Lord Fitzwilliam, 18 December 1816, ibid., ff.36(b to c) and Fitzwilliam MSS, 85/38, ff.1–3, N.R.O.; Lord Fitzwilliam to W. Wentworth, 25 December 1816, ibid., 85/38, ff.3–4 and Wentworth Papers, A757, f.1(b); W. Wentworth to Lord Fitzwilliam, 15 January 1817, Fitzwilliam MSS, 88/4, ff.1–4, N.R.O., and draft in Wentworth Papers, A756, ff.41–3; C. M. H. Clark, *A History of Australia*, vol. 2, p. 44; Fifer, *William Charles Wentworth*, pp. 25–7.

[20] W. Wentworth to Lord Fitzwilliam, 15 January 1817, Fitzwilliam MSS, 88/4, ff.1–4, N.R.O., and draft in Wentworth Papers, A756, ff.41–3; Lord Fitzwilliam to W. Wentworth, 16 January 1817, ibid., A757, ff.1 (e to f); W. Wentworth to Lord Bathurst, 18 January

Notes: Chapter 7

1817, ibid., A756, ff.77–80; to D. Wentworth, 22 March 1817, ibid., ff.53–60; Richards (ed.), *Blaxland-Lawson-Wentworth*, pp. 181–3.

[21] Certificate of Wentworth's admission to the Middle Temple, sealed on 23 January 1824, Wentworth Papers, A758, f.18(b); Liston, 'William Charles Wentworth', pp. 22–3; C. M. H. Clark, op. cit., vol. 2, pp. 44–5; Fifer, loc. cit., pp. 29–31; H. King, *Colonial Expatriates*, pp. 13–20; H. King, *Elizabeth Macarthur*, pp. 86–92; Melbourne, *Wentworth*, p. 23.

[22] *The Times*, 8 March 1817; House of Commons, *Parliamentary Debates*, 10 March 1817, vol. xxv, pp. 920–1; W. Wentworth to D. Wentworth, 5 February, 22 March, n.d. April, 10 and 28 April 1817, Wentworth Papers, A756, ff.45–8, 53–4, 55–9, 61–72 and 73–6; to H. G. Bennet, 10 March 1817, ibid., ff.49–51; C. Cookney to D. Wentworth, 18 March, 15 April and 21 August 1817, ibid., A754-2, ff.279, 283 and 287–8; J. Macarthur to T. K. Smith, 6 March 1817, Macarthur Papers, A2897, f.15(b); Richards, op. cit., pp. 183–6 and 189–90; Ritchie, *Macquarie*, p. 154; Ritchie, *Punishment and Profit*, pp. 1, 24, 66 and 69.

[23] H.R.A., I, ix, pp. 444–58, 487, 554–7 and 725; J. Wylde to L. Macquarie, 10 and 12 June 1817, Colonial Secretary, In Letters, 4/1737, ff.124–7 and 128–9; Minutes of Proceedings, Bench of Magistrates, 11 June 1817, CO201/121, ff.776–7; L. Macquarie to D. Wentworth, 25 June, 14, 18 and 21 September 1817, Wentworth Woodhouse Muniments, F114/59, ff.1, 13, 18–19 and 20–1; D. Wentworth to L. Macquarie, 27 August, 6, 8, 14 and 18 September 1817, ibid., F114/59, ff.1–3, 6–12, 15–18 and 19–20; G. Molle to L. Macquarie, 3 and 13 September 1817, ibid., F114/59, ff.3–6 and 14–15; to D. Wentworth. 9 September 1817, ibid., F114/59, f.12; J. Wylde to L. Macquarie, 14 September 1817, ibid., F114/59, f.13; Molle's charges against Wentworth, n.d., ibid., F114/59, ff.16–17; L. Macquarie, Memoranda, 12 to 19 September 1817, A772, ff.106–10; for copies of the pipes, see Wentworth Papers, A758, esp. ff.1–18; L. Macquarie to D. Wentworth, 25 June 1817, ibid., A752, f.27, and A753, ff.27 and 31; R. Murray's deposition, 4 July 1817, ibid., f.35; D. Wentworth to L. Macquarie, 29 August, 3 and 8 September 1817, ibid., A751, ff.193–5, A753, ff.51–5 and 61; Government and General Order, 12 September 1817, ibid., f.79; D. Wentworth's charges against

Molle, 12 September 1817, ibid., ff.83–5; H. Antill to D. Wentworth, 13 September 1817, ibid., ff.97–8; J. Wylde to D. Wentworth, 13 September 1817, ibid., f.89; D. Wentworth to Lord Fitzwilliam, 16 September and 16 December 1817, n.d. 1818, 20 July and 23 October 1819, Wentworth Woodhouse Muniments, F114/57–9 and Wentworth Papers, A753, ff.115–17 and 119–20; W. Wentworth to D. Wentworth, 25 May 1818, ibid., A756, ff.81–90; to J. Wentworth, 26 May 1818, ibid., ff.23–6; to A. Riley, 25 August 1818, ibid., ff.101–5; G. Johnston (jnr) to W. Wentworth, 1 March 1819, ibid., A757, ff.1(a to h); Melbourne, *Wentworth*, p. 14.

24 *H.R.A.*, I, ix, pp. 206–7, 385 and 495–501; *Sydney Gazette*, 28 March 1818; E. Macquarie to unnamed correspondent, 12 December 1817, Macquarie Papers, A797, f.137; L. Macquarie to S. Marsden, 8 January 1818, ibid., ff.141–4; L. Macquarie, Diary, 14 October 1816 and 8 January 1818, ibid., A773, ff.290 and 365; S. Marsden to W. Wilberforce, 5 February 1818, Appendix no. 2 in H. G. Bennet, *A Letter to Earl Bathurst*, London, 1820, pp. 117–22; Ritchie, *Punishment and Profit*, pp. 20–9, 68–9, 73–5, 79–81, 87–9 and 95–102; Ritchie, *Lachlan Macquarie*, pp. 148, 152–3, 165–6.

25 *H.R.A.*, 4, i, pp. 282–9 and 302–7; Ritchie, *Macquarie*, pp. 154–6; Ritchie, *Punishment and Profit*, pp. 69–71.

26 W. Wentworth to J. Wentworth, 26 May 1818, Wentworth Papers, A755, ff.673–4 and CY700, ff.23–6; J. Bigge to Lord Bathurst, 7 February 1823, CO201/142, ff.338–9; Will of D. Wentworth, 7 July 1827, Wentworth Papers, Miscellaneous Material, MSS 8/4, item 94, M.L., and Minter, Simpson & Co., Documents of Titles, A4026, no. 477, M.L.; J. Howard to J. Wentworth, 1 April 1819, Wentworth Papers, A753, f.299; W. Wentworth to D. Wentworth, 24 November 1819, ibid., A756, ff.151–9; J. C. Ross to D. Wentworth, 8 August 1820, ibid., A753, ff.473–7; J. Ritchie (ed.), *The Evidence to the Bigge Reports*, Melbourne, 1971, vol. 2, p. 184; see also Chapter 8, note 17 (below).

27 *H.R.A.*, I, ix, pp. 786–8 and 888–9; *Sydney Gazette*, 23 October 1819; D. Wentworth to L. Macquarie, 5 May 1818, Wentworth Papers, A753, ff.206–8; to Lord Bathurst, 5 and 20 May 1818, ibid., ff.257–8, and A754-2, f.307; L. Macquarie to D. Wentworth, 6 May 1818, ibid., A753, ff.210–12; D. Wentworth to Lord Fitzwilliam, 16 May 1818, ibid., ff.216–17; Lord Bathurst to Lord Fitzwilliam,

Notes: Chapters 7 and 8

14 December 1818, ibid., A754-2, f.313; W. Wentworth to D. Wentworth, 25 May 1818, 14 February and 13 April 1819, ibid., A756, ff.81–90, 119–21 and 139.

[28] C. M. H. Clark, op. cit., vol. 2, p. 45; Liston, 'William Charles Wentworth', p. 23; MacDonagh, *Austen*, pp. 146–66; Fifer, loc. cit., p. 23; H. King, *Elizabeth Macarthur*, pp. 88–91; Melbourne, *Wentworth*, pp. 26–8. For further sources, see note 29 (below).

[29] C. Cookney to D. Wentworth, 21 August and 8 December 1817, 18 March 1818, Wentworth Papers, A754-2, ff.287–8, 299–300 and 304; draft of a poem to a lady named Jane, n.d., ibid., A758, f.11; J. Foveaux to D. Wentworth, 20 February 1818, ibid., A753, ff.186–7; W. Wentworth to D. Wentworth, 25 May 1818 and 24 November 1819, ibid., A756, ff.81–90 and 151–9; to J. Wentworth, 26 May 1818, ibid., A755, ff.23–6; to J. Macarthur (jnr), 29 July and 24 August 1818, ibid., A756, ff.93–5 and 97–9; Lord Fitzwilliam to C. Cookney, 6 August 1818, ibid., A757, f.1(j); C. Cookney to W. Wentworth, 11 August 1818, ibid., f.1(h); W. Wentworth to A. Riley, 25 August and 19 November 1818, ibid., A756, ff.101–5 and 111–14; to D. Wentworth, 10 November 1818 and 13 April 1819, ibid., ff.107–10 and 140–1; A. Riley to W. Wentworth, 23 November 1818, ibid., f.203; C. Cookney to D. Wentworth, n.d. December 1818, ibid., A754-2, ff.311–13; Ritchie, *Punishment and Profit*, p. 51.

8 WHAT ONE IS

[1] H. G. Bennet, *Letter to Viscount Sidmouth*, London, 1819, pp. 77–9, 106, 108 and 110; Barker, D'Arcy Wentworth, pp. 216–18; C. M. H. Clark, *A History of Australia*, vol. 2, p. 46; Liston, 'William Charles Wentworth', pp. 25–7; Fifer, William Charles Wentworth, p. 54; Dermody, D'Arcy Wentworth, pp. 330–3; Melbourne, *Wentworth*, pp. 11 and 32.

[2] H. G. Bennet, *Letter to Viscount Sidmouth*, London, 1819, second ed., p. 110; House of Commons, *Parliamentary Debates*, 18 February 1819, vol. 39, pp. 471 and 481; W. Wentworth to H. G. Bennet, 12 February 1819, Wentworth Papers, A756, ff.115–18; to D. Wentworth, 14 February, 13 April, 8 August, 24 November and 6 December 1819, ibid., ff.119–21, 135–42, 143–9, 151–9 and

Notes: Chapter 8

161–5; H. G. Bennet to W. Wentworth, n.d. February 1819, ibid., A757, ff.99–102; Ritchie, *Punishment and Profit*, pp. 72–3.

[3] Ibid., pp. 76, 78 and 84–9; W. Wentworth to D. Wentworth, 13 and 15 April, 24 November, 6 and 8 December 1819, 1 May 1820, Wentworth Papers, A756, ff.123–4, 135–42, 151–9, 161–5, 167–70 and 171–84; H. Goulburn to W. Wentworth, 10 March 1820, ibid., A757, ff.3–6; House of Commons, *Parliamentary Debates*, 23 March 1819, vol. 39, pp. 1124–33; Report from the Select Committee on the State of Gaols, pp. 54, 56, 76, 91–2, 95, 121, 139, 147 and 439–51.

[4] W. C. Wentworth, *Statistical, Historical, and Political Description of The Colony of New South Wales, and Its dependent Settlements in Van Diemen's Land*, London, 1819, esp. pp. 166–71, 174–6, 336, 344, 356, 362, 364 and 375; C. M. H. Clark, op. cit., vol. 2, pp. 45–6; Fifer, loc. cit., pp. 33–50; Melbourne, *Wentworth*, p. 34; M. Hutchinson, 'W. C. Wentworth and the Sources of Australian Historiography', *J.R.A.H.S.*, vol. 77, part 4, April 1992, pp. 63–85.

[5] W. Wentworth to D. Wentworth, 25 May 1818, 13 April, 4 May, 8 July, 8 August and 24 November 1819, Wentworth Papers, A756, ff.81–90, 140, 125–7, 129–34, 143–9 and 151–9; J. T. Campbell to D. Wentworth, 21 October 1819, ibid., A753, ff.263–4; L. Macquarie to D. Wentworth, 13 November 1819, ibid., A754-2, f.369; J. Macarthur to J. Macarthur (jnr), 28 February 1820, Macarthur Papers, A2899, f.25; House of Commons, *Parliamentary Debates*, 23 March 1819, vol. 39, pp. 1124–8; *Edinburgh Review*, vol. 32, no. 63, 1819, pp. 44–7; *Quarterly Review*, vol. 24, no. 47, 1819, p. 56; Ritchie, *Punishment and Profit*, pp. 79–80; Fifer, loc. cit., pp. 51–3 and 56; Ellis, *Macarthur*, p. 470; N. D. McLachlan, 'Edward Eagar (1787–1866): A Colonial Spokesman in Sydney and London', in *Historical Studies*, vol. 10, no. 40, 1963, p. 435.

[6] Ritchie, *Punishment and Profit*, pp. 31–56; Ritchie, *Macquarie*, pp. 166–9.

[7] *H.R.A.*, I, x, pp. 146–7; *Sydney Gazette*, 23 October 1819; Government and General Order, 11 and 23 October 1819, Wentworth Papers, A753, ff.349–50, and A762, ff.55–8; J. T. Campbell to D. Wentworth, 11 and 23 October 1819, ibid., A753, ff.345–6 and A762, ff.53–4; L. Macquarie, Diary, 25 October 1819, Macquarie Papers, A774, f.76; C. Cookney to D. Wentworth,

Notes: Chapter 8

20 May 1819, Wentworth Papers, A754-2, ff.365–6; D. Wentworth to L. Macquarie, 13 May 1819, ibid., f.401; L. Macquarie to Wentworth, 25 January and 28 May 1820, 31 January 1821, ibid., ff.371, 402–3 and 436.

[8] Case of R. L. Murray, 26 October 1819, Colonial Secretary, In Letters, 4/1743, ff.50–70, A.O.N.S.W.; J. Wylde to L. Macquarie, 6 November 1819, ibid., ff.97–103; R. L. Murray to D. Wentworth, 26 July 1821, 26 January, 14 April and 20 June 1822, Wentworth Papers, A754-1, ff.27–9, 60, 83–6 and 105–6; Barker, loc. cit., p. 235; *A.D.B.*, vol. 2, pp. 272–4.

[9] *H.R.A.*, I, x, pp. 214–18 and 310–11; Ritchie, *Macquarie*, pp. 171–2.

[10] W. Wentworth to D. Wentworth, 14 February and 6 December 1819, 1 May and 1 July 1820, 18 March 1823, Wentworth Papers, A756, ff.119–21, 161–5, 171–84, 189–96 and 215(d); W. Johnstone to D. Wentworth, 8 November 1819, ibid., A753, ff.363–4; H. Goulburn to L. Macquarie, 17 July 1820, ibid., f.469; Government and General Order, 31 March 1820, ibid., ff.319–21; J. T. Campbell to D. Wentworth, 31 March 1820, ibid., A754-2, ff.373 and 375; L. Macquarie to D. Wentworth, 5 March 1821, ibid., A754-1, ff.13–15; *H.R.A.*, I, ix, pp. 814–15; ibid., I, x, pp. 68–9, 146–7 and 345; J. Bigge to Lord Bathurst, 7 February 1823, CO201/142, ff.340–1; *Sydney Gazette*, 18 November 1820; Barker, loc. cit., pp. 173, 245–8, 250 and 252–3; Dermody, loc. cit., pp. 343–6.

[11] *H.R.A.*, I, x, p. 345; D. Wentworth to L. Macquarie, 31 March 1820, Wentworth Papers, A753, ff.319–21; J. T. Campbell to D. Wentworth, 1 April 1820, ibid., ff.321–2; L. Macquarie to D. Wentworth, 1 April 1820, ibid., ff.323–4; D. Wentworth to L. Macquarie, 1 April 1820, ibid., ff.324–6; L. Macquarie to D. Wentworth, 1, 5, 7, 11 and 15 April 1820, ibid., A754-2, ff.377–9, 383–5, 387–9, and A753, ff.301–7, 311, 399–405 and 409; D. Wentworth to L. Macquarie, 3, 6, 8, 11 and 15 April 1820, B.T. Box 21, pp. 4063–4, 4125–8, 4134–43 and 4155, and B.T. Box 22, pp. 4170–1; D. Wentworth to L. Macquarie, 5, 7 and 11 April 1820, Wentworth Papers, A753, ff.328–31, 334–8 and 342; *Sydney Gazette*, 29 July 1820.

[12] Ritchie, *Macquarie*, pp. 169–71; Ritchie, *Punishment and Profit*, pp. 108–10 and 125–7.

Notes: Chapter 8

[13] Evidence of D. Wentworth, 10, 16, 19 and 23 November 1819, B.T. Box 2, pp. 560–610.

[14] Evidence of W. Cox, ibid., Box 1, pp. 180–91, and CO201/120, f.110; evidence of J. Harris, ibid., Box 1, pp. 264–81, Box 2, pp. 556–69, CO201/120, ff.157–9 and CO201/118, f.422; evidence of R. Cartwright, ibid., f.453; *H.R.A.*, 4, i, pp. 780, 789 and 810–11; J. Bigge to D. Wentworth, 5 and 6 July 1820, B.T. Box 23, pp. 4702 and 4736–7; Dermody, loc. cit., pp. 337–40 and 350–1.

[15] Evidence of H. Cowper, B.T. Box 6, pp. 2302–74, CO201/124, esp. ff.7, 14–15 and 36–49; evidence of W. Wakeman, R. W. Owen, D. West, W. Bland, J. Mileham and W. Evans, ibid., ff.64–5, 87–8, 118–23, 133, 146 and 158; Dermody, loc. cit., pp. 340 and 347–50; Ritchie, *Punishment and Profit*, p. 160.

[16] Evidence of D. Wentworth, undated, but probably after 26 June 1820, B.T. Box 6, pp. 2510–31, CO201/124, esp. ff.102–4 and 107; Ritchie (ed.), *The Evidence to the Bigge Reports*, vol. 1, pp. 121–2.

[17] W. Wentworth to D. Wentworth, 24 November and 6 December 1819, 1 July 1820, Wentworth Papers, A756, ff.151–9, 161–5 and 189–96; E. Crothers to D. Wentworth, 22 December 1819, ibid., A753, ff.373–5; J. C. Ross to D. Wentworth, 8 August 1820, ibid., ff.473–7; E. Macquarie to D. Wentworth, 5 October 1820, ibid., A754-2, ff.395–8; D. Wentworth to C. Cookney, 22 July 1821, ibid, A754, ff.23–6; M. Reibey, Journal, 13–14 October 1820, Safe 1/21a, f.55, M.L.; Bateson, *The Convict Ships*, pp. 342 and 382; *H.R.A.*, 1, x, p. 86; *D.N.B.*, vol. 7, p. 237.

[18] J. Bigge to D. Wentworth, 13 November 1820, 25 and 26 January 1821, Wentworth Papers, A754-2, ff.399–400, B.T. Box 26, pp. 5893–5 and 5901-2; D. Wentworth to J. Bigge, 26 January 1821, Wentworth Papers, A754-1, ff.7–12.

[19] W. Redfern to J. Bigge, 5 and 8 February 1821, B.T. Box 26, pp. 6186–6222, CO201/124, ff.183–91, B.T. Box 6, pp. 2502–9; L. Macquarie to J. Bigge, 4 February 1821, CO201/142, esp. ff.388–92, B.T. Box 11, pp. 4358–74.

[20] *H.R.A.*, 1, x, pp. 532 and 580; L. Macquarie, Diary, 8 February 1821, Macquarie Papers, A774, f.612; R. L. Murray to D. Wentworth, 21 April 1821, Wentworth Papers, A754-1, f.315; L. Macquarie to D. Wentworth, undated, ibid., ff.309–10;

Notes: Chapter 8

D. Wentworth to C. Cookney, 22 July 1821, ibid., A754, ff.23–6; F. Goulburn to D. Wentworth, 10 May and 7 July 1821, Colonial Secretary, Out Letters, 4/3054, f.43 and 4/5781, f.140, A.O.N.S.W.; *Sydney Gazette*, 31 March 1821; Barker, loc. cit., pp. 253–5; Dermody, loc. cit., pp. 355–6; *A.D.B.*, vol. 1, p. 358, and vol. 2, p. 234.

21 *H.R.A.*, 1, x, pp. 55–65 and 549–58; D. Wentworth to C. Cookney, 22 July 1821, Wentworth Papers, A754, ff.23–6; *A.D.B.*, vol. 2, p. 370; McLachlan, loc. cit., pp. 434–8.

22 *H.R.A.*, 1, x, p. 566; *Sydney Gazette*, 1, 8 and 15 December 1821, 15 February 1822; L. Macquarie to J. Jamison, 11 December 1821, Wentworth Papers, A754-1, ff.43–6; J. Jamison to D. Wentworth, 13 December 1821, ibid., ff.45–6; Statistics on population, land and stock, n.d. (probably December 1821), ibid., ff.48–52; L. Macquarie to D. Wentworth, 31 January 1821, ibid., A754-2, ff.402–3; L. Macquarie, Diary, 22 February 1821 and 31 January 1822, Macquarie Papers, A774, ff.619 and 672; S. Marsden to J. Bigge, 24 September 1821, Marsden Papers, A1993, f.74; Ritchie, *Macquarie*, pp. 158, 185–8 and 191; T. A. Coghlan, *Labour and Industry in Australia*, Melbourne, 1969, vol. 1, pp. 144–8, 277 and 282; *A.D.B.*, vol. 1, p. 463.

23 Bigge, State of the Colony, pp. 1–186; Judicial Establishments, pp. 1–90; Agriculture and Trade, pp. 1–112; Ritchie, *Punishment and Profit*, pp. 209–38; Ritchie, *Lachlan Macquarie*, p. 194.

24 Ibid., pp. 177–8.

25 Ibid., pp. 195–6.

26 Bigge, State of the Colony, pp. 49, 85–6, 101, 106–7 and 141; Bigge, Judicial Establishments, pp. 60, 62, 66, 69–71, 75–7, 81 and 83; Bigge, Agriculture and Trade, pp. 16, 41, 84–6 and 102–9.

27 J. Bigge to Lord Bathurst, 9 September 1822 and 7 February 1823, C.O. 201/142, ff.336–41; B.T. Box 28, pp. 6710–22, 7062–90 and 7162–70; Ritchie (ed.), *The Evidence to the Bigge Reports*, vol. 2, pp. 165–6, 168–70, 172–8 and 183–5.

28 R. Howe, Diary, 22 November 1822, B846-1, M.L.; *Sydney Gazette*, 29 November, 6, 13 and 20 December 1822, 6 and 13 February, 2 October 1823; J. Macarthur (jnr) to E. Macarthur, 18 August 1822, Macarthur Papers, A2911, ff.161–2; J. Macarthur to J. Macarthur (jnr), 31 January 1824, ibid., A2899, ff.97–9; Bigge,

Notes: Chapter 8

State of the Colony, p. 146; A.D.B., vol. 1, pp. 383–4 and 558–9; Ritchie, *Punishment and Profit*, pp. 244–5.

[29] Ibid., pp. 239–44; Ritchie, *Macquarie*, p. 196.

[30] J. Macarthur (jnr) to E. Macarthur, 18 August 1822, Macarthur Papers, A2911, ff.159–60; W. Redfern to D. Wentworth, 3 September 1822, Wentworth Papers, A754-1, ff.139–42; W. Wentworth to D. Wentworth, n.d. 1822, ibid., A756, ff.932–5; J. Bigge to Lord Bathurst, 29 July and 3 August 1822, B.T. Box 28, pp. 6694–7 and 6698–6700; Bigge, State of the Colony, pp. 148–9; House of Lords, *Parliamentary Papers*, vol. viii, no. 119, 1822, p. 148; Bigge, Judicial Establishments, p. 90; McLachlan, loc. cit., pp. 439–42; Ritchie, *Macquarie*, p. 196; Ritchie, *Punishment and Profit*, pp. 224–5 and 244. On 8 May 1823, to comply with a request in his father-in-law's will, Robert Wilmot obtained a royal licence to assume the name of Wilmot Horton. I have referred to him by this surname throughout.

[31] W. Wentworth to A. Riley, 27 October and 4 December 1820, Wentworth Papers, A756, ff.197–9 and 205–7; A. Riley to W. Wentworth, 31 October 1820, ibid., ff.201–2; W. Wentworth to Lord Fitzwilliam, 8 February 1821, Fitzwilliam MSS, 104/16, ff.1–4, N.R.O.; Lord Fitzwilliam to W. Wentworth, 9 February 1821, Wentworth Papers, A757, ff.6(b–c); certificate of Wentworth's admission to the Middle Temple, sealed on 23 January 1824, ibid., A758, f.18(b); W. Wentworth, love poem to Miss Taylor, 17 May 1823, ibid., A756, f.215 and A758, f.13; W. Wentworth to D. Wentworth, 1 May and 1 July 1820, 7 September 1822, ibid., A756, ff.171–84, 189–96 and 211–14; C. Cookney to D. Wentworth, 28 May 1820, 9 August and 28 December 1821, 4 March 1823, ibid., A754-2, ff.391, 406, 410–13 and 426–7; W. Redfern to D. Wentworth, 7 March and 3 September 1822, ibid., A754-1, ff.73–6 and 139–42; W. Wentworth's calling card, n.d. 1822, ibid., A758, f.207(a); E. Macquarie to D. Wentworth, undated, ibid., A757, ff.95–8; D. Wentworth (jnr) to W. Wentworth, 6 December 1823, ibid., A755, f.27; Ritchie, *Punishment and Profit*, p. 225; Ritchie, *Macquarie*, pp. 193–4, 206 and 224–5; A.D.B., vol. 1, pp. 421–2; Fifer, loc. cit., p. 58.

[32] Ibid., p. 59; C. Cookney to D. Wentworth, 4 March 1823, Wentworth Papers, A754-2, ff.426–7; T. A. Walker (ed.), *Admissions to Peterhouse or St Peter's College*, Cambridge, 1912, p. 417;

Notes: Chapters 8 and 9

T. R. Horne, *Peterhouse: the College and Chapel*, Cambridge, n.d., pp. 1–5; information from Dr Roderick Munday and Dr Roger Lovatt, members of staff, Peterhouse, 20 September 1993; Liston, 'William Charles Wentworth', pp. 29–34.

[33] W. Wentworth to D. Wentworth, Wentworth Papers, A756, ff.215(a–d); S. Tillbrook to W. Wentworth, 15 April 1823, ibid., A757, f.9; Lord Fitzwilliam to W. Wentworth, 31 December 1823, ibid., f.11; J. Macarthur (jnr) to E. Macarthur, 12 April and 1 May 1825, Macarthur Papers, A2911, CY752, ff.323–50 and A2911, ff.254–5; W. C. Wentworth, *Australasia*, London, 1823, see esp. pp. vii–xii; Melbourne, *Wentworth*, pp. 36–7; C. M. H. Clark, op. cit., vol. 2, pp. 47–9.

[34] C. Cookney to D. Wentworth, 30 August 1822, Wentworth Papers, A754-1, ff.135–7; J. B. Hirst, *Convict society*, pp. 161–2; McLachlan, loc. cit., pp. 441–3; Fifer, loc. cit., pp. 68–70; A. C. V. Melbourne, *Early Constitutional Development in Australia: New South Wales, 1788–1856*, St Lucia, 1963, pp. 98–103; Melbourne, *Wentworth*, p. 39; *D.N.B.*, vol. 7, p. 237; *A.D.B.*, vol. 2, pp. 169 and 570; *H.R.A.*, I, xi, p. 932.

9 Life's little day

[1] *H.R.A.*, I, x, pp. 784–94; *Sydney Gazette*, 3 February 1822; Liston, New South Wales Under Governor Brisbane, esp. pp. 42, 44, 63–4, 92 and 145; A. G. L. Shaw, *Sir George Arthur*, Melbourne, 1980, pp. 61–134; Ritchie, *Macquarie*, pp. 197, 201 and 223; *A.D.B.*, vol. 1, pp. 32–8 and 151–5; ibid., vol. 2, p. 461.

[2] *H.R.A.*, I, xi, pp. 96, 138, 252, 553 and 580; *Sydney Gazette*, 12 April 1822, 13 March and 4 December 1823, 16 December 1824 and 24 February 1825; F. Goulburn to D. Wentworth, 15 May 1822, Wentworth Papers, A754-1, f.97; R. L. Murray to D. Wentworth, 27 March 1824, ibid., ff.267–70; D. Wentworth to T. Brisbane, 15 June 1824, ibid., ff.205–6; payments of D. Wentworth's salary as superintendent of police, 1 October 1822 to 17 May 1824, ibid., A766, ff.2, 7 and 10; Magistrates' report to T. Brisbane on bushranging, 1 January 1825, Thomas Brisbane's Letterbook, Brisbane Papers, A1559, f.146, M.L.; Barker, *D'Arcy Wentworth*, pp. 260–4;

Dermody, D'Arcy Wentworth, pp. 362–3 and 365; A. McMartin, *Public Servants and Patronage*, Sydney, 1983, pp. 91–2 and 133.

3 H.R.A., I, x, p. 730; *Sydney Gazette*, 1 December 1821, 13 December 1822, 19 January 1825, 10 June 1826 and 20 March 1827; *Prospectus, Agricultural Society of New South Wales*, Sydney, 1822, p. 14; T. Brisbane to D. Wentworth, 1 November 1822 and 20 July 1824, Wentworth Papers, A754-1, ff.151(b) and 207; E. Wollstonecraft to D. Wentworth, 21 June 1822, ibid., f.123; G. Mills to D. Wentworth, 19 March 1825, ibid., ff.241–2; J. Wylde to D. Wentworth, 19 March 1824, ibid., A754-2, f.442; *Australasian Almanack*, 1823, p. 115, 1824, p. 140, and 1826, p. 111; R. Bourke's dispatch, 30 April 1834, Dispatches from Governors of New South Wales, A1267-13, f.1419(h), M.L.; Barker, loc. cit., pp. 268–70, 311–12 and 314–15; B. H. Fletcher, *Ralph Darling*, Melbourne, 1984, p. 263; *A.D.B.*, vol. 2, p. 620; Holder, *Bank of New South Wales*, p. 85.

4 M. A. Sinnamon to D. Wentworth, 6 May 1822, Wentworth Papers, A754-2, ff.414–16; W. Wentworth to D. Wentworth, 15 January 1824, ibid., ff.438–9; J. Dawson to D. Wentworth, 9 and 13 May 1822, ibid., ff.91–3 and 422–4; L. Dobbin to D. Wentworth, 22 May 1822, ibid., f.432; W. Wentworth to D. Wentworth, n.d. February 1822, MSS 8/4, item 93, M.L.; C. Cookney to D. Wentworth, 30 August 1822, Wentworth Papers, A754-1, ff.135–7; W. Wentworth to D. Wentworth, 7 September 1822 and 18 March 1823, ibid., A756, ff.906–8 and 215(a to d); J. James to D. Wentworth, 22 January 1823, ibid., A754, ff.135–7; W. Kerr to D. Wentworth, 21 November 1824, ibid., A754-1, ff.223–4; R. L. Murray to D. Wentworth, 26 January, 14 April and 20 June 1822, 18 May 1823, 27 March 1824, n.d. 1825, 5 January and 25 June 1825, and n.d. 1826, ibid., ff.59–63, 83–6, 117–20, 181 (a to d), 225–36, 247–8, 260, 267–70 and 321–4; Liston, *Sarah Wentworth*, pp. 16, 26–7 and 30.

5 H.R.A., I, xi, pp. 302 and 892–7; ibid., 4, i, pp. 500–4 and 509–20; *Sydney Gazette*, 22 July, 21 October and 4 November 1824; W. Pritchard to D. Wentworth, 14 April 1825, Wentworth Papers, A754-1, ff.245–6(a); D. Wentworth and J. Oxley to T. Brisbane, 4 August 1824, Forbes Papers, A741, ff.4–7; D. Wentworth to T. Brisbane, 24 August 1824, ibid., ff.21–3; W. Wentworth to

Notes: Chapter 9

D. Wentworth, 8 July 1819, Wentworth Papers, A756, ff.129–34; R. Jenkins to E. Eagar, 18 March 1819, C.O.201/126, f.602; Meeting of magistrates, 26 August 1824, Wentworth Papers, A754, f.217; *A.D.B.*, vol. 1, pp. 55 and 393; ibid., vol. 2, p. 477; C. H. Currey, *Sir Francis Forbes*, Sydney, 1968, pp. 113–20.

[6] *H.R.A.*, 1, xiii, pp. 730–2; *Sydney Gazette*, 6 June 1833; H. Scott to R. Scott, 8 August 1824, Scott Family Papers, A2264, and CY1587, ff.22–5, M.L.; J. Macarthur (jnr) to E. Macarthur, 12 April 1825, Macarthur Papers, A2911, CY752B, ff.323–30; Wentworth's pipe on Dr Halloran, 30 July 1824, Wentworth Papers, A758, f.21; W. Wentworth to T. Brisbane, 26 February 1825, Wentworth Papers, A1440, ff.22–5; to J. Ovens, 28 February 1825, ibid., f.35; Melbourne, *Wentworth*, pp. 40–2; *A.D.B.*, vol. 2, pp. 476–8 and 589; C. M. H. Clark, *A History of Australia*, vol. 3, Melbourne, 1973, p. 317; ibid., vol. 2, pp. 48, 50 and 52; Fifer, *William Charles Wentworth*, pp. 82 and 126–9; Liston, *Sarah Wentworth*, pp. 16 and 20; Fletcher, *Ralph Darling*, p. 265.

[7] *H.R.A.*, 1, xi, p. 407; *Sydney Gazette*, 26 August, 2 and 16 September 1824; W. Wentworth's Office Account Book, 1825–27, Wentworth Papers, A758, esp. ff.12–26, 57–9, 61–3, 66–76 and 193–5; W. Wentworth's Law Causes, 1825–26, ibid., A759, esp. ff.1–12 and 262; W. Wentworth's Legal Letterbook, 1825–26, ibid., A1440, passim; W. C. Wentworth, *Statistical Account of the British Settlements in Australasia*, London, 1824, vol. 1, p. 323; Liston, *Sarah Wentworth*, pp. 16 and 33; C. M. H. Clark, op. cit., vol. 2, p. 51; Melbourne, *Wentworth*, p. 42; Fifer, loc. cit., pp. 79–81.

[8] *H.R.A.*, 1, xi, pp. 470–1; ibid., 1, xii, pp. 16–17; *Australian*, 14, 21 and 28 October 1824, 13 January and 3 February, 6 and 13 October 1825; *Sydney Gazette*, 21 and 28 October, 2 December 1824, 24 February, 28 April, 9 and 16 June 1825; W. Wentworth, Bank of New South Wales passbook, 18 September 1824 to 24 August 1826, Wentworth Papers, B1344; W. Wentworth to S. Bannister, 25 August and 7 September 1825, 7 January 1826, ibid., A1440, ff.156, 165–7 and 260; Wentworth's draft of arguments for trial by jury, n.d. 1827(?), ibid., A758, fifteen unnumbered folios at the start of the volume; Bigge, *State of the Colony*, p. 153; B. Field to S. Marsden, 13 March 1827, Marsden Papers, A1992, ff.460–3; *A.D.B.*, vol. 1, p. 334; ibid., vol. 2, p. 585; Fifer, loc. cit., pp. 73, 80, 82, 84, 89,

Notes: Chapter 9

92–3, 130 and 160–3; C. M. H. Clark, op. cit., vol. 2, pp. 51 and 59; Ritchie, *Macquarie*, p. 224; Fletcher, *Ralph Darling*, p. 80; Barker, loc. cit., pp. 283–6 and 295; Currey, *Forbes*, p. 117; Holder, op. cit., pp. 28–9; R. B. Walker, *The Newspaper Press in New South Wales, 1803–1920*, Sydney, 1976, pp. 5–7.

[9] *Sydney Gazette*, 11 November 1824, 3 February and 3 March 1825; *Australian*, 28 October and 11 November 1824; Fifer, loc. cit., pp. 81 and 101–3; C. M. H. Clark, op. cit., vol. 2, pp. 52 and 55; Ritchie, *Macquarie*, pp. 223–6.

[10] *H.R.A.*, I, xi, pp. 352–6; W. Wentworth, *Statistical Account*, vol. 1, pp. 323–4, 348–50, 367–77, 389, 391, 403 and 409; *Australian*, 25 November, 16 and 23 December 1824, 16 June 1825, 5 September 1827; B. Field to S. Marsden, 21 November 1824, Marsden Papers, A1992, f.429; S. Marsden to D. Coates, 17 March 1825, B.T. Missionary, Box 53, pp. 1477–8; S. Marsden to J. Pratt, 24 June and 2 July 1825, ibid., pp. 1502–4 and 1518–19; W. Wentworth to J. Norton, n.d. May 1825, Wentworth Papers, A1440, f.81; Melbourne, *Wentworth*, p. 43; Fifer, loc. cit., pp. 60–72; C. M. H. Clark, op. cit., vol. 2, pp. 55–7; Liston, 'William Charles Wentworth', p. 32; Ritchie, *Punishment and Profit*, pp. 245–7; Ritchie, *Macquarie*, pp. 224–5.

[11] *Sydney Gazette*, 27 September 1826; *Australian*, 23 September 1829; Liston, *Sarah Wentworth*, pp. 7–17, 23 and 40–1.

[12] *H.R.A.*, I, xi, pp. 429–30, 589 and 605–6; *Sydney Gazette*, 12 July 1822; Lord Bathurst to T. Brisbane, 25 August 1825, Bathurst Papers, 57/64, f.15, B.L.; F. Goulburn to T. Brisbane, 21 November 1825, Brisbane Papers, MS4036, Box 3, N.L.A.; T. Brisbane to H. Crawford, 13 May 1825, ibid., Box 1; T. Brisbane to Duke of Wellington, 20 May 1825, ibid.; T. Brisbane to unnamed correspondent, 1 August 1825, ibid.; Ritchie, *Macquarie*, p. 222; Clark, op. cit., vol. 2, pp. 58–9; Dermody, loc. cit., pp. 362, 364–5 and 381.

[13] *H.R.A.*, I, xi, pp. 457–78; J. Ovens to D. Wentworth, n.d. May 1825, Mackaness Papers, A318, f.13, M.L.; Sydney magistrates to D. Wentworth, 19 May 1825, Wentworth Papers, A754-2, ff.450–2; *Sydney Gazette*, 26 May 1825; P. Cunningham, *Two Years in New South Wales*, ed. D. S. Macmillan, Sydney, 1966, pp. 39–40; Barker, loc. cit., pp. 264–6; *A.D.B.*, vol. 2, p. 399; McMartin, op. cit., p. 91.

Notes: Chapter 9

[14] *H.R.A.*, 4, i, pp. 627–33; *Australian*, 13, 20 and 27 October 1825; *Sydney Gazette*, 10, 13, 17 and 24 October 1825, 8 February 1827; C. Brooks, Diary, MS 1559/23, ff.19–21, N.L.A.; T. Scott to Lord Bathurst, 5 November 1825, CO201/168, ff.202–3; F. Forbes to R. Wilmot Horton, 26 November 1825, Catton Papers, Derby, A.J.C.P. M791, N.L.A.; Fifer, loc. cit., pp. 93–6, 99–101 and 105–12; Melbourne, *Wentworth*, pp. 44–5; *A.D.B.*, vol. 1, pp. 92–5.

[15] *H.R.A.*, 4, i, pp. 633–5; ibid., 1, xii, p. 85; J. Macarthur to Lord Bathurst, n.d. 1825, CO201/179, ff.220–1 and Macarthur Papers, A2988, ff.6–9; J. Macarthur (jnr) to R. Wilmot Horton, 11 July 1826, CO201/179, ff.218–19 and 230–1; J. Macarthur (jnr) to J. Macarthur, 18 July 1826, Macarthur Papers, A2911, ff.340–1; R. Stirling to W. Wentworth, 3 August 1826, Wentworth Papers, A757, ff.19–22; W. Moore to T. Brisbane, 23 October 1825, Brisbane Papers, A1559-1, ff.251–2; *Sydney Gazette*, 17, 20, 27 and 31 October, 3, 7 and 10 November 1825; Melbourne, *Wentworth*, pp. 45–7; C. M. H. Clark, op. cit., vol. 2, pp. 59–60; Dermody, loc. cit., pp. 381–3 and 386–8; Fifer, loc. cit., pp. 113–14; McMartin, op. cit., p. 71.

[16] *H.R.A.*, 1, xii, pp. 81–4 and 127; *Sydney Gazette*, 22 December 1825 and 5 January 1826; *Australian*, 22 December 1825; J. Macarthur (jnr) to J. Macarthur, 12 and 13 June 1825, Macarthur Papers, A2911, ff.297–9; C. M. H. Clark, op. cit., vol. 2, pp. 60–2; *A.D.B.*, vol. 1, pp. 282–6; Fletcher, *Ralph Darling*, pp. 69, 73, 221–2 and 237–8; Ritchie, *Macquarie*, pp. 222–3 and 275.

[17] *H.R.A.*, 1, xii, pp. 762–3 and 768; ibid., 1, xiv, p. 825; Fletcher, *Ralph Darling*, pp. 23, 25, 67, 77, 215–25, 239 and 248. The Bucknells arrived in October 1826.

[18] *H.R.A.*, 1, xi, pp. 563–8; ibid., 1, xii, pp. 18–19 and 128; *Australian*, 18 and 25 November, 30 December 1824, 27 January, 17, 24 and 31 March, 5 and 26 May, 27 July 1825; *A.D.B.*, vol. 2, pp. 177–8; C. M. H. Clark, op. cit., vol. 2, pp. 63–6; Fifer, loc. cit., p. 88; Melbourne, *Early Constitutional Development*, pp. 104–20; W. G. McMinn, *A Constitutional History of Australia*, Melbourne, 1979, p. 21; Ellis, *Macarthur*, pp. 493–4 and 503; J. F. Atchison, Port Stephens and Goonoo Goonoo—an early history of the Australian Agricultural Company, 1824–1849, Ph.D. thesis, Faculty of Arts, A.N.U., 1974; P. A. Pemberton, The London Connection: the

Notes: Chapter 9

formation and early years of the Australian Agricultural Company, Ph.D. thesis, Faculty of Arts, A.N.U., 1991.

[19] *H.R.A.*, 1, xii, pp. 144–8 and 210–11; ibid., 1, xiii, p. 99; *Sydney Gazette*, 29 December 1825, 2, 5, 12, 16 and 28 January 1826; *Australian*, 19 January 1826; D. Wentworth et al. to J. Mackaness, 22 December 1825, Wentworth Papers, A754-1, ff.253–4; members of deputation chosen on 16 January 1826, ibid., f.255; T. Scott to Lord Bathurst, 17 January 1826, CO201/179, ff.431–2; T. Scott to Bishop of London, 17 January 1826, B.T. Missionary, Box 53, p. 1595; R. Darling to R. Hay, 1 February 1826, CO201/179, ff.134–6; Fifer, loc. cit., pp. 114–18; C. M. H. Clark, op. cit., vol. 2, p. 65.

[20] *Sydney Gazette*, 28 January 1826; J. Macarthur to P. King, 22 August 1826, King Papers, A1976, f.442; C. M. H. Clark, op. cit., vol. 2, p. 66.

[21] D. Wentworth (jnr) to W. Wentworth, 6 December 1823 and 20 May 1825, Wentworth Papers, A755, ff.27 and 33; D. Wentworth (jnr) to D. Wentworth, 28 February 1826, ibid., ff.37–40; certificate of banns of marriage of D. Wentworth (jnr), 24 April 1826, ibid., f.41; D. Wentworth (jnr), matrimonial contract, 26 April 1826, ibid., ff.43–5; J. Beckett to D. Wentworth (jnr), 14 June 1824, ibid., f.31; J. Lloyd to Military Secretary, Dublin, n.d. 1828, ibid., f.49; J. Whyn to Military Secretary, Dublin, 3 July 1828, ibid., f.51; Lord Fitzwilliam to D. Wentworth, 14 July 1824, ibid., A754-2, ff.446–7; D. Wentworth (jnr) to D. Wentworth, 16 August 1824, ibid., ff.209–15.

[22] *H.R.A.*, 1, xii, pp. 210–11, 253–6, 467 and 522; *Australian*, 26 January, 16 February, 6 and 13 September, 10 October 1826; T. Scott to Lord Bathurst, 17 January 1826, CO201/179, ff.431–2; S. Marsden, *An Answer to certain calumnies in the late Governor Macquarie's pamphlet, and the third edition of Mr Wentworth's Account of Australasia*, London, 1826; Fifer, loc. cit., pp. 124–5; C. M. H. Clark, op. cit., vol. 2, pp. 57 and 67–9; A. T. Yarwood, *Samuel Marsden*, Melbourne, 1977, p. 254; Currey, *Forbes*, pp. 176–7; Ellis, *Macarthur*, p. 498.

[23] *H.R.A.*, 1, xii, pp. 528–34 and 725–9; *Sydney Gazette*, 4 and 18 November 1824, 2 June 1825, 6 and 17 May 1826; *Monitor*, 19 May and 2 June 1826; *Gleaner*, 5 and 12 April 1827; J. Macarthur

Notes: Chapter 9

to J. Macarthur (jnr), 27 May 1827, Macarthur Papers, A2899, f.162; Fifer, loc. cit., pp. 83, 91–3 and 132–4; C. M. H. Clark, op. cit., vol. 2, pp. 70 and 161–5; Walker, op. cit., pp. 5, 7–8, 11 and 13; *A.D.B.*, vol. 1, pp. 500–1, 506–7 and 558–9.

[24] *H.R.A.*, I, xii, pp. 716–24; Fletcher, *Ralph Darling*, pp. 245–6; Currey, *Forbes*, pp. 192–9; C. M. H. Clark, op. cit., vol. 2, p. 71; Walker, op. cit., p. 9; Melbourne, *Wentworth*, p. 48.

[25] *H.R.A.*, I, xii, pp. 716–17 and 763–4; ibid., I, xiii, p. 82; *Australian*, 29 November, 2, 6, 13 and 27 December 1826; *Monitor*, 1, 22 and 29 December 1826; *Sydney Gazette*, 2 and 16 December 1826; W. Wentworth to Lord Bathurst, 15 December 1826, CO201/179, f.516; Fletcher, *Ralph Darling*, pp. 245–59; Melbourne, *Wentworth*, p. 48; Fifer, loc. cit., pp. 131, 138 and 140–3; Walker, op. cit., pp. 9–11; Currey, *Forbes*, pp. 194–6.

[26] *H.R.A.*, I, xiii, pp. 50–8, 96–102 and 443; ibid., 4, i, pp. 680–1; W. and D. Wentworth to J. Mackaness, 16 January 1827, Wentworth Papers, A758, ff.77–78; A. McLeay to W. Wentworth, 5 February 1827, ibid., A757, ff.23–4; F. Forbes to R. Wilmot Horton, 6 February 1827, Forbes Papers, A1819, f.84; R. Darling to R. Hay, 20 April 1827, CO201/149, f.271; *Sydney Gazette*, 19, 20, 22 and 27 January 1827; *Monitor*, 20 and 27 January 1827; *Australian*, 20 January 1827; Melbourne, *Wentworth*, pp. 49–50; Fletcher, *Ralph Darling*, pp. 247–9; Currey, *Forbes*, pp. 196–9; Fifer, loc. cit., pp. 144–51; Dermody, loc. cit., pp. 393–5.

[27] *H.R.A.*, I, xii, pp. 17, 81 and 727–9; ibid., I, xiii, pp. 206–10, 277–82, 374–87 and 391–9; ibid., 4, i, pp. 703–17 and 718–29; J. Macarthur to J. Macarthur (jnr), 12 September 1826, Macarthur Papers, A2899, f.134; Walker, op. cit., pp. 12–14; C. M. H. Clark, op. cit., vol. 2, pp. 73–6; Fletcher, *Ralph Darling*, pp. 250–6; Currey, *Forbes*, pp. 199–234.

[28] Petitions of James Macneal, October 1824 and August 1825, Colonial Secretary, In Letters, 4/1782, ff.75–8, A.O.N.S.W.; notes by S. Bannister, 8 October and 18 November 1824, ibid.; Barker, loc. cit., p. 300; Dermody, loc. cit., pp. 395–6; *A.D.B.*, vol. 1, pp. 5–7.

[29] J. Dawson to D. Wentworth, 13 May 1822, Wentworth Papers, A754-2, ff.422–4; D. Masiere to D. Wentworth, 22 February 1826, ibid., A754-1, ff.257–8; M. Johnston to D. Wentworth, 3 February 1826, ibid., A754-2, ff.454–6; *Sydney Gazette*, 2 and 9 July 1827;

[292]

Notes: Chapters 9 and 10

Monitor, 10 July 1827; *Australian*, 11 July 1827; Will of D. Wentworth, 5 July 1827, Wentworth Papers, Miscellaneous Material, MSS8/4, item 94, M.L.; W. B. Yeats, 'When You Are Old'.

10 OF GRAVES AND EPITAPHS

[1] *Sydney Gazette*, 11 July 1827; *Australian*, 11 and 13 July 1827; *Monitor*, 12 July 1827; obituary of D. Wentworth, 9 July 1827, Wentworth Papers, A754, f.273 and A754-2, ff.450–2; C. M. H. Clark, *A History of Australia*, vol. 2, p. 77; Barker, *D'Arcy Wentworth*, p. 301; 'The Order for the Burial of the Dead', *The Book of Common Prayer*, Oxford, 1825, pp. 326–34. It is unclear which of the Campbells acted as a pall-bearer—John Thomas, Robert or Robert junior.

[2] Rev. W. J. Gunther, extract taken from burial records for 1827 in the parish of Parramatta, 13 March 1884, Wentworth Papers, A754-2, ff.458–61; D. Wentworth's epitaph, n.d. 1827, ibid., f.287; note on D. Wentworth's tombstone, St John's Cemetery, Parramatta, n.d., Miscellaneous Papers, A563, M.L.; C. M. H. Clark, op. cit., vol. 2, pp. 77–8; A. Pope, 'An Essay on Man', Ep. iv, line 247; R. Burns, 'The Cotter's Saturday Night', xix.

[3] *Sydney Gazette*, 9 July 1827; *Monitor*, 10 and 12 July 1827; *Australian*, 11 July 1827; *Gleaner*, 14 July 1827; Barker, loc. cit., pp. 302–3; *A.D.B.*, vol. 2, p. 582.

[4] Lady Fitzwilliam to Lord Fitzwilliam, n.d. 1828, Wentworth Woodhouse Muniments, F127/202; C. Cookney to Lord Fitzwilliam, n.d. July 1834, ibid., FM4/747; *Burke's Peerage*, p. 617.

[5] *H.R.A.*, I, xi, pp. 282, 457, 459 and 494; M. Johnston to D. Wentworth, 3 February 1826, Wentworth Papers, A754-2, ff.454–6.

[6] Melbourne, *Wentworth*, pp. 7–11; E. Ford, 'Medical Practice in Early Sydney', *Medical Journal of Australia*, vol. 2, no. 2, July 1955, p. 43.

[7] Will of D. Wentworth, 5 July 1827, Wentworth Papers, Miscellaneous Material, MSS8/4, item 94, and Minter, Simpson & Co., Documents of Titles, A4026, no. 477; Properties devised by D. Wentworth to W. C. Wentworth, 5 July 1827, Wentworth Papers, A754-1, ff.275–7 and 279–81; Will of Maria Ainslie, 15 April 1841, Probate Office, Series 1, no. 1311, A.O.N.S.W.; Dermody, *D'Arcy Wentworth*, pp. 398 and 406–7.

Notes: Chapter 10

[8] *Sydney Gazette*, 3 January and 24 August 1827; Barker, loc. cit., pp. 298–9 and 316.

[9] Liston, *Sarah Wentworth*, pp. 20 and 24–7.

[10] *Australian*, 22 and 27 June 1827, 7 and 24 March 1829; W. Wentworth to J. Piper, 30 May 1828, Piper Papers, A255, ff.71–4; C. M. H. Clark, op. cit., vol. 2, p. 78; Liston, *Sarah Wentworth*, pp. 18 and 30; Historic Houses Trust of New South Wales, *Vaucluse House*, Sydney, 1982, pp. 1–24; Vogue Australia, *Living*, June–July 1983, pp. 91–101; Melbourne, *Wentworth*, p. 54; C. H. Bertie, *The Story of Vaucluse House and Henry Browne Hayes*, Sydney, 1918; A.D.B., vol. 1, pp. 526–7.

[11] C. M. H. Clark, op. cit., vol. 2, p. 78; S. G. Foster, *Colonial Improver, Edward Deas Thomson 1800–1879*, Melbourne, 1978, p. 21.

Select bibliography

A full bibliography will accompany my next book on The Wentworths which is to be subtitled *His Father's Son*. All references have been acknowledged in full on their first citation in the footnotes to this volume. The vast majority of the surviving papers of D'Arcy and William Wentworth are located in three major holdings:

Fitzwilliam Manuscripts, 1810–1830, MSS 82 to 104, Northamptonshire Record Office, Wootton Hall Park, Northampton, England.

Wentworth Woodhouse Muniments, Letters and Papers of the 4th Earl Fitzwilliam, 1748–1833, F1 to F134, Archives, Sheffield City Libraries, Yorkshire, England.

Wentworth Family Papers, Mitchell Library, Sydney, which include

A751	D'Arcy Wentworth's Correspondence, 1785–1808
A752	D'Arcy Wentworth's Correspondence, 1809–16
A753	D'Arcy Wentworth's Correspondence, 1817–20
A754-1	D'Arcy Wentworth's Correspondence, 1821–27
A754-2	D'Arcy Wentworth, Supplementary Papers, 1785–1826
A755	Major D'Arcy Wentworth's Papers, 1785–1826
A756	Letters from William Charles Wentworth, 1804–63
A757	Letters to William Charles Wentworth
A758	William Charles Wentworth, Miscellaneous Papers
A759	D'Arcy Wentworth's Account Book, 1821–27
A761	Papers relating to the Sydney Hospital, 1810–17
A762	Medical stores, hospital returns, etc., 1803–20
A763	Treasury Orders etc., 1812–25

Select bibliography

A1410	D'Arcy Wentworth's Account Book, 1812–20
A1440	William Wentworth, Legal Letterbook, 1825–26
A4073	D'Arcy Wentworth Papers
Aw81	D'Arcy Wentworth, Papers relating to trial by jury
B196	D'Arcy Wentworth, Medical notebook, 1817 ff
FM4/747	Wentworth Woodhouse Muniments, 1796–1834, microfilm of some of the papers held at the Sheffield City Libraries
MS D1	D'Arcy Wentworth, Police Reports and Accounts, 1810–27
B149	D'Arcy Wentworth, Police Fund Account, 1821–22
MSS7	Wentworth Family, Legal Documents, 1799–1948
MSS8	Wentworth Family, Miscellaneous Material, 1674–1943

Index

Abbott, Edward, 33, 36, 58, 69, 105–6, 113, 117–18, 121
Abbott, Mrs, 94
Aborigines, 45, 117, 126, 142, 160–2
Acts: 4 Geo.IV, c.96 (British), 199, 202–3, 207, 211, 225; 8 Geo.IV, no. 2 (New South Wales), 227; 8 Geo. IV, no. 3 (New South Wales), 227
Addington, Henry, 97; *see also* Sidmouth
Admiralty, 43
Advertiser (newspaper), 64
Agricultural Society of New South Wales, 205
Agricultural Stock Club, 205
agriculture, 49, 51, 59, 62, 65–7, 73, 127, 130, 193
Aiken, George, 25
Ainslie, Maria, 104, 137, 159, 161, 172–3, 183, 201, 236
Aldred, William, 14–15
Alexander (ship), 97
Alfred (ship), 203, 208
Allen, George, 227
Alley, Richard, 25
Altree, John, 49, 54
Anderson, Andrew, 43
Anderson, Archibald, 12–13
An Historical Journal of the Transactions at Port Jackson and Norfolk Island, 64
Annandale, 111
Anson Bay (Norfolk Island), 51
Anstis, Nicholas, 32–3, 42
Argo (ship), 100–1
Armagh, County, 2

Armytage (publican), 163, 187
Arndell, Thomas, 121
Arnold, Joseph, 134, 154, 161
Arthur, George, 204, 206
Ascott, John, 58
Ashurst, Sir William, 20
Asia (ship), 68
Atkins, Richard, 81, 96, 102, 106, 108, 113, 116
Atlantic (ship), 60
Atlas (ship), 93
Austin, John, 109
Australasia (poem), 202
Australian (newspaper), 209, 211, 214–15, 222–5, 227, 232
Australian Agricultural Company, 218–19
Auxiliary Bible Society, 159

Bailey, Nicholas, 42
Bain, Reverend James, 63
Balcombe, William, 205
Ball, Henry, 49
Balmain, William, 59, 77–9, 81, 83, 85–8, 90–3, 95–6
Bank of Australia, 209
Bank of New South Wales, 144–5, 163–4, 191, 205, 209
Banks, Sir Joseph, 55, 60, 88, 102, 109–10, 116
Bann, River, 4–5, 24, 55
Bannister (soldier), 69
Bannister, Saxe, 207–8, 227
Barker, H. P., 146
Barrack Square, 113, 126

Index

Barrington, George, 22
Barwell (ship), 80
Bass, George, 87
Bastille (prison), 18
Batavia, 190
Batchelor, John, 49
Bathurst, Henry, 3rd Earl, 138, 149, 153–6, 165–6, 168, 170–4, 176, 180, 184–5, 192, 197, 199–200, 209, 211, 213, 215, 222, 225; character, 171
Bathurst (town and district), 143, 150, 206, 238
Baughan, John, 78
Baulkham Hills, 157
Bay of Biscay, 34
Bayly, Nicholas, 111–12, 114–18, 133
Bedlam, 12
beef, price of, (1810) 127, (1815) 130, (1821) 193, (1827) 144
Belbin, James, 64, 115
Beldon, George, 105, 107, 116
Bell, Archibald, 114, 154
Bennet, Henry Grey, 164, 167–8, 171, 177–80, 200
Bent, Ellis, 126, 133–4, 140, 143, 149, 152–4, 156; character, 149
Bent, Jeffery Hart, 149–50, 152–6, 161–2, 164; character, 149, 171, 177, 180, 200
Bent Street, Sydney, 212
Berry, Alexander, 214
Bessborough, 2nd Earl of, 2
Betsy (ship), 95
Bigge, John Thomas, 176–7, 180, 183–4, 192; character, 182–3; investigation in New South Wales, 186–93; reports, (confidential) 197–8, (official) 194–7, (reception of) 198–200, 204, 211, 219
Bird, Ann, 223
'Bird of Providence', 50–1
Black Caesar (bushranger), 64
Black Dog (inn), 141
Blacker, Reverend, 4
Blackheath, 12
Blake, William, 162, 181, 187
Bland, Dr William, 208
Blaxcell, Garnham, 111–12, 114–15, 133, 138, 145–8
Blaxland, Gregory, 109–12, 115, 118, 133, 142–3, 149, 226

Blaxland, John, 109–12, 114–15, 118–19, 121, 123, 132, 144, 149
Bletchley, Buckinghamshire, 93, 97, 99, 105
Bligh, Elizabeth, 103, 110, 134
Bligh, William: character, 103; governs New South Wales (1806–08), 101–3, 106–22, 125, 127–31, 133–4, 137, 154–5, 167, 175, 181, 234
Blue Mountains, 142–4, 150–1, 160
Bonaparte, Napoleon, 151
Bond, Nicholas, 15, 19
Bondel, 42
Borneo (ship), 190
Botany Bay, 49, 98, 108, 128, 171, 182
Bounty (ship), 103, 110
Bow Street, 10, 12, 14, 42, 214
Bow Street Runners, 10, 12, 14
Bowen, David, 143
Bowman, James, 174, 183–4, 191, 198, 204, 208, 210, 218, 222
Bradley, William, 52, 54
Branham, Mary, 57
Breakwell, Samuel, 239
Bridge Street, Sydney, 112, 141, 147
Bringelly, 160, 237
Brisbane, Sir Thomas, 198, 220; character, 204, 213–14, 217; governs New South Wales (1821–25), 193, 199, 204–16, 234
Britannia (ship), 68, 76–7
British criminal code, 16–17
Broken Bay, 237
Brooks, Richard, 93, 124, 130
Brothers (ship), 218
Brougham, Henry, Lord, 181
Broughton, William, 142, 153, 158
Brown, J., 215
Brown Bear (flash house), 18
Bucknell, Martha, 136, 168, 206, 217, 238
Bucknell, William, 168, 206, 217
Buffalo (ship), 102
Buller, Mr Justice, 16
Burns, Robert, 230
Burrough's Building, Peterhouse, Cambridge, 201
Burt, Samuel, 36
bushranging, 54, 64, 158, 192, 205

[298]

Index

Butler, Lawrence, 158
Byron, George Gordon, Lord, 167, 174, 210

Calcutta, 93, 138
Caley, George, 117
Cambridge, University of, 2, 167, 201–2
Camden, Calvert & King, 27–9, 32, 42–4
Camden, Lord, 99, 102, 119
Camden (district), 135, 198, 238
Campbell, John Thomas, 127, 164, 183, 210, 229, 236
Campbell, Robert, 104, 112, 114, 134, 217
Campbell, William, 148
Canning, George, 183, 203
Cape of Good Hope, 26, 37, 68
Cape Town, 37–9, 161
Carthy, Laurence, 84
Cartwright, Reverend Robert, 187–8
Cascade Bay (Norfolk Island), 51–3, 66
Cascades, the, 63
Castle Hill, 157; uprising at, 94
Castlereagh, Viscount, 107–8, 110, 120–2, 124–5, 130, 132, 137, 139, 168, 179
Castlereagh Street, Sydney, 208, 210
Catholic Emancipation, 67
cattle, number of, (1815) 130, (1821) 193
Caulfield, James, 1st Earl of Charlemont, 6
Cavendish, Caroline, Lady, 2
Censor (hulk), 22
Ceylon, 149, 159
Chambers, Charles, 208
Chapman, James, 110
Chapman, William Neate, 60, 63, 68
Chapman (ship), 157
Charles I, 2, 10
Charles II, 3
Charlotte (ship), 13
Charlotte Field (Norfolk Island), 51, 54–6, 59, 62, 75; *see also* Queenborough
Chartres, George, 153
Childe Harold, 174, 210
China, 93
Christ Church, Oxford, 166, 182
Christopher, William, 12
Church of England, 222–3, 229
Clarence, Duke of, 220

Clarendon, 2nd Earl of, 13
Clark, Alderman, 43
Clark, Betsy Alicia, 57; *see also* Trevan, Betsy
Clark, Ralph, 50–1, 54–7, 59–61, 63; character, 56
Clark, Zachariah, 64
Cleaveland, Thomas, 142
Coal River (Newcastle), 94, 115, 147–8, 157, 212
Cockle Bay, 144, 151, 237–8
Coe Fen, Cambridge, 201
Collingwood, William, 54
Collins, David, 25, 41–2, 46, 50, 55, 70, 76
Colonial Office, 116–17, 121, 124, 132, 134, 150, 154, 158, 164, 170, 174, 177, 179, 184, 186, 199, 202, 213, 216
Colquhoun, Patrick, 17
Commissariat, 68, 74, 95, 104, 136, 144, 206
Commission of Inquiry into New South Wales and Van Diemen's Land, 168, 171, 176; *see also* Bigge, John Thomas
Connell, John, 219
Considen, Dennis, 54–5, 59, 61, 96, 142
convict transportation, 25–44
convicts: clothing and rations of, 28; death rate on voyages, 40–1, 61; numbers, 103, 127, 151, 164; punishments of, 30, 36–7, 40, 54, 59–60, 63, 82, 94, 96, 127, 147, 211; rebellion, 94, 96
Cook, James, 48
Cook (district), 237–8
Cooke, Edward, 121–2, 124
Cookney, Charles, 22–3, 56, 79, 86, 159, 161, 237; D'Arcy Wentworth's agent, 22, 68, 96, 99, 134; helps Wentworth's children, 93, 97–9, 105, 120, 124, 136, 138, 165, 167, 174, 176, 178, 233; letters from D'Arcy Wentworth, 23, 75–6, 82–3, 86, 95, 97, 100, 107, 119, 123, 139, 190, 192; letters to D'Arcy Wentworth, 23, 68, 80, 87, 98–9, 101, 104, 108, 138–9, 183, 206
Cookney, Charles junior, 136
Cookney, George, 206, 239
Cookney, Mrs (wife of Charles senior), 94, 97, 99, 137, 165

[299]

Index

Cooper (convict), 69
Cooper, Daniel, 215, 219
Corsair, The (poem), 174
Court of Civil Jurisdiction, 79
Courts of Quarter Sessions, 207, 224, 226
Cowan, James, 37
Cowpastures, the, 102
Cowper, Henry, 146, 157, 188
Cowper, Reverend William, 126-7, 210
Cox, Elizabeth, 212, 238
Cox, Francis, 212
Cox, Henrietta, 212
Cox, James, 212
Cox, John, 212
Cox, Margaret (wife of Francis Cox), 212
Cox, Mary Maria, 212
Cox, Sarah, 211-14, 238
Cox, Thomasine (W. C. Wentworth's daughter), 213, 238
Cox, William, 143-4, 187
Cox, William Charles (W. C. Wentworth's son), 238
Creswell, John, 54, 58
Criminal Recorder (newspaper), 17
Crombie, Dr Alexander, 99, 120
Crook, Elizabeth, 183
Crook, Emma, 183-4
Crossley, George, 91-2, 102, 108, 115, 118, 152-3
Crothers, Elizabeth, 190
Crothers, John, 190
Crowley, Catherine (1772-1800, William Wentworth's mother), 31, 34, 40, 46-7, 52-3, 57, 62, 68, 71-2, 137, 159, 172, 197, 230, 235-6; death of, 83
Crowley, Dorset, 68, 83; *see also* Wentworth, D'Arcy (1793-1861)
Crowley, Martha, 68
Crowley, Mathew, 68, 83; *see also* Wentworth, John
Cruikshank, George, 174
Cubitt, Daniel, 158, 162
Cú Chulainn, 210
Cullen, Patrick, 155
Cunningham, Peter, 147
Curtis, William, 12-13
Cumberland, Duchess of, 19
Cumberland, Duke of, 19
Cumberland (ship), 148
Cumming's Hotel, 205

Cunningham, James, 49-50

Daily Universal Register (newspaper), 14-16; *see also Times, The*
Daphne, 183
Darling, Elizabeth, 216
Darling, Ralph, 213; character, 216-17; governs New South Wales (1825-31), 216-27, 234
Darnley, Lord, 116
Davidson, Walter, 102
Davis, John, 109
Dawes' Point, 146
Dawson, James, 8-9
Dawson, Robert, 218
Dawson, Thomas, 7
Day, Jack, 19
'Defenders', 81
Devonshire, Duke of, 2
Dickson, John, 151
Dinah, 64
Divine, Nicholas, 108
Dixon, Martha (D'Arcy's mother), *see* Wentworth, Martha
Dobbin, Leonard, 5
Dog and Duck (tavern), 11-12, 18, 97
Doidge, Denis, 59, 61, 63
Domain trespassers, 162, 171, 187
Donovan, Mr, 52
Douglass, Dr Henry Grattan, 208
Downey, Michael, 105
Draffin, Cadwallader, 116, 118
Dromedary (ship), 125, 191
Druitt, George, 187
Duchess of York (ship), 193
Duck River, 237
Dumaresq, Henry, 209-10, 225
Duncan, Mr, 12
Dundas, Henry (1st Viscount Melville), 43-4, 65, 70
Dunkirk (hulk), 22
Dunn, John, 16

Eagar, Edward, 152-3, 163-4, 182, 192-3, 198-200, 202-3, 207, 211
East India Company, 8, 27, 120, 136, 221
East Indies, 136
Edgar, Thomas, 25
Edge, Fane, 66
Edgeworth, Maria, 126

[300]

Index

Edinburgh Review (periodical), 182
Elizabeth Farm, 81
Ellerington, William, 35-7, 42-3, 47
Elm Court, 176
Elmsall Place (later Park), 150, 237
Ely, Bishop of, 201
emancipists, 103, 130-3, 151-4, 161, 163-4, 169, 171, 174, 177, 182, 184, 186, 192, 194-5, 199-200, 202-4, 209-11, 215-18, 222-4, 235, 239
Emu (ship), 160
Encyclopaedia Britannica, 100, 104
Erskine, James, 170, 192
Erskine, Thomas, 20
Eton, 2
Evans, Thomas, 42-3
Evans, William, 139
executive council, 215, 217, 218, 226

Faddy, William, 54, 58
False Bay, 37, 39
Farquhar, Sir Walter, 88, 102
Female Factory, Parramatta, 147, 206
Field, Barron, 156, 187-8, 193, 209
Fielding, Henry, 10
Fielding, John, 10
First Fleet, 13, 27, 29, 40, 54
Fitz, Robert, 110
Fitzgerald, Richard, 199
Fitzwilliam, Charles William, 5th Earl, 71, 233
Fitzwilliam, Charlotte, Lady (first wife of the 4th Earl), 2, 71, 160, 165, 190, 202
Fitzwilliam, Frances, Lady (sister of the 4th Earl), 232-3
Fitzwilliam, Louisa, Lady (second wife of the 4th Earl), 202
Fitzwilliam, William, 3rd Earl, 2-3
Fitzwilliam, William Wentworth, 4th Earl, 56, 64, 159, 178, 190, 202, 232, 237; birth and upbringing, 1-2; political career, 2, 65, 67, 101-2, 189; wealth and standing, 2, 20; character of, 24, 165-6; meets D'Arcy Wentworth, 13; becomes his patron, 20-22, further acts of patronage, 65, 68, 70-1, 80, 86, 96, 99, 100, 108, 122, 134-9, 166, 174, 220; letters from D'Arcy Wentworth, 65, 70-1, 75-6, 79-80, 82-3, 86, 88, 91-2, 96, 99, 102, 107, 116-21, 123, 132-3, 137, 143, 150, 154-5, 160, 165, 170; letters to D'Arcy Wentworth, 65, 87, 220; relations with William Charles Wentworth, 93, 98, 135, 165-6, 175-6, 182, 190, 201; death, 233
Fitzwilliam, Sir William, 1
Fitzwilliam family, 1-2, 201, 232, 239
Fitzwilliam Place, Parramatta, 123
Flattery, Phoebe, 54
flax, 48, 63-4, 66
Forbes, Charles, 181
Forbes, Francis, 199, 205, 207-8, 217, 225-7
Foster, Elizabeth, 212
Foveaux, Joseph, 83, 95, 99, 120, 122-3, 125, 128-9, 131-2, 135; character, 96-7, 120
Fox, Charles James, 2, 20
Francis, 64
freedom of the press, 209-11, 214, 220, 226-7
French revolution, 121
Friendly Islands, 148
Fulton, Reverend Henry, 104, 115-16, 123, 133-4, 200
Fyanstown, 3

Galloway (stallion), 144
Garden Court, Temple, London, 200
Garden Island, 130
Garling, Frederick, 156
Garrow, William, 20-1, 43
Gates, Samuel, 29, 35, 37
General Hewitt (ship), 157
General Stewart (ship), 190
George IV, 220
George Street, 84, 141, 147, 185, 190, 236
Gig (horse), 135, 142
Gilbert, Thomas, 24, 29, 32-5
Gilberthorpe, Thomas, 158
Ginders, Mary, 97, 236
Glatton (ship), 90
Gleaner (newspaper), 223-4, 232
Golden Grove (ship), 50
Goodenough, Philip, 148
Gordon, Lieutenant-Colonel, 110
Gordon Riots (1780), 10-11
Gore, William, 101, 104, 114-16, 130, 133-5, 137
Gorman, Ellen, 200

[301]

Index

Goulburn, Frederick, 193, 204, 208, 211, 213
Goulburn, Henry, 150, 171–2, 180
Governor King (ship), 101
Gow, John, 228
Gray, William, 33–4, 37, 46
Greenway, Francis, 145
Greenwich, 99, 105, 120
Grenville, William Wyndham, Lord, 27, 42, 60, 101
Griffin, Edmund, 104, 112, 114
Griffin, James, 105–6, 116
Grimes, Charles, 111–12, 114, 116, 118
Grimshaw, Richard, 92
Grose, Francis, 28–9, 67, 70, 72, 79, 83
Grose Farm, 128
Grundy, Ann, 14–17
Guardian (ship), 26–7, 38

Hall, Charlotte, 223
Hall, Edward, 158
Hall, Edward Smith, 219, 223, 225, 230–1
Halloran, Dr Laurence Hynes, 223, 232
Hamilton, Duke of, 20
Harpur, Thomas, 228
Harris, Dr John, 13, 33–4, 45–6, 109–10, 114, 147, 164, 184–5, 187–8, 230
Harris, John Prideaux, 127
Hart, G. V., 181
Hassall, Reverend Rowland, 108
Hawkesbury River district, 72–3, 102, 104, 108, 127, 133
Hayes, Sir Henry Browne, 238
Hector (stallion), 144
Henry V, 12
Henshall, William, 162, 187
Heritage, Charles, 49
Heywood, John Pemberton, 18, 20–1
Higgins, Mary, 59
Hill, James, 5
Hill, Mrs, 210, 220
Hill, Thomas, 23–4
Hill, William, 31–3, 37, 42, 46–7, 56, 58
Hobart, Lord, 91–2
Hobart Town, 160, 184, 192, 206; population (1806), 103
Hobby, Thomas, 89
Hogan, Michael, 81
Hogan, Patrick, 158
Holt, Joseph, 96–7

Home, Everard, 141
Home Bush, 81, 93, 137, 141, 143, 148, 172–3, 183, 185, 197, 206, 214, 227–9, 236–7
Home Office, 13, 18, 24, 27, 32, 43, 56, 64–5, 70–1, 74–5, 80, 86–7, 95–6, 164, 168, 199
Horace, 168
horse-racing, 135, 142, 235
Horsley, John, 158
Hottentots, 38
Hounslow Heath, 14, 154
House of Commons, 154, 162, 164, 167, 171, 179–81, 194, 225
House of Lords, 171, 181, 200
Howard, Captain, 183–4
Howard, Mr, 19–20
Howe, George, 92, 223
Howe, Robert, 198, 222–3, 230
Hughes, Edward, 14
Hume, Andrew, 63
Hungerford Coffee House, 175
Hunter, James, 188
Hunter, John, 51–5, 67, 70, 75, 95–6, 234; character, 74, 85; governs New South Wales (1795–1800), 74–6, 78–82, 84
Hurst, John, 14–17
Hutchinson, William, 187, 209, 219
Hutu, 64
Hyde Park, Sydney, 135, 210

Illawarra district, 206, 237
immigration, 151, 181, 206
income tax, 97
Indispensable (ship), 104
Inner Temple, 176
Innet, Ann, 49, 57, 91; *see also* Robinson, Ann
Ireland, conditions in, 3–7, 121, 206
Irving, John, 54
Irwin, Dr James, 12–13

Jack (stallion), 144
James, Mr (Cookney's brother-in-law), 206
Jamison, Dr Thomas, 49, 54–5, 59, 89, 92, 95, 100, 106, 109, 111–12, 116, 119, 132, 185
Jamison, Sir John, 142, 144, 154, 193, 225–6

[302]

Index

Jammond, Mrs, 142
Jenkins, Robert, 164
Jenkinson, Charles, 124
Jerry (horse), 142
John Barry (ship), 182, 184
Johnson, Mrs Richard, 45
Johnson, Reverend Richard, 41, 60–1, 76, 79
Johnson, Samuel (Dr), 11
Johnston, George, 54, 57–8, 81, 89, 94, 102, 106, 119–20, 123, 125, 127–8, 132–4; and rebellion against Bligh, 109–18, 122
Johnston, George junior, 135, 168
Johnstone, John, 54
Jolly Sailor (inn), 141
Jones, Frederick, 143
Jones, Richard, 223
Joseph, John, 42–3
Justicia (hulk), 22
Justinian (ship), 26–7, 51–2

Kable, Henry, 109, 115, 133, 148
Kellow, Robert, 54, 57
Kemp, Anthony Fenn, 110, 114, 116, 118, 133
Kennedy, John, 79, 84
Kent, William, 89, 95
Kerr, Warren, 206
Killaney, Lawrence, 105–6
King, Anna Josepha (née Coombe, P. G. King's wife), 60, 62, 66, 96, 102
King, Elizabeth, 96
King, John, 43, 65, 75
King, Philip Gidley, 72, 75–6, 80–1, 97, 110, 234; character, 49, 90; on Norfolk Island, 49–50, 57, 60–71; governs New South Wales (1800–06), 83–91, 94–5, 100–2, 104
King, Phillip Parker, 62
Kingdom, Elizabeth, 109
Kingston (Norfolk Island), 49–50, 54–5, 59, 69
Kitchen, Henry, 146
Knowlys, Mr, 15–16

Lady Juliana (ship), 25–6, 30–1, 41, 44
Lady Madeleine Sinclair (ship), 137
land grants, 72–3, 102, 104, 109, 115, 119, 123, 125, 128, 135, 143–5, 160, 163, 168, 186, 194–5, 197, 206, 211, 218, 222
Lansdowne, Marquis of, 171
Lapstone Hill, 224
Laurie, John, 158
Laverton, Mrs William, 212
Lawes, Mary Ann, 137, 159, 172–3, 183, 197, 206, 227, 229, 235–7
Lawson, William, 66, 116, 118, 133, 142, 219, 229, 236
Laycock, Thomas, 93, 116
le Carré, John, 151
Leach, Eleanor, 206–7
Leeds, Samuel, 74–5
legislative assembly, 181, 210, 214, 219–20, 223, 226
legislative council, 177, 181–2, 194, 199, 208, 215, 217–18, 220
Letter to Viscount Sidmouth, 177
Lewer, William, 14–15, 20
Lewin, John William, 189
Liberty Plains, 123
Lincoln's Inn, 8, 13, 18, 23
Lindwood, Miss, 136
Little, Thomas, 15
Little St Mary's Lane, Cambridge, 201
Liverpool, Lord, 124, 139
Liverpool, New South Wales, 192, 198, 237
Locke, John, 111
London, 9–12; metropolitan police, 10, 14; radical underworld, 10
Looking, May, 14–15
Lord, Edward, 160
Lord, Simeon, 92, 95, 102, 107, 109, 111–12, 115, 133, 135, 142, 153, 184, 198, 209, 219
Losh, James, 199
Louis XVI, 44
Low, Gustavus, 163
Lowe, Robert, 219
Lucas, Nathaniel, 64, 110
Lucas, Olive, 64
Luttrell, Dr Edward, 108
Lyons, Sarah, 60
Lyte, Henry, 204

Macarthur, Edward, 32–6, 39, 88, 112, 121
Macarthur, Elizabeth (John's daughter), 123, 167, 175

[303]

Index

Macarthur, Elizabeth (née Veale, John's wife), 32–6, 38–9, 44–6, 81, 94, 109–10, 123, 199
Macarthur, Hannibal (John's nephew), 204, 218
Macarthur, James (John's son), 218
Macarthur, John, 32–6, 38–9, 46, 49, 78, 81, 86, 88–9, 91, 93, 102–3, 123, 131, 134, 136, 144, 166–8, 175, 182, 198–200, 204, 208, 215, 217–18, 220, 222, 224; and rebellion against Bligh, 109–20, 122
Macarthur, John junior, 88, 166–8, 174–6, 180, 199–200, 202
McCann family, 4
McDonald, James, 105
McDowell, Mr, 5
McDuel, Jemima, 192
McDuel, John, 192
McGrigor, James, 141
Mackaness, John, 203, 208, 218, 230
Mackaness, Mrs (John's mother), 203
McKay, James, 54
Mackintosh, Sir James, 202–3, 211
McLeay, Alexander, 217–18, 220, 239
Macneal, James, 137, 227
Macneal, Mary Ann, *see* Lawes, Mary Ann
Macpherson, Charles, 221
Macpherson, Duncan, 221
Macpherson, Elizabeth, 221
Macpherson, George, 221
Macpherson, Margaret, 221
Macquarie, Charles, 154
Macquarie, Elizabeth Henrietta, 129, 131, 141, 150, 154, 190, 193–4, 200
Macquarie, Lachlan, 204, 211, 216, 220; birth and background, 129; commission and instructions, 124–5; installed as governor, 126; character, 129–30, 132, 161–2, 190, 217; governs New South Wales (1810–21), 127–94; emancipist policy, 130–2, 152–4, 169, 171, 174, 177, 184, 194–5, 210, 220; and J. T. Bigge, 184, 190; and Bigge's reports, 194–7, 199; visits London, 200; illnesses, 141; news of his death, 210
Macquarie, Lachlan junior, 150, 159, 194
Macquarie Place, Sydney, 144, 208
Madras, 159

Maidstone, 13, 15
Maidstone Journal (newspaper), 17
Maitland, Benjamin, 27
Malcolm, Sir Pulteney, 136
Maloney, Margaret, 192
Maluai, 64
Manning, William (highwayman), 12
Manning, William (politician), 181
Mansell, William, 139–40
manufacturing, 130, 151
Maoris, 64
Margarot, Maurice, 78, 82
Market Hill, Cambridge, 201
Marquis Cornwallis (ship), 81
Marsden, Elizabeth, 94
Marsden, Reverend Samuel, 77, 79, 81, 83, 93–4, 101, 108, 116, 131, 133–4, 144, 148, 153, 156, 170–1, 176–7, 179, 197, 204, 208, 211, 222, 229; his pamphlet (1826), 222
Marshall, John, 29, 36, 39
Mary Hope (ship), 216
Masiere, David, 227
Matilda (ship), 170
Mauritius, 216, 219
Maynard, Samuel, 14–16
Mealmaker, George, 116
medicine and hospitals, 6, 9, 55, 61, 76, 92–3, 95, 105–6, 139–40, 146, 156–9, 170, 180, 185, 188–91, 197–8; *see also* sickness and disease; Sydney Hospital
Meehan, James, 135
Melbourne, 2nd Viscount, 23
Melling, Catherine, 84
Methodist Society, 227
Middle Temple, 166–7, 176, 200, 203
Middleton, Sir Charles, 13, 27
Midgley, Reverend, 93, 98, 120
Mileham, James, 81, 96, 112, 116
Millwood, Sarah, 15
Milton, John, 168
Milton, Lord, *see* Fitzwilliam, Charles William
Milton, Viscount, 1
Minchin, William, 110, 113–15, 118, 185–6, 191
Molesworth, 3rd Viscount, 202
Molle, George, 149, 154, 161, 163, 168–70, 176, 179, 184, 200

[304]

Index

Money, W. T., 181
Monitor (newspaper), 223–5, 227, 231
Moore, Thomas, 163
Moore, William, 116
Moore, William Henry, 161–3, 170
Morisset, James, 157
Morley, Roger, 49
Morton, Frances, 212
Mount Pitt (Norfolk Island), 50, 55
Murray, Robert, 76
Murray, Robert Lathrop, 147, 169, 183–4, 192, 206
My Landlord (novel), 198

Napoleonic Wars, 44, 97, 101, 108, 151
Napthali, Michael, 224
Nash, John, 174
Nash's Inn, Parramatta, 215–16
Native Institution, 159, 205
Navy Board, 27, 32, 43
Navy Office, 28
Nelson, Horatio, 32
Nepean, Evan, 24, 27, 33, 60–1, 64–5
Nepean, Nicholas, 32–7, 46, 63
Neptune (ship), 22–4, 29–34, 36–43, 46, 56–7, 63, 233
Newcastle, *see* Coal River
Newgate (prison), 13, 19, 22, 25, 167, 209
Newman, John Henry, 48
New South Wales: population, (1790) 44, 233, (1796) 72, (1806) 103, (1810) 127, (1815) 151, (1821) 151, (1827) 233
New South Wales Charter of Justice, 207
New South Wales Corps (102nd Regiment from 1809), 22, 24, 28, 31, 34, 39, 58, 60, 62, 69, 73, 81–3, 95, 106, 116–17, 121–2, 126, 128, 134; and rebellion against Bligh, 103, 109–13
Newtown, 238
Nicol, John, 25–6
Nightingall, Miles, 123
Nore, mutiny at the, 103, 121
Norfolk Island, 47–71, 87, 95–100, 104, 143, 172, 178, 197, 234; population, (1788) 49, (1790) 50, 52, (1791) 60, (1796) 66, (1806) 103, (1810) 127
Norfolk Island pines, 48, 141
North, Lord (1732–92), 2
North Harbour, 237

Northumberland, Duke of, 117

Oakboys, 6
Oakes, Francis, 105, 107, 116
Obyns, John, 4
Ocean (ship), 158
O'Connell, Mary, 129, 137–8, 239; *see also* Putland, Mary
O'Connell, Maurice, 129, 138, 239
O'Donnell, Patrick, 228
O'Flynn, Father Jeremiah, 162
Old Bailey, 15–16, 20, 43, 135, 178, 197
Oriel College, Oxford, 166
Oxley, John, 207–8, 222

Pacific Ocean, 48, 148
Paine, Daniel, 76–7
Paine, John, 211–12
Paine, Thomas, 111
Palmer, John, 104, 112, 114, 116, 134
Paris, 168, 174–5
Parmeter, Thomas, 157
Parramatta, 72–3, 81–3, 90, 92–5, 105–6, 113, 116, 118, 123, 147–8, 158, 170, 177, 185, 192, 197–8, 204, 212–13, 216, 237–8
Parramatta (schooner), 111
Parry, John, 23
pastoral industry (in New South Wales), 73, 143, 151, 193, 195
Paterson, Elizabeth, 60, 122, 128
Paterson, William, 60–1, 63, 69, 72, 77, 79, 84–5, 88, 90, 120, 122–3, 125, 128, 132, 134
Patton, Dr Alexander, 6, 8–9, 54, 136, 206
Peel, Robert, 199
Perne Library, Peterhouse, Cambridge, 202
Perryn, Sir Richard, 16, 20
Peterhouse, Cambridge, 201–2
Peterloo massacre, 190
Petersham, 213, 238–9
Petrarch, 238
Philanthropic Society, 148, 159
Phillip, Arthur, governs New South Wales (1788–1792), 18, 24, 28, 42–5, 47–51, 55–6, 60–2, 64, 67, 72–4, 216, 220
Phillip Island, 69
Phillip Street, Sydney, 212
Phillipburgh, 51, 58, 60

Index

Phoenix (hulk), 224
Pimlico, 167
Piper, John, 64, 88, 95, 97, 110, 205, 213, 229, 239
'pipes', 82, 89–90, 110, 136, 168–9, 200
Pitt, Thomas, 26
Pitt, William, 26, 43, 67, 89, 101
police, 140, 156, 158, 180, 187–8, 192, 196–8, 205, 214
Pons (comet), 182
Ponsonby, Charlotte, Lady, *see* Fitzwilliam, Charlotte
Pope, Alexander, 168, 230
Porpoise (ship), 122
Port Dalrymple, 95, 110, 120; population (1806), 103
Port Jackson, 124–5, 144, 161, 239
Port Macquarie, 206
Portadown, 2, 4–5, 17, 24, 206, 228
Portland, 3rd Duke of, 67, 75, 80–1, 89
Portsmouth, 13, 22–4, 27, 30, 33–4, 124
Portugal, 108
Poyning's law, 7
Prentice, John Thomas, 33, 37, 58
Pritchard, William, 206–7
Pritchett, R. C., 219
prostitution, 10, 26, 30–1, 96–7, 184
Putland, John, 104
Putland, Mary (née Bligh), 102, 109, 112–13, 115; *see also* O'Connell, Mary
Pym, John, 111

Quarterly Review (periodical), 182
Queen (ship), 61
Queenborough, 59, 60–4, 67, 69, 80, 234; *see also* Charlotte Field

Raine, Thomas, 215, 219
Rarotonga, 148
Raven, William, 68, 77, 80, 157
Read, Daniel, 162
Redfern, Sarah, 104, 203
Redfern, William, 104, 133, 135, 139, 146, 157, 159, 163–4, 174, 179, 182, 184, 188–9, 191–3, 196, 198–201, 203, 208–10, 219–20, 228–9, 236
Redman, John, 110
Redmond, Miss, 211
regiments: 24th, 221; 36th, 7; 46th, 149, 153, 168–70; 48th, 170; 63rd, 233; 73rd, 123, 126, 128, 136–7, 140, 149, 200, 206, 212, 220; *see also* New South Wales Corps
Reibey, Mary, 144
Reid, Captain, 39
Reliance (ship), 71–2
Remnant, Stephen, 12–13
Resolution (ship), 48
Revolutionaire (ship), 161
Rhodes, Robert, 97
Richards, William (junior), 25, 27
Riley, Alexander, 138, 145–6, 148, 153, 162, 164, 168–9, 175–6, 180, 201
Riley, Edward, 138, 223
Rio de Janiero, 26
Riou, Edward, 26–7, 38
Robarts, Edward, 161
Roberts, John, 52
Robespierre, Maximilien de, 111
Robinson, Ann (née Innet), 92
Robinson, Michael Massey, 211
Robinson, Richard John, 91
Rockingham, 2nd Baron, 3
Rockingham, 1st Marquis of, 3
Rockingham, 2nd Marquis of, 2, 8
Rocks, The, 45, 140, 146, 196
Roscommon, 4th Earl of, 3
Rose (publican), 163, 187
Rose (ship), 119
Ross, J. C., 190
Ross, Robert, 50–5, 58–61
Rossi, Francis Nicholas, 214
Rotherham, 2
Roufigny, Abbé de, 105, 120
Rouse, Richard, 105, 116
Royal Botanical Gardens, Kew, 26
Royal Military College, Sandhurst, 220
Royal Oak (ship), 136
Russell, Henry, 13, 18, 20

Sadler's Wells, 98
St Bartholomew's Hospital, London, 9
St George's Fields, 11, 97
St Iago, 27
St James's Church, Sydney, 210, 213
St John's Church, Parramatta, 83, 229
St Martin-in-the-Fields, Westminster, 60
St Patrick, 205

Index

St Paul's Cathedral, London, 98
St Phillip's Church, Sydney, 126, 141, 210, 238
Sanderson, Edward, 169
Savage, John, 90
Scarborough (ship), 22, 24, 29, 33, 36, 38–41
Schell (pauper), 9
Scott, Claude, 12–13
Scott, Sir Walter, 174
Scott, Thomas Hobbes, 211, 213, 217–18, 220, 222–4
'Scottish Martyrs', 78
Scratch (horse), 142
scurvy, 39
Second Fleet, 22, 25–44, 58, 63
self-government, 181–2, 209, 211, 214, 216, 219
Settlers and Landholders Society (Norfolk Island), 65
Shakespeare, William, xv, 1, 11, 229
Shapcote, John, 28–30, 33–9, 46
Shea, John, 109
sheep, 102, 195, 197, 218; number of, (1815) 130, (1821) 193
Sheers, James, 63
Sheers, Mary Anne, 63
Sherwin, Ann, 96
sickness and disease, 61, 63, 92, 105; *see also* medicine
Sidmouth, 1st Viscount, 168, 177; *see also* Addington, Henry
Simon's Town, 37–8, 44, 161
Sinclair, Robert, 13, 21
Sinclair (ship), 120
Sirius (ship), 49–50, 52, 54–5
slavery, 27, 29, 32, 37–8, 42, 44, 171, 182
Smith, Joseph, 63
Smith, Sydney, 182, 199
Smythe, Thomas, 91
Sorell, William, 204
South Creek, 237
South Head, 238
South Sea Islanders, 142
Spain, 108, 216
Spithead, mutiny at, 121
spirits, 68, 73, 76, 79, 84–6, 92, 95, 97, 104, 108, 115, 124–5, 134, 138–40, 144–8, 153, 156, 158, 171, 177, 180, 187, 190–1, 196, 222
Sprotbrough, 1
Statesman (newspaper), 203
Statistical Account of the British Settlements in Australasia, 211
Statistical, Historical, and Political Description of The Colony of New South Wales, and Its dependent Settlements in Van Diemen's Land, 180–2
Steakham, Thomas, 105
steam-engine, 151
Stephen, Francis, 208
Stephen, James, 199
Stephen, John, 207–8
Stephen, John junior, 208
Stewart, William, 208, 217
Strafford family, 2–3, 232
Street, Thomas, 54
Sudds, Joseph, 224–5
Sullivan, John, 86
Supply (ship), 49–50, 55, 58, 68
Supreme Court of New South Wales, 152–3, 156, 171, 207–8, 211–12
Surprize (ship), 22, 24, 29, 31–3, 38–41, 47, 52
Surrey (ship), 194
Sussex, Duke of, 220
Suttor, George, 84, 115–16, 128, 134, 157
Sydney, Lord (Thomas Townshend), 11, 25
Sydney: descriptions of, 44–5, 72; population (1790), 44
Sydney Bay (Norfolk Island), 49–50, 52, 61
Sydney Cove, 49, 72, 84, 101, 119, 126, 149, 212
Sydney Gazette, 127–8, 132, 137, 148, 163, 171, 183, 192, 198, 205, 207, 209, 215, 222–3, 225, 230
Sydney Hospital, 138–9, 145–6, 150, 153, 157, 177, 184, 188–91, 197–8
Sydney Turf Club, 205

Table Bay, 26–7
Table Mountain, 37
Tank Stream, 45
Taylor, Miss, 201
Taylor, Mr, 93

Index

Temeraire (ship), 44
Tench, Watkin, 26, 44
Teneriffe, 25-6
Terry, Samuel, 163, 209, 219
The Rocks, *see* Rocks, The
Therry, Father John, 205
Third Fleet, 44, 61
Thompson (publican), 163, 187
Thompson, Andrew, 82, 111, 133, 153
Thompson, Patrick, 224-5
Thomson, James, 89, 101, 119
Thrale, Hester, 11
Three Horseshoe Yard, 16
Throsby, Charles, 144, 217, 230
Times, The (newspaper), 14, 19, 22, 27, 167
Timms, Martin, 64
Todhunter, William, 238
Toongabbie, 94, 237
Townson, John, 33, 36, 109, 111
Townson, Robert (Dr), 109-12, 117, 149
trade, 68-9, 73, 76-7, 84-5, 90-1, 95, 104, 108, 124, 130, 148, 158, 181
Trail, Donald, 29, 32-40, 42-4, 46-7
Trail, Elizabeth, 33-4
transportation system, 25-44, 61, 164, 167, 179; costs involved, 164-5, 171, 195
Traveller (schooner), 161
Treasury, 11, 43, 67-8, 104, 128, 164, 197, 199
Treasury bills, 74, 144, 197
Trevan, Betsy Alicia, 56; *see also* Clark, Betsy
trial by jury, 181, 193-4, 199, 207, 209-11, 214-16, 219-20, 226
Trinidad, 182
Trumpington Street, Cambridge, 201
Tuckey, James, 90
Tuki, 64
Turnbull, John, 79
Turner, Joseph Mallord William, 174
Tyler, Wat, 12

Ulster Volunteers, 6-7, 58
Underwood, James, 219
Underwood, Joseph, 109, 115, 133, 148-9
United Irishmen, 81-2
Uxbridge, Lord, 117

Vale, Reverend Benjamin, 161-3, 170-1
Vale–Moore petition, 162-3, 167, 170, 187
Van Diemen's Land, 95, 122, 129, 164, 166, 204, 211, 227; population, (1806) 103, (1810) 127, (1815) 151, (1821) 151
Van Linge, Bernard, 202
Vaucluse, 238-9
Vermont, 135
Victualling Board, 183-5, 198
Villiers, James, 13, 18-20, 23, 56, 64, 107

Walker, William, 219
Walker's Inn, Parramatta, 230
Walsh, Mary, 3
Waples, Margaret, 187
Wardell, Mrs, 203
Wardell, Robert, 203, 207-9, 212, 215, 223, 225-6, 230, 232, 239
Washington, George, 18
Waterhouse, Henry, 71, 96
Waterloo, battle of, 151, 158, 160
Wathen, Samuel, 42
Watt, James, 18
Welch, John, 26
Wellington, Duke of, 214
Welsh, William, 187
Wentworth, Charles (D'Arcy's nephew), 159
Wentworth, Charles John (D'Arcy's son), 137, 236-7
Wentworth, D'Arcy (b.1640), 3
Wentworth, D'Arcy (1722-1806, D'Arcy's father), 3, 5, 8-9, 84, 105, 232
Wentworth, D'Arcy (1762-1827)
 birth, 2-3; appearance, 6, 81; parents and siblings, 3-5, 105; childhood, 5, 235; schooling, 5; religion, 4, 118, 205, 235; politics, 235; apprenticeship, 6; service with Ulster Volunteers, 6-8, 58; drinking, 7; leaves Ireland, 8; in London, 8-22; raffish company, 10-11, 15, 18; lodgings in London, 9, 14-16, 19; highway robberies, 12, 14, 17, 19; arrested, 12, 14, 19; court appearances, 13, 15-16, 20-1, 27, 33; Fitzwilliam's patronage of, 20-2, 47, 65, 68, 70-1, 80, 86-7; sails from England for New South Wales, 23-4

[308]

Index

voyage (1790), 33–40; and Catherine Crowley, 34, 46–7, 53, 57, 197, 235–6; in Sydney, 44–6; sails for Norfolk Island, 47; acting assistant-surgeon, 47, 56; on Norfolk Island (1790–96), 53–71; character, 9–11, 18, 46, 53–4, 56, 61–2, 64–5, 74, 81, 94, 117–18, 137, 139–42, 148, 154, 159, 162, 172–3, 183–6, 232–6; medical practice, 6, 9, 54–5, 60–2, 66, 81, 92, 95, 105–6, 118, 141, 146, 156–9, 170–1, 180, 188–91, 197–8, 232; relations with his children, 68, 83, 93–4, 98–100, 124, 159–60, 172–3, 179, 190, 220–1, 235–7; and son, William, 53, 57, 119–20, 124, 134–5, 142–3, 149, 160–1, 167–9, 172–3, 175–82, 185, 190, 200–1, 207, 209, 216, 221–2, 228–30, 232, 235–7; kindness to convicts, 60, 63, 96, 148, 231, 235

superintendent of convicts at Queenborough, 61–2; appointed constable, 64; relations with John Hunter, 55, 64, 70, 81, 84, 96; relations with P. G. King, 61–2, 65–6, 76, 86, 88–91, 95–6, 102; farming, 57, 59, 65, 67–8, 93, 95; involved in trade, 68, 77–80, 84–7, 89, 92, 95, 100–1, 124, 136, 148, 158, 160, 206; deals in spirits, 79, 85–6, 92, 95, 100, 124–5, 134, 138–40, 144–8, 156, 158, 171, 180, 190–1, 196, 198; bonds with emancipists, 70, 133, 135, 197, 216, 222, 235; leaves Norfolk Island for Sydney (1796), 71

in New South Wales (1796–1804), 72–95; assistant-surgeon (1796), 74; land grants, 81, 123, 128, 132, 143, 194, 206; landholdings, 93, 104, 143–4, 186, 197, 231, 237; livestock, 93, 104, 123–4, 132, 144; unseemly behaviour, 83–4, 91–2, 97, 105–6, 139–40, 145, 197; litigation, 91, 148–9; acting-surgeon (1804), 95; again on Norfolk Island (1804–06), 95–100; recreations and interests, 100, 104, 142, 205–6, 228, 235; leaves Norfolk Island for Sydney (1806), 100; relations with Bligh, 103, 105–8, 110, 115–16; officially reprimanded, 106; involved in rebellion of 1808, 111–14, 121; and Maria Ainslie, 104, 137, 159, 161, 172–3, 183, 236; acting principal surgeon (1809), 119

relations with Macquarie, 132–3, 138, 140–1, 144, 149–50, 154, 162–3, 170, 174, 183, 185–6, 190–4, 210; principal surgeon (1810), 132, 141; treasurer of the police fund (1810), 133, 173–4, 190–1, 197; commissioner for the turnpike road (1810), 133, 205; justice of the peace (1810), 133, 147, 206–7, 231–2; and Ann Lawes, 137, 159, 172–3, 183, 197, 206, 227, 229, 235–7; hospital contractor (1810), 138–9, 145–6, 190–1; superintendent of police (1810), 140, 147, 156, 158, 187–8, 190, 196–8; other entrepreneurial activities, 144; rentier, 144; money-lender, 144; and Bank of New South Wales, 144–5, 163–4, 191, 205; and Jeffery Bent, 153–6; and George Molle, 169–70

and self-government, 182, 215; illnesses, 101–2, 173, 207, 216, 225, 228; resigns (as principal surgeon, 1819), 173, 183, (as superintendent of police, 1820), 173, 185, (as treasurer of the police fund, 1820), 185–6; examined by J. T. Bigge, 187–91; Bigge reports on, 196–9; serves again as superintendent of police (1821–25) and treasurer of the police fund (1821–24), 191–2, 205, 214; seeks a pension, 173–4, 183–6; attitude to trial by jury, 192, 207, 226; presents addresses, (to Sir Thomas Brisbane, 1825) 215, (to Governor Darling, 1825) 218–19; and James Macneal, 137, 227; wealth, 233, 237–8; will of, 227, 236–7; death, 227; funeral, 229–30; tombstone, 230; obituaries, 230–2; *see also* Cookney, Charles; Fitzwilliam, William Wentworth

Wentworth, D'Arcy (1793–1861, D'Arcy's son), 68, 71, 83, 93–4, 97–9, 102, 105,

[309]

Index

120, 124, 136–8, 149, 159, 179, 200, 206, 220–1, 233, 235–7
Wentworth, D'Arcy Charles (D'Arcy's son, known as Charles D'Arcy), 137, 235
Wentworth, Dorothy, 3, 8, 105, 159
Wentworth, Elizabeth (D'Arcy's sister-in-law), 24
Wentworth, George (D'Arcy's son), 137, 229, 236, 238
Wentworth, Gerrard, 3
Wentworth, John (1795–1820, D'Arcy's son), 68, 71, 83, 97, 99, 105, 120, 124, 136, 160–1, 163, 166, 168, 172–3, 235–6; death, 190
Wentworth, Katherine (D'Arcy's daughter), 137, 206, 237
Wentworth, Martha (D'Arcy's daughter), 137, 236–7
Wentworth, Martha (D'Arcy's niece), see Bucknell, Martha
Wentworth, Martha (D'Arcy's sister), 3, 105, 136, 159, 228, 233
Wentworth, Martha (née Dixon, 1727?–1803, D'Arcy's mother), 3, 105
Wentworth, Mary (D'Arcy's sister), 3, 136, 159
Wentworth, Mary Ann (D'Arcy's daughter), 137, 206, 237
Wentworth, Mary Anne (D'Arcy's sister), 3, 105, 136, 159, 206
Wentworth, Robert (D'Arcy's nephew), 136
Wentworth, Robert Charles (D'Arcy's son), 137, 237
Wentworth, Samuel, 5
Wentworth, Sophia (D'Arcy's daughter), 137, 237
Wentworth, Thomas (Earl of Strafford), 2–3
Wentworth, William (D'Arcy's brother), 3, 8, 84, 105, 136, 159, 190, 206
Wentworth, William Charles (1790–1872), 102, 119–20, 124, 149, 160, 221, 233
  birth, 52–3; childhood, 57, 62, 71, 83, 97; schooling, 68, 93–4, 97–9, 105, 120; appearance, 57, 83, 98–9, 208; character, 119–20, 135, 165–7, 174–5, 177–9, 200–1, 207–8, 237–9; religion, 167, 202; in New South Wales (1810–16), 134–5; acting provost marshal (1811), 135; land grants, 135, 143; close friends, 135; poetry and 'pipes', 135–6, 143, 166, 168–9, 175–6, 200–2, 213; crosses Blue Mountains (1813), 142–3, 150; voyage for sandalwood (1814), 148; voyages to England, (1802) 93, (1816) 160–1
  in London (1816–17), 165–8; in Paris (1817–18), 168, 174–5; again in England (1818–24), 175–82, 199–203; studies law, 165–7, 176; hopes to marry, 167, 175, 201; and Henry Grey Bennet, 167–8, 177–80; relations with Macquarie, 168, 181–2, 200, 202, 210, 214; writes book on New South Wales, 174–6, 180–2, 203, 206, 211; reaction to Bigge's reports, 199–200, 203, 211, 214, 219; called to the Bar (1822), 200; attends university, 201–2; sails (1824) for New South Wales, 203
  practises law, 200, 208; involved with the *Australian*, 209, 215; and Bank of New South Wales, 209; leads emancipist party, 200, 207, 209–11, 215–16, 219–20, 222; views on colonial politics (1824–27), 208–9, 211, 214–18, 225–6, 239; and Sarah Cox, 212–13, 238–9; address to Sir Thomas Brisbane, 214–15; attitude to Governor Darling, 217–19, 225–6; and Australian Agricultural Company, 218–19; Sudds and Thompson case (1826), 225; inherits property from his father, 237–8; as guardian, 238; and Vaucluse estate, 238–9
  see also Cookney, Charles; Fitzwilliam, William Wentworth; Wentworth, D'Arcy (1762–1827)
Wentworth Park, 150
Wentworth Woodhouse, Parramatta, 93
Wentworth Woodhouse, Yorkshire, 2–3, 20
Wesley, John, 12
Westbrook, William, 49–50
West Indies, 146, 216, 221
Westminster School, 182

Index

wheat, price of, (1810) 127, (1815) 130, (1821) 193
Wheeler, Thomas, 149
White, Catherine, 60
White, James, 59
White, John, 44
Whitefield, George, 12
Whitlam, Sarah, 26
Whittaker, G., 180, 182
Whittaker, W. B., 180, 182
Whittle, Thomas, 109
Wilberforce, William, 42, 116, 131, 170, 180
Wilbow, John, 162
Wilde, Oscar Fingal O'Flahertie Wills, 177
Wilkinson, Elizabeth, 16
Wilkinson, Mary, 15–16, 20, 236
William (ship), 65
Williams (convict), 50
Williams, Francis, 107
Williams, George, 163, 181
Williamson, James, 81, 89, 112
Wilmot Horton, Robert, 199–200
Wilson, George, 23
Wilson, Mrs, 19, 23, 236
Windham, William, 107, 115
Windsor, New South Wales, 198
Woolwich, 136
World (newspaper), 42
Wright, Sir Sampson, 14
Wyer, Michael, 155
Wylde, John, 156, 158, 163, 169–70, 184, 187–8
Wylde, Thomas, 164

Yeats, William Butler, 101
Yonge, Sir George, 28
York, Frederick, Duke of, 82–3, 137, 168, 220
York (ship), 218
York Street, Sydney, 224
Yorkshire Grey (inn), 91